The Expositor's Bible
The Epistles Of St. Paul To The Colossians And Philemon

by

Alexander Maclaren

Double 9
BOOKS

The Expositor's Bible
The Epistles Of St. Paul To The Colossians And Philemon

by Alexander Maclaren

ISBN: 978-93-61152-98-6

Published by

DOUBLE 9 BOOKS

2/13-B, Ansari Road
Daryaganj, New Delhi – 110002
info@double9books.com
www.double9books.com
Tel. 011-40042856

ABOUT THE AUTHOR

Alexander Maclaren was a Scottish Baptist clergyman who died on May 5, 1910. Maclaren was born in Glasgow, Scotland, the son of a merchant and Baptist lay preacher named David Maclaren. From 1837 to 1841, his father left his family in Edinburgh to serve as Resident Manager of the South Australian Company in Australia. Maclaren was converted and publicly baptized into the fellowship of the Hope St. Baptist Church, Glasgow, somewhere between the ages of 11 and 13. He attended Glasgow High School and Glasgow University before his family relocated to London when his father returned from Australia. Maclaren enrolled in Stepney College, a Baptist college in London, at the age of 16 in 1842. Dr. David Davies, an accomplished Hebrew scholar, affected him much, and he became a passionate student of Hebrew and Greek, among other disciplines. He completed his bachelor's degree at the University of London before the age of 20, appearing for arts degree examinations and receiving awards in Hebrew and Greek. Aside from his academic studies, he read extensively in literature, with a particular fondness for English poets. He began his ministry at Portland Chapel in Southampton the following year.

CONTENTS

THE EPISTLE TO PHILEMON

I
THE WRITER AND THE READERS

"Paul, an Apostle of Christ Jesus through the will of God, and Timothy our brother, to the saints and faithful brethren in Christ which are at Colossæ: Grace to you and peace from God our Father."—Col. i, 1, 2 (Rev. Ver.).

We may say that each of Paul's greater epistles has in it one salient thought. In that to the Romans, it is Justification by faith; in Ephesians, it is the mystical union of Christ and His Church; in Philippians, it is the joy of Christian progress; in this epistle, it is the dignity and sole sufficiency of Jesus Christ as the Mediator and Head of all creation and of the Church.

Such a thought is emphatically a lesson for the day.

The Christ whom the world needs to have proclaimed in every deaf ear and lifted up before blind and reluctant eyes, is not merely the perfect man, nor only the meek sufferer, but the Source of creation and its Lord, Who from the beginning has been the life of all that has lived, and before the beginning was in the bosom of the Father. The shallow and starved religion which contents itself with mere humanitarian conceptions of Jesus of Nazareth needs to be deepened and filled out by these lofty truths before it can acquire solidity and steadfastness sufficient to be the unmoved foundation of sinful and mortal lives. The evangelistic teaching which concentrates exclusive attention on the cross as "the work of Christ," needs to be led to the contemplation of them, in order to understand the cross, and to have its mystery as well as its meaning declared. This letter itself dwells upon two applications of its principles to two classes of error which, in somewhat changed forms, exist now as then—the error of the ceremonialist, to whom religion was mainly a matter of ritual, and the error of the speculative thinker, to whom the universe was filled with forces which left no room for the working of a personal Will. The vision of the living Christ Who fills all things, is held up before each of these two, as the antidote to his poison; and that same vision must be made clear to-day to the modern representatives of these ancient errors. If we are able to grasp with heart and mind the principles of this epistle for ourselves, we shall stand at the centre of things, seeing order where from any other position confusion only is apparent, and being at the point of rest instead of being hurried along by the wild whirl of conflicting opinions.

I desire, therefore, to present the teachings of this great epistle in a series of expositions.

Before advancing to the consideration of these verses, we must deal with one or two introductory matters, so as to get the frame and the background for the picture.

(1) First, as to the Church of Colossæ to which the letter is addressed.

Perhaps too much has been made of late years of geographical and topographical elucidations of Paul's epistles. A knowledge of the place to which a letter was sent cannot do much to help in understanding the letter, for local circumstances leave very faint traces, if any, on the Apostle's writings. Here and there an allusion may be detected, or a metaphor may gain in point by such knowledge; but, for the most part, local colouring is entirely absent. Some slight indication, however, of the situation and circumstances of the Colossian Church may help to give vividness to our conceptions of the little community to whom this rich treasure of truth was first entrusted.

Colossæ was a town in the heart of the modern Asia Minor, much decayed in Paul's time from its earlier importance. It lay in a valley of Phrygia, on the banks of a small stream, the Lycus, down the course of which, at a distance of some ten miles or so, two very much more important cities fronted each other, Hierapolis on the north, and Laodicea on the south bank of the river. In all three cities were Christian Churches, as we know from this letter, one of which has attained the bad eminence of having become the type of tepid religion for all the world. How strange to think of the tiny community in a remote valley of Asia Minor, eighteen centuries since, thus gibbeted for ever! These stray beams of light which fall upon the people in the New Testament, showing them fixed for ever in one attitude, like a lightning flash in the darkness, are solemn precursors of the last Apocalypse, when all men shall be revealed in "the brightness of His coming."

Paul does not seem to have been the founder of these Churches, or ever to have visited them at the date of this letter. That opinion is based on several of its characteristics, such, for instance, as the absence of any of those kindly greetings to individuals which in the Apostle's other letters are so abundant, and reveal at once the warmth and the delicacy of his affection: and the allusions which occur more than once to his having only "*heard*" of their faith and love, and is strongly supported by the expression in the second chapter where he speaks of the conflict in spirit which he had for "you, and for them at Laodicea, and for as many as have not seen my face in the flesh." Probably the teacher who planted the gospel in Colossæ was that Epaphras, whose visit to Rome occasioned the letter, and who is referred to in verse 7 of this chapter in terms which seem to suggest that he had first made known to them the fruit-producing "word of the truth of the gospel."

(2) Note the occasion and subject of the letter. Paul is a prisoner, in a certain sense, in Rome; but the word prisoner conveys a false impression of the amount of restriction of personal liberty to which he was subjected. We know from the last words of the Acts of the Apostles, and from the Epistle to the Philippians, that his "imprisonment" did not in the least interfere with his liberty of preaching, nor with his intercourse with friends. Rather, in the view of the facilities it gave that by him "the preaching might be fully known," it may be regarded, as indeed the writer of the Acts seems to regard it, as the very climax and topstone of Paul's work, wherewith his history may fitly end, leaving the champion of the gospel at the very heart of the world, with unhindered liberty to proclaim his message by the very throne of Cæsar. He was sheltered rather than confined beneath the wing of the imperial eagle. His imprisonment, as we call it, was, at all events at first, detention in Rome under military supervision rather than incarceration. So to his lodgings in Rome there comes a brother from this decaying little town in the far-off valley of the Lycus, Epaphras by name. Whether his errand was exclusively to consult Paul about the state of the Colossian Church, or whether some other business also had brought him to Rome, we do not know; at all events, he comes and brings with him bad news, which burdens Paul's heart with solicitude for the little community, which had no remembrances of his own authoritative teaching to fall back upon. Many a night would he and Epaphras spend in deep converse on the matter, with the stolid Roman legionary, to whom Paul was chained, sitting wearily by, while they two eagerly talked.

The tidings were that a strange disease, hatched in that hotbed of religious fancies, the dreamy East, was threatening the faith of the Colossian Christians. A peculiar form of heresy, singularly compounded of Jewish ritualism and Oriental mysticism—two elements as hard to blend in the foundation of a system as the heterogeneous iron and clay on which the image in Nebuchadnezzar's dream stood unstably—had appeared among them, and though at present confined to a few, was being vigorously preached. The characteristic Eastern dogma, that matter is evil and the source of evil, which underlies so much Oriental religion, and crept in so early to corrupt Christianity, and crops up to-day in so many strange places and unexpected ways, had begun to infect them. The conclusion was quickly drawn: "Well, then, if matter be the source of all evil, then, of course, God and matter must be antagonistic," and so the creation and government of this material universe could not be supposed to have come directly from Him. The endeavour to keep the pure Divinity and the gross world as far apart as possible, while yet an intellectual necessity forbad the entire breaking of the bond between them, led to the busy working of the imagination, which spanned the void gulf between God Who is good, and matter which is evil, with a bridge of cobwebs—a chain of intermediate beings, emanations, abstractions, each approaching more nearly to the material than his precursor, till at last the intangible and infinite was confined and curdled into actual earthly matter, and the pure was darkened thereby into evil.

Such notions, fantastic and remote from daily life as they look, really led by a very short cut to making wild work with the plainest moral teachings both of the natural conscience and of Christianity. For if matter be the source of all evil, then the fountain of each man's sin is to be found, not in his own perverted will, but in his body, and the cure of it is to be reached, not by faith which plants a new life in a sinful spirit, but simply by ascetic mortification of the flesh.

Strangely united with these mystical Eastern teachings, which might so easily be perverted to the coarsest sensuality, and had their heads in the clouds and their feet in the mud, were the narrowest doctrines of Jewish ritualism, insisting on circumcision, laws regulating food, the observance of feast days, and the whole cumbrous apparatus of a ceremonial religion. It is a monstrous combination, a cross between a Talmudical rabbi and a Buddhist priest, and yet it is not unnatural that, after soaring in these lofty regions of speculation where the air is too thin to support life, men should be glad to get hold of the externals of an elaborate ritual. It is not the first nor the last time that a misplaced philosophical religion has got close to a religion of outward observances, to keep it from shivering itself to death. Extremes meet. If you go far enough east, you are west.

Such, generally speaking, was the error that was beginning to lift its head in Colossæ. Religious fanaticism was at home in that country, from which, both in heathen and in Christian times, wild rites and notions emanated, and the Apostle might well dread the effect of this new teaching, as of a spark on hay, on the excitable natures of the Colossian converts.

Now we may say, "What does all this matter to us? We are in no danger of being haunted by the ghosts of these dead heresies." But the truth which Paul opposed to them is all important for every age. It was simply the Person of Christ as the only manifestation of the Divine, the link between God and the universe, its Creator and Preserver, the Light and Life of men, the Lord and Inspirer of the Church, Christ has come, laying His hand upon both God and man, therefore there is no need nor place for a misty crowd of angelic beings or shadowy abstractions to bridge the gulf across which His incarnation flings its single solid arch. Christ has been bone of our bone and flesh of our flesh, therefore that cannot be the source of evil in which the fulness of the Godhead has dwelt as in a shrine. Christ has come, the fountain of life and holiness, therefore there is no more place for ascetic mortifications on the one hand, nor for Jewish scrupulosities on the other. These things might detract from the completeness of faith in the complete redemption which Christ has wrought, and must becloud the truth that simple faith in it is all which a man needs.

To urge these and the like truths this letter is written. Its central principle is the sovereign and exclusive mediation of Jesus Christ, the God-man, the victorious antagonist of these dead speculations, and the destined conqueror of all the doubts and confusions of this day. If we grasp with mind and heart that truth, we can possess our souls in patience, and in its light see light where else is darkness and uncertainty.

So much then for introduction, and now a few words of comment on the superscription of the letter contained in these verses.

I. Notice the blending of lowliness and authority in Paul's designation of himself. "An Apostle of Christ Jesus through the will of God."

He does not always bring his apostolic authority to mind at the beginning of his letters. In his earliest epistles, those to the Thessalonians, he has not yet adopted the practice. In the loving and joyous letter to the Philippians, he has no need to urge his authority, for no man among them ever gainsaid it. In that to Philemon, friendship is uppermost, and though, as he says, he might be much bold to enjoin, yet he prefers to beseech, and will not command as "Apostle," but pleads as "the prisoner of Christ Jesus." In his other letters he put his authority in the foreground as here, and it may be noticed that it and its basis in the will of God are asserted with greatest emphasis in the Epistle to the Galatians, where he has to deal with more defiant opposition than elsewhere encountered him.

Here he puts forth his claim to the apostolate, in the highest sense of the word. He asserts his equality with the original Apostles, the chosen witnesses for the reality of Christ's resurrection. He, too, had seen the risen Lord, and heard the words of His mouth. He shared with them the prerogative of certifying from personal experience that Jesus is risen and lives to bless and rule. Paul's whole Christianity was built on the belief that Jesus Christ had actually appeared to him. That vision on the road to Damascus revolutionised his life. Because he had seen his Lord and heard his duty from His lips, he had become what he was.

"Through the will of God" is at once an assertion of Divine authority, a declaration of independence of all human teaching or appointment, and a most lowly disclaimer of individual merit, or personal power. Few religious teachers have had so strongly marked a character as Paul, or have so constantly brought their own experience into prominence; but the weight which he expected to be attached to his words was to be due entirely to their being the words which God spoke through him. If this opening clause were to be paraphrased it would be: I speak to you because God has sent me. I am not an Apostle by my own will, nor by my own merit. I am not worthy to be called an Apostle. I am a poor sinner like yourselves, and it is a miracle of love and mercy that God should put His words into such lips. But He does speak through me; my words are neither mine nor learned from any other man, but His. Never mind the cracked pipe through which the Divine breath makes music, but listen to the music.

So Paul thought of his message; so the uncompromising assertion of authority was united with deep humility. Do we come to his words, believing that we hear God speaking through Paul? Here is no formal doctrine of inspiration, but here is the claim to be the organ of the Divine will and mind, to which we ought to listen as indeed the voice of God.

The gracious humility of the man is further seen in his association with himself, as joint senders of the letter, of his young brother Timothy, who has no apostolic authority, but whose concurrence in its teaching might give it some additional weight. For the first few verses he remembers to speak in the plural, as in the name of both—"*we* give thanks," "Epaphras declared to *us* your love," and so on; but in the fiery sweep of his thoughts Timothy is soon left out of sight, and Paul alone pours out the wealth of his Divine wisdom and the warmth of his fervid heart.

II. We may observe the noble ideal of the Christian character set forth in the designations of the Colossian Church, as "saints and faithful brethren in Christ."

In his earlier letters Paul addresses himself to "the Church;" in his later, beginning with the Epistle to the Romans, and including the three great epistles from his captivity, namely, Ephesians, Philippians, and Colossians, he drops the word Church, and uses expressions which regard the individuals composing the community rather than the community which they compose. The slight change thus indicated in the Apostle's point of view is interesting, however it may be accounted for. There is no reason to suppose it done of set purpose, and certainly it did not arise from any lowered estimate of the sacredness of "the Church," which is nowhere put on higher ground than in the letter to Ephesus, which belongs to the later period; but it may be that advancing years and familiarity with his work, with his position of authority, and with his auditors, all tended to draw him closer to them, and insensibly led to the disuse of the more formal and official address to "the Church" in favour of the simpler and more affectionate superscription, to "the brethren."

Be that as it may, the lessons to be drawn from the names here given to the members of the Church are the more important matter for us. It would be interesting and profitable to examine the meaning of all the New Testament names for believers, and to learn the lessons which they teach; but we must for the present confine ourselves to those which occur here.

"Saints"—a word that has been wofully misapplied both by the Church and the world. The former has given it as a special honour to a few, and "decorated" with it mainly the possessors of a false ideal of sanctity—that of the ascetic and monastic sort. The latter uses it with a sarcastic intonation, as if it implied much cry and little wool, loud professions and small performance, not without a touch of hypocrisy and crafty self-seeking.

Saints are not people living in cloisters after a fantastic ideal, but men and women immersed in the vulgar work of every-day life and worried by the small prosaic anxieties which fret us all, who amidst the whirr of the spindle in the mill, and the clink of the scales on the counter, and the hubbub of the market-place and the jangle of the courts, are yet living lives of conscious devotion to God. The root idea of the word, which is an Old Testament word, is not moral purity, but separation to God. The holy things of the old covenant were things set apart from ordinary use for His service. So, on the high priest's mitre was written Holiness to the Lord. So the Sabbath was kept "holy," because set apart from the week in obedience to Divine command.

Sanctity, and *saint*, are used now mainly with the idea of moral purity, but that is a secondary meaning. The real primary signification is separation to God. Consecration to Him is the root from which the white flower of purity springs most surely. There is a deep lesson in the word as to the true method of attaining cleanness of life and spirit. We cannot make ourselves pure, but we can yield ourselves to God and the purity will come.

But we have not only here the fundamental idea of holiness, and the connection of purity of character with self-consecration to God, but also the solemn obligation on all so-called Christians thus to separate and devote themselves to Him. We are Christians as far as we give ourselves up to God, in the surrender of our wills and the practical obedience of our lives—so far and not one inch further. We are not merely bound to this consecration if we are Christians, but we are not Christians unless we thus consecrate ourselves. Pleasing self, and making my own will my law, and living for my own ends, is destructive of all Christianity. Saints are not an eminent sort of Christians, but all Christians are saints, and he who is not a saint is not a Christian. The true consecration is the surrender of the will, which no man can do for us, which needs no outward ceremonial, and the one motive which will lead us selfish and stubborn men to bow our necks to that gentle yoke, and to come out of the misery of pleasing self into the peace of serving God, is drawn from the great love of Him Who devoted Himself to God and man, and bought us for His own by giving Himself utterly to be ours. All sanctity begins with consecration to God. All consecration rests upon the faith of Christ's sacrifice. And if, drawn by the great love of Christ to us unworthy, we give ourselves away to God in Him, then He gives Himself in deep sacred communion to us. "I am thine" has ever for its chord which completes the fulness of its music, "Thou art mine." And so "saint" is a name of dignity and honour, as well as a stringent requirement. There is implied in it, too, safety from all that would threaten life or union with Him. He will not hold His possessions with a slack hand that negligently lets them drop, or with a feeble hand that cannot keep them from a foe. "Thou wilt not suffer him who is consecrated to Thee to see corruption." If I belong to God, having given myself to Him, then I am safe from the touch of evil and the taint of decay. "The Lord's portion is His people," and He will not lose even so worthless a part of that portion as I am. The great name "saints" carries with it the prophecy of victory over all evil, and the assurance that nothing can separate us from the love of God, or pluck us from His hand.

But these Colossian Christians are "faithful" as well as saints. That may either mean *trustworthy* and *true* to their stewardship, or *trusting*. In the parallel verses in the Epistle to the Ephesians (which presents so many resemblances to this epistle) the latter meaning seems to be required, and here it is certainly the more natural, as pointing to the very foundation of all Christian consecration and brotherhood in the act of believing. We are united to Christ by our faith. The Church is a family of faithful, that is to say of believing, men. Faith underlies consecration and is the parent of holiness, for he only will yield himself to God who trustfully grasps the mercies of God and rests on Christ's great gift of Himself. Faith weaves the bond that unites men in the brotherhood of the Church, for it brings all who share it into a common relation to the Father. He who is faithful, that is, believing, will be faithful in the sense of being worthy of confidence and true to his duty, his profession, and his Lord.

They were *brethren* too. That strong new bond of union among men the most unlike, was a strange phenomenon in Paul's time, when the Roman world was falling to pieces, and rent by deep clefts of hatreds and jealousies such as modern society scarcely knows; and men might well wonder as they saw the slave and his master sitting at the same table, the Greek and the barbarian learning the same wisdom in the same tongue, the Jew and the Gentile bowing the knee in the same worship, and the hearts of all fused into one great glow of helpful sympathy and unselfish love.

But "brethren" means more than this. It points not merely to Christian love, but to the common possession of a new life. If we are brethren, it is because we have one Father, because in us all there is one life. The name is often regarded as sentimental and metaphorical. The obligation of mutual love is supposed to be the main idea in it, and there is a melancholy hollowness and unreality in the very sound of it as applied to the usual average Christians of to-day. But the name leads straight to the doctrine of regeneration, and proclaims that all Christians are born again through their faith in Jesus Christ, and thereby partake of a common new life, which makes all its possessors children of the Highest, and therefore brethren one of another. If regarded as an expression of the affection of Christians for one another, "brethren" is an exaggeration, ludicrous or tragic, as we view it; but if we regard it as the expression of the real bond which gathers all believers into one family, it declares the deepest mystery and mightiest privilege of the gospel that "to as many as received Him, to them gave He power to become the Sons of God."

They are "in Christ." These two words may apply to all the designations or to the last only. They are saints in Him, believers in Him, brethren in Him. That mystical but most real union of Christians with their Lord is never far away from the Apostle's thoughts, and in the twin Epistle to the Ephesians is the very burden of the whole. A shallower Christianity tries to weaken that great phrase to something more intelligible to the unspiritual temper and the poverty-stricken experience proper to it; but no justice can be done to Paul's teaching unless it be taken in all its depth as expressive of that same mutual indwelling and interlacing of spirit with spirit which is so prominent in the writings of the Apostle John. *There* is one point of contact between the Pauline and the Johannean conceptions, on the differences between which so much exaggeration has been expended: to both the inmost essence of the Christian life is union to Christ, and abiding in Him. If we are Christians, we are in Him, in yet profounder sense than creation lives and moves and has its being in God. We are in Him as the earth with all its living things is in the atmosphere, as the branch is in the vine, as the members are in the body. We are in Him as inhabitants in a house, as hearts that love in hearts that love, as parts in the whole. If we are Christians, He is in us, as life in every vein, as the fruit-producing sap and energy of the vine is in every branch, as the air in every lung, as the sunlight in every planet.

This is the deepest mystery of the Christian life. To be "in Him" is to be complete. "In Him" we are "blessed with all spiritual blessings." "In Him", we are "chosen," "In Him," God "freely bestows His grace upon us." "In Him" we "have redemption through His blood." "In Him" "all things in heaven and earth are gathered." "In Him we have obtained an inheritance." In Him is the better life of all who live. In Him we have peace though the world be seething with change and storm. In Him we conquer though earth and our own evil be all in arms against us. If we live in Him, we live in purity and joy. If we die in Him, we die in tranquil trust. If our gravestones may truly carry the sweet old inscription carved on so many a nameless slab in the catacombs, "In Christo," they will also bear the other "In pace" (In peace). If we sleep in Him, our glory is assured, for them also that sleep in Jesus, will God bring with Him.

III. A word or two only can be devoted to the last clause of salutation, the apostolic wish, which sets forth the high ideal to be desired for Churches and individuals: "Grace be unto and peace from God our Father." The Authorized Version reads, "and the Lord Jesus Christ," but the Revised Version follows the majority of recent text-critics and their principal authorities in omitting these words, which are supposed to have been imported into our passage from the parallel place in Ephesians. The omission of these familiar words which occur so uniformly in the similar introductory salutations of Paul's other epistles, is especially singular here, where the main subject of the letter is the office of Christ as channel of all blessings. Perhaps the previous word, "brethren" was lingering in his mind, and so instinctively he stopped with the kindred word "Father."

"Grace and peace"—Paul's wishes for those whom he loves, and the blessings which he expects every Christian to possess, blend the Western and the Eastern forms of salutation, and surpass both. All that the Greek meant by his "Grace," all that the Hebrew meant by his "Peace," the ideally happy condition which differing nations have placed in different blessings, and which all loving words have vainly wished for dear ones, is secured and conveyed to every poor soul that trusts in Christ.

"Grace"—what is that? The word means first—love in exercise to those who are below the lover, or who deserve something else; stooping love that condescends, and patient love that forgives. Then it means the gifts which such love bestows, and then it means the effects of these gifts in the beauties of character and conduct developed in the receivers. So there are here invoked, or we may call it, proffered and promised, to every believing heart, the love and gentleness of that Father whose love to us sinful atoms is a miracle of lowliness and longsuffering; and, next, the outcome of that love which never visits the soul emptyhanded, in all varied spiritual gifts, to strengthen weakness, to enlighten ignorance, to fill the whole being; and as last result of all, every beauty of mind, heart, and temper which can adorn the character, and refine a man into the likeness of God. That great gift will come in continuous bestowment if we are "saints in Christ." Of His fulness we all receive and grace for grace, wave upon wave as the ripples press shoreward and each in turn pours its tribute on the beach, or as pulsation after pulsation makes one golden beam of unbroken light, strong winged enough to come all the way from the sun, gentle enough to fall on the sensitive eyeball without pain. That one beam will decompose into all colours and brightnesses. That one "grace" will part into sevenfold gifts and be the life in us of whatsoever things are lovely and of good report.

"Peace be unto you." That old greeting, the witness of a state of society when every stranger seen across the desert was probably an enemy, is also a witness to the deep unrest of the heart. It is well to learn the lesson that peace comes after grace, that for tranquillity of soul we must go to God, and that He gives it by giving us His love and its gifts, of which, and of which only, peace is the result. If we have that grace for ours, as we all may if we will, we shall be still, because our desires are satisfied and all our needs met. To seek is unnecessary when we are conscious of possessing. We may end our weary quest, like the dove when it had found the green leaf, though little dry land may be seen as yet, and fold our wings and rest by the cross. We may be lapped in calm repose, even in the midst of toil and strife, like John resting on the heart of his Lord. There must be first of all, peace *with* God, that there may be peace *from* God. Then, when we have been won from our alienation and enmity by the power of the cross, and have learned to know that God is our Lover, Friend and Father, we shall possess the peace of those whose hearts have found their home, the peace of spirits no longer at war within—conscience and choice tearing them asunder in their strife, the peace of obedience which banishes the disturbance of self-will, the peace of security shaken by no fears, the peace of a sure future across the brightness of which no shadows of sorrow nor mists of uncertainty can fall, the peace of a heart in amity with all mankind. So living in peace, we shall lay ourselves down and die in peace, and enter into "that country, afar beyond the stars," where "grows the flower of peace."

> "The Rose that cannot wither,
> Thy fortress and thy ease."

All this may be ours. Paul could only wish it for these Colossians. We can only long for it for our dearest. No man can fulfil his wishes or turn them into actual gifts. Many precious things we can give, but not peace. But our brother, Jesus Christ, can do more than wish it. He can bestow it, and when we need it most, He stands ever beside us, in our weakness and unrest, with His strong arm stretched out to help, and on His calm lips the old words—"My grace is sufficient for thee," "My peace I give unto you."

Let us keep ourselves in Him, believing in Him and yielding ourselves to God for His dear sake, and we shall find His grace ever flowing into our emptiness and His settled "peace keeping our hearts and minds in Christ Jesus."

II
THE PRELUDE

"We give thanks to God the Father of our Lord Jesus Christ, praying always for you, having heard of your faith in Christ Jesus, and of the love which ye have toward all the saints, because of the hope which is laid up for you in the heavens, whereof ye heard before in the word of the truth of the gospel, which is come unto you; even as it is also in all the world bearing fruit and increasing, as it doth in you also, since the day ye heard and knew the grace of God in truth; even as ye learned of Epaphras our beloved fellow-servant, who is a faithful minister of Christ on our behalf, who also declared to us your love in the Spirit." —Col. i. 3–8. (Rev. Ver.).

This long introductory section may at first sight give the impression of confusion, from the variety of subjects introduced. But a little thought about it shows it to be really a remarkable specimen of the Apostle's delicate tact, born of his love and earnestness. Its purpose is to prepare a favourable reception for his warnings and arguments against errors which had crept in, and in his judgment were threatening to sweep away the Colossian Christians from their allegiance to Christ, and their faith in the gospel as it had been originally preached to them by Epaphras. That design explains the selection of topics in these verses, and their weaving together.

Before he warns and rebukes, Paul begins by giving the Colossians credit for all the good which he can find in them. As soon as he opens his mouth, he asserts the claims and authority, the truth and power of the gospel which he preaches, and from which all this good in them had come, and which had proved that it came from God by its diffusiveness and fruitfulness. He reminds them of their beginnings in the Christian life, with which this new teaching was utterly inconsistent, and he flings his shield over Epaphras, their first teacher, whose words were in danger of being neglected now for newer voices with other messages.

Thus skilfully and lovingly these verses touch a prelude which naturally prepares for the theme of the epistle. Remonstrance and rebuke would more often be effective if they oftener began with showing the rebuker's love, and with frank acknowledgment of good in the rebuked.

I. We have first a thankful recognition of Christian excellence as introductory to warnings and remonstrances.

Almost all Paul's letters begin with similar expressions of thankfulness for the good that was in the Church he is addressing. Gentle rain softens the ground and prepares it to receive the heavier downfall which would else mostly run off the hard surface. The exceptions are, 2 Corinthians; Ephesians, which was probably a circular letter; and Galatians, which is too hot throughout for such praises. These expressions are not compliments, or words of course. Still less are they flattery used for personal ends. They are the uncalculated and uncalculating expression of affection which delights to see white patches in the blackest character, and of wisdom which knows that the nauseous medicine of blame is most easily taken if administered wrapped in a capsule of honest praise.

All persons in authority over others, such as masters, parents, leaders of any sort, may be the better for taking the lesson—"provoke not your"—inferiors, dependents, scholars—"to wrath, lest they be discouraged"—and deal out praise where you can, with a liberal hand. It is nourishing food for many virtues, and a powerful antidote to many vices.

This praise is cast in the form of thanksgiving to God, as the true fountain of all that is good in men. How all that might be harmful in direct praise is strained out of it, when it becomes gratitude to God! But we need not dwell on this, nor on the principle underlying these thanks, namely that Christian men's excellences are God's gift, and that therefore, admiration of the man should ever be subordinate to thankfulness to God. The fountain, not the pitcher filled from it, should have the credit of the crystal purity and sparkling coolness of the water. Nor do we need to do more than point to the inference from that phrase "having *heard* of your faith," an inference confirmed by other statements in the letter, namely, that the Apostle himself had never *seen* the Colossian Church. But we briefly emphasize the two points which occasioned his thankfulness. They are the familiar two, *faith* and *love*.

Faith is sometimes spoken of in the New Testament as "*towards* Christ Jesus," which describes that great act of the soul by its direction, as if it were a going out or flight of the man's nature to the true goal of all active being. It is sometimes spoken of as "*on* Christ Jesus," which describes it as reposing on Him as the end of all seeking, and suggests such images as that of a hand that leans or of a burden borne, or a weakness upheld by contact with Him. But more sweet and great is the blessedness of faith considered as "*in*

Him," as its abiding place and fortress-home, in union with, and indwelling in whom the seeking spirit may fold its wings, and the weak heart may be strengthened to lift its burden cheerily, heavy though it be, and the soul may be full of tranquillity and soothed into a great calm. *Towards, on,* and *in*—so manifold are the phases of the relation between Christ and our faith.

In all, faith is the same,—simple confidence, precisely like the trust which we put in one another. But how unlike are the objects!—broken reeds of human nature in the one case, and the firm pillar of that Divine power and tenderness in the other, and how unlike, alas! is the fervency and constancy of the trust we exercise in each other and in Christ! "Faith" covers the whole ground of man's relation to God. All religion, all devotion, everything which binds us to the unseen world is included in or evolved from faith. And mark that this faith is, in Paul's teaching, the foundation of love to men and of everything else good and fair. We may agree or disagree with that thought, but we can scarcely fail to see that it is the foundation of all his moral teaching. From that fruitful source all good will come. From that deep fountain sweet water will flow, and all drawn from other sources has a tang of bitterness. Goodness of all kinds is most surely evolved from faith—and that faith lacks its best warrant of reality which does not lead to whatsoever things are lovely and of good report. Barnabas was a "good man," because, as Luke goes on to tell us by way of analysis of the sources of his goodness, he was "full of the Holy Ghost," the author of all goodness, "and of faith" by which that Inspirer of all beauty of purity dwells in men's hearts. Faith then is the germ of goodness, not because of anything in itself, but because by it we come under the influence of the Divine Spirit whose breath is life and holiness.

Therefore we say to every one who is seeking to train his character in excellence, begin with trusting Christ, and out of that will come all lustre and whiteness, all various beauties of mind and heart. It is hard and hopeless work to cultivate our own thorns into grapes, but if we will trust Christ, He will sow good seed in our field and "make it soft with showers and bless the springing thereof."

As faith is the foundation of all virtue, so it is the parent of love, and as the former sums up every bond that knits men to God, so the latter includes all relations of men to each other, and is the whole law of human conduct packed into one word. But the warmest place in a Christian's heart will belong to those who are in sympathy with his deepest self, and a true faith in Christ, like a true loyalty to a prince, will weave a special bond between all fellow-subjects. So the sign, on the surface of earthly relations, of the deep-lying central fire of faith to Christ, is the fruitful vintage of brotherly love, as the vineyards bear the heaviest clusters on the slopes of Vesuvius.

Faith in Christ and love to Christians—that is the Apostle's notion of a good man. That is the ideal of character which we have to set before ourselves. Do we desire to be good? Let us trust Christ. Do we profess to trust Christ? Let us show it by the true proof—our goodness and especially our love.

So we have here two members of the familiar triad, Faith and Love, and their sister Hope is not far off. We read in the next clause, "because of the hope which is laid up for you in the heavens." The connection is not altogether plain. Is the hope the reason for the Apostle's thanksgiving, or the reason in some sense of the Colossians' love? As far as the language goes, we may either read "We give thanks ... because of the hope," or "the love which ye have ... because of the hope." But the long distance which we have to go back for the connection, if we adopt the former explanation, and other considerations which need not be entered on here, seem to make the latter the preferable construction if it yields a tolerable sense. Does it? Is it allowable to say that the hope which is laid up in heaven is in any sense a reason or motive for brotherly love? I think it is.

Observe that "hope" here is best taken as meaning not the emotion, but the object on which the emotion is fixed; not the faculty, but the thing hoped for; or in other words, that it is objective not subjective; and also that the ideas of futurity and security are conveyed by the thought of this object of expectation being laid up. This future blessedness, grasped by our expectant hearts as assured for us, does stimulate and hearten to all well-doing. Certainly it does not supply the main reason; we are not to be loving and good because we hope to win heaven thereby. The deepest motive for all the graces of Christian character is the will of God in Christ Jesus, apprehended by loving hearts. But it is quite legitimate to draw subordinate motives for the strenuous pursuit of holiness from the anticipation of future blessedness, and it is quite legitimate to use that prospect to reinforce the higher motives. He who seeks to be good only for the sake of the heaven which he thinks he will get for his goodness—if there be any such a person existing anywhere but in the imaginations of the caricaturists of Christian teaching—is not good and will not get his heaven; but he who feeds his devotion to Christ and his earnest cultivation of holiness with the animating hope of an unfading crown will find in it a mighty power to intensify and ennoble all life, to bear him up as on angel's hands that lift over all stones of stumbling, to diminish sorrow and dull pain, to kindle love to men into a brighter flame, and to purge holiness to a more radiant whiteness. The hope laid up in heaven is not the deepest reason or motive for faith and love—but both are made more vivid when it is strong. It is not the light at which their lamps are lit, but it is the odorous oil which feeds their flame.

II. The course of thought passes on to a solemn reminder of the truth and worth of that Gospel which was threatened by the budding heresies of the Colossian Church.

That is contained in the clauses from the middle of the fifth verse to the end of the sixth, and is introduced with significant abruptness, immediately after the commendation of the Colossians' faith. The Apostle's mind and heart are so full of the dangers which he saw them to be in, although they did not know it, that he cannot refrain from setting forth an impressive array of considerations, each of which should make them hold to the gospel with an iron grasp. They are put with the utmost compression. Each word almost might be beaten out into a long discourse, so that we can only indicate the lines of thought. This somewhat tangled skein may, on the whole, be taken as the answer to the question, Why should we cleave to Paul's gospel, and dread and war against tendencies of opinion that would rob us of it? They are preliminary considerations adapted to prepare the way for a patient and thoughtful reception of the arguments which are to follow, by showing how much is at stake, and how the readers would be poor indeed if they were robbed of that great Word.

He begins by reminding them that to that gospel they owed all *their knowledge and hope of heaven*—the hope "whereof ye heard before in the word of the truth of the gospel." That great word alone gives light on the darkness. The sole certainty of a life beyond the grave is built on the Resurrection of Jesus Christ, and the sole hope of a blessed life beyond the grave for the poor soul that has learned its sinfulness is built on the Death of Christ. Without this light, that land is a land of darkness, lighted only by glimmering sparks of conjectures and peradventures. So it is to-day, as it was then; the centuries have only made more clear the entire dependence of the living conviction of immortality on the acceptance of Paul's gospel, "how that Christ died for our sins according to the Scriptures, and that He was raised again the third day." All around us, we see those who reject the fact of Christ's resurrection finding themselves forced to surrender their faith in any life beyond. They cannot sustain themselves on that height of conviction, unless they lean on Christ. The black mountain wall that rings us poor mortals round about is cloven in one place only. Through one narrow cleft there comes a gleam of light. There and there only is the frowning barrier passable. Through that grim cañon, narrow and black, where there is only room for the dark river to run, bright-eyed Hope may travel, letting our her golden thread as she goes, to guide us. Christ has cloven the rock, "the Breaker has gone up before" us, and by His resurrection alone we have the knowledge which is certitude, and the hope which is confidence, of an inheritance in light. If Paul's gospel goes, that goes like morning mist.

Before you throw away the "word of the truth of the gospel," at all events understand that you fling away all assurance of a future life along with it.

Then, there is another motive touched in these words just quoted. The gospel is a word of which the whole substance and content is truth. You may say that is the whole question, whether the gospel is such a word? Of course it is; but observe how here, at the very outset, the gospel is represented as having a distinct dogmatic element in it. It is of value, not because it feeds sentiment or regulates conduct only, but first and foremost because it gives us true though incomplete knowledge concerning all the deepest things of God and man about which, but for its light, we know nothing. That truthful word is opposed to the argumentations and speculations and errors of the heretics. The gospel is not speculation but fact. It is truth, because it is the record of a Person who is the Truth. The history of His life and death is the one source of all certainty and knowledge with regard to man's relations to God, and God's loving purposes to man. To leave it and Him of whom it speaks in order to listen to men who spin theories out of their own brains is to prefer will-o'-the-wisps to the sun. If we listen to Christ, we have the truth; if we turn from Him, our ears are stunned by a Babel. "To whom shall we go? Thou hast the words of eternal life."

Further, this gospel had been already received by them. Ye *heard before*, says he, and again he speaks of the gospel as "come unto" them, and reminds them of the past days in which they "heard and knew the grace of God." That appeal is, of course, no argument except to a man who admits the truth of what he had already received, nor is it meant for argument with others, but it is equivalent to the exhortation, "You have heard that word and accepted it, see that your future be consistent with your past." He would have the life a harmonious whole, all in accordance with the first glad grasp which they had laid on the truth. Sweet and calm and noble is the life which preserves to its close the convictions of its beginning, only deepened and expanded. Blessed are they whose creed at last can be spoken in the lessons they learned in childhood, to which experience has but given new meaning! Blessed they who have been able to store the treasure of a life's thought and learning in the vessels of the early words, which have grown like the magic coffers in a fairy tale, to hold all the increased wealth that can be lodged in them! Beautiful is it when the little children and the young men and the fathers possess the one faith, and when he who began as a child, "knowing the Father," ends as an old man with the same knowledge of the same God, only apprehended now in a form which has gained majesty from the fleeting years, as "Him that is from the beginning." There is no need to leave the Word long since heard in order to get novelty. It will open out into all new depths, and blaze in new radiance as men grow. It will give new answers as the years ask new questions. Each epoch of individual experience, and each phase of society, and all changing forms of opinion will find what meets them in the gospel as it is in Jesus. It is good for Christian men often to recall the beginnings of their faith, to live over again their early emotions, and when they may be getting stunned with the din of controversy, and confused as to the relative importance of different parts of Christian truth, to remember *what* it was that first filled their heart with joy like that of the finder of a hidden treasure, and with what a leap of gladness they first laid hold of Christ.

That spiritual discipline is no less needful than is intellectual, in facing the conflicts of this day.

Again, this gospel was filling the world: "it is in all the world bearing fruit, and increasing." There are two marks of life—it is fruitful and it spreads. Of course such words are not to be construed as if they occurred in a statistical table. "All the world" must be taken with an allowance for rhetorical statement; but making such allowance, the rapid spread of Christianity in Paul's time, and its power to influence character and conduct among all sorts and conditions of men, were facts that needed to be accounted for, if the gospel was not true.

That is surely a noteworthy fact, and one which may well raise a presumption in favour of the truth of the message, and make any proposal to cast it aside for another gospel, a serious matter. Paul is not suggesting the vulgar argument that a thing must be true because so many people have so quickly believed it. But what he is pointing to is a much deeper thought than that. All schisms and heresies are essentially local, and partial. They suit coteries and classes. They are the product of special circumstances acting on special casts of mind, and appeal to such. Like parasitical plants they each require a certain species to grow on, and cannot spread where these are not found. They are not for all time, but for an age. They are not for all men, but for a select few. They reflect the opinions or wants of a layer of society or of a generation, and fade away. But the gospel goes through the world and draws men to itself out of every land and age. Dainties and confections are for the few, and many of them are like pickled olives to unsophisticated palates, and the delicacies of one country are the abominations of another; but everybody likes bread and lives on it, after all.

The gospel which tells of Christ belongs to all and can touch all, because it brushes aside superficial differences of culture and position, and goes straight to the depths of the one human heart, which is alike in us all, addressing the universal sense of sin, and revealing the Saviour of us all, and in Him the universal Father. Do not fling away a gospel that belongs to all, and can bring forth fruit in all kinds of people, for the sake of accepting what can never live in the popular heart, nor influence more than a handful of very select and "superior persons." Let who will have the dainties, do you stick to the wholesome wheaten bread.

Another plea for adherence to the gospel is based upon its continuous and universal fruitfulness. It brings about results in conduct and character which strongly attest its claim to be from God. That is a rough and ready test, no doubt, but a sensible and satisfactory one. A system which says that it will make men good and pure is reasonably judged of by its fruits, and Christianity can stand the test. It did change the face of the old world. It has been the principal agent in the slow growth of "nobler manners, purer laws" which give the characteristic stamp to modern as contrasted with pre-Christian nations. The threefold abominations of the old world—slavery, war, and the degradation of woman—have all been modified, one of them abolished, and the others growingly felt to be utterly un-Christian. The main agent in the change has been the gospel. It has wrought wonders, too, on single souls; and though all Christians must be too conscious of their own imperfections to venture on putting themselves forward as specimens of its power, still the gospel of Jesus Christ has lifted men from the dungheaps of sin and self to "set them with princes," to make them kings and priests; has tamed passions, ennobled pursuits, revolutionised the whole course of many a life, and mightily works to-day in the same fashion, in the measure in which we submit to its influence. Our imperfections are our own; our good is its. A medicine is not shown to be powerless, though it does not do as much as is claimed for it, if the sick man has taken it irregularly and sparingly. The failure of Christianity to bring forth full fruit arises solely from the failure of professing Christians to allow its quickening powers to fill their hearts. After all deductions we may still say with Paul, "it bringeth forth fruit in all the world." This rod has budded, at all events; have any of its antagonists' rods done the same? Do not cast it away, says Paul, till you are sure you have found a better.

This tree not only fruits, but grows. It is not exhausted by fruit-bearing, but it makes wood as well. It is "increasing" as well as "bearing fruit," and that growth in the circuit of its branches that spread through the world, is another of its claims on the faithful adhesion of the Colossians.

Again, they have heard a gospel which reveals the "true grace of God," and that is another consideration urging to steadfastness.

In opposition to it there were put then, as there are put to-day, man's thoughts, and man's requirements, a human wisdom and a burdensome code. Speculations and arguments on the one hand, and laws and rituals on the other, look thin beside the large free gift of a loving God and the message which tells of it. They are but poor bony things to try to live on. The soul wants something more nourishing than such bread made out of sawdust. We want a loving God to live upon, whom we can love because He loves us. Will anything but the gospel give us that? Will anything be our stay, in all weakness, weariness, sorrow and sin, in the fight of life and the agony of death, except the confidence that in Christ we "know the grace of God in truth"?

So, if we gather together all these characteristics of the gospel, they bring out the gravity of the issue when we are asked to tamper with it, or to abandon the old lamp for the brand new ones which many eager voices are proclaiming as the light of the future. May any of us who are on the verge of the precipice lay to heart these serious thoughts! To that gospel we owe our peace; by it alone can the fruit of lofty devout lives be formed and ripened; it has filled the world with its sound, and is revolutionising humanity; it and it only brings to men the good news and the actual gift of the love and mercy of God. It is not a small matter to fling away all this.

We do not prejudge the question of the truth of Christianity; but, at all events, let there be no mistake as to the fact that to give it up is to give up the mightiest power that has ever wrought for the world's good, and that if its light be quenched there will be darkness that may be felt, not dispelled but made more sad and dreary by the ineffectual flickers of some poor rushlights that men have lit, which waver and shine dimly over a little space for a little while, and then die out.

III. We have the Apostolic endorsement of Epaphras, the early teacher of the Colossian Christians.

Paul points his Colossian brethren, finally, to the lessons which they had received from the teacher who had first led them to Christ. No doubt his authority was imperiled by the new direction of thought in the Church, and Paul was desirous of adding the weight of his attestation to the complete correspondence between his own teaching and that of Epaphras.

We know nothing about this Epaphras except from this letter and that to Philemon. He is "one of you," a member of the Colossian Church (iv. 12), whether a Colossian born or not. He had come to the prisoner in Rome, and had brought the tidings of their condition which filled the Apostle's heart with strangely mingled feelings—of joy for their love and Christian walk (verses 4, 8), and of anxiety lest they should be swept from their steadfastness by the errors that he heard were assailing them. Epaphras shared this anxiety, and during his stay in Rome was much in thought, and care, and prayer for them (iv. 12). He does not seem to have been the bearer of this letter to Colossæ. He was in some sense Paul's fellow-servant, and in Philemon he is called by the yet more intimate, though somewhat obscure, name of his fellow-prisoner. It is noticeable that he alone of all Paul's companions receives the name of "fellow-servant," which may perhaps point to some very special piece of service of his, or may possibly be only an instance of Paul's courteous humility, which ever delighted to lift others to his own level—as if he had said, Do not make differences between your own Epaphras and me, we are both slaves of one Master.

The further testimony which Paul bears to him is so emphatic and pointed as to suggest that it was meant to uphold an authority that had been attacked, and to eulogize a character that had been maligned. "He is a faithful minister of Christ on our behalf." In these words the Apostle endorses his teaching, as a true representation of his own. Probably Epaphras founded the Colossian Church and did so in pursuance of a commission given him by Paul. He "also declared to us your love in the Spirit." As he had truly represented Paul and his message to them, so he lovingly represented them and their kindly affection to him. Probably the same people who questioned Epaphras' version of Paul's teaching would suspect the favourableness of his report of the Colossian Church, and hence the double witness borne from the Apostle's generous heart to both parts of his brother's work. His unstinted praise is ever ready. His shield is swiftly flung over any of his helpers who are maligned or assailed. Never was a leader truer to his subordinates, more tender of their reputation, more eager for their increased influence, and freer from every trace of jealousy, than was that lofty and lowly soul.

It is a beautiful though a faint image which shines out on us from these fragmentary notices of this Colossian Epaphras—a true Christian bishop, who had come all the long way from his quiet valley in the depths of Asia Minor, to get guidance about his flock from the great Apostle, and who bore them on his heart day and night, and prayed much for them, while so far away from them. How strange the fortune which has made his name and his solicitudes and prayers immortal! How little he dreamed that such embalming was to be given to his little services, and that they were to be crowned with such exuberant praise!

The smallest work done for Jesus Christ lasts for ever, whether it abide in men's memories or no. Let us ever live as those who, like painters in fresco, have with swift hand to draw lines and lay on colours which will never fade, and let us, by humble faith and holy life, earn such a character from Paul's master. He is glad to praise, and praise from His lips is praise indeed. If He approves of us as faithful servants on His behalf, it matters not what others may say. The Master's "Well done" will outweigh labours and toils, and the depreciating tongues of fellow-servants, or of the Master's enemies.

III
THE PRAYER

"For this cause we also, since the day we heard it, do not cease to pray and to make request for you, that ye may be filled with the knowledge of His will, in all spiritual wisdom and understanding, to walk worthily of the Lord unto all pleasing, bearing fruit in every good work, and increasing in the knowledge of God; strengthened with all power, according to the might of His glory, unto all patience and longsuffering with joy; giving thanks unto the Father."—Col. i. 9–12 (Rev. Ver.).

We have here to deal with one of Paul's prayers for his brethren. In some respects these are the very topmost pinnacles of his letters. Nowhere else does his spirit move so freely, in no other parts are the fervour of his piety and the beautiful simplicity and depth of his love more touchingly shown. The freedom and heartiness of our prayers for others are a very sharp test of both our piety to God and our love to men. Plenty of people can talk and vow who would find it hard to pray. Paul's intercessory prayers are the high-water mark of the epistles in which they occur. He must have been a good man and a true friend of whom so much can be said.

This prayer sets forth the ideal of Christian character. What Paul desired for his friends in Colossæ is what all true Christian hearts should chiefly desire for those whom they love, and should strive after and ask for themselves. If we look carefully at these words we shall see a clear division into parts which stand related to each other as root, stem, and fourfold branches, or as fountain, undivided stream, and "four heads" into which this "river" of Christian life "is parted." To be filled with the knowledge of God's will is the root or fountain-source of all. From it comes a walk worthily of the Lord unto all pleasing—the practical life being the outcome and expression of the inward possession of the will of God. Then we have four clauses, evidently co-ordinate, each beginning with a participle, and together presenting an analysis of this worthy walk. It will be fruitful in all outward work. It will be growing in all inward knowledge of God. Because life is not all doing and knowing, but is suffering likewise, the worthy walk must be patient and long-suffering, because strengthened by God Himself. And to crown all, above work and knowledge and suffering it must be thankfulness to the Father. The magnificent massing together of the grounds of gratitude which follows, we must leave for future consideration, and pause, however abruptly, yet not illogically, at the close of the enumeration of these four branches of the tree, the four sides of the firm tower of the true Christian life.

I. Consider the Fountain or Root of all Christian character—"that ye may be filled with the knowledge of His will in all spiritual wisdom and understanding."

One or two remarks in the nature of verbal exposition may be desirable. Generally speaking, the thing desired is the perfecting of the Colossians in religious knowledge, and the perfection is forcibly expressed in three different aspects. The idea of completeness up to the height of their capacity is given in the prayer that they may be "filled," like some jar charged with sparkling water to the brim. The advanced degree of the knowledge desired for them is given in the word here employed, which is a favourite in the Epistles of the Captivity, and means additional or mature knowledge, that deeper apprehension of God's truth which perhaps had become more obvious to Paul in the quiet growth of his spirit during his life in Rome. And the rich variety of forms which that advanced knowledge would assume is set forth by the final words of the clause, which may either be connected with its first words, so meaning "filled ... so that ye may abound in ... wisdom and understanding;" or with "the knowledge of His will," so meaning a "knowledge which is manifested in." That knowledge will blossom out into *every kind* of "wisdom" and "understanding," two words which it is hard to distinguish, but of which the former is perhaps the more general and the latter the more special, the former the more theoretical and the latter the more practical: and both are the work of the Divine Spirit whose sevenfold perfection of gifts illuminates with perfect light each waiting heart. So perfect, whether in regard to its measure, its maturity, or its manifoldness, is the knowledge of the will of God, which the Apostle regards as the deepest good which his love can ask for these Colossians.

Passing by many thoughts suggested by the words, we may touch one or two large principles which they involve. The first is, that the foundation of all Christian character and conduct is laid in the knowledge of the will of God. Every revelation of God is a law. What it concerns us to know is not abstract truth, or a revelation for speculative thought, but God's *will*. He does not show Himself to us in order merely that we may know, but in order that, knowing, we may do, and, what is more than either knowing or doing, in order that we may be. No revelation from God has accomplished its purpose when a man has simply understood it, but every fragmentary flash of light which comes from Him in nature and providence, and still more the steady radiance that pours from Jesus, is meant indeed to teach us how we should think of God, but to do that mainly as a means to the end that we may live in conformity with His will. The light is knowledge, but it is a light to guide our feet, knowledge which is meant to shape practice.

If that had been remembered, two opposite errors would have been avoided. The error that was threatening the Colossian Church, and has haunted the Church in general ever since, was that of fancying Christianity to be merely a system of truth to be believed, a rattling skeleton of abstract dogmas, very many and very dry. An unpractical heterodoxy was their danger. An unpractical orthodoxy is as real a peril. You may swallow all the creeds bodily, you may even find in God's truth the food of very sweet and real feeling: but neither knowing nor feeling is enough. The one all-important question for us is—does our Christianity *work*? It is knowledge of His *will*, which becomes an ever active force in our lives! Any other kind of religious knowledge is windy food; as Paul says, it "puffeth up;" the knowledge which feeds the soul with wholesome nourishment is the knowledge of His *will*.

The converse error to that of unpractical knowledge, that of an unintelligent practice, is quite as bad. There is always a class of people, and they are unusually numerous to-day, who profess to attach no importance to Christian doctrines, but to put all the stress on Christian morals. They swear by the "Sermon on the Mount," and are blind to the deep doctrinal basis laid in that "sermon" itself, on which its lofty moral teaching is built. What God hath joined together, let no man put asunder. Why pit the parent against the child? why wrench the blossom from its stem? Knowledge is sound when it moulds conduct. Action is good when it is based on knowledge. The knowledge of God is wholesome when it shapes the life. Morality has a basis which makes it vigorous and permanent when it rests upon the knowledge of His will.

Again: Progress in knowledge is the law of the Christian life. There should be a continual advancement in the apprehension of God's will, from that first glimpse which saves, to the mature knowledge which Paul here desires for his friends. The progress does not consist in leaving behind old truths, but in a profounder conception of what is contained in these truths. How differently a Fijian just saved, and a Paul on earth, or a Paul in heaven, look at that verse, "God so loved the world that He gave His only begotten Son"! The truths which are dim to the one, like stars seen through a mist, blaze to the other like the same stars to an eye that has travelled millions of leagues nearer them, and sees them to be suns. The law of the Christian life is continuous increase in the knowledge of the depths that lie in the old truths, and of their far-reaching applications. We are to grow in knowledge of the Christ by coming ever nearer to Him, and learning more of the infinite meaning of our earliest lesson that He is the Son of God who has died for us. The constellations that burn in our nightly sky looked down on Chaldean astronomers, but though these are the same, how much more is known about them at Greenwich than was dreamed at Babylon!

II. Consider the River or Stem of Christian conduct.

The purpose and outcome of this full knowledge of the will of God in Christ is to "walk worthily of the Lord unto all pleasing." By "walk" is of course meant the whole active life; so that the principle is brought out here very distinctly, that the last result of knowledge of the Divine will is an outward life regulated by that will. And the sort of life which such knowledge leads to, is designated in most general terms as "worthy of the Lord unto all pleasing," in which we have set forth two aspects of the true Christian life.

"Worthily of the Lord!" The "Lord" here, as generally, is Christ, and "worthily" seems to mean, in a manner corresponding to what Christ is to us, and has done for us. We find other forms of the same thought in such expressions as "worthy of the vocation wherewith ye are called" (Eph. iv. 1), "worthily of saints" (Rom. xvi. 2), "worthy of the gospel" (Phil. i. 27), "worthily of God" (1 Thess. ii. 12), in all of which there is the idea of a standard to which the practical life is to be conformed. Thus the Apostle condenses into one word all the manifold relations in which we stand to Christ, and all the multifarious arguments for a holy life which they yield.

These are mainly two. The Christian should "walk" in a manner corresponding to what Christ has done for him. "Do ye thus requite the Lord, O foolish people, and unwise?" was the mournful wondering question of the dying Moses to his people, as he summed up the history of unbroken tenderness and love on the one side, and of disloyalty almost as uninterrupted on the other. How much more pathetically and emphatically might the question be asked of us! We say that we are not our own, but bought with a price. Then how do we repay that costly purchase? Do we not requite His blood and tears, His unquenchable, unalterable love, with a little tepid love which grudges sacrifices and has scarcely power enough to influence conduct at all, with a little trembling faith which but poorly corresponds to His firm promises, with a little reluctant obedience? The richest treasure of heaven has been freely lavished for us, and we return a sparing expenditure of our hearts and ourselves, repaying fine gold with tarnished copper, and the flood of love from the heart of Christ with a few niggard drops grudgingly squeezed from ours. Nothing short of complete self-surrender, perfect obedience, and unwavering unfaltering love can characterize the walk that corresponds with our profound obligations to Him. Surely there can be no stronger cord with which to bind us as sacrifices to the horns of the altar than the cords of love. This is the unique glory and power of Christian ethics, that it brings in this tender personal element to transmute the coldness of duty into the warmth of gratitude, so throwing rosy light over the snowy summits of abstract virtue. Repugnant duties become tokens of love, pleasant as every sacrifice made at its bidding ever is. The true Christian spirit says: Thou hast given Thyself wholly for me: help me to yield myself to Thee. Thou hast loved me perfectly: help me to love Thee with all my heart.

The other side of this conception of a worthy walk is, that the Christian should act in a manner corresponding to Christ's character and conduct. We profess to be His by sacredest ties: then we should set our watches by that dial, being conformed to His likeness, and in all our daily life trying to do as He has done, or as we believe He would do if He were in our place. Nothing less than the effort to tread in His footsteps is a walk worthy of the Lord. All unlikeness to His pattern is a dishonour to Him and to ourselves. It is neither worthy of the Lord, nor of the vocation wherewith we are called, nor of the name of saints. Only when these two things are brought about in my experience—when the glow of His love melts my heart and makes it flow down in answering affection, and when the beauty of His perfect life stands ever before me, and though it be high above me, is not a despair, but a stimulus and a hope—only then do I "walk worthy of the Lord."

Another thought as to the nature of the life in which the knowledge of the Divine will should issue, is expressed in the other clause—"unto all pleasing," which sets forth the great aim as being to please Christ in everything. That is a strange purpose to propose to men, as the supreme end to be ever kept in view, to satisfy Jesus Christ by their conduct. To make the good opinion of men our aim is to be slaves; but to please this Man ennobles us, and exalts life. Who or what is He, whose judgment of us is thus all-important, whose approbation is praise indeed, and to win whose smile is a worthy object for which to use life, or even to lose it? We should ask ourselves, Do we make it our ever present object to satisfy Jesus Christ? We are not to mind about other people's approbation. We can do without that. We are not to hunt after the good word of our fellows. Every life into which that craving for man's praise and good opinion enters is tarnished by it. It is a canker, a creeping leprosy, which eats sincerity and nobleness and strength out of a man. Let us not care to trim our sails to catch the shifting winds of this or that man's favour and eulogium, but look higher and say, "With me it is a very small matter to be judged of man's judgment." "I appeal unto Cæsar." He, the true Commander and Emperor, holds our fate in His hands; we have to please Him and Him only. There is no thought which will so reduce the importance of the babble around us, and teach us such brave and wholesome contempt for popular applause, and all the strife of tongues, as the constant habit of trying to act as ever in our great Taskmaster's eye. What does it matter who praise, if He frowns? or who blame, if His face lights with a smile? No thought will so spur us to diligence, and make all life solemn and grand as the thought that "we labour, that whether present or absent, we may be well pleasing to Him." Nothing will so string the muscles for the fight, and free us from being entangled with the things of this life, as the ambition to "please Him who has called us to be soldiers."

Men have willingly flung away their lives for a couple of lines of praise in a despatch, or for a smile from some great commander. Let us try to live and die so as to get "honourable mention" from our captain. Praise from His lips is praise indeed. We shall not know how much it is worth, till the smile lights His face, and the love comes into His eyes, as He looks at us, and says, "Well done! good and faithful servant."

III. We have finally the fourfold streams or branches into which this general conception of Christian character parts itself.

There are four participial clauses here, which seem all to stand on one level, and to present an analysis in more detail of the component parts of this worthy walk. In general terms it is divided into fruitfulness in work, increase in knowledge, strength for suffering, and, as the climax of all, thankfulness.

The first element is—"bearing fruit in every good work." These words carry us back to what was said in ver. 6 about the fruitfulness of the gospel. Here the man in whom that word is planted is regarded as the producer of the fruit, by the same natural transition by which, in our Lord's Parable of the Sower, the men in whose hearts the seed was sown are spoken of as themselves on the one hand, bringing no fruit to perfection, and on the other, bringing forth fruit with patience. The worthy walk will be first manifested in the production of a rich variety of forms of goodness. All profound knowledge of God, and all lofty thoughts of imitating and pleasing Christ, are to be tested at last by their power to make men good, and that not after any monotonous type, nor on one side of their nature only.

One plain principle implied here is that the only true fruit is goodness. We may be busy, as many a man in our great commercial cities is busy, from Monday morning till Saturday night for a long lifetime, and may have had to build bigger barns for our "fruits and our goods," and yet, in the high and solemn meaning of the word here, our life may be utterly empty and fruitless. Much of our work and of its results is no more fruit than the galls on the oak-leaves are. They are a swelling from a puncture made by an insect, a sign of disease, not of life. The only sort of work which can be called fruit, in the highest meaning of the word, is that which corresponds to a man's whole nature and relations; and the only work which does so correspond is a life of loving service of God, which cultivates all things lovely and of good report. Goodness, therefore, alone deserves to be called fruit—as for all the rest of our busy lives, they and their toils are like the rootless, lifeless chaff that is whirled out of the threshing-floor by every gust. A life which has not in it holiness and loving obedience, however richly productive it may be in lower respects, is in inmost reality blighted and barren, and is "nigh unto burning." Goodness is fruit; all else is nothing but leaves.

Again: the Christian life is to be "fruitful in *every* good work." This tree is to be like that in the apocalyptic vision, which "bare twelve manner of fruits," yielding every month a different sort. So we should fill the whole circuit of the year with various holiness, and seek to make widely different forms of goodness our own. We have all certain kinds of excellence which are more natural and easier for us than others are. We should seek to cultivate the kind which is hardest for us. The thorn stock of our own character should bear not only grapes, but figs too, and olives as well, being grafted upon the true olive-tree, which is Christ. Let us aim at this all-round and multiform virtue, and not be like a scene for a stage, all gay and bright on one side, and dirty canvas and stretchers hung with cobwebs on the other.

The second element in the analysis of the true Christian life is— "increasing in the knowledge of God." The figure of the tree is probably continued here. If it fruits, its girth will increase, its branches will spread, its top will mount, and next year its shadow on the grass will cover a larger circle. Some would take the "knowledge" here as the instrument or means of growth, and would render "increasing by the knowledge of God," supposing that the knowledge is represented as the rain or the sunshine which minister to the growth of the plant. But perhaps it is better to keep to the idea conveyed by the common rendering, which regards the words "in knowledge" as the specification of that region in which the growth enjoined is to be realized. So here we have the converse of the relation between work and knowledge which we met in the earlier part of the chapter. There, knowledge led to a worthy walk; here, fruitfulness in good works leads to, or at all events is accompanied with, an increased knowledge. And both are true. These two work on each other a reciprocal increase. All true knowledge which is not mere empty notions, naturally tends to influence action, and all true action naturally tends to confirm the knowledge from which it proceeds. Obedience gives insight: "If any man wills to do My will, he shall know of the doctrine." If I am faithful up to the limits of my present knowledge, and have brought it all to bear on character and conduct, I shall find that in the effort to make my every thought a deed, there have fallen from my eyes as it were scales, and I see some things clearly which were faint and doubtful before. Moral truth becomes dim to a bad man. Religious truth grows bright to a good one, and whosoever strives to bring all his creed into practice, and all his practice under the guidance of his creed, will find that the path of obedience is the path of growing light.

Then comes the third element in this resolution of the Christian character into its component parts—"strengthened with all power, according to the might of His glory, unto all patience and longsuffering with joyfulness." Knowing and doing are not the whole of life: there are sorrow and suffering too.

Here again we have the Apostle's favourite "all," which occurs so frequently in this connection. As he desired for the Colossians, all wisdom, unto all pleasing, and fruitfulness in every good work, so he prays for all power to strengthen them. Every kind of strength which God can give and man can receive, is to be sought after by us, that we may be "girded with strength," cast like a brazen wall all round our human weakness. And that Divine power is to flow into us, having this for its measure and limit—"the might of His glory." His "glory" is the lustrous light of His self-revelation; and the far-flashing energy revealed in that self-manifestation is the immeasurable measure of the strength that may be ours. True, a finite nature can never contain the infinite, but man's finite nature is capable of indefinite expansion. Its elastic walls stretch to contain the increasing gift. The more we desire, the more we receive, and the more we receive, the more we are able to receive. The amount which filled our hearts to-day should not fill them to-morrow. Our capacity is at each moment the working limit of the measure of the strength given us. But it is always shifting, and may be continually increasing. The only real limit is "the might of His glory," the limitless omnipotence of the self-revealing God. To that we may indefinitely approach, and till we have exhausted God we have not reached the furthest point to which we should aspire.

And what exalted mission is destined for this wonderful communicated strength? Nothing that the world thinks great: only helping some lone widow to stay her heart in patience, and flinging a gleam of brightness, like sunrise on a stormy sea, over some tempest-tossed life. The strength is worthily employed and absorbed in producing "all patience and longsuffering with joy." Again the favourite "all" expresses the universality of the patience and longsuffering. Patience here is not merely passive endurance.

It includes the idea of perseverance in the right course, as well as that of uncomplaining bearing of evil. It is the "steering right onward," without bating one jot of heart or hope; the temper of the traveller who struggles forward, though the wind in his face dashes the sleet in his eyes, and he has to wade through deep snow. While "patience" regards the evil mainly as sent by God, and as making the race set before us difficult, "longsuffering" describes the temper under suffering when considered as a wrong or injury done by man. And whether we think of our afflictions in the one or the other light, God's strength will steal into our hearts, if we will, not merely to help us to bear them with perseverance and with meekness as unruffled as Christ's, but to crown both graces—as the clouds are sometimes rimmed with flashing gold—with a great light of joy. That is the highest attainment of all. "Sorrowful, yet always rejoicing." Flowers beneath the snow, songs in the night, fire burning beneath the water, "peace subsisting at the heart of endless agitation," cool airs in the very crater of Vesuvius—all these paradoxes may be surpassed in our hearts if they are strengthened with all might by an indwelling Christ.

The crown of all, the last of the elements of the Christian character, is thankfulness—"giving thanks unto the Father." This is the summit of all; and is to be diffused through all. All our progressive fruitfulness and insight, as well as our perseverance and unruffled meekness in suffering, should have a breath of thankfulness breathed through them. We shall see the grand enumeration of the reasons for thankfulness in the next verses. Here we pause for the present, with this final constituent of the life which Paul desired for the Colossian Christians. Thankfulness should mingle with all our thoughts and feelings, like the fragrance of some perfume penetrating through the common scentless air. It should embrace all events. It should be an operating motive in all actions. We should be clear-sighted and believing enough to be thankful for pain and disappointment and loss. That gratitude will add the crowning consecration to service and knowledge and endurance. It will touch our spirits to the finest of all issues, for it will lead to glad self-surrender, and make of our whole life a sacrifice of praise. "I beseech you, brethren, by the mercies of God, that ye present your bodies a living sacrifice." Our lives will then exhale in fragrance and shoot up in flashing tongues of ruddy light and beauty, when kindled into a flame of gratitude by the glow of Christ's great love. Let us lay our poor selves on that altar, as sacrifices of thanksgiving; for with such sacrifices God is well-pleased.

IV
THE FATHER'S GIFTS THROUGH THE SON

"The Father, who made us meet to be partakers of the inheritance of the saints in light; who delivered us out of the power of darkness, and translated us into the kingdom of the Son of His love; in whom we have our redemption, the forgiveness of our sins." — Col. i. 12–14 (Rev. Ver.).

We have advanced thus far in this Epistle without having reached its main subject. We now, however, are on its verge. The next verses to those now to be considered lead us into the very heart of Paul's teaching, by which he would oppose the errors rife in the Colossian Church. The great passages describing the person and work of Jesus Christ are at hand, and here we have the immediate transition to them.

The skill with which the transition is made is remarkable. How gradually and surely the sentences, like some hovering winged things, circle more and more closely round the central light, till in the last words they touch it, ... "the Son of His love!" It is like some long procession heralding a king. They that go before, cry Hosanna, and point to him who comes last and chief. The affectionate greetings which begin the letter, pass into prayer; the prayer into thanksgiving. The thanksgiving, as in these words, lingers over and recounts our blessings, as a rich man counts his treasures, or a lover dwells on his joys. The enumeration of the blessings leads, as by a golden thread, to the thought and name of Christ, the fountain of them all, and then, with a burst and a rush, the flood of the truths about Christ which he had to give them sweeps through Paul's mind and heart, carrying everything before it. The name of Christ always opens the floodgates in Paul's heart.

We have here then the deepest grounds for Christian thanksgiving, which are likewise the preparations for a true estimate of the worth of the Christ who gives them. These grounds of thanksgiving are but various aspects of the one great blessing of "Salvation." The diamond flashes greens and purples, and yellows and reds, according to the angle at which its facets catch the eye.

It is also to be observed, that all these blessings are the present possession of Christians. The language of the first three clauses in the verses before us points distinctly to a definite past act by which the Father, at some definite point of time, made us meet, delivered and translated us, while the present tense in the last clause shows that "our redemption" is not only begun by some definite act in the past, but is continuously and progressively possessed in the present.

We notice, too, the remarkable correspondence of language with that which Paul heard when he lay prone on the ground, blinded by the flashing light, and amazed by the pleading remonstrance from heaven which rung in his ears. "I send thee to the Gentiles ... that they may turn from *darkness* to *light*, and from the power of Satan unto God, that they may receive *remission of sins*, and an *inheritance* among them which are sanctified." All the principal phrases are there, and are freely recombined by Paul, as if unconsciously his memory was haunted still by the sound of the transforming words heard so long ago.

I. The first ground of thankfulness which all Christians have is, that they are fit for the inheritance. Of course the metaphor here is drawn from the "inheritance" given to the people of Israel, namely, the land of Canaan. Unfortunately, our use of "heir" and "inheritance" confines the idea to possession by succession on death, and hence some perplexity is popularly experienced as to the force of the word in Scripture. There, it implies possession by lot, if anything more than the simple notion of possession; and points to the fact that the people did not win their land by their own swords, but because "God had a favour unto them." So the Christian inheritance is not won by our own merit, but given by God's goodness. The words may be literally rendered, "fitted us for the portion of the lot," and taken to mean the share or portion which consists in the lot; but perhaps it is clearer, and more accordant with the analogy of the division of the land among the tribes, to take them as meaning "for our (individual) share in the broad land which, as a whole, is the allotted possession of the saints." This possession belongs to them, and is situated in the world of "light." Such is the general outline of the thoughts here. The first question that arises is, whether this inheritance is present or future. The best answer is that it is both; because, whatever additions of power and splendour as yet unspeakable may wait to be revealed in the future, the essence of all which heaven can bring is ours to-day, if we live in the faith and love of Christ. The difference between a life of communion with God here and yonder is one of degree and not of kind. True, there are differences of which we cannot speak, in enlarged capacities, and a "spiritual body," and sins cast out, and nearer approach to "the fountain itself of heavenly radiance;" but he who can say, while he walks amongst the shadows of earth, "The Lord is the portion of my inheritance," will neither leave his treasures behind him when he dies, nor enter on the possession of a wholly new inheritance, when he passes into the heavens. But while this is true, it is also true that that future possession of God will be so deepened and enlarged that its beginnings here are but the "earnest," of the same nature indeed as the estate, but limited in comparison as is the tuft of grass which used to be given to a new possessor, when set against the broad lands from which it was plucked. Here certainly the predominant idea is that of a present fitness for a mainly future possession.

We notice again—where the inheritance is situated—"in the light." There are several possible ways of connecting that clause with the preceding. But without discussing these, it may be enough to point out that the most satisfactory seems to be to regard it as specifying the region in which the inheritance lies. It lies in a realm where purity and knowledge and gladness dwell undimmed and unbounded by an envious ring of darkness. For these three are the triple rays into which, according to the Biblical use of the figure, that white beam may be resolved.

From this there follows that it is capable of being possessed only by *saints*. There is no merit or desert which makes men worthy of the inheritance, but there is a congruity, or correspondence between character and the inheritance. If we rightly understand what the essential elements of "heaven" are, we shall have no difficulty in seeing that the possession of it is utterly incompatible with anything but holiness. The vulgar ideas of what heaven is, hinder people from seeing how to get there. They dwell upon the mere outside of the thing, they take symbols for realities and accidents for essentials, and so it appears an arbitrary arrangement that a man must have faith in Christ to enter heaven. If it be a kingdom of light, then only souls that love the light can go thither, and until owls and bats rejoice in the sunshine, there will be no way of being fit for the inheritance which is light, but by ourselves being "light in the Lord." Light itself is a torture to diseased eyes. Turn up any stone by the roadside and we see how unwelcome light is to crawling creatures that have lived in the darkness till they have come to love it.

Heaven is God and God is heaven. How can a soul possess God, and find its heaven in possessing Him? Certainly only by likeness to Him, and loving Him. The old question, "Who shall stand in the Holy Place?" is not answered in the gospel by reducing the conditions, or negativing the old reply. The common sense of every conscience answers, and Christianity answers, as the Psalmist does, "He that hath clean hands and a pure heart."

One more step has to be taken to reach the full meaning of these words, namely, the assertion that men who are not yet perfectly pure are already fit to be partakers of the inheritance. The tense of the verb in the original points back to a definite act by which the Colossians were made meet, namely, their conversion; and the plain emphatic teaching of the New Testament is that incipient and feeble faith in Christ works a change so great, that through it we are fitted for the inheritance by the impartation of a new nature, which, though it be but as a grain of mustard seed, shapes from henceforth the very inmost centre of our personal being. In due time that spark will convert into its own fiery brightness the whole mass, however green and smokily it begins to burn. Not the absence of sin, but the presence of faith working by love, and longing for the light, makes fitness. No doubt flesh and blood cannot inherit the Kingdom of God, and we must put off the vesture of the body which has wrapped us during the wild weather here, before we can be fully fit to enter the banqueting hall; nor do we know how much evil which has not its seat in the soul may drop away therewith—but the spirit is fit for heaven as soon as a man turns to God in Christ. Suppose a company of rebels, and one of them, melted by some reason or other, is brought back to loyalty. He is fit by that inward change, although he has not done a single act of loyalty, for the society of loyal subjects, and unfit for that of traitors. Suppose a prodigal son away in the far off land. Some remembrance comes over him of what home used to be like, and of the bountiful house-keeping that is still there; and though it may begin with nothing more exalted than an empty stomach, if it ends in "I will arise and go to my Father," at that instant a gulf opens between him and the riotous living of "the citizens of that country," and he is no longer fitted for their company. He is meet for the fellowship of his father's house, though he has a weary journey before he gets there, and needs to have his rags changed, and his filth washed off him, ere he can sit down at the feast.

So whoever turns to the love of God in Christ, and yields in the inmost part of his being to the power of His grace, is already "light in the Lord." The true home and affinities of his real self are in the kingdom of the light, and he is ready for his part in the inheritance, either here or yonder. There is no breach of the great law, that character makes fitness for heaven—might we not say that character makes heaven?—for the very roots of character lie in disposition and desire, rather than in action. Nor is there in this principle anything inconsistent with the need for continual growth in congruity of nature with that land of light. The light within, if it be truly there, will, however slowly, spread, as surely as the grey of twilight brightens to the blaze of noonday. The heart will be more and more filled with it, and the darkness driven back more and more to brood in remote corners, and at last will vanish utterly. True fitness will become more and more fit. We shall grow more and more capable of God. The measure of our capacity is the measure of our possession, and the measure in which we have become light, is the measure of our capacity for the light. The land was parted among the tribes of Israel according to their strength; some had a wider, some a narrower strip of territory. So, as there are differences in Christian character here, there will be differences in Christian participation in the inheritance hereafter. "Star differeth from star." Some will blaze in brighter radiance and glow with more fervent heat because they move in orbits closer to the sun.

But, thank God, we are "fit for the inheritance," if we have ever so humbly and poorly trusted ourselves to Jesus Christ and received His renewing life into our spirits. Character alone fits for heaven. But character may be in germ or in fruit. "If any man be in Christ, he *is* a new creature." Do we trust ourselves to Him? Are we trying, with His help, to live as children of the light? Then we need not droop or despair by reason of evil that may still haunt our lives. Let us give it no quarter, for it diminishes our fitness for the full possession of God; but let it not cause our tongue to falter in "giving thanks to the Father who made us meet to be partakers of the inheritance of the saints in light."

II. The second ground of thankfulness is, the change of king and country. God "delivered us out of the power of darkness, and translated us into the kingdom of the Son of His love." These two clauses embrace the negative and positive sides of the same act which is referred to in the former ground of thankfulness, only stated now in reference to our allegiance and citizenship in the present rather than in the future. In the "deliverance" there maybe a reference to God's bringing Israel out of Egypt, suggested by the previous mention of the inheritance, while the "translation" into the other kingdom may be an illustration drawn from the well known practice of ancient warfare, the deportation of large bodies of natives from conquered kingdoms to some other part of the conqueror's realm.

We notice then the two kingdoms and their kings. "The power of darkness," is an expression found in Luke's Gospel (xxii. 18), and it may be used here as a reminiscence of our Lord's solemn words. "Power" here seems to imply the conception of harsh, arbitrary dominion, in contrast with the gracious rule of the other kingdom. It is a realm of cruel and grinding sway. Its prince is personified in an image that Æschylus or Dante might have spoken. Darkness sits sovereign there, a vast and gloomy form on an ebon throne, wielding a heavy sceptre over wide regions wrapped in night. The plain meaning of that tremendous metaphor is just this—that the men who are not Christians live in a state of subjection to darkness of ignorance, darkness of misery, darkness of sin. If I am not a Christian man, that black three-headed hound of hell sits baying on my doorstep.

What a wonderful contrast the other kingdom and its King present! "The kingdom of"—not "the light," as we are prepared to hear, in order to complete the antithesis, but—"the Son of His love," who is the light. The Son who is the object of His love, on whom it all and ever rests, as on none besides. He has a kingdom in existence now, and not merely hoped for, and to be set up at some future time. Wherever men lovingly obey Christ, there is His kingdom. The subjects make the kingdom, and we may to-day belong to it, and be free from all other dominion because we bow to His. There then sit the two kings, like the two in the old story, "either of them on his throne, clothed in his robes, at the entering in of the gate of the city." Darkness and Light, the ebon throne and the white throne, surrounded each by their ministers; there Sorrow and Gloom, here Gladness and Hope; there Ignorance with blind eyes and idle aimless hands, here Knowledge with the sunlight on her face, and Diligence for her handmaid; here Sin, the pillar of the gloomy realm, there Righteousness, in robes so as no fuller on earth could white them. Under which king, my brother?

We notice the transference of subjects. The sculptures on Assyrian monuments explain this metaphor for us. A great conqueror has come, and speaks to us as Sennacherib did to the Jews (2 Kings xviii. 31, 32), "Come out to me ... and I will take you away to a land of corn and wine, that ye may live and not die."

If we listen to His voice, He will lead away a long string of willing captives and plant them, not as pining exiles, but as happy naturalized citizens, in the kingdom which the Father has appointed for "the Son of His love."

That transference is effected on the instant of our recognising the love of God in Jesus Christ, and yielding up the heart to Him. We too often speak as if the "entrance ministered at last to" a believing soul "into the kingdom of our Lord and Saviour," were its first entrance therein, and forget that we enter it as soon as we yield to the drawings of Christ's love and take service under the king. The change then is greater than at death. When we die, we shall change provinces, and go from an outlying colony to the mother city and seat of empire, but we shall not change kingdoms. We shall be under the same government, only then we shall be nearer the King and more loyal to Him. That change of king is the real fitness for heaven. We know little of what profound changes death may make, but clearly a physical change cannot effect a spiritual revolution. They who are not Christ's subjects will not become so by dying. If here we are trying to serve a King who has delivered us from the tyranny of darkness, we may be very sure that He will not lose His subjects in the darkness of the grave. Let us choose our king. If we take Christ for our heart's Lord, every thought of Him here, every piece of partial obedience and stained service, as well as every sorrow and every joy, our fading possessions and our undying treasures, the feeble new life that wars against our sins, and even the very sins themselves as contradictory of our deepest self, unite to seal to us the assurance, "Thine eyes shall see the King in His beauty. They shall behold the land that is very far off."

III. The heart and centre of all occasions for thankfulness is the Redemption which we receive in Christ.

"In whom we have our redemption, the forgiveness of our sins." The Authorized Version reads "redemption *through His blood*," but these words are not found in the best manuscripts, and are regarded by the principal modern editors as having been inserted from the parallel place in Ephesians (i. 7), where they are genuine. The very heart then of the blessings which God has bestowed, is "redemption," which consists primarily, though not wholly, in "forgiveness of sins," and is received by us in "the Son of His love."

"Redemption," in its simplest meaning, is the act of delivering a slave from captivity by the payment of ransom. So that it contains in its application to the effect of Christ's death, substantially the same figure as in the previous clause which spoke of a deliverance from a tyrant, only that what was there represented as an act of Power is here set forth as the act of self-sacrificing Love which purchases our freedom at a heavy cost. That ransom price is said by Christ Himself to be "His life," and His Incarnation to have the paying of that price as one of its two chief objects. So the words added here by quotation from the companion Epistle are in full accordance with New Testament teaching; but even omitting them, the meaning of the clause is unmistakable. Christ's death breaks the chains which bind us, and sets us free. By it He acquires us for Himself. That transcendent act of sacrifice has such a relation to the Divine government on the one hand, and to the "sin of the world," as a whole, on the other, that by it all who trust in Him are delivered from the most real penal consequences of sin and from the dominion of its darkness over their natures. We freely admit that we cannot penetrate to the understanding of *how* Christ's death thus avails. But just because the *rationale* of the doctrine is avowedly beyond our limits, we are barred from asserting that it is incompatible with God's character, or with common justice, or that it is immoral, and the like. When we know God through and through, to all the depths and heights and lengths and breadths of His nature, and when we know man in like manner, and when, consequently, we know the relation between God and man as perfectly, and not till then, we shall have a right to reject the teaching of Scripture on this matter, on such grounds. Till then, let our faith lay hold on the fact, though we do not understand the "how" of the fact, and cling to that cross which is the great power of God unto salvation, and the heart-changing exponent of the love of Christ which passeth knowledge.

The essential and first element in this redemption is "the forgiveness of sins." Possibly some misconception of the nature of redemption may have been associated with the other errors which threatened the Colossian Church, and thus Paul may have been led to this emphatic declaration of its contents. Forgiveness, and not some mystic deliverance by initiation or otherwise from the captivity of flesh and matter, is redemption. There is more than forgiveness in it, but forgiveness lies on the threshold; and that not only the removal of legal penalties inflicted by a specific act, but the forgiveness of a father. A sovereign pardons when he remits the sentence which law has pronounced. A father forgives when the free flow of his love is unhindered by his child's fault, and he may forgive and punish at the same moment. The truest "penalty" of sin is that death which consists in separation from God; and the conceptions of judicial pardon and fatherly forgiveness unite when we think of the "remission of sins" as being the removal of that separation, and the deliverance of heart and conscience from the burden of guilt and of a father's wrath.

Such forgiveness leads to that full deliverance from the power of darkness, which is the completion of redemption. There is deep meaning in the fact that the word here used for "forgiveness," means literally, "sending away." Pardon has a mighty power to banish sin, not only as guilt, but as habit. The waters of the gulf stream bear the warmth of the tropics to the icy north, and lave the foot of the glaciers on its coast till they melt and mingle with the liberating waves. So the flow of the forgiving love of God thaws the hearts frozen in the obstinacy of sin, and blends our wills with itself in glad submission and grateful service.

But we must not overlook the significant words in which the condition of possessing this redemption is stated: "in Whom." There must be a real living union with Christ, by which we are truly "in Him" in order to our possession of redemption. "Redemption through His blood" is not the whole message of the Gospel; it has to be completed by "*In Whom* we have redemption through His blood." That real living union is effected by our faith, and when we are thus "in Him," our wills, hearts, spirits joined to Him, then, and only then are we borne away from "the kingdom of the darkness" and partake of redemption. We cannot get His gifts without Himself.

We observe, in conclusion, how redemption appears here as a present and growing possession. There is emphasis on "we *have*." The Colossian

Christians had by one definite act in the past been fitted for a share in the inheritance, and by the same act had been transferred to the kingdom of Christ. Already they possess the inheritance, and are in the kingdom, although both are to be more gloriously manifested in the future. Here, however, Paul contemplates rather the reception, moment by moment, of redemption. We might almost read "we are having," for the present tense seems used on purpose to convey the idea of a continual communication from Him to Whom we are to be united by faith. Daily we may draw what we daily need—daily forgiveness for daily sins, the washing of the feet which even he who has been bathed requires after each day's march through muddy roads, daily bread for daily hunger, and daily strength for daily effort. So day unto day may, in our narrow lives, as in the wide heavens with all their stars, utter speech, and night unto night show knowledge of the redeeming love of our Father. Like the rock that followed the Israelites in the wilderness, according to Jewish legend, and poured out water for their thirst, His grace flows ever by our sides and from its bright waters we may daily draw with joy.

And so let us lay to heart humbly these two lessons; that all our Christianity must begin with forgiveness, and that, however far advanced we may be in the Divine life, we never get beyond the need for a continual bestowal upon us of God's pardoning mercy.

Many of us, like some of these Colossians, are ready to call ourselves in some sense followers of Christ. The speculative side of Christian truth may have attractions for some of us, its lofty morality for others. Some of us may be mainly drawn to it by its comforts for the weary; some may be looking to it chiefly in hope of a future heaven. But whatever we are, and however we may be disposed to Christ and His Gospel, here is a plain message for us; we must begin by going to Him for pardon. It is not enough for any of us to find in Him "wisdom," or even "righteousness," for we need "redemption" which is "forgiveness," and unless He is to us forgiveness, He will not be either righteousness or wisdom.

We can climb a ladder that reaches to heaven, but its foot must be in "the horrible pit and miry clay" of our sins. Little as we like to hear it, the first need for us all is forgiveness. Everything begins with that. "The inheritance of the saints," with all its wealth of glory, its immortal life and unfading joys, its changeless security, and its unending progress deeper and deeper into the light and likeness of God, is the goal, but the *only* entrance is through the strait gate of penitence. Christ will forgive on our cry for pardon, and that is the first link of a golden chain unwinding from His hand by which we may ascend to the perfect possession of our inheritance in God. "Whom He justified, them," and them only, He will glorify.

V

THE GLORY OF THE SON IN HIS RELATION TO THE FATHER, THE UNIVERSE AND THE CHURCH

"Who is the image of the invisible God, the firstborn of all creation; for in Him were all things created, in the heavens and upon the earth, things visible and things invisible, whether thrones or dominions or principalities or powers, all things have been created through Him and unto Him; and He is before all things, and in Him all things consist. And He is the head of the body, the church: who is the beginning, the firstborn from the dead; that in all things He might have the pre-eminence."—Col. i. 15–18 (Rev. Ver.).

As has already been remarked, the Colossian Church was troubled by teachers who had grafted on Jewish belief many of the strange speculations about matter and creation which have always had such a fascination for the Eastern mind. To us, they are apt to seem empty dreams, baseless and bewildering; but they had force enough to shake the early Church to its foundation, and in some forms they still live.

These teachers in Colossæ seem to have held that all matter was evil and the seat of sin; that therefore the material creation could not have come directly from a good God, but was in a certain sense opposed to Him, or, at all events, was separated from Him by a great gulf. The void space was bridged by a chain of beings, half abstractions and half persons, gradually becoming more and more material. The lowest of them had created the material universe and now governed it, and all were to be propitiated by worship.

Some such opinions must be presupposed in order to give point and force to these great verses in which Paul opposes the solid truth to these dreams, and instead of a crowd of Powers and angelic Beings, in whom the effulgence of Deity was gradually darkened, and the spirit became more and more thickened into matter, lifts high and clear against that background of fable, the solitary figure of the one Christ. He fills all the space between God and man. There is no need for a crowd of shadowy beings to link heaven with earth. Jesus Christ lays His hand upon both. He is the head and source of creation; He is the head and fountain of life to His Church. Therefore He is first in all things, to be listened to, loved and worshipped by men. As when the full moon rises, so when Christ appears, all the lesser stars with which Alexandrian and Eastern speculation had peopled the abysses of the sky are lost in the mellow radiance, and instead of a crowd of flickering ineffectual lights there is one perfect orb, "and heaven is overflowed." "We see no *creature* any more save Jesus only."

We have outgrown the special forms of error which afflicted the Church at Colossæ, but the truths which are here set over against them are eternal, and are needed to-day in our conflicts of opinion as much as then. There are here three grand conceptions of Christ's relations. We have Christ and God, Christ and Creation, Christ and the Church, and, built upon all these, the triumphant proclamation of His supremacy over all creatures in all respects.

I. We have the relation of Christ to God set forth in these grand words, "the image of the invisible God."

Apparently Paul is here using for his own purposes language which was familiar on the lips of his antagonists. We know that Alexandrian Judaism had much to say about the "Word," and spoke of it as the Image of God: and probably some such teaching had found its way to Colossæ. An "image" is a likeness or representation, as of a king's head on a coin, or of a face reflected in a mirror. Here it is that which makes the invisible visible. The God who dwells in the thick darkness, remote from sense and above thought, has come forth and made Himself known to man, even in a very real way has come within the reach of man's senses, in the manhood of Jesus Christ. Where then is there a place for the shadowy abstractions and emanations with which some would bind together God and man?

The first thought involved in this statement is, that the Divine Being in Himself is inconceivable and unapproachable. "No man hath seen God at any time, nor can see Him." Not only is He beyond the reach of sense, but above the apprehension of the understanding. Direct and immediate knowledge of Him is impossible. There may be, there is, written on every human spirit a dim consciousness of His presence, but that is not knowledge. Creatural limitations prevent it, and man's sin prevents it. He is "the King invisible," because He is the "Father of Lights" dwelling in "a glorious privacy of light," which is to us darkness because there is in it "no darkness at all."

Then, the next truth included here is, that Christ is the perfect manifestation and image of God. In Him we have the invisible becoming visible. Through Him we know all that we know of God, as distinguished from what we guess or imagine or suspect of Him. On this high theme, it is not wise to deal much in the scholastic language of systems and creeds. Few words, and these mainly His own, are best, and he is least likely to speak wrongly who confines himself most to Scripture in his presentation of the truth. All the great streams of teaching in the New Testament concur in the truth which Paul here proclaims. The conception in John's Gospel of the Word which is the utterance and making audible of the Divine mind, the conceptions in the Epistle to the Hebrews of the effulgence or forthshining of God's glory, and the very image, or stamped impress of His substance, are but other modes of representing the same facts of full likeness and complete manifestation, which Paul here asserts by calling the man Christ Jesus, the image of the Invisible God. The same thoughts are involved in the name by which our Lord called Himself, the Son of God; and they cannot be separated from many words of His, such as "he that hath seen Me hath seen the Father." In Him the Divine nature comes near to us in a form that once could be grasped in part by men's senses, for it was "that of the Word of life" which they saw with their eyes and their hands handled, and which is to-day and for ever a form that can be grasped by mind and heart and will. In Christ we have the revelation of a God who can be known, and loved, and trusted, with a knowledge which, though it be not complete, is real and valid, with a love which is solid enough to be the foundation of a life, with a trust which is conscious that it has touched rock and builds secure. Nor is that fact that He is the revealer of God, one that began with His incarnation, or ends with His earthly life. From the beginning and before the creatural beginning, as we shall see in considering another part of these great verses, the Word was the agent of all Divine activity, the "arm of the Lord," and the source of all Divine illumination, "the face of the Lord," or, as we have the thought put in the remarkable words of the Book of Proverbs, where the celestial and pure Wisdom is more than a personification though not yet distinctly conceived as a person, "The Lord possessed me in the beginning of His way. I was by Him as one brought up—or as a master worker—with Him, and I was daily *His* delight ... and *My* delights were with the sons of men." And after the veils of flesh and sense are done away, and we see face to face, I believe that the face which we shall see, and seeing, shall have beauty born of the vision passing into our faces, will be the face of Jesus Christ, in which the light of the glory of God shall shine for the redeemed and perfected sons of God, even as it did for them when they groped amid the shows of earth. The law for time and for eternity is, "I have declared Thy name unto My brethren and will declare it." That great fathomless, shoreless ocean of the Divine nature is like a "closed sea"—Christ is the broad river which brings its waters to men, and "everything liveth whithersoever the river cometh."

In these brief words on so mighty a matter, I must run the risk of appearing to deal in unsupported statements. My business is not so much to try to prove Paul's words as to explain them, and then to press them home. Therefore I would urge that thought, that we depend on Christ for all true knowledge of God. Guesses are not knowledge. Speculations are not knowledge. Peradventures, whether of hope or fear, are not knowledge. What we poor men need, is a certitude of a God who loves us and cares for us, has an arm that can help us, and a heart that will. The God of "pure theism" is little better than a phantom, so unsubstantial that you can see the stars shining through the pale form, and when a man tries to lean on him for support, it is like leaning on a wreath of mist. There is nothing. There is no certitude firm enough for us to find sustaining power against life's trials in resting upon it, but in Christ. There is no warmth of love enough for us to thaw our frozen limbs by, apart from Christ. In Him, and in Him alone, the far off, awful, doubtful God becomes a God very near, of Whom we are sure, and sure that He loves and is ready to help and cleanse and save.

And that is what we each need. "My soul crieth out for God, for the *living* God." And never will that orphaned cry be answered, but in the possession of Christ, in Whom we possess the Father also. No dead abstractions—no reign of law—still less the dreary proclamation, "Behold we know not anything," least of all, the pottage of material good, will hush that bitter wail that goes up unconsciously from many an Esau's heart—"My father, my father!" Men will find Him in Christ. They will find Him nowhere else. It seems to me that the only refuge for this generation from atheism—if it is still allowable to use that unfashionable word—is the acceptance of Christ as the revealer of God. On any other terms religion is rapidly becoming impossible for the cultivated class. The great word which Paul opposed to the cobwebs of Gnostic speculation is the word for our own time with all its perplexities—Christ is the Image of the Invisible God.

II. We have the relation of Christ to Creation set forth in that great name, "the firstborn of all creation," and further elucidated by a magnificent series of statements which proclaim Him to be agent or medium, and aim or goal of creation, prior to it in time and dignity, and its present upholder and bond of unity.

"The firstborn of all creation." At first sight, this name seems to include Him in the great family of creatures as the eldest, and clearly to treat Him as one of them, just because He is declared to be in some sense the first of them.

That meaning has been attached to the words; but it is shown not to be their intention by the language of the next verse, which is added to prove and explain the title. It distinctly alleges that Christ was "before" all creation, and that He is the agent of all creation. To insist that the words must be explained so as to include Him in "creation" would be to go right in the teeth of the Apostle's own justification and explanation of them. So that the true meaning is that He is the firstborn, in comparison with, or in reference to, all creation. Such an understanding of the force of the expression is perfectly allowable grammatically, and is necessary unless this verse is to be put in violent contradiction to the next. The same construction is found in Milton's

> "Adam, the goodliest man of men since born,
> His sons, the fairest of her daughters, Eve."

where "of" distinctly means "in comparison with," and not "belonging to."

The title implies priority in existence, and supremacy. It substantially means the same thing as the other title of "the only begotten Son," only that the latter brings into prominence the relation of the Son to the Father, while the former lays stress on His relation to Creation. Further it must be noted, that this name applies to the Eternal Word and not to the incarnation of that Word, or to put it in another form, the divinity and not the humanity of the Lord Jesus is in the Apostle's view. Such is the briefest outline of the meaning of this great name.

A series of clauses follow, stating more fully the relation of the firstborn Son to Creation, and so confirming and explaining the title.

The whole universe is, as it were, set in one class, and He alone over against it. No language could be more emphatically all-comprehensive. Four times in one sentence we have "all things"—the whole universe—repeated, and traced to Him as Creator and Lord. "In the heavens and the earth" is quoted from Genesis, and is intended here, as there, to be an exhaustive enumeration of the creation according to place. "Things visible or invisible" again includes the whole under a new principle of division—there are visible things in heaven, as sun and stars, there may be invisible on earth, but wherever and of whatever sort they are, He made them. "Whether thrones or dominions, or principalities or powers," an enumeration evidently alluding to the dreamy speculations about an angelic hierarchy filling the space between the far off God, and men immersed in matter. There is a tone of contemptuous impatience in Paul's voice, as he quotes the pompous list of sonorous titles which a busy fancy had coined. It is as if he had said, You are being told a great deal about these angel hierarchies, and know all about their ranks and gradations. I do not know anything about them; but this I know, that if, amid the unseen things in the heavens or the earth, there be any such, my Lord made them, and is their master. So he groups together the whole universe of created beings, actual or imaginary, and then high above it, separate from it, its Lord and Creator, its upholder and end, he points to the majestic person of the only begotten Son of God, His Firstborn, higher than all the rulers of the earth, whether human or superhuman.

The language employed brings into strong relief the manifold variety of relations which the Son sustains to the universe, by the variety of the prepositions used in the sentence. The whole sum of created things (for the Greek means not only "all things," but "all things considered as a unity") was in the original act, created *in* Him, *through* Him, and *unto* Him. The first of these words, "in Him," regards Him as the creative centre, as it were, or element in which as in a storehouse or reservoir all creative force resided, and was in a definite act put forth. The thought may be parallel with that in the prologue to John's Gospel, "In Him was life." The Word stands to the universe as the incarnate Christ does to the Church; and as all spiritual life is in Him, and union to Him is its condition, so all physical takes its origin within the depths of His Divine nature. The error of the Gnostics was to put the act of creation and the thing created, as far away as possible from God, and it is met by this remarkable expression, which brings creation and the creatures in a very real sense within the confines of the Divine nature, as manifested in the Word, and asserts the truth of which pantheism so called is the exaggeration, that all things are in Him, like seeds in a seed vessel, while yet they are not identified with Him.

The possible dangers of that profound truth, which has always been more in harmony with Eastern than with Western modes of thought, are averted by the next preposition used, "all things have been created *through* Him." That presupposes the full, clear demarcation between creature and creator, and so on the one hand extricates the person of the Firstborn of all creation from all risk of being confounded with the universe, while on the other it emphasizes the thought that He is the medium of the Divine energy, and so brings into clear relief His relation to the inconceivable Divine nature. He is the image of the invisible God, and accordingly, *through* Him have all things been created. The same connection of ideas is found in the parallel passage in the Epistle to the Hebrews, where the words, "*through* Whom also He made the worlds," stand in immediate connection with "being the effulgence of His glory."

But there remains yet another relation between Him and the act of creation. "*For* Him" they have been made. All things come from and tend towards Him. He is the Alpha and the Omega, the beginning and the ending. All things spring from His will, draw their being from that fountain, and return thither again. These relations which are here declared of the Son, are in more than one place declared of the Father. Do we face the question fairly—what theory of the person of Jesus Christ explains that fact?

But further, His existence before the whole creation is repeated, with a force in both the words, "He is," which can scarcely be given in English. The former is emphatic—He Himself—and the latter emphasizes not only pre-existence, but absolute existence. "He *was* before all things" would not have said so much as "He *is* before all things." We are reminded of His own words, "Before Abraham was, I am."

"In Him all things consist" or hold together. He is the element in which takes place and by which is caused that continued creation which is the preservation of the universe, as He is the element in which the original creative act took place of old. All things came into being and form an ordered unity in Him. He links all creatures and forces into a co-operant whole, reconciling their antagonisms, drawing all their currents into one great tidal wave, melting all their notes into music which God can hear, however discordant it may sometimes sound to us. He is "the bond of perfectness," the key-stone of the arch, the centre of the wheel.

Such, then, in merest outline is the Apostle's teaching about the Eternal Word and the Universe. What sweetness and what reverential awe such thoughts should cast around the outer world and the providences of life! How near they should bring Jesus Christ to us! What a wonderful thought that is, that the whole course of human affairs and of natural processes is directed by Him who died upon the cross! The helm of the universe is held by the hands which were pierced for us. The Lord of Nature and the Mover of all things is that Saviour on whose love we may pillow our aching heads.

We need these lessons to-day, when many teachers are trying hard to drive all that is spiritual and Divine out of creation and history, and to set up a merciless law as the only God. Nature is terrible and stern sometimes, and the course of events can inflict crushing blows; but we have not the added horror of thinking both to be controlled by no will. Christ is King in either region, and with our elder brother for the ruler of the land, we shall not lack corn in our sacks, nor a Goshen to dwell in. We need not people the void, as these old heretics did, with imaginary forms, nor with impersonal forces and laws—nor need we, as so many are doing to-day, wander through its many mansions as through a deserted house, finding nowhere a Person who welcomes us; for everywhere we may behold our Saviour, and out of every storm and every solitude hear His voice across the darkness saying, "It is I; be not afraid."

III. The last of the relations set forth in this great section is that between Christ and His Church. "He is the head of the body, the Church; who is the beginning, the firstborn from the dead."

A parallel is plainly intended to be drawn between Christ's relation to the material creation and to the Church, the spiritual creation. As the Word of God before incarnation is to the universe, so is the incarnate Christ to the Church. As in the former, He is prior in time and superior in dignity, so is He in the latter. As in the universe He is source and origin of all being, so in the Church He is the beginning, both as being first and as being origin of all spiritual life. As the glowing words which described His relation to creation began with the great title "the Firstborn," so those which describe His relation to the Church close with the same name in a different application. Thus the two halves of His work are as it were moulded into a golden circle, and the end of the description bends round towards the beginning.

Briefly, then, we have here first, Christ the head, and the Church His body. In the lower realm the Eternal Word was the power which held all things together, and similar but higher in fashion is the relation between Him and the whole multitude of believing souls. Popular physiology regards the head as the seat of life. So the fundamental idea in the familiar metaphor, when applied to our Lord is that of the source of the mysterious spiritual life which flows from Him into all the members, and is sight in the eye, strength in the arm, swiftness in the foot, colour in the cheek, being richly various in its manifestations but one in its nature, and all His. The same mysterious derivation of life from Him is taught in His own metaphor of the Vine, in which every branch, however far away from the root, lives by the common life circulating through all, which clings in the tendrils, and reddens in the clusters, and is not theirs though it be in them.

That thought of the source of life leads necessarily to the other, that He is the centre of unity, by Whom the "many members" become "one body," and the maze of branches one vine. The "head," too, naturally comes to be the symbol for authority—and these three ideas of seat of life, centre of unity, and emblem of absolute power, appear to be those principally meant here.

Christ is further the *beginning* to the Church. In the natural world He was before all, and source of all. The same double idea is contained in this name, "the Beginning." It does not merely mean the first member of a series who begins it, as the first link in a chain does, but it means the power which causes the series to begin. The root is the beginning of the flowers which blow in succession through the plant's flowering time, though we may also call the first flower of the number the beginning. But Christ is root; not merely the first flower, though He is also that.

He is head and beginning to His Church by means of His resurrection. He is the firstborn from the dead, and His communication of spiritual life to His Church requires the historical fact of His resurrection as its basis, for a dead Christ could not be the source of life; and that resurrection completes the manifestation of the incarnate Word, by our faith in which, His spiritual life flows into our spirits. Unless He has risen from the dead, all His claims to be anything else than a wise teacher and fair character crumble into nothing, and to think of Him as a source of life is impossible.

He is the beginning through His resurrection, too, in regard of His raising us from the dead. He is the first-fruits of them that slept, and bears the promise of a mighty harvest. He has risen from the dead, and therein we have not only the one demonstration for the world that there is a life after death, but the irrefragable assurance to the Church that because He lives it shall live also. A dead body and a living head cannot be. We are knit to Him too closely for the Fury "with the abhorred shears" to cut the thread. He has risen that He might be the firstborn among many brethren.

So the Apostle concludes that in all things He is first—and all things are, that He *may* be first. Whether in nature or in grace, that pre-eminence is absolute and supreme. The end of all the majesty of creation and of all the wonders of grace is that His solitary figure may stand clearly out as centre and lord of the universe, and His name be lifted high over all.

So the question of questions for us all is, What think ye of Christ? Our thoughts now have necessarily been turned to subjects which may have seemed abstract and remote—but these truths which we have been trying to make clear and to present in their connection, are not the mere terms or propositions of a half mystical theology far away from our daily life, but bear most gravely and directly on our deepest interests. I would fain press on every conscience the sharp-pointed appeal—What is this Christ to us? Is He *any* thing to us but a name? Do our hearts leap up with a joyful Amen when we read these great words of this text? Are we ready to crown Him Lord of all? Is He our head, to fill us with vitality, to inspire and to command? Is He the goal and the end of our individual life? Can we each say—I live by Him, in Him, and for Him?

Happy are we, if we give to Christ the pre-eminence, and if our hearts set "Him first, Him last, Him midst and without end."

VI
THE RECONCILING SON

"For it was the good pleasure *of the Father* that in Him should all the fulness dwell; and through Him to reconcile all things unto Himself, having made peace through the blood of His cross; through Him, *I say*, whether things upon the earth, or things in the heavens. And you, being in time past alienated and enemies in your mind in your evil works, yet now hath He reconciled in the body of His flesh through death." — Col. i. 19–22 (Rev. Ver.).

These words correspond to those which immediately precede them, inasmuch as they present the same sequence, and deal with Christ in His relation to God, to the universe, and to the Church. The strata of thought are continuous, and lie here in the same order as we found them there. There we had set forth the work of the pre-incarnate Word as well as of the incarnate Christ; here we have mainly the reconciling power of His cross proclaimed as reaching to every corner of the universe, and as culminating in its operations on the believing souls to whom Paul speaks. There we had the fact that He was the image of God laid as basis of His relation to men and creatures; here that fact itself apprehended in somewhat different manner, namely, as the dwelling in Him of all "fulness," is traced to its ground in the "good pleasure" of the Father, and the same Divine purpose is regarded as underlying Christ's whole reconciling work. We observe, also, that all this section with which we have now to deal is given as the explanation and reason of Christ's pre-eminence. These are the principal links of connection with the previous words, and having noted them, we may proceed to attempt some imperfect consideration of the overwhelming thoughts here contained.

I. As before, we have Christ in relation to God. "It was the good pleasure of the Father that in Him should all the fulness dwell."

Now, we may well suppose from the use of the word "fulness" here, which we know to have been a very important term in later full-blown Gnostic speculations, that there is a reference to some of the heretical teachers' expressions, but such a supposition is not needed either to explain the meaning, or to account for the use of the word.

"The fulness"—what fulness? I think, although it has been disputed, that the language of the next chapter (ii. 9), where we read "In Him dwelleth all the fulness of the Godhead bodily," should settle that.

It seems most improbable that with two out of three significant words the same, the ellipse should be supplied by anything but the third. The meaning then will be—the whole abundance, or totality of Divine powers and attributes. That is, to put it in homelier words, that all that Divine nature in all its sweet greatness, in all its infinite wealth of tenderness and power and wisdom, is embodied in Jesus Christ. We have no need to look to heavens above or to earth beneath for fragmentary revelations of God's character. We have no need to draw doubtful inferences as to what God is from the questionable teachings of nature, or from the mysteries of human history with its miseries. No doubt these do show something of Him to observant hearts, and most to those who have the key to their meaning by their faith in a clearer revelation. At sundry times and in divers manners, God has spoken to the world by these partial voices, to each of which some syllables of His name have been committed. But He has put His whole name in that messenger of a New Covenant by whom He has finally declared His whole character to us, even His Son, in whom "it was the good pleasure of the Father that all the fulness should dwell."

The word rendered "dwell" implies a permanent abode, and may have been chosen in order to oppose a view which we know to have prevailed later, and may suspect to have been beginning to appear thus early, namely, that the union of the Divine and the human in the person of Christ was but temporary. At all events, emphasis is placed here on the opposite truth that that indwelling does not end with the earthly life of Jesus, and is not like the shadowy and transient incarnations of Eastern mythology or speculation—a mere assumption of a fleshly nature for a moment, which is dropped from the re-ascending Deity, but that, for evermore, manhood is wedded to divinity in the perpetual humanity of Jesus Christ.

And this indwelling is the result of the Father's good pleasure. Adopting the supplement in the Authorized and Revised Versions, we might read "the Father pleased"—but without making that change, the force of the words remains the same. The Incarnation and whole work of Christ are referred to their deepest ground in the will of the Father. The word rendered "pleased" implies both counsel and complacency; it is both pleasure and good pleasure. The Father determined the work of the Son, and delighted in it. Caricatures intentional or unintentional of New Testament teaching have often represented it as making Christ's work the means of pacifying an unloving God and moving Him to mercy. That is no part of the Pauline doctrine. But he, as all his brethren, taught that the love of God is the cause of the mission of Christ, even as Christ Himself had taught that "God so loved the world that He sent His Son." On that Rock-foundation of the will—the loving will of the Father, is built the whole work of His Incarnate Son. And as that work was the issue of His eternal purpose, so it is the object of His eternal delight. That is the wonderful meaning of the word which fell gently as the dove descending on His head, and lay on His locks wet from His baptism, like a consecrating oil—"This is My beloved Son, in whom *I am well pleased*." God willed that so He should be; He delighted that so He was. Through Christ, the Father purposed that His fulness should be communicated to us, and through Christ the Father rejoices to pour His abundance into our emptiness, that we may be filled with all the fulness.

II. Again, we have here, as before Christ and the Universe, of which He is not only Maker, Sustainer, and Lord, but through "the blood of His cross" reconciles "all things unto Himself."

Probably these same false teachers had dreams of reconciling agents among the crowd of shadowy phantoms with which they peopled the void. Paul lifts up in opposition to all these the one Sovereign Mediator, whose cross is the bond of peace for all the universe.

It is important for the understanding of these great words to observe their distinct reference to the former clauses which dealt with our Lord's relation to the universe as Creator. The same words are used in order to make the parallelism as close as may be, "Through Him" was creation; "through Him" is reconciliation. "All things"—or as the Greek would rather suggest, "the universe"—all things considered as an aggregate—were made and sustained through Him and subordinated to Him; the same "all things" are reconciled. A significant change in the order of naming the elements of which these are composed is noticeable. When creation is spoken of, the order is "in the heavens and upon the earth"—the order of creation; but when reconciliation is the theme, the order is reversed, and we read "things upon the earth and things in the heavens"—those coming first which stand nearest to the reconciling cross, and are first to feel the power which streams from it.

This obvious intentional correspondence between these two paragraphs shows us that whatever be the nature of the "reconciliation" spoken of here, it is supposed to affect not only rational and responsible creatures who alone in the full sense of the word can be reconciled, as they only in the full sense of the word can be enemies, but to extend to *things*, and to send its influence through the universe. The width of the reconciliation is the same as that of the creation; they are conterminous. That being the case, "reconciliation" here must have a different shade of meaning when applied to the sum total of created things from what it has when applied to persons. But not only are inanimate creatures included in the expression; it may even be made a question whether the whole of mankind is not excluded from it, not only by the phrase "all *things*" but also from the consideration that the effect of Christ's death on men is the subject of the following words, which are not an explanation of this clause, but an addition to it, introducing an entirely different department of Christ's reconciling work. Nor should we lose sight of the very significant omission in this section of the reference to the angelic beings who were named in the creation section. We hear nothing now about thrones or dominions or principalities or powers. The division into "visible and invisible" is not reproduced. I suggest the possibility that the reason may be the intention to represent this "reconciliation" as taking effect exclusively on the regions of creation below the angelic and below the human, while the "reconciliation," properly so called, which is brought to pass on alienated men is dealt with first in the following words.

If this be so, then these words refer mainly to the restitution of the material universe to its primal obedience, and represent Christ the Creator removing by His cross the shadow which has passed over nature by reason of sin. It has been well said, "How far this restoration of universal nature may be subjective, as involved in the changed perceptions of man thus brought into harmony with God, and how far it may have an objective and independent existence, it were vain to speculate."[1]

Scripture seems to teach that man's sin has made the physical world "subject to vanity"; for, although much of what it says on this matter is unquestionably metaphor only, portraying the Messianic blessings in poetical language never meant for dogmatic truth, and although unquestionably physical death reigned among animals, and storms and catastrophes swept over the earth long before man or sin were here, still— seeing that man by his sin has compelled dead matter to serve his lusts and to be his instrument in acts of rebellion against God, making "a league with the stones of the field" against his and their Master—seeing that he has used earth to hide heaven and to shut himself out from its glories, and so has made it an unwilling antagonist to God and temptress to evil—seeing that he has actually polluted the beauty of the world and has stained many a lovely scene with his sin, making its rivers run red with blood—seeing that he has laid unnumbered woes on the living creatures—we may feel that there is more than poetry in the affirmation that "the whole creation groaneth and travaileth in pain together," and may hear a deep truth, the extent of which we cannot measure, in Milton's majestic lines—

"Disproportioned Sin
Jarred against Nature's chime, and with harsh din
Brake the fair music that all creatures made
To their great Lord, whose love their motion swayed."

Here we have held forth in words, the extent of which we can measure as little, the counter-hope that wherever and however any such effect has come to pass on the material universe, it shall be done away by the reconciling power of the blood shed on the cross. That reconciling power goes as far as His creative power. The universe is one, not only because all created by the one personal Divine Word, nor because all upheld by Him, but because in ways to us unknown, the power of the cross pierces its heights and depths. As the impalpable influences of the sun bind planets and comets into one great system, so from Him on His cross may stream out attractive powers which knit together far off regions, and diverse orders, and bring all in harmonious unity to God, who has made peace by the blood shed on the cross, and has thereby been pleased to reconcile all things to Himself.

"And a Priest's hand through creation
Waveth calm and consecration."

It may be that the reference to things in heaven is like the similar reference in the previous verses, occasioned by some dreams of the heretical teachers. He may merely mean to say: You speak much about heavenly things, and have filled the whole space between God's throne and man's earth with creatures thick as the motes in the sunbeam. I know nothing about them; but this I know, that, if they are, Christ made them, and that if among them there be antagonism to God, it can be overcome by the cross. As to reconciliation proper,—in the heavens, meaning by that, among spiritual beings who dwell in that realm, it is clear there can be no question of it. There is no enmity among the angels of heaven, and no place for return to union with God among their untroubled bands, who "hearken to the voice of His word." But still if the hypothetical form of the clause and the use of the neuter gender permit any reference to intelligent beings in the heavens, we know that to the principalities and powers in heavenly places the cross has been the teacher of before unlearned depths in the Divine nature and purposes, the knowledge of which has drawn them nearer the heart of God, and made even their blessed union with Him more blessed and more close.

On no subject is it more necessary to remember the limitations of our knowledge than on this great theme. On none is confident assertion more out of place. The general truth taught is clear, but the specific applications of it to the various regions of the universe is very doubtful. We have no source of knowledge on that subject but the words of Scripture, and we have no means of verifying or checking the conclusions we may draw from them. We are bound, therefore, if we go beyond the general principle, to remember that *it* is one thing, and our reckoning up of what it includes is quite another. Our inferences have not the certainty of God's word. *It* comes to us with "Verily, verily." *We* have no right to venture on more than Perhaps.

Especially is this the case when we have but one or two texts to build on, and these most general in their language. And still more, when we find other words of Scripture which seem hard to reconcile with them, if pressed to their utmost meaning. In such a case our wisdom is to recognise that God has not been pleased to give us the means of constructing a dogma on the subject, and rather to seek to learn the lessons taught by the obscurity that remains than rashly and confidently to proclaim our inferences from half of our materials as if they were the very heart of the gospel.

Sublime and great beyond all our dreams, we may be sure, shall be the issue. Certain as the throne of God is it that His purposes shall be accomplished—and at last this shall be the fact for the universe, as it has ever been the will of the Father—"Of Him, and through Him, and to Him are all things, to whom be glory for ever." To that highest hope and ultimate vision for the whole creation, who will not say, Amen? The great sight which the seer beheld in Patmos is the best commentary on our text. To him the eternal order of the universe was unveiled—the great white throne, a snowy Alp in the centre; between the throne and the creatures, the Lamb, through Whom blessing and life passed outwards to them, and their incense and praise passed inwards to the throne; and all around the "living creatures," types of the aggregate of creatural life, the "elders," representatives of the Church redeemed from among men, and myriads of the firstborn of heaven. The eyes of all alike wait upon that slain Lamb. In Him they see God in clearest light of love and gentlest might—and as they look and learn and are fed, each according to his hunger, from the fulness of Christ, "every creature which is in heaven, and on the earth, and under the earth, and such as are in the sea, and all that are in them," will be heard saying "Blessing, and honour, and glory, and power, be unto Him, that sitteth upon the throne, and unto the Lamb for ever."

III. Christ, and His Reconciling Work in the Church. We have still the parallel kept up between the reconciling and the creative work of Christ. As in verse 18 He was represented as the giver of life to the Church, in a higher fashion than to the universe, so, and probably with a similar heightening of the meaning of "reconciliation," He is here set forth as its giver to the Church.

Now observe the solemn emphasis of the description of the condition of men before that reconciling work has told upon their hearts. They are "alienated"—not "aliens," as if that were their original condition, but "alienated," as having become so. The same thought that man's sin and separation from God is a fall, something abnormal and superinduced on humanity, which is implied in "reconciliation" or restoration to an original concord, is implied in this expression. "And enemies in your mind"—the seat of the enmity is in that inner man which thinks, reflects, and wills, and its sphere of manifestation is "in evil works" which are religiously acts of hostility to God because morally they are bad. We should not read "*by* wicked works," as the Authorized Version does, for the evil deeds have not made them enemies, but the enmity has originated the evil deeds, and is witnessed to by them.

That is a severe indictment, a plain, rough, and as it is thought now-a-days, a far too harsh description of human nature. Our forefathers no doubt were tempted to paint the "depravity of human nature" in very black colours—but I am very sure that we are tempted just in the opposite direction. It sounds too harsh and rude to press home the old-fashioned truth on cultured, respectable ladies and gentlemen. The charge is not that of conscious, active hostility, but of practical want of affection, as manifested by habitual disobedience or inattention to God's wishes, and by indifference and separation from Him in heart and mind.

And are these not the habitual temper of multitudes? The signs of love are joy in the company of the beloved, sweet memories and longings if parted, eager fulfilment of their lightest wish, a quick response to the most slender association recalling them to our thoughts. Have we these signs of love to God? If not, it is time to consider what temper of heart and mind towards the most loving of Hearts and the most unwearied of Givers, is indicated by the facts that we scarcely ever think of Him, that we have no delight in His felt presence, that most of our actions have no reference whatever to Him and would be done just the same if there were no God at all. Surely such a condition is liker hostility than love.

Further, here, as uniformly, God Himself is the Reconciler. "He"— that is, God, not Christ, "has reconciled us." Some, indeed, read "ye have been reconciled," but the preponderance of authority is in favour of the text as it stands, which yields a sense accordant with the usual mode of representation. It is we who are reconciled. It is God who reconciles. It is we who are enemies. The Divine patience loves on through all our enmity, and though perfect love meeting human sin must become wrath, which is consistent with love, it never becomes hatred, which is love's opposite.

Observe finally the great means of reconciliation: "In the body of His flesh"—that is, of course, Christ's flesh—God has reconciled us. Why does the Apostle use this apparently needless exuberance of language—"the body of His flesh"? It may have been in order to correct some erroneous tendencies towards a doctrine which we know was afterwards eagerly embraced in the Eastern Churches, that our Lord's body was not truly flesh, but only a phantasm or appearance. It may have been to guard against risk of confounding it with His "body the Church," spoken of in the 18th verse, though that supposes a scarcely credible dulness in his readers. Or it may more naturally be accounted for as showing how full his own mind was of the overwhelming wonder of the fact that He, Whose majesty he has been setting forth in such deep words, should veil His eternal glories and limit His far reaching energies within a fleshly body. He would point the contrast between the Divine dignity of the Eternal Word, the Creator and Lord of the universe, and the lowliness of His incarnation. On these two pillars, as on two solid piers, one on either continent, with a great gulf between, the Divinity of Christ on one side, His Manhood on the other, is built the bridge by which we pass over the river into the glory.

But that is not all. The Incarnation is not the whole gospel. The body of His flesh becomes the means of our reconciliation "through death." Christ's death has so met the requirements of the Divine law that the Divine love can come freely forth, and embrace and forgive sinful men. That fact is the very centre of the revelation of God in Christ, the very secret of His power. He has died. Voluntarily and of His own love, as well as in obedience to the Father's loving will, He has borne the consequences of the sin which He had never shared, in that life of sorrow and sympathy, in that separation from God which is sin's deepest penalty, and of which the solemn witness comes to us in the cry that rent the darkness, "My God, My God, why hast Thou forsaken Me?" and in that physical death which is the parable in the material sphere of the true death of the spirit. We do not know all the incidence of Christ's death. The whole manner of its operation has not been told us, but the fact has been. It does not affect the Divine heart. *That* we know, for "God so loved the world, that He sent His Son." But it does affect the Divine government. Without it, forgiveness could not have been. Its influence extends to all the years before, as to all after, Calvary, for the fact that Man continued to be after Man had sinned, was because the whole Divine government from the first had respect to the sacrifice that was to be, as now it all is moulded by the merit of the sacrifice that has been. And in this aspect of the case, the previous thoughts as to the blood of the cross having power in the material universe derive a new meaning, if we regard the whole history of the world as shaped by Christ's sacrifice, and the very continuance of humanity from the first moment of transgression as possible, because He was "the Lamb slain before the foundation of the world," whose cross, as an eternal fact in the Divine purpose, influenced the Divine government long before it was realized in time.

For us, that wondrous love—mightier than death, and not to be quenched by many waters—is the one power that can change our alienation to glad friendship, and melt the frost and hard-ribbed ice of indifference and dread into love. That, and that alone, is the solvent for stubborn wills, the magnet for distant hearts. The cross of Christ is the key-stone of the universe and the conqueror of all enmity.

If religion is to have sovereign power in our lives, it must be the religion built upon faith in the Incarnate Son of God, who reconciles the world to God upon His cross. That is the only faith which makes men love God and binds them to Him with bands which cannot be broken. Other types of Christianity are but tepid; and lukewarm water is an abomination. The one thing that makes us ground our rebellious arms and say, Lord, I surrender, Thou hast conquered, is to see in Christ's life the perfect image of God, and in His death the all-sufficient sacrifice for sin.

What does it avail for us that the far-reaching power of Christ's cross shoots out magnetic forces to the uttermost verge of the heavens, and binds the whole universe by silken blood-red cords to God, if it does not bind me to Him in love and longing? What does it avail that God is in Christ, reconciling the world to Himself, if I am unconscious of the enmity, and careless of the friendship? Each man has to ask himself, Am I reconciled to God? Has the sight of His great love on the cross won *me*, body and soul, to His love and service? Have I flung away self-will, pride and enmity, and yielded myself a glad captive to the loving Christ who died? His cross draws us, His love beckons us. God pleads with all hearts. He who has made peace by so costly means as the sacrifice of His Son, condescends to implore the rebels to come into amity with Him, and "prays us with much entreaty to receive the gift." God beseeches us to be reconciled to Himself.

FOOTNOTES:

[1] Bp. Lightfoot, *On Coloss.*, p. 226.

VII
THE ULTIMATE PURPOSE OF RECONCILIATION
AND ITS HUMAN CONDITIONS

"To present you holy and without blemish and unreproveable before Him: if so be that ye continue in the faith, grounded and stedfast, and not moved away from the hope of the gospel which ye heard, which was preached in all creation under heaven; whereof I Paul was made a minister."—Col. i. 22, 23 (Rev. Ver.).

The Apostle has been sketching in magnificent outline a vast system, which we may almost call the scheme of the universe. He has set forth Christ as its Lord and centre, through Whom all things at first came into being, and still continue to be. In parallel manner he has presented Christ as Lord and Centre of the Church, its lifegiving Head. And finally he has set forth Christ as the Reconciler of all discords in heaven and earth, and especially of that which parts sinful men from God.

And now he shows us here, in the first words of our text, the purpose of this whole manifestation of God in Christ to be the presenting of men perfect in purity, before the perfect judgment of God. He then appends the condition on which the accomplishment of this ultimate purpose in each man depends—namely, the man's continuance in the faith and hope of the Gospel. That leads him to gather up, in a series of clauses characterizing the Gospel, certain aspects of it which constitute subordinate motives and encouragements to such stedfastness. That is, I think, the outline connection of the words before us, which at first sight seem somewhat tangled and difficult to unravel.

I. We have then, first, to consider the ultimate purpose of God in the work of Christ.

"To present you holy and without blemish and unreproveable before Him." It may be a question whether these words should be connected with "now hath He reconciled," or whether we are to go farther back in the long paragraph, and make them dependent on "it was the good pleasure of the Father." The former seems the more natural—namely, to see here a statement of the great end contemplated in our reconciliation to God; which, indeed, whatever may be the grammatical construction preferred here, is also, of course, the ultimate object of the Father's good pleasure. In the word "present" there is possibly a sacrificial allusion, as there is unquestionably in its use in Rom. xii., "Present your bodies a living sacrifice"; or there may be another and even more eloquent metaphor implied, that of the bringing of the bride to the husband by the friend of the bridegroom. That lovely figure is found in two instances of the use of the word in Paul's epistle (2 Cor. ii. 2, "to present you as a chaste virgin to Christ," and Eph. v. 27, "that He might present it to Himself a glorious Church"), and possibly in others. It certainly gives an appropriate and beautiful emblem here if we think of the presentation of the bride in virginal beauty and purity to her Lord at that last great day which is the bridal day of the perfected Church.

There is, however, no need to suppose any metaphor at all, nor any allusion beyond the general meaning of the word — *to set in the presence of.* The sacrificial reference is incongruous here, and the bridal one not indicated by anything in the context, as it is in the instances just quoted. One thing is clear, that the reference is to a future presentation in the day of judgment, as in another place, where Paul says, "He ... shall raise up us also ... and shall present us" (2 Cor. iv. 14). In the light of that revealing day, His purpose is that we shall stand "holy," that is, devoted to God and therefore pure — "without blemish," as the offerings had to be, and "unreproveable," against whom no charge can be brought. These three express a regular sequence; first, the inward principle of consecration and devotion to God, then its visible issue in stainless conduct and character, and then its last consequence, that in the judgment of God and of men we shall stand acquitted of blame, and every accusation drop away from our dazzling purity, like muddy water from the white wing of the sea-bird as it soars. And all this moral perfectness and unblameableness is to be not merely in the judgment of men, but "before Him," the light of whose "pure eyes and perfect judgment" discovers all stains and evils. They must be spotless indeed who are "without fault before the throne of God."

Such, then, is the grand conception of the ultimate purpose and issue of Christ's reconciling work. All the lines of thought in the preceding section lead up to and converge in this peak. The meaning of God in creation and redemption cannot be fully fathomed without taking into view the future perfecting of men. This Christian ideal of the possibilities for men is the noblest vision that can animate our hopes. Absolute moral purity which shall be recognised as perfect by the perfect Judge, and a close approach to God, so as that we shall be "before Him" in a manner unknown here — are hopes as much brighter than those which any other systems of belief print on the dim canvass curtain of the future, as the Christian estimate of man's condition apart from Christ is sadder and darker than theirs. Christianity has a much more extended scale of colours than they have. It goes further down into blackness for the tints with which it paints man as he is, and further up into flashing glories of splendour for the gleaming hues with which it paints him as he may become. They move within narrow limits of neutral tints. The Gospel alone does not try to minimise man's evil, because it is triumphantly confident of its power to turn all that evil into good.

Nothing short of this complete purity and blamelessness satisfies God's heart. We may travel back to the beginning of this section, and connect its first words with these, "It pleased the Father, to present us holy and spotless and blameless." It delights Him thus to effect the purifying of sinful souls, and He is glad when He sees Himself surrounded by spirits thus echoing His will and reflecting His light. This is what he longs for. This is what He aims at in all His working—to make good and pure men. The moral interest is uppermost in His heart and in His doings. The physical universe is but the scaffolding by which the true house of God may be built. The work of Christ is the means to that end, and when God has got us, by such lavish expenditure, to be white like Himself, and can find nothing in us to condemn, then, and not till then, does He brood over us satisfied and glad at heart, resting in His love, and rejoicing over us with singing.

Nor will anything short of this complete purity exhaust the power of the Reconciling Christ. His work is like an unfinished column, or Giotto's Campanile, all shining with marbles and alabasters and set about with fair figures, but waiting for centuries for the glittering apex to gather its glories into a heaven-piercing point. His cross and passion reach no adequate result, short of the perfecting of saints, nor was it worth Christ's while to die for any less end. His cross and passion have evidently power to effect this perfect purity, and cannot be supposed to have done all that is in them to do, until they have done that with every Christian.

We ought then to keep very clear before us this as the crowning object of Christianity: not to make men happy, except as a consequence of holiness; not to deliver from penalty, except as a means to holiness; but to make them holy, and being holy, to set them close by the throne of God. No man understands the scope of Christianity, or judges it fairly, who does not give full weight to that as its own statement of its purpose. The more distinctly we, as Christians, keep that purpose prominent in our thoughts, the more shall we have our efforts stimulated and guided, and our hopes fed, even when we are saddened by a sense of failure. We have a power working in us which can make us white as the angels, pure as our Lord is pure. If it, being able to produce perfect results, has produced only such imperfect ones, we may well ask, where the reason for the partial failure lies. If we believed more vividly that the real purpose and use of Christianity was to make us good men, we should surely labour more earnestly to secure that end, should take more to heart our own responsibility for the incompleteness with which it has been attained in us, and should submit ourselves more completely to the operation of the "might of the power" which worketh in us.

Nothing less than our absolute purity will satisfy God about us. Nothing less should satisfy ourselves. The only worthy end of Christ's work for us is to present us holy, in complete consecration, and without blemish, in perfect homogeneousness and uniformity of white purity and unreproveable in manifest innocence in His sight. If we call ourselves Christians let us make it our life's business to see that that end is being accomplished in us in some tolerable and growing measure.

II. We have next set forth the conditions on which the accomplishment of that purpose depends: "If so be that ye continue in the faith, grounded and stedfast, and not moved away from the hope of the Gospel."

The condition is, generally speaking, a stedfast adherence to the Gospel which the Colossians had received. "If ye continue in the faith," means, I suppose, if ye continue to live in the *exercise* of your faith. The word here has its ordinary subjective sense, expressing the act of the believing man, and there is no need to suppose that it has the later ecclesiastical objective sense, expressing the believer's creed, a meaning in which it may be questioned whether the word is ever employed in the New Testament. Then this continuance in the faith is further explained as to its manner, and that first positively, and then negatively. They are to be grounded, or more picturesquely and accurately, "founded," that is, built into a foundation, and therefore "stedfast," as banded into the firm rock, and so partaking of its fixedness. Then, negatively, they are not to be "moved away"; the word by its form conveying the idea, that this is a process which may be continually going on, and in which, by some force constantly acting from without, they may be gradually and imperceptibly pushed off from the foundation—that foundation is the hope evoked or held out by the Gospel, a representation which is less familiar than that which makes the Gospel itself the foundation, but is substantially equivalent to it, though with a different colour.

One or two plain lessons may be drawn from these words. There is an "if," then. However great the powers of Christ and of His work, however deep the desire and fixed the purpose of God, no fulfilment of these is possible except on condition of our habitual exercise of faith. The Gospel does not work on men by magic. Mind, heart and will must be exercised on Christ, or all His power to purify and bless will be of no avail to us. We shall be like Gideon's fleece, dry when the dew is falling thick, unless we are continually putting forth living faith. That attracts the blessing and fits the soul to receive it. There is nothing mystical about the matter. Common sense tells us, that if a man never thinks about any truth, that truth will do him no good in any way. If it does not find its road into his heart through his mind, and thence into his life, it is all one as if there were no such truth, or as if he did not believe it. If our creed is made up of truths which we do not think about, we may just as well have no creed. If we do not bring ourselves into contact with the motives which the Gospel brings to bear on character, the motives will not mould our character. If we do not, by faith and meditation, realize the principles which flow from the truth as it is in Jesus, and obtain the strength which is stored in Him, we shall not grow by Him or like Him. No matter how mighty be the renewing powers of the Gospel wielded by the Divine Spirit, they can only work on the nature that is brought into contact with and continues in contact with them by faith. The measure in which we trust Jesus Christ will be the measure in which He helps us. "He could do no mighty works because of their unbelief." He cannot do what He can do, if we thwart Him by our want of faith. God will present us holy before Him *if* we continue in the faith.

And it must be present faith which leads to present results. We cannot make an arrangement by which we exercise faith wholesale once for all, and secure a delivery of its blessings in small quantities for a while after, as a buyer may do with goods. The moment's act of faith will bring the moment's blessings; but to-morrow will have to get its own grace by its own faith. We cannot lay up a stock for the future. There must be present drinking for present thirst; we cannot lay in a reserve of the water of life, as a camel can drink at a draught enough for a long desert march. The Rock follows us all through the wilderness, but we have to fill our pitchers day by day. Many Christians seem to think that they can live on past acts of faith. No wonder that their Christian character is stunted, and their growth stopped, and many a blemish visible, and many a "blame" to be brought against them. Nothing but continual exercise of faith, day by day, moment by moment, in every duty, and every temptation, will secure the continual entrance into our weakness of the strength which makes strong and the purity which makes pure.

Then again, if we and our lives are to be firm and stable, we must have a foundation outside of ourselves on which to rest. That thought is involved in the word "grounded" or "founded." It is possible that this metaphor of the foundation is carried on into the next clause, in which case "the hope of the Gospel" would be the foundation. Strange to make a solid foundation out of so unsubstantial a thing as "hope!" That would be indeed to build a castle on the air, a palace on a soap-bubble, would it not? Yes, it would, if this hope were not "the hope produced by the Gospel," and therefore as solid as the ever-enduring Word of the Lord on which it is founded. But, more probably, the ordinary application of the figure is preserved here, and Christ is the foundation, the Rock, on which builded, our fleeting lives and our fickle selves may become rock-like too, and every impulsive and changeable Simon Bar Jonas rise to the mature stedfastness of a Peter, the pillar of the Church.

Translate that image of taking Christ for our foundation into plain English, and what does it come to? It means, let our minds find in Him, in His Word, and whole revealing life, the basis of our beliefs, the materials for thought; let our hearts find in Him their object, which brings calmness and unchangeableness into their love; let our practical energies take Him as their motive and pattern, their strength and their aim, their stimulus and their reward; let all hopes and joys, emotions and desires, fasten themselves on Him; let Him occupy and fill our whole nature, and mould and preside over all our actions. So shall we be "founded" on Christ.

And so "founded," we shall, as Paul here beautifully puts it, be "stedfast." Without that foundation to give stability and permanence, we never get down to what abides, but pass our lives amidst fleeting shadows, and are ourselves transient as they. The mind whose thoughts about God and the unseen world are not built on the personal revelation of God in Christ will have no solid certainties which cannot be shaken, but, at the best, opinions which cannot have more fixedness than belongs to human thoughts upon the great problem. If my love does not rest on Christ, it will flicker and flutter, lighting now here and now there, and even where it rests most secure in human love, sure to have to take wing some day, when Death with his woodman's axe fells the tree where it nestles. If my practical life is not built on Him, the blows of circumstance will make it reel and stagger. If we are not well joined to Jesus Christ, we shall be driven by gusts of passion and storms of trouble, or borne along on the surface of the slow stream of all-changing time like thistle-down on the water. If we are to be stable, it must be because we are fastened to something outside of ourselves that is stable, just as they have to lash a man to the mast or other fixed things on deck, if he is not to be washed overboard in the gale. If we are lashed to the unchangeable Christ by the "cords of love" and faith, we too shall, in our degree, be stedfast.

And, says Paul, that Christ-derived stedfastness will make us able to resist influences that would move us away from the hope of the Gospel. That process which their stedfastness would enable the Colossians successfully to resist, is described by the language of the Apostle as continuous, and as one which acted on them from without. Intellectual dangers arose from false teachings. The ever acting tendencies of worldliness pressed upon them, and they needed to make a distinct effort to keep themselves from being overcome by these.

If we do not take care that imperceptible, steady pressure of the all-surrounding worldliness, which is continually acting on us, will push us right off the foundation without our knowing that we have shifted at all. If we do not look well after our moorings we shall drift away down stream, and never know that we are moving, so smooth is the motion, till we wake up to see that everything round about is changed. Many a man is unaware how completely his Christian faith has gone till some crisis comes when he needs it, and when he opens the jar there is nothing. It has evaporated. When white ants eat away all the inside of a piece of furniture, they leave the outside shell apparently solid, and it stands till some weight is laid upon it, and then goes down with a crash. Many people loose their Christianity in that fashion, by its being nibbled away in tiny flakes by a multitude of secretly working little jaws, and they never know that the pith is out of it till they want to lean on it, and then it gives under them.

The only way to keep firm hold of hope is to keep fast on the foundation. If we do not wish to slide imperceptibly away from Him who alone will make our lives stedfast and our hearts calm with the peacefulness of having found our All, we must continuously make an effort to tighten our grasp on Him, and to resist the subtle forces which, by silent pressure or by sudden blows, seek to get us off the one foundation.

III. Then lastly, we have a threefold motive for adherence to the Gospel.

The three clauses which close these verses seem to be appended as secondary and subordinate encouragements to stedfastness, which encouragements are drawn from certain characteristics of the Gospel. Of course, the main reason for a man's sticking to the Gospel, or to anything else, is that it is true. And unless we are prepared to say that we believe it true, we have nothing to do with such subordinate motives for professing adherence to it, except to take care that they do *not* influence us. And that one sole reason is abundantly wrought out in this letter. But then, its truth being established, we may fairly bring in other subsidiary motives to reinforce this, seeing that there may be a certain coldness of belief which needs the warmth of such encouragements.

The first of these lies in the words, "the Gospel, which ye heard." That is to say, the Apostle would have the Colossians, in the face of these heretical teachers, remember the beginning of their Christian life, and be consistent with that. They had heard it at their conversion. He would have them recall what they had heard then, and tamper with no teaching inconsistent with it. He also appeals to their experience. "Do you remember what the Gospel did for you? Do you remember the time when it first dawned upon your astonished hearts, all radiant with heavenly beauty, as the revelation of a Heart in heaven that cared for you, and of a Christ Who, on earth, had died for you? Did it not deliver you from your burden? Did it not set new hope before you? Did it not make earth as the very portals of heaven? And have these truths become less precious because familiar? Be not moved away from the Gospel 'which ye have heard.'"

To us the same appeal comes. This word has been sounding in our ears ever since childhood. It has done everything for some of us, something for all of us. Its truths have sometimes shone out for us like suns, in the dark, and brought us strength when nothing else could sustain us. If they are not truths, of course they will have to go. But they are not to be abandoned easily. They are interwoven with our very lives. To part with them is a resolution not to be lightly undertaken.

The argument of experience is of no avail to convince others, but is valid for ourselves. A man has a perfect right to say, "I have heard Him myself, and I know that this is indeed the Christ, the Saviour of the world." A Christian may wisely decline to enter on the consideration of many moot questions which he may feel himself incompetent to handle, and rest upon the fact that Christ has saved his soul. The blind man beat the Pharisees in logic when he sturdily took his stand on experience, and refused to be tempted to discuss subjects which he did not understand, or to allow his ignorance to slacken his grasp of what he did know. "Whether this man be a sinner or no, I know not: one thing I know, that, whereas I was blind, now I see." There was no answering that, so by excommunicating him they confessed themselves beaten.

A second encouragement to stedfast adherence to the Gospel lies in the fact that it "was preached in all creation under heaven." We need not be pedantic about literal accuracy, and may allow that the statement has a rhetorical colouring. But what the Apostle means is, that the gospel had spread so widely, through so many phases of civilisation, and had proved its power by touching men so unlike each other in mental furniture and habits, that it had showed itself to be a word for the whole race. It is the same thought as we have already found in verse 6. His implied exhortation is, "Be not moved away from what belongs to humanity by teachings which can only belong to a class." All errors are transient in duration and limited in area. One addresses itself to one class of men, another to another. Each false, or exaggerated, or partial representation of religious truth, is congenial to some group with idiosyncrasies of temperament or mind. Different tastes like different spiced meats, but the gospel, "human nature's daily food," is the bread of God that everybody can relish, and which everybody must have for healthy life. What only a certain class or the men of one generation or of one stage of culture can find nourishment in, cannot be meant for all men. But the great message of God's love in Jesus Christ commends itself to us because it can go into any corner of the world, and there, upon all sorts of people, work its wonders. So we will sit down with the women and children upon the green grass, and eat of *it*, however fastidious people whose appetites have been spoiled by high-spiced meat, may find it coarse and insipid. It would feed them too, if they would try—but whatever they may do, let us take it as more than our necessary food.

The last of these subsidiary encouragements to stedfastness lies in, "whereof I Paul was made a minister." This is not merely an appeal to their affection for him, though that is perfectly legitimate. Holy words may be holier because dear lips have taught them to us, and even the truth of God may allowably have a firmer hold upon our hearts because of our love for some who have ministered it to us. It is a poor commentary on a preacher's work if, after long service to a congregation, his words do not come with power given to them by old affection and confidence. The humblest teacher who has done his Master's errand will have some to whom he can appeal as Paul did, and urge them to keep hold of the message which he has preached.

But there is more than that in the Apostle's mind. He was accustomed to quote the fact that he, the persecutor, had been made the messenger of Christ, as a living proof of the infinite mercy and power of that ascended Lord, whom his eyes saw on the road to Damascus. So here, he puts stress on the fact that he *became* a minister of the gospel, as being an "evidence of Christianity." The history of his conversion is one of the strongest proofs of the resurrection and ascension of Jesus Christ. You know, he seems to say, what turned me from being a persecutor into an apostle. It was because I saw the living Christ, and "heard the words of His mouth," and, I beseech you, listen to no words which make His dominion less sovereign, and His sole and all sufficient work on the cross less mighty as the only power that knits earth to heaven.

So the sum of this whole matter is—abide in Christ. Let us root and ground our lives and characters in Him, and then God's inmost desire will be gratified in regard to us, and He will bring even us stainless and blameless into the blaze of His presence. There we shall all have to stand, and let that all-penetrating light search us through and through. How do we expect to be then "found of Him in peace, without spot and blameless"? There is but one way—to live in constant exercise of faith in Christ, and grip Him so close and sure that the world, the flesh and the devil cannot make us loosen our fingers. Then He will hold us up, and His great purpose, which brought Him to earth, and nailed Him to the cross, will be fulfilled in us, and at last, we shall lift up voices of wondering praise "to Him who is able to keep us from falling, and to present us faultless before the presence of His glory with exceeding joy."

VIII

JOY IN SUFFERING, AND TRIUMPH IN THE MANIFESTED MYSTERY

"Now I rejoice in my sufferings for your sake, and fill up on my part that which is lacking of the afflictions of Christ in my flesh for His body's sake, which is the Church; whereof I was made a minister according to the dispensation of God which was given me to you-ward to fulfil the word of God, even the mystery which hath been hid from all ages and generations; but now hath it been manifested to His Saints, to Whom God was pleased to make known what is the riches of the glory of this mystery among the Gentiles, which is Christ in you, the hope of glory."—Col. i. 24–27 (Rev. Ver.).

There are scarcely any personal references in this Epistle, until we reach the last chapter. In this respect it contrasts strikingly with another of Paul's epistles of the captivity, that to the Philippians, which is running over with affection and with allusions to himself. This sparseness of personal details strongly confirms the opinion that he had not been to Colossæ. Here, however, we come to one of the very few sections which may be called personal, though even here it is rather Paul's office than himself which is in question. He is led to speak of himself by his desire to enforce his exhortations to faithful continuance in the gospel, and, as is so often the case with him in touching on his apostleship, he as it were, catches fire, and blazes up in a grand flame, which sheds a bright light on his lofty enthusiasm and evangelistic fervour The words to be considered now are plain enough in themselves, but they are run together, and thought follows thought in a fashion which makes them somewhat obscure; and there are also one or two difficulties in single words which require to be cleared up. We shall perhaps best bring out the course of thought by dealing with these verses in three groups, of which the three words, Suffering, Service, and Mystery, are respectively the centres. First, we have a remarkable view taken by the prisoner of the meaning of his sufferings, as being endured for the Church. That leads him to speak of his relation to the Church generally as being that of a servant or steward appointed by God, to bring to its completion the work of God; and then, as I said, he takes fire, and, forgetting himself, flames up in rapturous magnifying of the grand message hid so long, and now entrusted to him to preach. So we have his Sufferings for the Church, his service of Stewardship to the Church, and the great Mystery which in that stewardship he had to unveil. It may help us to understand both Paul and his message, as well as our own tasks and trials, if we try to grasp his thoughts here about his work and his sorrows.

I. We have the Apostle's triumphant contemplation of his sufferings. "I rejoice in my sufferings for your sake, and fill up on my part that which is lacking of the afflictions of Christ in my flesh for His body's sake, which is the Church."

The Revised Version, following the best authorities, omits the "who" with which the Authorized Version begins this verse, and marks a new sentence and paragraph, as is obviously right.

The very first word is significant: "*Now* I rejoice." Ay; it is easy to say fine things about patience in sufferings and triumph in sorrow when we are prosperous and comfortable; but it is different when we are in the furnace. This man, with the chain on his wrist, and the iron entering into his soul, with his life in danger, and all the future uncertain, can say, "*Now* I rejoice." This bird sings in a darkened cage.

Then come startling words, "I on my part fill up that which is lacking (a better rendering than 'behind') of the afflictions of Christ." It is not surprising that many explanations of these words have tried to soften down their boldness; as, for instance, "afflictions borne for Christ," or "imposed by Him," or "like His." But it seems very clear that the startling meaning is the plain meaning, and that "the sufferings of Christ" here, as everywhere else, are "the sufferings borne by Christ."

Then at once the questions start up, Does Paul mean to say that in any sense whatever the sufferings which Christ endured have anything "lacking" in them? or does he mean to say that a Christian man's sufferings, however they may benefit the Church, can be put alongside of the Lord's, and taken to eke out the incompleteness of His? Surely that cannot be! Did He not say on the cross, "It is finished"? Surely that sacrifice needs no supplement, and can receive none, but stands "the one sacrifice for sins for ever"! Surely, His sufferings are absolutely singular in nature and effect, unique and all-sufficient and eternal. And does this Apostle, the very heart of whose gospel was that these were the life of the world, mean to say that anything which he endures can be tacked on to them, a bit of the old rags to the new garment?

Distinctly not! To say so would be contradictory of the whole spirit and letter of the Apostle's teaching. But there is no need to suppose that he means anything of the sort. There is an idea frequently presented in Scripture, which gives full meaning to the words, and is in full accordance with Pauline teaching; namely, that Christ truly participates in the sufferings of His people borne for Him. He suffers with them. The head feels the pangs of all the members; and every ache may be thought of as belonging, not only to the limb where it is located, but to the brain which is conscious of it. The pains and sorrows and troubles of His friends and followers to the end of time are one great whole. Each sorrow of each Christian heart is one drop more added to the contents of the measure which has to be filled to the brim, ere the purposes of the Father who leads through suffering to rest are accomplished; and all belong to Him. Whatsoever pain or trial is borne in fellowship with Him is felt and borne by Him. Community of sensation is established between Him and us. Our sorrows are transferred to Him. "In all our afflictions He is afflicted," both by His mystical but most real oneness with us, and by His brother's sympathy.

So for us all, and not for the Apostle only, the whole aspect of our sorrows may be changed, and all poor struggling souls in this valley of weeping may take comfort and courage from the wonderful thought of Christ's union with us, which makes our griefs His, and our pain touch Him. Bruise your finger, and the pain pricks and stabs in your brain. Strike the man that is joined to Christ here, and Christ up yonder feels it. "He that toucheth you toucheth the apple of His eye." Where did Paul learn this deep lesson, that the sufferings of Christ's servants were Christ's sufferings? I wonder whether, as he wrote these words of confident yet humble identification of himself the persecuted with Christ the Lord, there came back to his memory what he heard on that fateful day as he rode to Damascus, "Saul, Saul, why persecutest thou Me?" The thought so crushing to the persecutor had become balm and glory to the prisoner,—that every blow aimed at the servant falls on the Master, who stoops from amid the glory of the throne to declare that whatsoever is done, whether it be kindness or cruelty, to the least of His brethren, is done to Him. So every one of us may take the comfort and strength of that wonderful assurance, and roll all our burdens and sorrows on Him.

Again, there is prominent here the thought that the good of sorrow does not end with the sufferer. His sufferings are borne in his *flesh* for the *body's* sake, which is the Church,—a remarkable antithesis between the Apostle's flesh in which, and Christ's body for which, the sufferings are endured. Every sorrow rightly borne, as it will be when Christ is felt to be bearing it with us, is fruitful of blessing. Paul's trials were in a special sense "for His body's sake," for of course, if he had not preached the gospel, he would have escaped them all; and on the other hand, they have been especially fruitful of good, for if he had not been persecuted, he would never have written these precious letters from Rome. The Church owes much to the violence which has shut up confessors in dungeons. Its prison literature, beginning with this letter, and ending with "Pilgrim's Progress," has been among its most cherished treasures.

But the same thing is true about us all, though it may be in a narrower sphere. No man gets good for himself alone out of his sorrows. Whatever purifies and makes gentler and more Christlike, whatever teaches or builds up—and sorrows rightly borne do all these—is for the common good. Be our trials great or small, be they minute and every-day—like gnats that hum about us in clouds, and may be swept away by the hand, and irritate rather than hurt where they sting—or be they huge and formidable, like the viper that clings to the wrist and poisons the life blood, they are meant to give us good gifts, which we may transmit to the narrow circle of our homes, and in ever widening rings of influence to all around us. Have we never known a household, where some chronic invalid, lying helpless perhaps on a sofa, was a source of the highest blessing and the centre of holy influence, that made every member of the family gentler, more self-denying and loving? We shall never understand our sorrows, unless we try to answer the question, What good to others is meant to come through me by this? Alas, that grief should so often be self-absorbed, even more than joy is! The heart sometimes opens to unselfish sharing of its gladness with others; but it too often shuts tight over its sorrow, and seeks solitary indulgence in the luxury of woe. Let us learn that our brethren claim benefit from our trials, as well as from our good things, and seek to ennoble our griefs by bearing them for "His body's sake, which is the Church."

Christ's sufferings on His cross are the satisfaction for a world's sins, and in that view can have no supplement, and stand alone in kind. But His "afflictions"—a word which would not naturally be applied to His death—do operate also to set the pattern of holy endurance, and to teach many a lesson; and in that view every suffering borne for Him and with Him may be regarded as associated with His, and helping to bless the Church and the world. God makes the rough iron of our natures into shining, flexible, sharp steel, by heavy hammers and hot furnaces, that He may shape us as His instruments to help and heal.

It is of great moment that we should have such thoughts of our sorrows whilst their pressure is upon us, and not only when they are past. "I *now* rejoice." Most of us have had to let years stretch between us and the blow before we could attain to that clear insight. We can look back and see how our past sorrows tended to bless us, and how Christ was with us in them: but as for this one, that burdens us to-day, we cannot make *it* out. We can even have a solemn thankfulness not altogether unlike joy as we look on those wounds that we remember; but how hard it is to feel it about those that pain us now! There is but one way to secure that calm wisdom, which feels their meaning even while they sting and burn, and can smile through tears, as sorrowful and yet always rejoicing; and that is to keep in very close communion with our Lord. Then, even when we are in the whitest heat of the furnace, we may have the Son of man with us; and if we have, the fiercest flames will burn up nothing but the chains that bind us, and we shall "walk at liberty" in that terrible heat, because we walk with Him. It is a high attainment of Christian fortitude and faith to feel the blessed meaning, not only of the six tribulations which are past, but of the present seventh, and to say, even while the iron is entering the quivering flesh, "I *now* rejoice in my sufferings," and try to turn them to others' good.

II. These thoughts naturally lead on to the statement of the Apostle's lowly and yet lofty conception of his office—"whereof (that is, of which *Church*) I was made a minister, according to the dispensation of God, which was given me to you-ward, to fulfil the word of God."

The first words of this clause are used at the close of the preceding section in verse 23, but the "whereof" there refers to the gospel, not as here to the Church. He is the servant of both, and because he is the servant of the Church he suffers, as he has been saying. The representation of himself as servant gives the reason for the conduct described in the previous clause. Then the next words explain what makes him the Church's servant. He is so in accordance with, or in pursuance of, the stewardship, or office of administrator, of His household, to which God has called him, "to you-ward," that is to say, with especial reference to the Gentiles. And the final purpose of his being made a steward is "to fulfil the word of God"; by which is not meant "to accomplish or bring to pass its predictions," but "to bring it to completion," or "to give full development to it," and that possibly in the sense of preaching it fully, without reserve, and far and wide throughout the whole world.

So lofty and yet so lowly was Paul's thought of his office. He was the Church's servant, and therefore bound to suffer cheerfully for its sake. He was so, because a high honour had been conferred on him by God, nothing less than the stewardship of His great household the Church, in which he had to give to every man his portion, and to exercise authority. He is the Church's servant indeed, but it is because he is the Lord's steward. And the purpose of his appointment goes far beyond the interests of any single Church; for while his office sends him especially to the Colossians, its scope is as wide as the world.

One great lesson to be learned from these words is that Stewardship means service; and we may add that, in nine cases out of ten, service means suffering. What Paul says, if we put it into more familiar language, is just this: "Because God has given me something that I can impart to others, I am their servant, and bound, not only by my duty to Him, but by my duty to them, to labour that they may receive the treasure." That is true for us all. Every gift from the great Householder involves the obligation to impart it. It makes us His stewards and our brethren's servants. We have that we may give. The possessions are the Householder's, not ours, even after He has given them to us. He gives us truths of various kinds in our minds, the gospel in our hearts, influence from our position, money in our pockets, not to lavish on self, nor to hide and gloat over in secret, but that we may transmit His gifts, and "God's grace fructify through us to all." "It is required of stewards that a man be found faithful"; and the heaviest charge, "that he had wasted his Lord's goods," lies against every one of us who does not use all that he possesses, whether of material or intellectual or spiritual wealth, for the common advantage.

But that common obligation of stewardship presses with special force on those who say that they are Christ's servants. If we are, we know something of His love and have felt something of His power; and there are hundreds of people around us, many of whom we can influence, who know nothing of either. That fact makes us their servants, not in the sense of being under their control, or of taking orders from them, but in the sense of gladly working for them, and recognising our obligation to help them. Our resources may be small. The Master of the house may have entrusted us with little. Perhaps we are like the boy with the five barley loaves and two small fishes; but even if we had only a bit of the bread and a tail of one of the fishes, we must not eat our morsel alone. Give it those who have none, and it will multiply as it is distributed, like the barrel of meal, which did not fail because its poor owner shared it with the still poorer prophet. Give, and not only give, but "pray them with much entreaty to receive the gift"; for men need to have the true Bread pressed on them, and they will often throw it back, or drop it over a wall, as soon as your back is turned, as beggars do in our streets. We have to win them by showing that we are their servants, before they will take what we have to give. Besides this, if stewardship is service, service is often suffering; and he will not clear himself of his obligations to his fellows, or of his responsibility to his Master, who shrinks from seeking to make known the love of Christ to his brethren, because he has often to "go forth weeping" whilst he bears the precious seed.

III. So we come to the last thought here, which is of the grand Mystery of which Paul is the Apostle and Servant. Paul always catches fire when he comes to think of the universal destination of the gospel, and of the honour put upon him as the man to whom the task was entrusted of transforming the Church from a Jewish sect to a world-wide society. That great thought now sweeps him away from his more immediate object, and enriches us with a burst which we could ill spare from the letter.

His task, he says, is to give its full development to the word of God, to proclaim a certain mystery long hid, but now revealed to those who are consecrated to God. To these it has been God's good pleasure to show the wealth of glory which is contained in this mystery, as exhibited among the Gentile Christians, which mystery is nothing else than the fact that Christ dwells in or among these Gentiles, of whom the Colossians are part, and by His dwelling in them gives them the confident expectation of future glory.

The mystery then of which the Apostle speaks so rapturously is the fact that the Gentiles were fellow-heirs and partakers of Christ. "Mystery" is a word borrowed from the ancient systems, in which certain rites and doctrines were communicated to the initiated. There are several allusions to them in Paul's writings, as for instance in the passage in Philippians iv. 12, which the Revised Version gives as "I have learned the secret both to be filled and to be hungry," and probably in the immediate context here, where the characteristic word "perfect" means "initiated." Portentous theories which have no warrant have been spun out of this word. The Greek mysteries implied secrecy; the rites were done in deep obscurity; the esoteric doctrines were muttered in the ear. The Christian mysteries are spoken on the housetop, nor does the word imply anything as to the comprehensibility of the doctrines or facts which are so called.

We talk about "mysteries," meaning thereby truths that transcend human faculties; but the New Testament "mystery" may be, and most frequently is, a fact perfectly comprehensible when once spoken. "Behold I show you a mystery: We shall not all sleep, but we shall all be changed." There is nothing incomprehensible in that. We should never have known it if we had not been told; but when told it is quite level with our faculties. And as a matter of fact, the word is most frequently used in connection with the notion, not of concealment, but of declaring. We find too that it occurs frequently in this Epistle, and in the parallel letter to the Ephesians, and in every instance but one refers as it does here, to a fact which was perfectly plain and comprehensible when once made known; namely, the entrance of the Gentiles into the Church.

If that be the true meaning of the word, then "a steward of the mysteries" will simply mean a man who has truths, formerly unknown but now revealed, in charge to make known to all who will hearken, and neither the claims of a priesthood nor the demand for the unquestioning submission of the intellect have any foundation in this much abused term.

But turning from this, we may briefly consider what was the substance of this grand mystery which thrilled Paul's soul. It is the wonderful fact that all barriers were broken down, and that Christ dwelt in the hearts of these Colossians. He saw in that the proof and the prophecy of the world-wide destination of the gospel. No wonder that his heart burned as he thought of the marvellous work which God had wrought by him. For there is no greater revolution in the history of the world than that accomplished through him, the cutting loose of Christianity from Judaism and widening the Church to the width of the race. No wonder that he was misunderstood and hated by Jewish Christians all his days!

He thinks of these once heathens and now Christians at Colossæ, far away in their lonely valley, and of many another little community—in Judæa, Asia, Greece, and Italy; and as he thinks of how a real solid bond of brotherhood bound them together in spite of their differences of race and culture, the vision of the oneness of mankind in the Cross of Christ shines out before him, as no man had ever seen it till then, and he triumphs in the sorrows that had helped to bring about the great result.

That dwelling of Christ among the Gentiles reveals the exuberant abundance of glory. To him the "mystery" was all running over with riches, and blazing with fresh radiance. To us it is familiar and somewhat worn. The "vision splendid," which was manifestly a revelation of hitherto unknown Divine treasures of mercy and lustrous light when it first dawned on the Apostle's sight, has "faded" somewhat "into the light of common day" for us, to whom the centuries since have shown so slow a progress. But let us not lose more than we can help, either by our familiarity with the thought, or by the discouragements arising from the chequered history of its partial realization. Christianity is still the only religion which has been able to make permanent conquests. It is the only one that has been able to disregard latitude and longitude, and to address and guide condition of civilization and modes of life quite unlike those of its origin. It is the only one that sets itself the task of conquering the world without the sword, and has kept true to the design for centuries. It is the only one whose claims to be world-wide in its adaptation and destiny would not be laughed out of court by its history. It is the only one which is to-day a missionary religion. And so, notwithstanding the long centuries of arrested growth and the wide tracts of remaining darkness, the mystery which fired Paul's enthusiasm is still able to kindle ours, and the wealth of glory that lies in it has not been impoverished nor stricken with eclipse.

One last thought is here,—that the possession of Christ is the pledge of future blessedness. "Hope" here seems to be equivalent to "the source" or "ground" of the hope. If we have the experience of His dwelling in our hearts, we shall have, in that very experience of His sweetness and of the intimacy of His love, a marvellous quickener of our hope that such sweetness and intimacy will continue for ever. The closer we keep to Him, the clearer will be our vision of future blessedness. If He is throned in our hearts, we shall be able to look forward with a hope, which is not less than certainty, to the perpetual continuance of His hold of us and of our blessedness in Him. Anything seems more credible to a man who habitually has Christ abiding in him, than that such a trifle as death should have power to end such a union. To have Him is to have life. To have Him will be heaven. To have Him is to have a hope certain as memory and careless of death or change.

That hope is offered to us all. If by our faith in His great sacrifice we grasp the great truth of "Christ for us," our fears will be scattered, sin and guilt taken away, death abolished, condemnation ended, the future a hope and not a dread. If by communion with Him through faith, love, and obedience, we have "Christ in us," our purity will grow, and our experience will be such as plainly to demand eternity to complete its incompleteness and to bring its folded buds to flower and fruit. If Christ be in us, His life guarantees ours, and we cannot die whilst He lives. The world has come, in the persons of its leading thinkers, to the position of proclaiming that all is dark beyond and above. "Behold! we know not anything," is the dreary "end of the whole matter"—infinitely sadder than the old Ecclesiastes, which from "vanity of vanities" climbed to "fear God and keep His commandments," as the sum of human thought and life. "I find no God; I know no future." Yes! Paul long ago told us that if we were "without Christ" we should "have no hope, and be without God in the world." And cultivated Europe is finding out that to fling away Christ and to keep a faith in God or in a future life is impossible.

But if we will take Him for our Saviour by simple trust, He will give us His own presence in our hearts, and infuse there a hope full of immortality. If we live in close communion with Him, we shall need no other assurance of an eternal life beyond than that deep, calm blessedness springing from the imperfect fellowship of earth which must needs lead to and be lost in the everlasting and completed union of heaven.

IX
THE CHRISTIAN MINISTRY IN ITS THEME, METHODS AND AIM

"Whom we proclaim, admonishing every man and teaching every man in all wisdom, that we may present every man perfect in Christ; whereunto I labour also, striving according to His working, which worketh in me mightily,"—Col. i. 28, 29 (Rev. Ver.).

The false teachers at Colossæ had a great deal to say about a higher wisdom reserved for the initiated. They apparently treated the Apostolic teaching as trivial rudiments, which might be good for the vulgar crowd, but were known by the possessors of this higher truth to be only a veil for it. They had their initiated class, to whom their mysteries were entrusted in whispers.

Such absurdities excited Paul's special abhorrence. His whole soul rejoiced in a gospel for all men. He had broken with Judaism on the very ground that it sought to enforce a ceremonial exclusiveness, and demanded circumcision and ritual observances along with faith. That was, in Paul's estimate, to destroy the gospel. These Eastern dreamers at Colossæ were trying to enforce an intellectual exclusiveness quite as much opposed to the gospel. Paul fights with all his might against that error. Its presence in the Church colours this context, where he uses the very phrases of the false teachers in order to assert the great principles which he opposes to their teaching. "Mystery," "perfect" or initiated, "wisdom,"—these are the key-words of the system which he is combating; and here he presses them into the service of the principle that the gospel is for all men, and the most recondite secrets of its deepest truth the property of every single soul that wills to receive them. Yes, he says in effect, we have mysteries. We have our initiated. We have wisdom. But we have no whispered teachings, confined to a little coterie; we have no inner chamber closed to the many. We are not muttering hierophants, cautiously revealing a little to a few, and fooling the rest with ceremonies and words. Our whole business is to tell out as fully and loudly as we can what we know of Christ, to tell to *every* man *all* the wisdom that we have learned. We fling open the inmost sanctuary, and invite all the crowd to enter.

This is the general scope of the words before us which state the object and methods of the Apostle's work; partly in order to point the contrast with those other teachers, and partly in order to prepare the way, by this personal reference, for his subsequent exhortations.

I. We have here the Apostle's own statement of what he conceived his life work to be.

"Whom we proclaim." All three words are emphatic. "Whom," not what—a person, not a system; we "proclaim," not we argue or dissertate about. "We" preach—the Apostle associates himself with all his brethren, puts himself in line with them, points to the unanimity of their testimony— "whether it were they or I, so we preach." We have all one message, a common type of doctrine.

So then—the Christian teacher's theme is not to be a theory or a system, but a living Person. One peculiarity of Christianity is that you cannot take its message, and put aside Christ, the speaker of the message, as you may do with all men's teachings. Some people say: "We take the great moral and religious truths which Jesus declared. They are the all-important parts of His work. We can disentangle them from any further connection with Him. It matters comparatively little who first spoke them." But that will not do. His person is inextricably intertwined with His teaching, for a very large part of His teaching is exclusively concerned with, and all of it centres in, Himself. He is not only true, but He is the truth. His message is, not only what He said with His lips about God and man, but also what He said about Himself, and what He did in His life, death, and resurrection. You may take Buddha's sayings, if you can make sure that they are his, and find much that is beautiful and true in them, whatever you may think of him; you may appreciate the teaching of Confucius, though you know nothing about him but that he said so and so; but you cannot do thus with Jesus. Our Christianity takes its whole colour from what we think of Him. If we think of Him as less than this chapter has been setting Him forth as being, we shall scarcely feel that *He* should be the preacher's theme; but if He is to us what He was to this Apostle, the sole Revealer of God, the Centre and Lord of creation, the Fountain of life to all which lives, the Reconciler of men with God by the blood of His cross, then the one message which a man may be thankful to spend his life in proclaiming will be, Behold the Lamb! Let who will preach abstractions, the true Christian minister has to preach the person and the office—Jesus the Christ.

To preach Christ is to set forth the person, the facts of His life and death, and to accompany these with that explanation which turns them from being merely a biography into a gospel. So much of "theory" must go with the "facts," or they will be no more a gospel than the story of another life would be. The Apostle's own statement of "the gospel which he preached" distinctly lays down what is needed—"how that Jesus Christ died." That is biography, and to say that and stop there is not to preach Christ; but add, "For our sins, according to the Scriptures, and that He was raised again the third day,"—preach *that*, the fact and its meaning and power, and you will preach Christ.

Of course there is a narrower and a wider sense of this expression. There is the initial teaching, which brings to a soul, who has never seen it before, the knowledge of a Saviour, whose Cross is the propitiation for sin; and there is the fuller teaching, which opens out the manifold bearings of that message in every region of moral and religious thought. I do not plead for any narrow construction of the words. They have been sorely abused, by being made the battle-cry for bitter bigotry and a hard system of abstract theology, as unlike what Paul means by "Christ" as any cobwebs of Gnostic heresy could be. Legitimate outgrowths of the Christian ministry have been checked in their name. They have been used as a cramping iron, as a shibboleth, as a stone to fling at honest and especially at young preachers. They have been made a pillow for laziness. So that the very sound of the words suggests to some ears, because of their use in some mouths, ignorant narrowness.

But for all that, they are a standard of duty for all workers for God, which it is not difficult to apply, if the will to do so be present, and they are a touch-stone to try the spirits, whether they be of God. A ministry of which the Christ who lived and died for us is manifestly the centre to which all converges and from which all is viewed, may sweep a wide circumference, and include many themes. The requirement bars out no province of thought or experience, nor does it condemn the preacher to a parrot-like repetition of elementary truths, or a narrow round of commonplace. It does demand that all themes shall lead up to Christ, and all teaching point to Him; that He shall be ever present in all the preacher's words, a diffused even when not a directly perceptible presence; and that His name, like some deep tone on an organ, shall be heard sounding on through all the ripple and change of the higher notes. Preaching Christ does not exclude any theme, but prescribes the bearing and purpose of all; and the widest compass and richest variety are not only possible but obligatory for him who would in any worthy sense take this for the motto of his ministry, "I determined not to know anything among you, save Jesus Christ and Him crucified."

But these words give us not only the theme but something of the manner of the Apostle's activity. "We *proclaim*." The word is emphatic in its form, meaning *to tell out*, and representing the proclamation as full, clear, earnest. "We are no muttering mystery-mongers. From full lungs and in a voice to make people hear, we shout aloud our message. We do not take a man into a corner, and whisper secrets into his ear; we cry in the streets, and our message is for 'every man.'"

And the word not only implies the plain, loud earnestness of the speaker, but also that what he speaks is a *message*, that he is not a speaker of his own words or thoughts, but of what has been told him to tell. His gospel is a good message, and a messenger's virtue is to say exactly what he has been told, and to say it in such a way that the people to whom he has to carry it cannot but hear and understand it.

This connection of the Christian minister's office contrasts on the one hand with the priestly theory. Paul had known in Judaism a religion of which the altar was the centre, and the official function of the "minister" was to sacrifice. But now he has come to see that "the one sacrifice for sins for ever" leaves no room for a sacrificing priest in that Church of which the centre is the Cross. We sorely need that lesson to be drilled into the minds of men to-day, when such a strange resurrection of priestism has taken place, and good, earnest men, whose devotion cannot be questioned, are looking on preaching as a very subordinate part of their work. For three centuries there has not been so much need as now to fight against the notion of a priesthood in the Church, and to urge this as the true definition of the minister's office: "we preach," not "we sacrifice," not "we *do*" anything; "we preach," not "we work miracles at any altar, or impart grace by any rites," but by manifestation of the truth discharge our office and spread the blessings of Christ.

This conception contrasts on the other hand, with the false teachers' style of speech, which finds its parallel in much modern talk. Their business was to argue and refine and speculate, to spin inferences and cobwebby conclusions. They sat in a lecturer's chair; we stand in a preacher's pulpit. The Christian minister has not to deal in such wares; he has a message to proclaim, and if he allows the "philosopher" in him to overpower the "herald," and substitutes his thoughts about the message, or his arguments in favour of the message, for the message itself, he abdicates his highest office and neglects his most important function.

We hear many demands to-day for a "higher type of preaching," which I would heartily echo, if only it be *preaching*; that is, the proclamation in loud and plain utterance of the great facts of Christ's work. But many who ask for this really want, not preaching, but something quite different; and many, as I think, mistaken Christian teachers are trying to play up to the requirements of the age by turning their sermons into dissertations, philosophical or moral or æsthetic. We need to fall back on this "we preach," and to urge that the Christian minister is neither priest nor lecturer, but a herald, whose business is to tell out his message, and to take good care that he tells it faithfully. If, instead of blowing his trumpet and calling aloud his commission, he were to deliver a discourse on acoustics and the laws of the vibration of sonorous metal, or to prove that he had a message, and to dilate on its evident truth or on the beauty of its phrases, he would scarcely be doing his work. No more is the Christian minister, unless he keeps clear before himself as the guiding star of his work this conception of his theme and his task—*Whom we preach*—and opposes that to the demands of an age, one half of which "require a sign," and would again degrade him into a priest, and the other calls for "wisdom," and would turn him into a professor.

II. We have here the varying methods by which this one great end is pursued. "Admonishing every man and teaching every man in all wisdom."

There are then two main methods—"admonishing" and "teaching." The former means "admonishing with blame," and points, as many commentators remark, to that side of the Christian ministry which corresponds to repentance, while the latter points to that side which corresponds to faith. In other words, the former rebukes and warns, has to do with conduct and the moral side of Christian truth; the latter has chiefly to do with doctrine, and the intellectual side. In the one Christ is proclaimed as the pattern of conduct, the "new commandment"; in the other, as the creed of creeds, the new and perfect knowledge.

The preaching of Christ then is to be unfolded into all "warning," or admonishing. The teaching of morality and the admonishing of the evil and the end of sin are essential parts of preaching Christ. We claim for the pulpit the right and the duty of applying the principles and pattern of Christ's life to all human conduct. It is difficult to do, and is made more so by some of the necessary conditions of our modern ministry, for the pulpit is not the place for details; and yet moral teaching which is confined to general principles is woefully like repeating platitudes and firing blank cartridges. Everybody admits the general principles, and thinks they do not apply to his specific wrong action; and if the preacher goes beyond these toothless generalities, he is met with the cry of "personalities." If a man preaches a sermon in which he speaks plainly about tricks of trade or follies of fashion, somebody is sure to say, going down the chapel steps, "Oh! ministers know nothing of business," and somebody else to add, "It is a pity he was so personal," and the chorus is completed by many other voices, "He should preach Christ, and leave secular things alone."

Well! whether a sermon of that sort be preaching Christ or not depends on the way in which it is done. But sure I am that there is no "preaching Christ" completely, which does not include plain speaking about plain duties. Everything that a man can either do rightly or wrongly belongs to the sphere of morals, and everything within the sphere of morals belongs to Christianity and to "preaching Christ."

Nor is such preaching complete without plain warning of the end of sin, as death here and hereafter. This is difficult, for many people like to have the smooth side of truth always put uppermost. But the gospel has a rough side, and is by no means a "soothing syrup" merely. There are no rougher words about what wrongdoers come to than some of Christ's words; and he has only given half his Master's message who hides or softens down the grim saying, "The wages of sin is death."

But all this moral teaching must be closely connected with and built upon Christ. Christian morality has Jesus for its perfect exemplar, His love for its motive, and His grace for its power. Nothing is more impotent than mere moral teaching. What is the use of perpetually saying to people, Be good, be good? You may keep on at that for ever, and not a soul will listen, any more than the crowds on our streets are drawn to church by the bell's monotonous call. But if, instead of a cold ideal of duty, as beautiful and as dead as a marble statue, we preach the Son of man, whose life is our law incarnate; and instead of urging to purity by motives which our own evil makes feeble, we re-echo His heart-touching appeal, "If ye love Me, keep My commandments;" and if, instead of mocking lame men with exhortations to walk, we point those who despairingly cry, "Who shall deliver us from the body of this death?" to Him who breathes His living spirit into us to set us free from sin and death, then our preaching of morality will be "preaching the gospel" and be "preaching Christ."

This gospel is also to be unfolded into "teaching." In the facts of Christ's life and death, as we ponder them and grow up to understand them, we get to see more and more the key to all things. For thought, as for life, He is the alpha and omega, the beginning and the ending. All that we can or need know about God or man, about present duty or future destiny, about life, death, and the beyond,—all is in Jesus Christ, and to be drawn from Him by patient thought and by abiding in Him. The Christian minister's business is to be ever learning and ever teaching more and more of the "manifold wisdom" of God. He has to draw for himself from the deep, inexhaustible fountains; he has to bear the water, which must be fresh drawn to be pleasant or refreshing, to thirsty lips. He must seek to present all sides of the truth, teaching *all* wisdom, and so escaping from his own limited mannerisms. How many ministers' Bibles are all dog-eared and thumbed at certain texts, at which they almost open of themselves, and are as clean in most of their pages as on the day when they were bought!

The Christian ministry, then, in the Apostle's view, is distinctly educational in its design. Preachers and hearers equally need to be reminded of this. We preachers are poor scholars ourselves, and in our work are tempted, like other people, to do most frequently what we can do with least trouble. Besides which, we many of us know, and all suspect, that our congregations prefer to hear what they have heard often before, and what gives them the least trouble. We often hear the cry for "simple preaching," by which one school intends "simple instruction in plain, practical matters, avoiding mere dogma," and another intends "the simple gospel," by which is meant the repetition over and over again of the great truth, "Believe on the Lord Jesus Christ, and thou shalt be saved." God forbid that I should say a word which might even seem to under-estimate the need for that proclamation being made in its simple form, as the staple of the Christian ministry, to all who have not welcomed it into their hearts, or to forget that, however dimly understood, it will bring light and hope and new loves and strengths into a soul! But the New Testament draws a distinction between evangelists and teachers, and common sense insists that Christian people need more than the reiteration of that message from him whom they call their "teacher." If he is a teacher, he should teach; and he cannot do that, if the people who listen to him suspect everything that they do not know already, and are impatient of anything that gives them the trouble of attending and thinking in order to learn. I fear there is much unreality in the name, and that nothing would be more distasteful to many of our congregations than the preacher's attempt to make it truly descriptive of his work. Sermons should not be "quiet resting places." Nor is it quite the ideal of Christian teaching that busy men should come to church or chapel on a Sunday, and not be fatigued by being made to think, but perhaps to be able to sleep for a minute or two and pick up the thread when they wake, quite sure that they have missed nothing of any consequence. We are meant to be teachers, as well as evangelists, though we fulfil the function so poorly; but our hearers often make that task more difficult by ill-concealed impatience with sermons which try to discharge it.

Observe too the emphatic repetition of "every man" both in these two clauses and in the following. It is Paul's protest against the exclusiveness of the heretics, who shut out the mob from their mysteries. An intellectual aristocracy is the proudest and most exclusive of all. A Church built upon intellectual qualifications would be as hard and cruel a *coterie* as could be imagined. So there is almost vehemence and scorn in the persistent repetition in each clause of the obnoxious word, as if he would thrust down his antagonists' throats the truth that his gospel has nothing to do with cliques and sections, but belongs to the world. To it philosopher and fool are equally welcome. Its message is to all. Brushing aside surface diversities, it goes straight to deep-lying wants, which are the same in all men. Below king's robe and professor's gown, and workman's jacket and prodigal's rags, beats the same heart with the same wants, wild longings, and weariness. Christianity knows no hopeless classes. But its highest wisdom can be spoken to the little child and the barbarian, and it is ready to deal with the most forlorn and foolish, knowing its own power to "warn every man and to teach every man in all wisdom."

III. We have here the ultimate aim of these diverse methods. "That we may present every man perfect in Christ Jesus."

We found this same word "present" in verse 22. The remarks made there will apply here. There the Divine purpose of Christ's great work, and here Paul's purpose in his, are expressed alike. God's aim is Paul's aim too. The Apostle's thoughts travel on to the great coming day, when we shall all be manifested at the judgment seat of Christ, and preacher and hearer, Apostle and convert, shall be gathered there. That solemn period will test the teacher's work, and should ever be in his view as he works. There is a real and indissoluble connection between the teacher and his hearers, so that in some sense he is to blame if they do not stand perfect then, and he in some sense has to present them as in his work—the gold, silver, and precious stones which he has built on the foundation. So each preacher should work with that end clear in view, as Paul did. He is always toiling in the light of that great vision. One sees him, in all his letters, looking away yonder to the horizon, where he expects the breaking of its morning low down in the eastern sky. Ah! how many formal pulpit and how many a languid pew would be galvanised into intense action if only their occupants once saw burning in on them, in their decorous deadness, the light of that great white throne! How differently we should preach if we always felt "the terror of the Lord," and under its solemn influence sought to "persuade men!" How differently we should hear if we felt we must appear before the Judge, and give account to Him of our profitings by His word!

And the purpose which the true minister of Christ has in view is to "present every man *perfect in Christ Jesus*." "Perfect" may be used here with the technical signification of "initiated," but it means absolute moral completeness. Negatively, it implies the entire removal of all defects; positively, the complete possession of all that belongs to human nature as God meant it to be. The Christian aim, for which the preaching of Christ supplies ample power, is to make the whole race possess, in fullest development, the whole circle of possible human excellences. There is to be no one-sided growth but men are to grow like a tree in the open, which has no barrier to hinder its symmetry, but rises and spreads equally on all sides, with no branch broken or twisted, no leaf worm-eaten or wind-torn, no fruit blighted or fallen, no gap in the clouds of foliage, no bend in the straight stem,—a green and growing completeness. This absolute completeness is attainable "in Christ," by union with Him of that vital sort brought about by faith, which will pour His Spirit into our spirits. The preaching of Christ is therefore plainly the direct way to bring about this perfecting. That is the Christian theory of the way to make perfect men.

And this absolute perfection of character is, in Paul's belief, possible for every man, no matter what his training or natural disposition may have been. The gospel is confident that it can change the Ethiopian's skin, because it can change his heart, and the leopard's spots will be altered when it "eats straw like the ox." There are no hopeless classes, in the glad, confident view of the man who has learned Christ's power.

What a vision of the future to animate work! What an aim! What dignity, what consecration, what enthusiasm it would give, making the trivial great and the monotonous interesting, stirring up those who share it to intense effort, overcoming low temptations, and giving precision to the selection of means and use of instruments! The pressure of a great, steady purpose consolidates and strengthens powers, which, without it, become flaccid and feeble. We can make a piece of calico as stiff as a board by putting it under an hydraulic press. Men with a fixed purpose are terrible men. They crash through conventionalities like a cannon ball. They, and they only, can persuade and arouse and impress their own enthusiasm on the inert mass. "Behold, how great a matter a little fire kindleth!" No Christian minister will work up to the limits of his power, nor do much for Christ or man, unless his whole soul is mastered by this high conception of the possibilities of his office, and unless he is possessed with the ambition to present every man "perfect in Christ Jesus."

IV. Note the struggle and the strength with which the Apostle reaches toward this aim. "Whereunto I labour also, striving according to His working, which worketh in me mightily."

As to the object, theme, and method of the Christian ministry, Paul can speak, as he does in the previous verses, in the name of all his fellow workers: "*We* preach, admonishing and teaching, that we may present." There was substantial unity among them. But he adds a sentence about his own toil and conflict in doing his work. He will only speak for himself now. The others may say what their experience has been. He has found that he cannot do his work easily. Some people may be able to get through it with little toil of body or agony of mind, but for himself it has been laborious work. He has not learned to "take it easy." That great purpose has been ever before him, and made a slave of him. "I labour *also*"; I do not only preach, but I *toil*—as the word literally implies—like a man tugging at an oar, and putting all his weight into each stroke. No great work for God will be done without physical and mental strain and effort. Perhaps there were people in Colossæ who thought that a man who had nothing to do but to preach had a very easy life, and so the Apostle had to insist that most exhausting work is brain work and heart work. Perhaps there were preachers and teachers there who worked in a leisurely, dignified fashion, and took great care always to stop a long way on the safe side of weariness; and so he had to insist that God's work cannot be done at all in that fashion, but has to be done "with both hands, earnestly." The "immortal garland" is to be run for, "not without dust and heat." The racer who takes care to slack his speed whenever he is in danger of breaking into a perspiration will not win the prize. The Christian minister who is afraid of putting all his strength into his work, up to the point of weariness, will never do much good.

There must be not only toil, but conflict. He labours, "*striving*"—that is to say, contending—with hindrances, both without and within, which sought to mar his work. There is the struggle with one's self, with the temptations to do high work from low motives, or to neglect it, and to substitute routine for inspiration and mechanism for fervour. One's own evil, one's weaknesses and fears and falsities, and laziness and torpor and faithlessness, have all to be fought, besides the difficulties and enemies without. In short, all good work is a battle.

The hard strain and stress of this life of effort and conflict made this man "Paul the aged" while he was not old in years. Such soul's agony and travail is indispensable for all high service of Christ. How can any true, noble Christian life be lived without continuous effort and continual strife? Up to the last particle of our power, it is our duty to work. As for the sleepy, languid, self-indulgent service of modern Christians, who seem to be chiefly anxious not to overstrain themselves, and to manage to win the race set before them without turning a hair, I am afraid that a large deduction will have to be made from it in the day that shall "try every man's work, of what sort it is."

So much for the struggle; now for the strength. The toil and the conflict are to be carried on "according to His working, which worketh in me mightily." The measure of our power then is Christ's power in us. He whose presence makes the struggle necessary, by His presence strengthens us for it. He will dwell in us and work in us, and even our weakness will be lifted into joyful strength by Him. We shall be mighty because that mighty Worker is in our spirits. We have not only His presence beside us as an ally, but His grace within us. We may not only have the vision of our Captain standing at our side as we front the foe—an unseen presence to them, but inspiration and victory to us—but we may have the consciousness of His power welling up in our spirits and flowing, as immortal strength, into our arms. It is much to know that Christ fights for us; it is more to know that He fights in us.

Let us take courage then for all work and conflict; and remember that if we have not "striven according to the power"—that is, if we have not utilised *all* our Christ-given strength in His service—we have not striven enough. There may be a double defect in us. We may not have taken all the power that he Has given, and we may not have used all the power that we have taken. Alas, for us! we have to confess both faults. How weak we have been when Omnipotence waited to give Itself to us! How little we have made our own of the grace that flows so abundantly past us, catching such a small part of the broad river in our hands, and spilling so much even of that before it reached our lips! And how little of the power given, whether natural or spiritual, we have used for our Lord! How many weapons have hung rusty and unused in the fight! He has sowed much in our hearts, and reaped little. Like some unkindly soils, we have "drunk in the rain which cometh oft upon it," and have "*not* brought forth herbs fit for Him by whom it is dressed." Talents hid, the Master's goods squandered, power allowed to run to waste, languid service and half-hearted conflict, we have all to acknowledge. Let us go to Him and confess that, "we have most unthankful been," and are unprofitable servants indeed, coming far short of duty. Let us yield our spirits to His influence, that He may work in us that which is pleasing in His sight, and may encircle us with ever-growing completeness of beauty and strength, until He "present us faultless before the presence of His glory with exceeding joy."

X
PAUL'S STRIVING FOR THE COLOSSIANS

"For I would have you know how greatly I strive for you, and for them at Laodicea, and for as many as have not seen my face in the flesh; that their hearts may be comforted, they being knit together in love, and unto all riches of the full assurance of understanding, that they may know the mystery of God, even Christ, in Whom are all the treasures of wisdom and knowledge hidden." — Col. ii. 1–3 (Rev. Ver.).

We have seen that the closing portion of the previous chapter is almost exclusively personal. In this context the same strain is continued, and two things are dwelt on: the Apostle's agony of anxiety for the Colossian Church, and the joy with which, from his prison, he travelled in spirit across mountain and sea, and saw them in their quiet valley, cleaving to the Lord. The former of these feelings is expressed in the words now before us; the latter, in the following verses.

All this long outpouring of self-revelation is so natural and characteristic of Paul that we need scarcely look for any purpose in it, and yet we may note with what consummate art he thereby prepares the way for the warnings which follow. The unveiling of his own throbbing heart was sure to work on the affections of his readers and to incline them to listen. His profound emotion in thinking of the preciousness of his message would help to make them feel how much was at stake, and his unfaltering faith would give firmness to their less tenacious grasp of the truth which, as they saw, he gripped with such force. Many truths may be taught coolly, and some must be. But in religious matters, arguments wrought in frost are powerless, and earnestness approaching to passion is the all-conquering force. A teacher who is afraid to show his feelings, or who has no feelings to show, will never gather many disciples.

So this revelation of the Apostle's heart is relevant to the great purposes of the whole letter—the warning against error, and the exhortation to stedfastness. In the verses which we are now considering, we have the conflict which Paul was waging set forth in three aspects: first, in itself; second, in regard to the persons for whom it was waged; and, finally and principally, in regard to the object or purpose in view therein. The first and second of these points may be dealt with briefly. The third will require further consideration.

I. There is first the conflict, which he earnestly desired that the Colossian Christians might know to be "great." The word rendered in the Authorised Version "conflict," belongs to the same root as that which occurs in the last verse of the previous chapter, and is there rendered "striving." The Revised Version rightly indicates this connection by its translation, but fails to give the construction as accurately as the older translation does. "What great strife I have" would be nearer the Greek, and more forcible than the somewhat feeble "how greatly I strive," which the Revisers have adopted. The conflict referred to is, of course, that of the arena, as so often in Paul's writings.

But how could he, in Rome, wage conflict on behalf of the Church at Colossæ? No external conflict can be meant. He could strike no blows on their behalf. What he could do in that way, he did, and he was now taking part in their battle by this letter. If he could not fight by their side, he could send them ammunition, as he does in this great Epistle, which was, no doubt, to the eager combatants for the truth at Colossæ, what it has been ever since, a magazine and arsenal in all their warfare. But the real struggle was in his own heart. It meant anxiety, sympathy, an agony of solicitude, a passion of intercession. What he says of Epaphras in this very Epistle was true of himself. He was "always striving in prayer for them." And by these wrestlings of spirit he took his place among the combatants, though they were far away, and though in outward seeming, his life was untouched by any of the difficulties and dangers which hemmed them in. In that lonely prison-cell, remote from their conflict, and with burdens enough of his own to carry, with his life in peril, his heart yet turned to them and, like some soldier left behind to guard the base while his comrades had gone forward to the fight, his ears listened for the sound of battle, and his thoughts were in the field. His prison cell was like the focus of some reverberating gallery in which every whisper spoken all round the circumference was heard, and the heart that was held captive there was set vibrating in all its chords by every sound from any of the Churches.

Let us learn the lesson, that, for all Christian people, sympathy in the battle for God, which is being waged all over the world, is plain duty. For all Christian teachers of every sort, an eager sympathy in the difficulties and struggles of those whom they would try to teach is indispensable. We can never deal wisely with any mind until we have entered into its peculiarities. We can never help a soul fighting with errors and questionings until we have ourselves felt the pinch of the problems, and have shown that soul that we know what it is to grope and stumble. No man is ever able to lift a burden from another's shoulders except on condition of bearing the burden himself. If I stretch out my hand to some poor brother struggling in "the miry clay," he will not grasp it, and my well-meant efforts will be vain, unless he can see that I too have felt with him the horror of great darkness, and desire him to share with me the benedictions of the light.

Wheresoever our prison or our workshop may be, howsoever Providence or circumstances—which is but a heathenish word for the same thing—may separate us from active participation in any battle for God, we are bound to take an eager share in it by sympathy, by interest, by such help as we can render, and by that intercession which may sway the fortunes of the field, though the uplifted hands grasp no weapons, and the spot where we pray be far from the fight. It is not only the men who bear the brunt of the battle in the high places of the field who are the combatants. In many a quiet home, where their wives and mothers sit, with wistful faces waiting for the news from the front, are an agony of anxiety, and as true a share in the struggle as amidst the battery smoke and the gleaming bayonets. It was a law in Israel, "As his part is that goeth down to the battle, so shall his part be that abideth by the stuff. They shall part alike." They were alike in recompense, because they were rightly regarded as alike in service. So all Christians who have in heart and sympathy taken part in the great battle shall be counted as combatants and crowned as victors, though they themselves have struck no blows. "He that receiveth a prophet in the name of a prophet shall receive a prophet's reward."

II. We notice the persons for whom this conflict was endured. They are the Christians of Colossæ, and their neighbours of Laodicea, and "as many as have not seen my face in the flesh." It may be a question whether the Colossians and Laodiceans belong to those who have not seen his face in the flesh, but the most natural view of the words is that the last clause "introduces the whole class to which the persons previously enumerated belong,"[2] and this conclusion is confirmed by the silence of the Acts of the Apostles as to any visit of Paul's to these Churches, and by the language of the Epistle itself, which, in several places, refers to his knowledge of the Colossian Church as derived from hearing of them, and never alludes to personal intercourse. That being so, one can understand that its members might easily think that he cared less for them than he did for the more fortunate communities which he had himself planted or watered, and might have suspected that the difficulties of the Church at Ephesus, for instance, lay nearer his heart than theirs in their remote upland valley. No doubt, too, their feelings to him were less warm than to Epaphras and to other teachers whom they had heard. They had never felt the magnetism of his personal presence, and were at a disadvantage in their struggle with the errors which were beginning to lift their snaky heads among them, from not having had the inspiration and direction of his teaching.

It is beautiful to see how, here, Paul lays hold of that very fact which seemed to put some film of separation between them, in order to make it the foundation of his especial keenness of interest in them. Precisely because he had never looked them in the eyes, they had a warmer place in his heart, and his solicitude for them was more tender. He was not so enslaved by sense that his love could not travel beyond the limits of his eyesight. He was the more anxious about them because they had not the recollections of his teaching and of his presence to fall back upon.

III. But the most important part of this section is the Apostle's statement of the great subject of his solicitude, that which he anxiously longed that the Colossians might attain. It is a prophecy, as well as a desire. It is a statement of the deepest purpose of his letter to them, and being so, it is likewise a statement of the Divine desire concerning each of us, and of the Divine design of the gospel. Here is set forth what God would have all Christians to be, and, in Jesus Christ, has given them ample means of being.

(1) The first element in the Apostle's desire for them is "that their hearts may be comforted." Of course the Biblical use of the word "heart" is much wider than the modern popular use of it. We mean by it, when we use it in ordinary talk, the hypothetical seat of the emotions, and chiefly, the organ and throne of love; but Scripture means by the word, the whole inward personality, including thought and will as well as emotion. So we read of the "thoughts and intents of the heart," and the whole inward nature is called "the hidden man of the heart."

And what does he desire for this inward man? That it may be "comforted." That word again has a wider signification in Biblical, than in nineteenth century English. It is much more than consolation in trouble. The cloud that hung over the Colossian Church was not about to break in sorrows which they would need consolation to bear, but in doctrinal and practical errors which they would need strength to resist. They were called to fight rather than to endure, and what they needed most was courageous confidence. So Paul desires for them that their hearts should be *encouraged* or strengthened, that they might not quail before the enemy, but go into the fight with buoyancy, and be of good cheer.

Is there any greater blessing in view both of the conflict which Christianity has to wage to-day, and of the difficulties and warfare of our own lives, than that brave spirit, which plunges into the struggle with the serene assurance that victory sits on our helms and waits upon our swords, and knows that anything is possible rather than defeat? That is the condition of overcoming—even our faith. "The sad heart tires in a mile," but the strong hopeful heart carries in its very strength the prophecy of triumph.

Such a disposition is not altogether a matter of temperament, but may be cultivated, and though it may come easier to some of us than to others, it certainly ought to belong to all who have God to trust to, and believe that the gospel is His truth. They may well be strong who have Divine power ready to flood their hearts, who know that everything works for their good, who can see, above the whirl of time and change, one strong loving Hand which moves the wheels. What have we to do with fear for ourselves, or wherefore should our "hearts tremble for the ark of God," seeing that One fights by our sides who will teach our hands to war and cover our heads in the day of battle? "Be of good courage, and He shall strengthen thine heart."

(2) The way to secure such joyous confidence and strength is taught us here, for we have next, *Union in love*, as part of the means for obtaining it—"They being knit together in love." The persons, not the hearts, are to be thus united. Love is the true bond which unites men—the bond of perfectness, as it is elsewhere called. That unity in love would, of course, add to the strength of each. The old fable teaches us that little fagots bound together are strong, and the tighter the rope is pulled, the stronger they are. A solitary heart is timid and weak, but many weaknesses brought together make a strength, as slimly built houses in a row hold each other up, or dying embers raked closer burst into flame. Loose grains of sand are light and moved by a breath; compacted they are rock against which the Atlantic beats in vain. So, a Church, of which the members are bound together by that love which is the only real bond of Church life, presents a front to threatening evils through which they cannot break. A real moral defence against even intellectual error will be found in such a close compaction in mutual Christian love. A community so interlocked will throw off many evils, as a Roman legion with linked shields roofed itself over against missiles from the wall of a besieged city, or the imbricated scales on a fish keep it dry in the heart of the sea.

But we must go deeper than this in interpreting these words. The love which is to knit Christian men together is not merely love to one another, but is common love to Jesus Christ. Such common love to Him is the true bond of union, and the true strengthener of men's hearts.

(3) This compaction in love will lead to a wealth of certitude in the possession of the truth.

Paul is so eagerly desirous for the Colossians' union in love to each other and all to God, because He knows that such union will materially contribute to their assured and joyful possession of the truth. It tends, he thinks, unto "all riches of the full assurance of understanding," by which he means the wealth which consists in the entire, unwavering certitude which takes possession of the understanding, the confidence that it has the truth and the life in Jesus Christ. Such a joyful stedfastness of conviction that I have grasped the truth is opposed to hesitating half belief. It is attainable, as this context shows, by paths of moral discipline, and amongst them, by seeking to realize our unity with our brethren, and not proudly rejecting the "common faith" because it is common. Possessing that assurance, we shall be rich and heart-whole. Walking amid certainties we shall walk in paths of peace, and re-echo the triumphant assurance of the Apostle, to whom love had given the key of knowledge:—"we know that we are of God, and we know that the Son of God is come, and hath given us an understanding, that we may know Him that is true."

In all times of religious unsettlement, when an active propaganda of denial is going on, Christian men are tempted to lower their own tone, and to say, "It is so," with somewhat less of certainty, because so many are saying, "It is not so." Little Rhoda needs some courage to affirm constantly that "it was even so," when apostles and her masters keep assuring her that she has only seen a vision. In this day, many professing Christians falter in the clear assured profession of their faith, and it does not need a keen ear to catch an undertone of doubt making their voices tremulous. Some even are so afraid of being thought "narrow," that they seek for the reputation of liberality by talking as if there were a film of doubt over even the truths which used to be "most surely believed." Much of the so-called faith of this day is all honeycombed with secret misgivings, which have in many instances no other intellectual basis than the consciousness of prevalent unbelief and a second-hand acquaintance with its teachings. Few things are more needed among us now than this full assurance and satisfaction of the understanding with the truth as it is in Jesus. Nothing is more wretched than the slow paralysis creeping over faith, the fading of what had been stars into darkness. A tragedy is being wrought in many minds which have had to exchange Christ's "Verily, verily," for a miserable "perhaps," and can no longer say "I know," but only, "I would fain believe," or at the best, "I incline to think still." On the other hand, the "full assurance of the understanding" brings wealth. It breathes peace over the soul, and gives endless riches in the truths which through it are made living and real.

This wealth of conviction is attained by living in the love of God. Of course, there is an intellectual discipline which is also needed. But no intellectual process will lead to an assured grasp of spiritual truth, unless it be accompanied by love. As soon may we lay hold of truth with our hands, as of God in Christ with our understandings alone. This is the constant teaching of Scripture—that, if we would know God and have assurance of Him, we must love Him. "In order to love human things, it is necessary to know them. In order to know Divine things, it is necessary to love them." When we are rooted and grounded in love, we shall be able to know—for what we have most need to know and what the gospel has mainly to teach us is the love, and "unless the eye with which we look is love, how shall we know love?" If we love, we shall possess an experience which verifies the truth for us, will give us an irrefragable demonstration which will bring certitude to ourselves, however little it may avail to convince others. Rich in the possession of this confirmation of the gospel by the blessings which have come to us from it, and which witness of their source, as the stream that dots some barren plain with a line of green along its course is revealed thereby, we shall have the right to oppose to many a doubt the full assurance born of love, and while others are disputing whether there be any God, or any living Christ, or any forgiveness of sins, or any guiding providence, we shall know that they are, and are ours, because we have felt the power and wealth which they have brought into our lives.

(4) This unity of love will lead to full knowledge of the mystery of God. Such seems to be the connection of the next words, which may be literally read "unto the full knowledge of the mystery of God," and may be best regarded as a co-ordinate clause with the preceding, depending like it on "being knit together in love." So taken, there is set forth a double issue of that compaction in love to God and one another, namely, the calm assurance in the grasp of truth already possessed, and the more mature and deeper insight into the deep things of God. The word for knowledge here is the same as in i. 9, and here as there means a full knowledge. The Colossians had known Christ at first, but the Apostle's desire is that they may come to a fuller knowledge, for the object to be known is infinite, and endless degrees in the perception and possession of His power and grace are possible. In that fuller knowledge they will not leave behind what they knew at first, but will find in it deeper meaning, a larger wisdom and a fuller truth.

Among the large number of readings of the following words, that adopted by the Revised Version is to be preferred, and the translation which it gives is the most natural and is in accordance with the previous thought in chapter i. 27, where also "the mystery" is explained to be "Christ in you." A slight variation in the conception is presented here. The "mystery" is Christ, not "in you," but "in Whom are hid all the treasures of wisdom and knowledge." The great truth long hidden, now revealed, is that the whole wealth of spiritual insight (knowledge), and of reasoning on the truths thus apprehended so as to gain an ordered system of belief and a coherent law of conduct (wisdom), is stored for us in Christ.

Such being in brief the connection and outline meaning of these great words, we may touch upon the various principles embodied in them. We have seen, in commenting upon a former part of the Epistle, the force of the great thought that Christ in His relations to us is the mystery of God, and need not repeat what was then said. But we may pause for a moment on the fact that the knowledge of that mystery has its stages. The revelation of the mystery is complete. No further stages are possible in that. But while the revelation is, in Paul's estimate, finished, and the long concealed truth now stands in full sunshine, our apprehension of it may grow, and there is a mature knowledge possible. Some poor ignorant soul catches through the gloom a glimpse of God manifested in the flesh, and bearing his sins. That soul will never outgrow that knowledge, but as the years pass, life and reflection and experience will help to explain and deepen it. God so loved the world that He gave His only begotten Son—there is nothing beyond that truth. Grasped however imperfectly, it brings light and peace. But as it is loved and lived by, it unfolds undreamed-of depths, and flashes with growing brightness. Suppose that a man could set out from the great planet that moves on the outermost rim of our system, and could travel slowly inwards towards the central sun, how the disc would grow, and the light and warmth increase with each million of miles that he crossed, till what had seemed a point filled the whole sky! Christian growth is into, not away from Christ, a penetrating deeper into the centre, and a drawing out into distinct consciousness as a coherent system, all that was wrapped, as the leaves in their brown sheath, in that first glimpse of Him which saves the soul.

These stages are infinite, because in Him are all the treasures of wisdom and knowledge. These four words, *treasures, wisdom, knowledge, hidden,* are all familiar on the lips of the latter Gnostics, and were so, no doubt, in the mouths of the false teachers at Colossæ. The Apostle would assert for his gospel all which they falsely claimed for their dreams. As in several other places of this Epistle, he avails himself of his antagonists' special vocabulary, transferring its terms, from the illusory phantoms which a false knowledge adorned with them, to the truth which he had to preach. He puts special emphasis on the predicate "hidden" by throwing it to the end of the sentence—a peculiarity which is reproduced with advantage in the Revised Version.

All wisdom and knowledge are in Christ. He is the Light of men, and all thought and truth of every sort come from Him Who is the Eternal Word, the Incarnate Wisdom. That Incarnate Word is the perfect Revelation of God, and by His one completed life and death has declared the whole name of God to His brethren, of which all other media of revelation have but uttered broken syllables. That ascended Christ breathes wisdom and knowledge into all who love Him, and still pursues, by giving us the Spirit of wisdom, His great work of revealing God to men, according to His own word, which at once asserted the completeness of the revelation made by His earthly life and promised the perpetual continuance of the revelation from His heavenly seat: "I have declared Thy name unto My brethren, and will declare it."

In Christ, as in a great storehouse, lie all the riches of spiritual wisdom, the massive ingots of solid gold which when coined into creeds and doctrines are the wealth of the Church. All which we can know concerning God and man, concerning sin and righteousness and duty, concerning another life, is in Him Who is the home and deep mine where truth is stored.

In Christ these treasures are "hidden," but not, as the heretics' mysteries were hidden, in order that they might be out of reach of the vulgar crowd. This mystery is hidden indeed, but it is revealed. It is hidden only from the eyes that will not see it. It is hidden that seeking souls may have the joy of seeking and the rest of finding. The very act of revealing is a hiding, as our Lord has said in His great thanksgiving because these things are (by one and the same act) "hid from the wise and prudent, and revealed to babes." They are hid, as men store provisions in the Arctic regions, in order that the bears may not find them and the shipwrecked sailors may.

Such thoughts have a special message for times of agitation such as the Colossian Church was passing through, and such as we have to face. We too are surrounded by eager confident voices, proclaiming profounder truths and a deeper wisdom than the gospel gives us. In joyful antagonism to these, Christian men have to hold fast by the confidence that all Divine wisdom is laid up in their Lord. We need not go to others to learn new truth. The new problems of each generation to the end of time will find their answers in Christ, and new issues of that old message which we have heard from the beginning will continually be discerned. Let us not wonder if the lessons which the earlier ages of the Church drew from that infinite storehouse fail at many points to meet the eager questionings of to-day. Nor let us suppose that the stars are quenched because the old books of astronomy are in some respects out of date. We need not cast aside the truths that we learned at our mother's knees. The central fact of the universe and the perfect encyclopædia of all moral and spiritual truth is Christ, the Incarnate Word, the Lamb slain, the ascended King. If we keep true to Him and strive to widen our minds to the breadth of that great message, it will grow as we gaze, even as the nightly heavens expand to the eye which stedfastly looks into them, and reveal violet abysses sown with sparkling points, each of which is a sun. "Lord, to whom shall we go? Thou hast the words of eternal life."

The ordinary type of Christian life is contented with a superficial acquaintance with Christ. Many understand no more of Him and of His gospel than they did when first they learned to love Him. So completely has the very idea of a progressive knowledge of Jesus Christ faded from the horizon of the average Christian that "edification," which ought to mean the progressive building up of the character course by course, in new knowledge and grace, has come to mean little more than the sense of comfort derived from the reiteration of old and familiar words which fall on the ear with a pleasant murmur. There is sadly too little first-hand and growing knowledge of their Lord, among Christian people, too little belief that fresh treasures may be found hidden in that field which, to each soul and each new generation struggling with its own special forms of the burdens and problems that press upon humanity, would be cheaply bought by selling all, but may be won at the easier rate of earnest desire to possess them, and faithful adherence to Him in whom they are stored for the world. The condition of growth for the branch is abiding in the vine. If our hearts are knit together with Christ's heart in that love which is the parent of communion, both as delighted contemplation and as glad obedience, then we shall daily dig deeper into the mine of wealth which is hid in Him that it may be found, and draw forth an unfailing supply of things new and old.

FOOTNOTES:

[2] Bishop Lightfoot, *in loc.*

XI
CONCILIATORY AND HORTATORY
TRANSITION TO POLEMICS

"This I say, that no one may delude you with persuasiveness of speech. For though I am absent in the flesh, yet am I with you in the spirit, joying and beholding your order, and the stedfastness of your faith in Christ.

"As therefore ye received Christ Jesus the Lord, so walk in Him, rooted and builded up in Him, and stablished in your faith, even as ye were taught, abounding in thanksgiving."— Col. ii. 4–7 (Rev. Ver.).

Nothing needs more delicacy of hand and gentleness of heart than the administration of warning or reproof, especially when directed against errors of religious opinion. It is sure to do harm unless the person reproved is made to feel that it comes from true kindly interest in him, and does full justice to his honesty. Warning so easily passes into scolding, and sounds to the warned so like it even when the speaker does not mean it so, that there is special need to modulate the voice very carefully.

So in this context, the Apostle has said much about his deep interest in the Colossian Church, and has dwelt on the passionate earnestness of his solicitude for them, his conflict of intercession and sympathy, and the large sweep of his desires for their good. But he does not feel that he can venture to begin his warnings till he has said something more, so as to conciliate them still further, and to remove from their minds other thoughts unfavourable to the sympathetic reception of his words. One can fancy some Colossians saying, "What need is there for all this anxiety? Why should Paul be in such a taking about us? He is exaggerating our danger, and doing scant justice to our Christian character." Nothing stops the ear to the voice of warning more surely than a feeling that it is pitched in too solemn a key, and fails to recognise the good.

So before he goes further, he gathers up his motives in giving the following admonitions, and gives his estimate of the condition of the Colossians, in the two first of the verses now under consideration. All that he has been saying has been said not so much because he thinks that they have gone wrong, but because he knows that there are heretical teachers at work, who may lead them astray with plausible lessons. He is not combating errors which have already swept away the faith of the Colossian Christians, but putting them on their guard against such as threaten them. He is not trying to pump the water out of a water-logged vessel, but to stop a little leak which is in danger of gaping wider. And, in his solicitude, he has much confidence and is encouraged to speak because, absent from them as he is, he has a vivid assurance, which gladdens him, of the solidity and firmness of their faith.

So with this distinct definition of the precise danger which he feared, and this soothing assurance of his glad confidence in their stedfast order, the Apostle at last opens his batteries. The 6th and 7th verses are the first shot fired, the beginning of the monitions so long and carefully prepared for They contain a general exhortation, which may be taken as the keynote for the polemical portion of the Epistle, which occupies the rest of the chapter.

I. We have then first, the purpose of the Apostle's previous self-revelation. "This I say"—this namely which is contained in the preceding verses, the expression of his solicitude, and perhaps even more emphatically, the declaration of Christ as the revealed secret of God, the inexhaustible storehouse of all wisdom and knowledge. The purpose of the Apostle, then, in his foregoing words has been to guard the Colossians against the danger to which they were exposed, of being deceived and led astray by "persuasiveness of speech." That expression is not necessarily used in a bad sense, but here it evidently has a tinge of censure, and implies some doubt both of the honesty of the speakers and of the truthfulness of their words. Here we have an important piece of evidence as to the then condition of the Colossian Church. There were false teachers busy amongst them who belonged in some sense to the Christian community. But probably these were not Colossians, but wandering emissaries of a Judaizing Gnosticism, while certainly the great mass of the Church was untouched by their speculations. They were in danger of getting bewildered, and being *deceived*, that is to say, of being induced to accept certain teaching because of its speciousness, without seeing all its bearings, or even knowing its real meaning. So error ever creeps into the Church. Men are caught by something fascinating in some popular teaching, and follow it without knowing where it will lead them. By slow degrees its tendencies are disclosed, and at last the followers of the heresiarch wake to find that everything which they once believed and prized has dropped from their creed.

We may learn here, too, the true safeguard against specious errors. Paul thinks that he can best fortify these simple-minded disciples against all harmful teaching by exalting his Master and urging the inexhaustible significance of His person and message. To learn the full meaning and preciousness of Christ is to be armed against error. The positive truth concerning Him, by preoccupying mind and heart, guards beforehand against the most specious teachings. If you fill the coffer with gold, nobody will want, and there will be no room for, pinchbeck. A living grasp of Christ will keep us from being swept away by the current of prevailing popular opinion, which is always much more likely to be wrong than right, and is sure to be exaggerated and one-sided at the best. A personal consciousness of His power and sweetness will give an instinctive repugnance to teaching that would lower His dignity and debase His work. If He be the centre and anchorage of all our thoughts, we shall not be tempted to go elsewhere in search of the "treasures of wisdom and knowledge" which "are hid in Him." He who has found the one pearl of great price, needs no more to go seeking goodly pearls, but only day by day more completely to lose self, and give up all else, that he may win more and more of Christ his All. If we keep our hearts and minds in communion with our Lord, and have experience of His preciousness, that will preserve us from many a snare, will give us a wisdom beyond much logic, will solve for us many of the questions most hotly debated to-day, and will show us that many more are unimportant and uninteresting to us. And even if we should be led to wrong conclusions on some matters, "if we drink any deadly thing, it shall not hurt us."

II. We see here the joy which blended with the anxiety of the solitary prisoner, and encouraged him to warn the Colossians against impending dangers to their faith.

We need not follow the grammatical commentators in their discussion of how Paul comes to invert the natural order here, and to say "joying and beholding," instead of "beholding and rejoicing" as we should expect. No one doubts that what he saw in spirit was the cause of his joy. The old man in his prison, loaded with many cares, compelled to be inactive in the cause which was more to him than life, is yet full of spirit and buoyancy. His prison-letters all partake of that "rejoicing in the Lord," which is the keynote of one of them. Old age and apparent failure, and the exhaustion of long labours, and the disappointments and sorrows which almost always gather like evening clouds round a life as it sinks in the west had not power to quench his fiery energy or to blunt his keen interest in all the Churches. His cell was like the centre of a telephonic system. Voices spoke from all sides. Every Church was connected with it, and messages were perpetually being brought. Think of him sitting there, eagerly listening, and thrilling with sympathy at each word, so self-oblivious was he, so swallowed up were all personal ends in the care for the Churches, and in the swift, deep fellow-feeling with them? Love and interest quickened his insight, and though he was far away, he had them so vividly before him that he was as if a spectator. The joy which he had in the thought of them made him dwell on the thought—so the apparently inverted order of the words may be the natural one and he may have looked all the more fixedly because it gladdened him to look.

What did he see? "Your order." That is unquestionably a military metaphor, drawn probably from his experiences of the Prætorians, while in captivity. He had plenty of opportunities of studying both the equipment of the single legionary, who, in the 6th chapter of Ephesians, sat for his portrait to the prisoner to whom he was chained, and also the perfection of discipline in the whole which made the legion so formidable. It was not a multitude but a unit, "moving altogether if it move at all," as if animated by one will. Paul rejoices to know that the Colossian Church was thus welded into a solid unity.

Further, he beholds "the stedfastness of your faith in Christ." This may be a continuation of the military metaphor, and may mean "the solid front, the close phalanx" which your faith presents. But whether we suppose the figure to be carried on or dropped, we must, I think, recognise that this second point refers rather to the inward condition than to the outward discipline of the Colossians.

Here then is set forth a lofty ideal of the Church, in two respects. First there is outwardly, an ordered disciplined array; and secondly, there is a stedfast faith.

As to the first, Paul was no martinet, anxious about the pedantry of the parade ground, but he knew the need of organization and drill. Any body of men united in order to carry out a specific purpose have to be organized. That means a place for every man, and every man in his place. It means co-operation to one common end, and therefore division of function and subordination. Order does not merely mean obedience to authority. There may be equal "order" under widely different forms of polity. The legionaries were drawn up in close ranks, the light-armed skirmishers more loosely. In the one case the phalanx was more and the individual less; in the other there was more play given to the single man, and less importance to corporate action; but the difference between them was not that of order and disorder, but that of two systems, each organized but on somewhat different principles and for different purposes. A loosely linked chain is as truly a chain as a rigid one. The main requirement for such "order" as gladdened the Apostle is conjoint action to one end, with variety of office, and unity of spirit.

Some Churches give more weight to the principle of authority; others to that of individuality. They may criticise each other's polity, but the former has no right to reproach the latter as being necessarily defective in "order." Some Churches are all drill and their favourite idea of discipline is, Obey them that have the rule over you. The Churches of looser organization, on the other hand, are no doubt in danger of making too little of organization. But both need that all their members should be more penetrated by the sense of unity, and should fill each his place in the work of the body. It was far easier to secure the true order—a place and a task for every man and every man in his place and at his task—in the small homogeneous communities of apostolic times than it is now, when men of such different social position, education, and ways of thinking are found in the same Christian community. The proportion of idlers in all Churches is a scandal and a weakness. However highly organized and officered a Church may be, no joy would fill an apostle's heart in beholding it, if the mass of its members had no share in its activities. Every society of professing Christians should be like a man of war's crew, each of whom knows the exact inch where he has to stand when the whistle sounds, and the precise thing he has to do in the gun drill.

But the perfection of discipline is not enough. That may stiffen into routine if there be not something deeper. We want life even more than order. The description of the soldiers who set David on the throne should describe Christ's army—"men that could keep rank, they were not of double heart." They had discipline and had learned to accommodate their stride to the length of their comrades' step; but they had whole-hearted enthusiasm, which was better. Both are needed. If there be not courage and devotion there is nothing worth disciplining. The Church that has the most complete order and not also stedfastness of faith will be like the German armies, all pipeclay and drill, which ran like hares before the ragged shoeless levies whom the first French Revolution flung across the border with a fierce enthusiasm blazing in their hearts. So the Apostle beholds with joy the stedfastness of the Colossians' faith toward Christ.

If the rendering "stedfastness" be adopted as in the Rev. Ver., the phrase will be equivalent to the "firmness which characterizes or belongs to your faith." But some of the best commentators deny that this meaning of the word is ever found, and propose "foundation" (that which is made stedfast). The meaning then will either be "the firm foundation (for your lives) which consists of your faith," or, more probably, "the firm foundation which your faith has." He rejoices, seeing that their faith towards Jesus Christ has a basis unshaken by assaults.

Such a rock foundation, and consequent stedfastness, must faith have, if it is to be worthy of the name and to manifest its true power. A tremulous faith may, thank God! be a true faith, but the very idea of faith implies solid assurance and fixed confidence. Our faith should be able to resist pressure and to keep its ground against assaults and gainsaying. It should not be like a child's card castle, that the light breath of a scornful laugh will throw down, but

> "a tower of strength
> That stands foursquare to all the winds that blow."

We should seek to make it so, nor let the fluctuations of our own hearts cause it to fluctuate. We should try so to control the ebb and flow of religious emotion that it may always be near high water with our faith, a tideless but not stagnant sea. We should oppose a settled conviction and unalterable confidence to the noisy voices which would draw us away.

And that we may do so we must keep up a true and close communion with Jesus Christ. The faith which is ever going out "towards" Him, as the sunflower turns sunwards, will ever draw from Him such blessed gifts that doubt or distrust will be impossible. If we keep near our Lord and wait expectant on Him, He will increase our faith and make our "hearts fixed, trusting in the Lord." So a greater than Paul may speak even to us, as He walks in the midst of the golden candlesticks, words which from *His* lips will be praise indeed: "Though I am absent in the flesh, yet am I with you in the spirit, joying and beholding your order and the stedfastness of your faith in Me."

III. We have here, the exhortation which comprehends all duty, and covers the whole ground of Christian belief and practice.

"Therefore"—the following exhortation is based upon the warning and commendation of the preceding verses. There is first a wide general injunction. "As ye received Christ Jesus the Lord, so walk in Him," *i.e.* let your active life be in accord with what you learned and obtained when you first became Christians. Then this exhortation is defined or broken up into four particulars in the following clauses, which explain in detail how it is to be kept.

The general exhortation is to a true Christian walk. The main force lies upon the "as." The command is to order all life in accordance with the early lessons and acquisitions. The phrase "ye received Christ Jesus the Lord" presents several points requiring notice. It is obviously parallel with "as ye were taught" in the next verse; so that it was from their first teachers, and probably from Epaphras (i. 7) that they had "received Christ." So then what we receive, when, from human lips, we hear the gospel and accept it, is not merely the word about the Saviour, but the Saviour Himself. This expression of our text is no mere loose or rhetorical mode of speech, but a literal and blessed truth. Christ is the sum of all Christian teaching and, where the message of His love is welcomed, He Himself comes in spiritual and real presence, and dwells in the spirit.

The solemnity of the full name of our Saviour in this connection is most significant. Paul reminds the Colossians, in view of the teaching which degraded the person and curtailed the work of Christ, that they had received the man Jesus, the promised Christ, the universal Lord. As if he had said, Remember whom you received in your conversion—*Christ*, the Messiah, anointed, that is, fitted by the unmeasured possession of the Divine Spirit to fulfil all prophecy and to be the world's deliverer. Remember *Jesus*, the man, our brother;—therefore listen to no misty speculations nor look to whispered mysteries nor to angel hierarchies for knowledge of God or for help in conflict. Our gospel is not theory spun out of men's brains, but is, first and foremost, the history of a brother's life and death. You received *Jesus*, so you are delivered from the tyranny of these unsubstantial and portentous systems, and relegated to the facts of a human life for your knowledge of God. You received Jesus Christ as *Lord*. He was proclaimed as Lord of men, angels, and the universe, Lord and Creator of the spiritual and material worlds, Lord of history and providence. Therefore you need not give heed to those teachers who would fill the gulf between men and God with a crowd of powers and rulers. You have all that your mind or heart or will can need in the human Divine Jesus, who is the Christ and the Lord for you and all men. You have received Him in the all-sufficiency of His revealed nature and offices. You have Him for your very own. Hold fast that which you have, and let no man take this your crown and treasure. The same exhortation has emphatic application to the conflicts of to-day. The Church has had Jesus set forth as Christ and Lord. His manhood, the historical reality of His Incarnation with all its blessed issues, His Messiahship as the fulfiller of prophecy and symbol, designated and fitted by the fulness of the Spirit, to be man's deliverer, His rule and authority over all creatures and events have been taught, and the tumults of present unsettlement make it hard and needful to keep true to that threefold belief, and to let nothing rob us of any of the elements of the full gospel which lies in the august name, Christ Jesus the Lord.

To that gospel, to that Lord, the walk, the active life, is to be conformed, and the manner thereof is more fully explained in the following clauses.

"Rooted and built up in Him." Here again we have the profound "in Him," which appears so frequently in this and in the companion Epistle to the Ephesians, and which must be allowed its proper force, as expressing a most real indwelling of the believer in Christ, if the depth of the meaning is to be sounded.

Paul drives his fiery chariot through rhetorical proprieties, and never shrinks from "mixed metaphors" if they more vigorously express his thought. Here we have three incongruous ones close on each other's heels. The Christian is to *walk*, to be *rooted* like a tree, to be *built up* like a house. What does the incongruity matter to Paul as the stream of thought and feeling hurries him along?

The tenses of the verbs, too, are studiously and significantly varied. Fully rendered they would be "having been rooted and being builded up." The one is a past act done once for all, the effects of which are permanent; the other is a continuous resulting process which is going on now. The Christian has been rooted in Jesus Christ at the beginning of his Christian course. His faith has brought him into living contact with the Saviour, who has become as the fruitful soil into which the believer sends his roots, and both feeds and anchors there. The familiar image of the first Psalm may have been in the writer's mind, and naturally recurs to ours. If we draw nourishment and stability from Christ, round whom the roots of our being twine and cling, we shall flourish and grow and bear fruit. No man can do without some person beyond himself on whom to repose, nor can any of us find in ourselves or on earth the sufficient soil for our growth. We are like seedlings dropped on some great rock, which send their rootlets down the hard stone and are stunted till they reach the rich leaf-mould at its base. We blindly feel through all the barrenness of the world for something into which our roots may plunge that we may be nourished and firm. In Christ we may be "like a tree planted by the river of water;" out of Him we are "as the chaff," rootless, lifeless, profitless, and swept at last by the wind from the threshing floor. The choice is before every man—either to be rooted in Christ by faith, or to be rootless.

"Being built up in Him." The gradual continuous building up of the structure of a Christian character is doubly expressed in this word by the present tense which points to a process, and by the prefixed preposition represented by "up," which points to the successive laying of course of masonry upon course. We are the architects of our own characters. If our lives are based on Jesus Christ as their foundation, and every deed is in vital connection with Him, as at once its motive, its pattern, its power, its aim, and its reward, then we shall build holy and fair lives, which will be temples. Men do not merely grow as a leaf which "grows green and broad, and takes no care." The other metaphor of a building needs to be taken into account, to complete the former. Effort, patient continuous labour must be put forth. More than "forty and six years is this temple in building." A stone at a time is fitted into its place, and so after much toil and many years, as in the case of some mediæval cathedral unfinished for centuries, the topstone is brought forth at last. This choice, too, is before all men—to build on Christ and so to build for eternity, or on sand and so to be crushed below the ruins of their fallen houses.

"Stablished in your faith, even as ye were taught." This is apparently simply a more definite way of putting substantially the same thoughts as in the former clauses. Possibly the meaning is "stablished by faith," the Colossians' faith being the instrument of their establishment. But the Revised Version is probably right in its rendering, "stablished in," or as to, "your faith." Their faith, as Paul had just been saying, was stedfast, but it needed yet increased firmness. And this exhortation, as it were, translates the previous ones into more homely language, that if any man stumbled at the mysticism of the thoughts there, he might grasp the plain practicalness here. If we are established and confirmed in our faith, we shall be rooted and built up in Jesus, for it is faith which joins us to Him, and its increase measures our growth in and into Him.

There then is a very plain practical issue of these deep thoughts of union with Jesus. A progressive increase of our faith is the condition of all Christian progress. The faith which is already the firmest, and by its firmness may gladden an Apostle, is still capable of and needs strengthening. Its range can be enlarged, its tenacity increased, its power over heart and life reinforced. The eye of faith is never so keen but that it may become more longsighted; its grasp never so close but that it may be tightened; its realisation never so solid but that it may be more substantial; its authority never so great but that it may be made more absolute. This continual strengthening of faith is the most essential form of a Christian's effort at self-improvement. Strengthen faith and you strengthen all graces; for it measures our reception of Divine help.

And the furthest development which faith can attain should ever be sedulously kept in harmony with the initial teaching—"even as ye were taught." Progress does not consist in dropping the early truths of Jesus Christ the Lord for newer wisdom and more speculative religion, but in discovering ever deeper lessons and larger powers in these rudiments which are likewise the last and highest lessons which men can learn.

Further, as the daily effort of the believing soul ought to be to strengthen the quality of his faith, so it should be to increase its amount—"abounding in it with thanksgiving." Or if we adopt the reading of the Revised Version, we shall omit the "in it," and find here only an exhortation to thanksgiving.

That is, in any case, the main idea of the clause, which adds to the former the thought that thanksgiving is an inseparable accompaniment of vigorous Christian life. It is to be called forth, of course, mainly by the great gift of Christ, in whom we are rooted and builded, and, in Paul's judgment it is the very spring of Christian progress.

That constant temper of gratitude implies a habitual presence to the mind, of God's great mercy in His unspeakable gift, a continual glow of heart as we gaze, a continual appropriation of that gift for our very own, and a continual outflow of our heart's love to the Incarnate and Immortal Love. Such thankfulness will bind us to glad obedience, and will give swiftness to the foot and eagerness to the will, to run in the way of God's commandments. It is like genial sunshine, all flowers breathe perfume and fruits ripen under its influence. It is the fire which kindles the sacrifice of life and makes it go up in fragrant incense-clouds, acceptable to God. The highest nobleness of which man is capable is reached when, moved by the mercies of God, we yield ourselves living sacrifices, thank-offerings to Him Who yielded Himself the sin-offering for us. The life which is all influenced by thanksgiving will be pure, strong, happy, in its continual counting of its gifts, and in its thoughts of the Giver, and not least happy and beautiful in its glad surrender of itself to Him who has given Himself for and to it. The noblest offering that we can bring, the only recompense which Christ asks, is that our hearts and our lives should say, We thank thee, O Lord. "By Him, therefore, let us offer the sacrifice of praise to God continually," and the continual thanksgiving will ensure continuous growth in our Christian character, and a constant increase in the strength and depth of our faith.

XII
THE BANE AND THE ANTIDOTE

"Take heed lest there shall be any one that maketh spoil of you through his philosophy and vain deceit, after the tradition of men, after the rudiments of the world, and not after Christ: for in Him dwelleth all the fulness of the Godhead bodily, and in Him ye are made full, Who is the head of all principality and power."—Col. ii. 8–10 (Rev. Ver.).

We come now to the first plain reference to the errors which were threatening the peace of the Colossian community. Here Paul crosses swords with the foe. This is the point to which all his previous words have been steadily converging. The immediately preceding context contained the positive exhortation to continue in the Christ Whom they had received, having been rooted in Him as the tree in a fertile place "by the rivers of water," and being continually builded up in Him, with ever-growing completeness of holy character. The same exhortation in substance is contained in the verses which we have now to consider, with the difference that it is here presented negatively, as warning and dehortation, with distinct statement of the danger which would uproot the tree and throw down the building, and drag the Colossians away from union with Christ.

In these words the Bane and Antidote are both before us. Let us consider each.

I. The Poison against which Paul warns the Colossians is plainly described in our first verse, the terms of which may require a brief comment.

"Take heed lest there shall be." The construction implies that it is a real and not a hypothetical danger which he sees threatening. He is not crying "wolf" before there is need.

"Any one"—perhaps the tone of the warning would be better conveyed if we read the more familiar "somebody"; as if he had said—"I name no names—it is not the persons but the principles that I fight against—but you know whom I mean well enough. Let him be anonymous, you understand who it is." Perhaps there was even a single "somebody" who was the centre of the mischief.

"That maketh spoil of you." Such is the full meaning of the word — and not "injure" or "rob," which the translation in the Authorized Version suggests to an English reader. Paul sees the converts in Colossæ taken prisoners and led away with a cord round their necks, like the long strings of captives on the Assyrian monuments. He had spoken in the previous chapter (ver. 13) of the merciful conqueror who had "translated" them from the realm of darkness into a kingdom of light, and now he fears lest a robber horde, making a raid upon the peaceful colonists in their happy new homes, may sweep them away again into bondage.

The instrument which the man-stealer uses, or perhaps we may say, the cord, whose fatal noose will be tightened round them, if they do not take care, is "philosophy and vain deceit." If Paul had been writing in English, he would have put "philosophy" in inverted commas, to show that he was quoting the heretical teachers' own name for their system, if system it may be called, which was really a chaos. For the true love of wisdom, for any honest, humble attempt to seek after her as hid treasure, neither Paul nor Paul's Master have anything but praise and sympathy and help. Where he met real, however imperfect, searchers after truth, he strove to find points of contact between them and his message, and to present the gospel as the answer to their questionings, the declaration of that which they were groping to find. The thing spoken of here has no resemblance but in name to what the Greeks in their better days first called philosophy, and nothing but that mere verbal coincidence warrants the representation — often made both by narrow-minded Christians, and by unbelieving thinkers — that Christianity takes up a position of antagonism or suspicion to it.

The form of the expression in the original shows clearly that "vain deceit," or more literally "empty deceit," describes the "philosophy" which Paul is bidding them beware of. They are not two things, but one. It is like a blown bladder, full of wind, and nothing else. In its lofty pretensions, and if we take its own account of itself, it is a love of and search after wisdom; but if we look at it more closely, it is a swollen nothing, empty and a fraud. This is what he is condemning. The genuine thing he has nothing to say about here.

He goes on to describe more closely this impostor, masquerading in the philosopher's cloak. It is "after the traditions of men." We have seen in a former chapter what a strange heterogeneous conglomerate of Jewish ceremonial and Oriental dreams the false teachers in Colossæ were preaching. Probably both these elements are included here. It is significant that the very expression, "the traditions of men," is a word of Christ's, applied to the Pharisees, whom He charges with "leaving the commandment of God, and holding fast the tradition of men" (Mark vii. 8). The portentous undergrowth of such "traditions" which, like the riotous fertility of creepers in a tropical forest, smother and kill the trees round which they twine, is preserved for our wonder and warning in the Talmud, where for thousands and thousands of pages, we get nothing but Rabbi So and So said this, but Rabbi So and So said that; until we feel stifled, and long for one Divine Word to still all the babble.

The Oriental element in the heresy, on the other hand, prided itself on a hidden teaching which was too sacred to be entrusted to books, and was passed from lip to lip in some close conclave of muttering teachers and listening adepts. The fact that all this, be it Jewish, be it Oriental teaching, had no higher source than men's imaginings and refinings, seems to Paul the condemnation of the whole system. His theory is that in Jesus Christ, every Christian man has the full truth concerning God and man, in their mutual relations, — the authoritative Divine declaration of all that can be known, the perfect exemplar of all that ought to be done, the sun-clear illumination and proof of all that dare be hoped. What an absurd descent, then, from the highest of our prerogatives, to "turn away from Him that speaketh from heaven," in order to listen to poor human voices, speaking men's thoughts!

The lesson is as needful to-day as ever. The special forms of men's traditions in question here have long since fallen silent, and trouble no man any more. But the tendency to give heed to human teachers and to suffer them to come between us and Christ is deep in us all. There is at one extreme the man who believes in no revelation from God, and, smiling at us Christians who accept Christ's words as final and Himself as the Incarnate truth, often pays to his chosen human teacher a deference as absolute as that which he regards as superstition, when we render it to our Lord. At the other extremity are the Christians who will not let Christ and the Scripture speak to the soul, unless the Church be present at the interview, like a jailer, with a bunch of man-made creeds jingling at its belt. But it is not only at the two ends of the line, but all along its length, that men are listening to "traditions" of men and neglecting "the commandment of God." We have all the same tendency in us. Every man carries a rationalist and a traditionalist under his skin. Every Church in Christendom, whether it has a formal creed or no, is ruled as to its belief and practice, to a sad extent, by the "traditions of the elders." The "freest" of the Nonconformist Churches, untrammelled by any formal confession, may be bound with as tight fetters, and be as much dominated by men's opinions, as if it had the straitest of creeds. The mass of our religious beliefs and practices has ever to be verified, corrected and remodelled, by harking back from creeds, written or unwritten, to the one Teacher, the endless significance of Whose person and work is but expressed in fragments by the purest and widest thoughts even of those who have lived nearest to Him, and seen most of His beauty. Let us get away from men, from the Babel of opinions and the strife of tongues, that we may "hear the words of His mouth!" Let us take heed of the empty fraud which lays the absurd snare for our feet, that we can learn to know God by any means but by listening to His own speech in His Eternal Word, lest it lead us away captive out of the Kingdom of the Light! Let us go up to the pure spring on the mountain top, and not try to slake our thirst at the muddy pools at its base! "Ye are Christ's, be not the slave of men." "This is My beloved Son, hear ye Him."

Another mark of this empty pretence of wisdom which threatens to captivate the Colossians is, that it is "after the rudiments of the world." The word rendered "rudiments" means the letters of the alphabet, and hence comes naturally to acquire the meaning of "elements," or "first principles," just as we speak of the A B C of a science. The application of such a designation to the false teaching, is, like the appropriation of the term "mystery" to the gospel, an instance of turning the tables and giving back the teachers their own words. They boasted of mysterious doctrines reserved for the initiated, of which the plain truths that Paul preached were but the elements, and they looked down contemptuously on his message as "milk for babes." Paul retorts on them, asserting that the true mystery, the profound truth long hidden and revealed, is the word which he preached, and that the poverty-stricken elements, fit only for infants, are in that swelling inanity which called itself wisdom and was not. Not only does he brand it as "rudiments," but as "rudiments of the *world*," which is worse—that is to say, as belonging to the sphere of the outward and material, and not to the higher region of the spiritual, where Christian thought ought to dwell. So two weaknesses are charged against the system: it is the mere alphabet of truth, and therefore unfit for grown men. It moves, for all its lofty pretensions, in the region of the visible and mundane things and is therefore unfit for spiritual men. What features of the system are referred to in this phrase? Its use in the Epistle to the Galatians (iv. 3), as a synonyme for the whole system of ritual observances and ceremonial precepts of Judaism, and the present context, which passes on immediately to speak of circumcision, point to a similar meaning here, though we may include also the ceremonial and ritual of the Gentile religions, in so far as they contributed to the outward forms which the Colossian heresy sought to impose on the Church. This then is Paul's opinion about a system which laid stress on ceremonial and busied itself with forms. He regards it as a deliberate retrogression to an earlier stage. A religion of rites had come first, and was needed for the spiritual infancy of the race—but in Christ we ought to have outgrown the alphabet of revelation, and, being men, to have put away childish things. He regards it further as a pitiable descent into a lower sphere, a fall from the spiritual realm to the material, and therefore unbecoming for those who have been enfranchised from dependence upon outward helps and symbols, and taught the spirituality and inwardness of Christian worship.

We need the lesson in this day no less than did these Christians in the little community in that remote valley of Phrygia. The forms which were urged on them are long since antiquated, but the tendency to turn Christianity into a religion of ceremonial is running with an unusually powerful current to-day. We are all more interested in art, and think we know more about it than our fathers did. The eye and the ear are more educated than they used to be, and a society as "æsthetic" and "musical" as much cultured English society is becoming, will like an ornate ritual. So, apart altogether from doctrinal grounds, much in the conditions of to-day works towards ritual religion. Nonconformist services are less plain; some go from their ranks because they dislike the "bald" worship in the chapel, and prefer the more elaborate forms of the Anglican Church, which in its turn is for the same reason left by others who find their tastes gratified by the complete thing, as it is to be enjoyed full blown in the Roman Catholic communion. We may freely admit that the Puritan reaction was possibly too severe, and that a little more colour and form might with advantage have been retained. But enlisting the senses as the allies of the spirit in worship is risky work. They are very apt to fight for their own hand when they once begin, and the history of all symbolic and ceremonial worship shows that the experiment is much more likely to end in sensualising religion than in spiritualising sense. The theory that such aids make a ladder by which the soul may ascend to God is perilously apt to be confuted by experience, which finds that the soul is quite as likely to go down the ladder as up it. The gratification of taste, and the excitation of æsthetic sensibility, which are the results of such aids to worship, are not worship, however they may be mistaken as such. All ceremonial is in danger of becoming opaque instead of transparent as it was meant to be, and of detaining mind and eye instead of letting them pass on and up to God. Stained glass is lovely, and white windows are "barnlike," and "starved," and "bare"; but perhaps, if the object is to get light and to see the sun, these solemn purples and glowing yellows are rather in the way. I for my part believe that of the two extremes, a Quaker's meeting is nearer the ideal of Christian worship than High Mass, and so far as my feeble voice can reach, I would urge, as eminently a lesson for the day, Paul's great principle here, that a Christianity making much of forms and ceremonies is a distinct retrogression and descent. You are men in Christ, do not go back to the picture book A B C of symbol and ceremony, which was fit for babes. You have been brought in to the inner sanctuary of worship in spirit; do not decline to the beggarly elements of outward form.

Paul sums up his indictment in one damning clause, the result of the two preceding. If the heresy have no higher source than men's traditions, and no more solid contents than ceremonial observances, it cannot be "after Christ." He is neither its origin, nor its substance, nor its rule and standard. There is a fundamental discord between every such system, however it may call itself Christian, and Christ. The opposition may be concealed by its teachers. They and their victims may not be aware of it. They may not themselves be conscious that by adopting it they have slipped off the foundation; but they have done so, and though in their own hearts they be loyal to Him, they have brought an incurable discord into their creeds which will weaken their lives, if it do not do worse. Paul cared very little for the dreams of these teachers, except in so far as they carried them and others away from his Master. The Colossians might have as many ceremonies as they liked, and welcome; but when these interfered with the sole reliance to be placed on Christ's work, then they must have no quarter. It is not merely because the teaching was "after the traditions of men, after the rudiments of the world," but because being so, it was "not after Christ," that Paul will have none of it. He that touches his Master touches the apple of his eye, and shades of opinion, and things indifferent in practice, and otherwise unimportant forms of worship, have to be fought to the death if they obscure one corner of the perfect and solitary work of the One Lord, who is at once the source, the substance, and the standard of all Christian teaching.

II. The Antidote.—"For in Him dwelleth all the fulness of the Godhead bodily, and in Him ye are made full, who is the head of all principality and power."

These words may be a reason for the warning—"Take heed, *for*"; or they may be a reason for the implied exclusion of any teaching which is not after Christ. The statement of its characteristics carries in itself its condemnation. Anything "not after Christ" is *ipso facto* wrong, and to be avoided—"for," etc. "In Him" is placed with emphasis at the beginning, and implies "and nowhere else." "Dwelleth," that is, has its permanent abode; where the tense is to be noticed also, as pointing to the ascended Christ. "All the fulness of the Godhead," that is, the whole unbounded powers and attributes of Deity, where is to be noted the use of the abstract term *Godhead*, instead of the more usual *God*, in order to express with the utmost force the thought of the indwelling in Christ of the whole essence and nature of God. "Bodily," that points to the Incarnation, and so is an advance upon the passage in the former chapter (ver. 19), which speaks of "the fulness" dwelling in the Eternal Word, whereas this speaks of the Eternal Word in whom the fulness dwelt becoming flesh. So we are pointed to the glorified corporeal humanity of Jesus Christ in His exaltation as the abode, now and for ever, of all the fulness of the Divine nature, which is thereby brought very near to us. This grand truth seems to Paul to shiver to pieces all the dreams of these teachers about angel mediators, and to brand as folly every attempt to learn truth and God anywhere else but in Him.

If He be the one sole temple of Deity in whom all Divine glories are stored, why go anywhere else in order to *see* or to *possess* God? It is folly; for not only are all these glories stored in Him, but they are so stored on purpose to be reached by us. Therefore the Apostle goes on, "and in Him ye are made full;" which sets forth two things as true in the inward life of all Christians, namely, their living incorporation in and union with Christ, and their consequent participation in His fulness. Every one of us may enter into that most real and close union with Jesus Christ by the power of continuous faith in Him. So may we be grafted into the Vine, and builded into the Rock. If thus we keep our hearts in contact with His heart and let Him lay His lip on our lips, He will breathe into us the breath of His own life, and we shall live because He lives, and in our measure, as He lives. All the fulness of God is in Him, that from Him it may pass into us. We might start back from such bold words if we did not remember that the same apostle who here tells us that that fulness dwells in Jesus, crowns his wonderful prayer for the Ephesian Christians with that daring petition, "that ye may be filled with all the fulness of God." The treasure was lodged in the earthen vessel of Christ's manhood that it might be within our reach. He brings the fiery blessing of a Divine life from Heaven to earth enclosed in the feeble reed of His manhood, that it may kindle kindred fire in many a heart. Freely the water of life flows into all cisterns from the ever fresh stream, into which the infinite depth of that unfathomable sea of good pours itself. Every kind of spiritual blessing is given therein. That stream, like a river of molten lava, holds many precious things in its flaming current, and will cool into many shapes and deposit many rare and rich gifts. According to our need it will vary itself, being to each what the moment most requires,—wisdom, or strength, or beauty, or courage, or patience. Out of it will come whatsoever things are lovely, whatsoever things are of good report, as Rabbinical legends tell us that the manna tasted to each man like the food for which he wished most.

This process of receiving of all the Divine fulness is a continuous one. We can but be approximating to the possession of the infinite treasure which is ours in Christ; and since the treasure is infinite, and we can indefinitely grow in capacity of receiving God, there must be an eternal continuance of the filling and an eternal increase of the measure of what fills us. Our natures are elastic, and in love and knowledge, as well as in purity and capacity for blessedness, there are no bounds to be set to their possible expansion. They will be widened by bliss into a greater capacity for bliss. The indwelling Christ will "enlarge the place of His habitation," and as the walls stretch and the roofs soar, He will fill the greater house with the light of His presence and the fragrance of His name. The condition of this continuous reception of the abundant gift of a Divine life is abiding in Jesus. It is "in Him" that we are "being filled full" — and it is only so long as we continue in Him that we continue full. We cannot bear away our supplies, as one might a full bucket from a well, and keep it full. All the grace will trickle out and disappear unless we live in constant union with our Lord, whose Spirit passes into our deadness only so long as we are joined to Him.

From all such thoughts Paul would have us draw the conclusion—how foolish, then, it must be to go to any other source for the supply of our needs! Christ is "the head of all principality and power," he adds, with a reference to the doctrine of angel mediators, which evidently played a great part in the heretical teaching. If He is sovereign head of all dignity and power on earth and heaven, why go to the ministers, when we have access to the King; or have recourse to erring human teachers, when we have the Eternal Word to enlighten us; or flee to creatures to replenish our emptiness, when we may draw from the depths of God in Christ? Why should we go on a weary search after goodly pearls when the richest of all is by us, if we will have it? Do we seek to know God? Let us behold Christ, and let men talk as they list. Do we crave a stay for our spirit, guidance and impulse for our lives? Let us cleave to Christ, and we shall be no more lonely and bewildered. Do we need a quieting balm to be laid on conscience, and the sense of guilt to be lifted from our hearts? Let us lay our hands on Christ, the one sacrifice, and leave all other altars and priests and ceremonies. Do we look longingly for some light on the future? Let us stedfastly gaze on Christ as He rises to heaven bearing a human body into the glory of God.

Though all the earth were covered with helpers and lovers of my soul, "as the sand by the sea shore innumerable," and all the heavens were sown with faces of angels who cared for me and succoured me, thick as the stars in the milky way—all could not do for me what I need. Yea, though all these were gathered into one mighty and loving creature, even he were no sufficient stay for one soul of man. We want more than creature help. We need the whole fulness of the Godhead to draw from. It is all there in Christ, for each of us. Whosoever will, let him draw freely. Why should we leave the fountain of living waters to hew out for ourselves, with infinite pains, broken cisterns that can hold no water? All we need is in Christ. Let us lift our eyes from the low earth and all creatures, and behold "no man any more," as Lord and Helper, "save Jesus only," "that we may be filled with all the fulness of God."

XIII
THE TRUE CIRCUMCISION

"In whom ye were also circumcised with a circumcision not made with hands, in the putting off of the body of the flesh, in the circumcision of Christ, having been buried with Him in baptism, wherein ye were also raised with Him through faith in the working of God, who raised Him from the dead. And you, being dead through your trespasses and the uncircumcision of your flesh, you, *I say*, did he quicken together with Him, having forgiven us all our trespasses." — Col. ii. 11–13 (Rev. Ver.).

There are two opposite tendencies ever at work in human nature to corrupt religion. One is of the intellect; the other of the senses. The one is the temptation of the cultured few; the other, that of the vulgar many. The one turns religion into theological speculation; the other, into a theatrical spectacle. But, opposite as these tendencies usually are, they were united in that strange chaos of erroneous opinion and practice which Paul had to front at Colossæ. From right and from left he was assailed, and his batteries had to face both ways. Here he is mainly engaged with the error which insisted on imposing circumcision on these Gentile converts.

I. To this teaching of the necessity of circumcision, he first opposes the position that all Christian men, by virtue of their union with Christ, have received the true circumcision, of which the outward rite was a shadow and a prophecy, and that therefore the rite is antiquated and obsolete.

His language is emphatic and remarkable. It points to a definite past time—no doubt the time when they became Christians—when, because they were in Christ, a change passed on them which is fitly paralleled with circumcision. This Christian circumcision is described in three particulars: as "not made with hands;" as consisting in "putting off the body of the flesh;" and as being "of Christ."

It is "not made with hands," that is, it is not a rite but a reality, not transacted in flesh but in spirit. It is not the removal of ceremonial impurity, but the cleansing of the heart. This idea of ethical circumcision, of which the bodily rite is the type, is common in the Old Testament, as, for instance, "The Lord thy God will circumcise thine heart ... to love the Lord thy God with all thine heart" (Deut. xxx. 6). This is the true Christian circumcision.

It consists in the "putting off the body of the flesh"—for "the sins of" is an interpolation. Of course a man does not shuffle off this mortal coil when he becomes a Christian, so that we have to look for some other meaning of the strong words. They are very strong, for the word "putting off" is intensified so as to express a complete stripping off from oneself, as of clothes which are laid aside, and is evidently intended to contrast the partial outward circumcision as the removal of a small part of the body, with the entire removal effected by union with Christ. If that removal of "the body of the flesh" is "not made with hands," then it can only be in the sphere of the spiritual life, that is to say, it must consist in a change in the relation of the two constituents of a man's being, and that of such a kind that, for the future, the Christian shall not live after the flesh, though he live in the flesh. "Ye are not in the flesh, but in the Spirit," says Paul, and again he uses an expression as strong as, if not stronger than that of our text, when he speaks of "the body" as "being destroyed," and explains himself by adding "that henceforth we should not serve sin." It is not the body considered simply as material and fleshly that we put off, but the body considered as the seat of corrupt and sinful affections and passions. A new principle of life comes into men's hearts which delivers them from the dominion of these, and makes it possible that they should live in the flesh, not "according to the lusts of the flesh, but according to the will of God." True, the text regards this divesting as complete, whereas, as all Christian men know only too sadly, it is very partial, and realised only by slow degrees. The ideal is represented here,—what we receive "in Him," rather than what we actually possess and incorporate into our experience. On the Divine side the change is complete. Christ gives complete emancipation from the dominion of sense, and if we are not in reality completely emancipated, it is because we have not taken the things that are freely given to us, and are not completely "in Him." So far as we are, we have put off "the flesh." The change has passed on us if we are Christians. We have to work it out day by day. The foe may keep up a guerilla warfare after he is substantially defeated, but his entire subjugation is certain if we keep hold of the strength of Christ.

Finally, this circumcision is described as "of Christ," by which is not meant that He submitted to it, but that He instituted it.

Such being the force of this statement, what is its bearing on the Apostle's purpose? He desires to destroy the teaching that the rite of circumcision was binding on the Christian converts, and he does so by asserting that the gospel has brought the reality, of which the rite was but a picture and a prophecy. The underlying principle is that when we have the thing signified by any Jewish rites, which were all prophetic as well as symbolic, the rite may—must go. Its retention is an anachronism, "as if a flower should shut, and be a bud again." That is a wise and pregnant principle, but as it comes to the surface again immediately hereafter, and is applied to a whole series of subjects, we may defer the consideration of it, and rather dwell briefly on other matters suggested by this verse.

We notice, then, the intense moral earnestness which leads the Apostle here to put the true centre of gravity of Christianity in moral transformation, and to set all outward rites and ceremonies in a very subordinate place. What had Jesus Christ come from heaven for, and for what had He borne His bitter passion? To what end were the Colossians knit to Him by a tie so strong, tender and strange? Had they been carried into that inmost depth of union with Him, and were they still to be laying stress on ceremonies? Had Christ's work, then, no higher issue than to leave religion bound in the cords of outward observances? Surely Jesus Christ, who gives men a new life by union with Himself, which union is brought about through faith alone, has delivered men from that "yoke of bondage," if He has done anything at all. Surely they who are joined to Him should have a profounder apprehension of the means and the end of their relation to their Lord than to suppose that it is either brought about by any outward rite, or has any reality unless it makes them pure and good. From that height all questions of external observances dwindle into insignificance, and all question of sacramental efficacy drops away of itself. The vital centre lies in our being joined to Jesus Christ—the condition of which is faith in Him, and the outcome of it a new life which delivers us from the dominion of the flesh. How far away from such conceptions of Christianity are those which busy themselves on either side with matters of detail, with punctilios of observance, and pedantries of form? The hatred of forms may be as completely a form as the most elaborate ritual—and we all need to have our eyes turned away from these to the far higher thing, the worship and service offered by a transformed nature.

We notice again, that the conquest of the animal nature and the material body is the certain outcome of true union with Christ, and of that alone.

Paul did not regard matter as necessarily evil, as these teachers at Colossæ did, nor did he think of the body as the source of all sin. But he knew that the fiercest and most fiery temptations came from it, and that the foulest and most indelible stains on conscience were splashed from the mud which it threw. We all know that too. It is a matter of life and death for each of us to find some means of taming and holding in the animal that is in us all. We all know of wrecked lives, which have been driven on the rocks by the wild passions belonging to the flesh. Fortune, reputation, health, everything are sacrificed by hundreds of men, especially young men, at the sting of this imperious lust. The budding promise of youth, innocence, hope, and all which makes life desirable and a nature fair, are trodden down by the hoofs of the brute. There is no need to speak of that. And when we come to add to this the weaknesses of the flesh, and the needs of the flesh, and the limitations of the flesh, and to remember how often high purposes are frustrated by its shrinking from toil, and how often mists born from its undrained swamps darken the vision that else might gaze on truth and God, we cannot but feel that we do not need to be Eastern Gnostics, to believe that goodness requires the flesh to be subdued. Every one who has sought for self-improvement recognises the necessity. But no asceticisms and no resolves will do what we want. Much repression may be effected by sheer force of will, but it is like a man holding a wolf by the jaws. The arms begin to ache and the grip to grow slack, and he feels his strength ebbing, and knows that, as soon as he lets go, the brute will fly at his throat. Repression is not taming. Nothing tames the wild beast in us but the power of Christ. He binds it in a silken lash, and that gentle constraint is strong, because the fierceness is gone. "The wolf also shall dwell with the lamb, and a little child shall lead them." The power of union with Christ, and that alone, will enable us to put off the body of the flesh. And such union will certainly lead to such crucifying of the animal nature. Christianity would be easy if it were a round of observances; it would be comparatively easy if it were a series of outward asceticisms. Anybody can fast or wear a hair shirt, if he have motive sufficient; but the "putting off the body of the flesh" which is "not made with hands," is a different and harder thing. Nothing else avails. High-flown religious emotion, or clear theological definitions, or elaborate ceremonial worship, may all have their value; but a religion which includes them all, and leaves out the plain moralities of subduing the flesh, and keeping our heel well pressed down on the serpent's head, is worthless. If we are in Christ, we shall not live in the flesh.

II. The Apostle meets the false teaching of the need for circumcision, by a second consideration; namely, a reference to Christian Baptism, as being the Christian sign of that inward change.

Ye were circumcised, says he—being buried with Him in baptism. The form of expression in the Greek implies that the two things are cotemporaneous. As if he had said—Do you want any further rite to express that mighty change which passed on you when you came to be "in Christ"? You have been baptised, does not that express all the meaning that circumcision ever had, and much more? What can you want with the less significant rite when you have the more significant? This reference to baptism is quite consistent with what has been said as to the subordinate importance of ritual. Some forms we must have, if there is to be any outward visible Church, and Christ has yielded to the necessity, and given us two, of which the one symbolises the initial spiritual act of the Christian life, and the other the constantly repeated process of Christian nourishment. They are symbols and outward representations, nothing more. They convey grace, in so far as they help us to realise more clearly and to feel more deeply the facts on which our spiritual life is fed, but they are not channels of grace in any other way than any other outward acts of worship may be.

We see that the form of baptism here presupposed is by immersion, and that the form is regarded as significant. All but entire unanimity prevails among commentators on this point. The burial and the resurrection spoken of point unmistakably to the primitive mode of baptism, as Bishop Lightfoot, the latest and best English expositor of this book, puts it in his paraphrase: "Ye were buried with Christ to your old selves beneath the baptismal waters, and were raised with Him from these same waters, to a new and better life."

If so, two questions deserve consideration—first, is it right to alter a form which has a meaning that is lost by the change? second, can we alter a significant form without destroying it? Is the new thing rightly called by the old name? If baptism be immersion, and immersion express a substantial part of its meaning, can sprinkling or pouring be baptism?

Again, baptism is associated in time with the inward change, which is the true circumcision. There are but two theories on which these two things are cotemporaneous. The one is the theory that baptism effects the change, the other is the theory that baptism goes with the change as its sign. The association is justified if men are "circumcised," that is, changed when they are baptised, or if men are baptised when they have been "circumcised." No other theory gives full weight to these words.

The former theory elevates baptism into more than the importance of which Paul sought to deprive circumcision, it confuses the distinction between the Church and the world, it lulls men into a false security, it obscures the very central truth of Christianity—namely that faith in Christ, working by love, makes a Christian—it gives the basis for a portentous reproduction of sacerdotalism, and it is shivered to pieces against the plain facts of daily life. But it may be worth while to notice in a sentence, that it is conclusively disposed of by the language before us—it is "through faith in the operation of God" that we are raised again in baptism. Not the rite, then, but faith is the means of this participation with Christ in burial and resurrection. What remains but that baptism is associated with that spiritual change by which we are delivered from the body of the flesh, because in the Divine order it is meant to be the outward symbol of that change which is effected by no rite or sacrament, but by faith alone, uniting us to the transforming Christ?

We observe the solemnity and the thoroughness of the change thus symbolised. It is more than a circumcision. It is burial and a resurrection, an entire dying of the old self by union with Christ, a real and present rising again by participation in His risen life. This and nothing less makes a Christian. We partake of His death, inasmuch as we ally ourselves to it by our faith, as the sacrifice for our sins, and make it the ground of all our hope. But that is not all. We partake of His death, inasmuch as, by the power of His cross, we are drawn to sever ourselves from the selfish life, and to slay our own old nature; dying for His dear sake to the habits, tastes, desires and purposes in which we lived. Self-crucifixion for the love of Christ is the law for us all. His cross is the pattern for our conduct, as well as the pledge and means of our acceptance. We must die to sin that we may live to righteousness. We must die to self, that we may live to God and our brethren. We have no right to trust in Christ *for* us, except as we have Christ *in* us. His cross is not saving us from our guilt, unless it is moulding our lives to some faint likeness of Him who died that we might live, and might live a real life by dying daily to the world, sin, and self.

If we are thus made conformable to His death, we shall know the power of His resurrection, in all its aspects. It will be to us the guarantee of our own, and we shall know its power as a prophecy for our future. It will be to us the seal of His perfect work on the cross, and we shall know its power as God's token of acceptance of His sacrifice in the past. It will be to us the type of our spiritual resurrection now, and we shall know its power as the pattern and source of our supernatural life in the present. Thus we must die in and with Christ that we may live in and with Him, and that twofold process is the very heart of personal religion. No lofty participation in the immortal hopes which spring from the empty grave of Jesus is warranted, unless we have His quickening power raising us to-day by a better resurrection; and no participation in the present power of His heavenly life is possible, unless we have such a share in His death, as that by it the world is crucified to us, and we unto the world.

III. The Apostle adds another phase of this great contrast of life and death, which brings home still more closely to his hearers, the deep and radical change which passes upon all Christians. He has been speaking of a death and burial followed by a resurrection. But there is another death from which Christ raises us, by that same risen life imparted to us through faith—a darker and grimmer thing than the self-abnegation before described.

"And you, being dead through your trespasses, and the uncircumcision of your flesh." The separate acts of transgression of which they had been guilty, and the unchastened, unpurified, carnal nature from which these had flowed, were the reasons of a very real and awful death; or, as the parallel passage in Ephesians (ii. 2) puts it with a slight variation, they made the condition or sphere in which that death inhered. That solemn thought, so pregnant in its dread emphasis in Scripture, is not to be put aside as a mere metaphor. All life stands in union with God. The physical universe exists by reason of its perpetual contact with His sustaining hand, in the hollow of which all Being lies, and it is, because He touches it. "In Him we live." So also the life of mind is sustained by His perpetual inbreathing, and in the deepest sense "we see light" in His light. So, lastly, the highest life of the spirit stands in union in still higher manner with Him, and to be separated from Him is death to it. Sin breaks that union, and therefore sin is death, in the very inmost centre of man's being. The awful warning, "In the day thou eatest thereof, thou shalt surely die," was fulfilled. That separation by sin, in which the soul is wrenched from God, is the real death, and the thing that men call by the name is only an outward symbol of a far sadder fact—the shadow of that which is the awful substance, and as much less terrible than it as painted fires are less than the burning reality.

So men may live in the body, and toil and think and feel, and be dead. The world is full of "sheeted dead," that "squeak and gibber" in "our streets," for every soul that lives to self and has rent itself away from God, so far as a creature can, is "dead while he liveth." The other death, of which the previous verse spoke, is therefore but the putting off of a death. We lose nothing of real life in putting off self, but only that which keeps us in a separation from God, and slays our true and highest being. To die to self is but "the death of death."

The same life of which the previous verse spoke as coming from the risen Lord is here set forth as able to raise us from that death of sin. "He hath quickened you together with Him." Union with Christ floods our dead souls with His own vitality, as water will pour from a reservoir through a tube inserted in it. There is the actual communication of a new life when we touch Christ by faith. The prophet of old laid himself upon the dead child, the warm lip on the pallid mouth, the throbbing heart on the still one, and the contact rekindled the extinguished spark. So Christ lays His full life on our deadness, and does more than recall a departed glow of vitality. He communicates a new life kindred with His own. That life makes us free here and now from the law of sin and death, and it shall be perfected hereafter when the working of His mighty power shall change the body of our humiliation into the likeness of the body of His glory, and the leaven of His new life shall leaven the three measures in which it is hidden, body, soul, and spirit, with its own transforming energy. Then, in yet higher sense, death shall die, and life shall be victor by His victory.

But to all this one preliminary is needful—"having forgiven us all trespasses." Paul's eagerness to associate himself with his brethren, and to claim his share in the forgiveness, as well as to unite in the acknowledgment of sin, makes him change his word from "you" to "us." So the best manuscripts give the text, and the reading is obviously full of interest and suggestiveness. There must be a removal of the cause of deadness before there can be a quickening to new life. That cause was sin, which cannot be cancelled as guilt by any self-denial however great, nor even by the impartation of a new life from God for the future. A gospel which only enjoined dying to self would be as inadequate as a gospel which only provided for a higher life in the future. The stained and faultful past must be cared for. Christ must bring pardon for it, as well as a new spirit for the future. So the condition prior to our being quickened together with Him is God's forgiveness, free and universal, covering all our sins, and given to us without anything on our part. That condition is satisfied. Christ's death brings to us God's pardon, and when the great barrier of unforgiven sin is cleared away, Christ's life pours into our hearts, and "everything lives whithersoever the river cometh."

Here then we have the deepest ground of Paul's intense hatred of every attempt to make anything but faith in Christ and moral purity essential to the perfect Christian life. Circumcision and baptism and all other rites or sacraments of Judaism or Christianity are equally powerless to quicken dead souls. For that, the first thing needed is the forgiveness of sins, and that is ours through simple faith in Christ's death. We are quickened by Christ's own life in us, and He "dwells in our hearts by faith." All ordinances may be administered to us a hundred times, and without faith they leave us as they found us—dead. If we have hold of Christ by faith we live, whether we have received the ordinances or not. So all full blown or budding sacramentarianism is to be fought against to the uttermost, because it tends to block the road to the City of Refuge for a poor sinful soul, and the most pressing of all necessities is that that way of life should be kept clear and unimpeded.

We need the profound truth which lies in the threefold form which Paul gives to one of his great watchwords: "Circumcision is nothing, and uncircumcision is nothing, but the keeping of the commandments of God."

And how, says my despairing conscience, shall I keep the commandments? The answer lies in the second form of the saying—"In Christ Jesus neither circumcision availeth anything, nor uncircumcision, but a new creature." And how, replies my saddened heart, can I become a new creature? The answer lies in the final form of the saying—"In Jesus Christ neither circumcision availeth anything nor uncircumcision, but faith which worketh." Faith brings the life which makes us new men, and then we can keep the commandments. If we have faith, and are new men and do God's will, we need no rites but as helps. If we have not faith, all rites are nothing.

XIV

THE CROSS THE DEATH OF LAW AND THE TRIUMPH OVER EVIL POWERS

> "Blotting out the handwriting of ordinances that was against us, which was contrary to us, and took it out of the way, nailing it to His cross; and having spoiled principalities and powers, He made a show of them openly, triumphing over them in it." —Col. ii. 14, 15 (Rev. Ver.).

The same double reference to the two characteristic errors of the Colossians which we have already met so frequently, presents itself here. This whole section vibrates continually between warnings against the Judaising enforcement of the Mosaic law on Gentile Christians, and against the Oriental figments about a crowd of angelic beings filling the space betwixt man and God, betwixt pure spirit and gross matter. One great fact is here opposed to these strangely associated errors. The cross of Christ is the abrogation of the Law; the cross of Christ is the victory over principalities and powers. If we hold fast by it, we are under no subjection to the former, and have neither to fear nor reverence the latter.

I. The Cross of Christ is the death of Law.

The law is a written document. It has an antagonistic aspect to us all, Gentiles as well as Jews. Christ has blotted it out. More than that, He has taken it out of the way, as if it were an obstacle lying right in the middle of our path. More than that, it is "nailed to the cross." That phrase has been explained by an alleged custom of repealing laws and cancelling bonds by driving a nail into them, and fixing them up in public, but proof of the practice is said to be wanting. The thought seems to be deeper than that. This antagonistic "law" is conceived of as being, like "the world," crucified in the crucifixion of our Lord. The nails which fastened Him to the cross fastened it, and in His death it was done to death. We are free from it, "that being dead in which we were held."

We have first, then, to consider the "handwriting," or, as some would render the word, "the bond." Of course, by *law* here is primarily meant the Mosaic ceremonial law, which was being pressed upon the Colossians. It is so completely antiquated for us, that we have difficulty in realising what a fight for life and death raged round the question of its observance by the primitive Church. It is always harder to change customs than creeds, and religious observances live on, as every maypole on a village green tells us, long after the beliefs which animated them are forgotten. So there was a strong body among the early believers to whom it was flat blasphemy to speak of allowing the Gentile Christian to come into the Church, except through the old doorway of circumcision, and to whom the outward ceremonial of Judaism was the only visible religion. That is the point directly at issue between Paul and these teachers.

But the modern distinction between moral and ceremonial law had no existence in Paul's mind, any more than it has in the Old Testament, where precepts of the highest morality and regulations of the merest ceremonial are interstratified in a way most surprising to us moderns. To him the law was a homogeneous whole, however diverse its commands, because it was all the revelation of the will of God for the guidance of man. It is the law as a whole, in all its aspects and parts, that is here spoken of, whether as enjoining morality, or external observances, or as an accuser fastening guilt on the conscience, or as a stern prophet of retribution and punishment.

Further, we must give a still wider extension to the thought. The principles laid down are true not only in regard to "*the* law," but about all law, whether it be written on the tables of stone, or on "the fleshy tables of the heart" or conscience, or in the systems of ethics, or in the customs of society. Law, as such, howsoever enacted and whatever the bases of its rule, is dealt with by Christianity in precisely the same way as the venerable and God-given code of the Old Testament. When we recognise that fact, these discussions in Paul's Epistles flash up into startling vitality and interest. It has long since been settled that Jewish ritual is nothing to us. But it ever remains a burning question for each of us, What Christianity does for us in relation to the solemn law of duty under which we are all placed, and which we have all broken?

The antagonism of law is the next point presented by these words. Twice, to add to the emphasis, Paul tells us that the law is against us. It stands opposite us fronting us and frowning at us, and barring our road. Is "law" then become our "enemy because it tells us the truth?" Surely this conception of law is a strange contrast to and descent from the rapturous delight of psalmists and prophets in the "law of the Lord." Surely God's greatest gift to man is the knowledge of His will, and law is beneficent, a light and a guide to men, and even its strokes are merciful. Paul believed all that too. But nevertheless the antagonism is very real. As with God, so with law, if we be against Him, He cannot but be against us. We may make Him our dearest friend or our foe. "They rebelled ... therefore He was turned to be their enemy and fought against them." The revelation of duty to which we are not inclined is ever unwelcome. Law is against us, because it comes like a taskmaster, bidding us do, but neither putting the inclination into our hearts, nor the power into our hands. And law is against us, because the revelation of unfulfilled duty is the accusation of the defaulter and a revelation to him of his guilt. And law is against us, because it comes with threatenings and foretastes of penalty and pain. Thus as standard, accuser and avenger, it is—sad perversion of its nature and function though such an attitude be—against us.

We all know that. Strange and tragic it is, but alas! it is true, that God's law presents itself before us as an enemy. Each of us has seen that apparition, severe in beauty, like the sword-bearing angel that Balaam saw "standing in the way" between the vineyards, blocking our path when we wanted to "go frowardly in the way of our heart." Each of us knows what it is to see our sentence in the stern face. The law of the Lord should be to us "sweeter than honey and the honeycomb," but the corruption of the best is the worst, and we can make it poison. Obeyed, it is as the chariot of fire to bear us heavenward. Disobeyed, it is an iron car that goes crashing on its way, crushing all who set themselves against it. To know what we ought to be and to love and try to be it, is blessedness, but to know it and to refuse to be it, is misery. In herself she "wears the Godhead's most benignant grace," but if we turn against her, Law, the "daughter of the voice of God," gathers frowns upon her face and her beauty becomes stern and threatening.

But the great principle here asserted is—the destruction of law in the cross of Christ. The cross ends the law's power of *punishment*. Paul believed that the burden and penalty of sin had been laid on Jesus Christ and borne by Him on His cross. In deep, mysterious, but most real identification of Himself with the whole race of man, He not only Himself took our infirmities and bare our sicknesses, by the might of His sympathy and the reality of His manhood, but "the Lord made to meet upon Him the iniquity of us all"; and He, the Lamb of God, willingly accepted the load, and bare away our sins by bearing their penalty.

To philosophise on that teaching of Scripture is not my business here. It is my business to assert it. We can never penetrate to a full understanding of the rationale of Christ's bearing the world's sins, but that has nothing to do with the earnestness of our belief in the fact. Enough for us that in His person He willingly made experience of all the bitterness of sin: that when He agonised in the dark on the cross, and when from out of the darkness came that awful cry, so strangely compact of wistful confidence and utter isolation, "My God, My God, why hast Thou forsaken Me?" it was something deeper than physical pain or shrinking from physical death that found utterance—even the sin-laden consciousness of Him who in that awful hour gathered into His own breast the spear-points of a world's punishment. The cross of Christ is the endurance of the penalty of sin, and therefore is the unloosing of the grip of the law upon us, in so far as threatening and punishment are concerned. It is not enough that we should only intellectually recognise that as a principle—it is the very heart of the gospel, the very life of our souls. Trusting ourselves to that great sacrifice, the dread of punishment will fade from our hearts, and the thunder-clouds melt out of the sky, and the sense of guilt will not be a sting, but an occasion for lowly thankfulness, and the law will have to draw the bolts of her prison-house and let our captive souls go free.

Christ's cross is the end of law as *ceremonial*. The whole elaborate ritual of the Jew had sacrifice for its vital centre, and the prediction of the Great Sacrifice for its highest purpose. Without the admission of these principles, Paul's position is unintelligible, for he holds, as in this context, that Christ's coming puts the whole system out of date, because it fulfils it all. When the fruit has set, there is no more need for petals; or, as the Apostle himself puts it, "when that which is perfect is come, that which is in part is done away." We have the reality, and do not need the shadow. There is but one temple for the Christian soul—the "temple of His body." Local sanctity is at an end, for it was never more than an external picture of that spiritual fact which is realised in the Incarnation. Christ is the dwelling-place of Deity, the meeting-place of God and man, the place of sacrifice; and, built on Him, we in Him become a spiritual house. There are none other temples than these. Christ is the great priest, and in His presence all human priesthood loses its consecration, for it could offer only external sacrifice, and secure a local approach to a "worldly sanctuary." He is the real Aaron, and we in Him become a royal priesthood. There are none other priests than these. Christ is the true sacrifice. His death is the real propitiation for sin, and we in Him become thank-offerings, moved by His mercies to present ourselves living sacrifices. There are none other offerings than these. So the law as a code of ceremonial worship is done to death in the cross, and, like the temple veil, is torn in two from the top to the bottom.

Christ's cross is the end of law as *moral* rule. Nothing in Paul's writings warrants the restriction to the ceremonial law of the strong assertion in the text, and its many parallels. Of course, such words do not mean that Christian men are freed from the obligations of morality, but they do mean that we are not bound to do the "things contained in the law" because they are there. Duty is duty now because we see the pattern of conduct and character in Christ. Conscience is not our standard, nor is the Old Testament conception of the perfect ideal of manhood. We have neither to read law in the fleshy tables of the heart, nor in the tables graven by God's own finger, nor in men's parchments and prescriptions. Our law is the perfect life and death of Christ, who is at once the ideal of humanity and the reality of Deity.

The weakness of all law is that it merely commands, but has no power to get its commandments obeyed. Like a discrowned king, it posts its proclamations, but has no army at its back to execute them. But Christ puts His own power within us, and His love in our hearts; and so we pass from under the dominion of an external commandment into the liberty of an inward spirit. He is to His followers both "law and impulse." He gives not the "law of a carnal commandment, but the power of an endless life." The long schism between inclination and duty is at an end, in so far as we are under the influence of Christ's cross. The great promise is fulfilled, "I will put My law into their minds and write it in their hearts"; and so, glad obedience with the whole power of the new life, for the sake of the love of the dear Lord who has bought us by His death, supersedes the constrained submission to outward precept. A higher morality ought to characterise the partakers of the life of Christ, who have His example for their code, and His love for their motive. The tender voice that says, "If ye love Me, keep My commandments," wins us to purer and more self-sacrificing goodness than the stern accents that can only say, "Thou shalt—or else!" can ever enforce. He came "not to destroy, but to fulfil." The fulfilment was destruction in order to reconstruction in higher form. Law died with Christ on the cross in order that it might rise and reign with Him in our inmost hearts.

II. The Cross is the triumph over all the powers of evil.

There are considerable difficulties in the interpretation of verse 15; the main question being the meaning of the word rendered in the Authorized Version "spoiled," and in the R. V. "having put off from Himself." It is the same word as is used in iii. 9, and is there rendered "have put off"; while a cognate noun is found in verse 11 of this chapter, and is there translated "the putting off." The form here must either mean "having put off from oneself," or "having stripped (others) *for* oneself." The former meaning is adopted by many commentators, as well as by the R. V., and is explained to mean that Christ having assumed our humanity, was, as it were, wrapped about and invested with Satanic temptations, which He finally flung from Him for ever in His death, which was His triumph over the powers of evil. The figure seems far-fetched and obscure, and the rendering necessitates the supposition of a change in the person spoken of, which must be God in the earlier part of the period, and Christ in the latter.

But if we adopt the other meaning, which has equal warrant in the Greek form, "having stripped for Himself," we get the thought that in the cross, God has, for His greater glory, stripped principalities and powers. Taking this meaning, we avoid the necessity of supposing with Bishop Lightfoot that there is a change of subject from God to Christ at some point in the period including verses 13 to 15—an expedient which is made necessary by the impossibility of supposing that God "divested Himself of principalities or powers"—and also avoid the other necessity of referring the whole period to Christ, which is another way out of that impossibility. We thereby obtain a more satisfactory meaning than that Christ in assuming humanity was assailed by temptations from the powers of evil which were, as it were, a poisoned garment clinging to Him, and which He stripped off from Himself in His death. Further, such a meaning as that which we adopt makes the whole verse a consistent metaphor in three stages, whereas the other introduces an utterly incongruous and irrelevant figure. What connection has the figure of stripping off a garment with that of a conqueror in his triumphal procession? But if we read "spoiled for Himself principalities and powers," we see the whole process before our eyes—the victor stripping his foes of arms and ornaments and dress, then parading them as his captives, and then dragging them at the wheels of his triumphal car.

The words point us into dim regions of which we know nothing more than Scripture tells us. These dreamers at Colossæ had much to say about a crowd of beings, bad and good, which linked men and matter with spirit and God. We have heard already the emphasis with which Paul has claimed for his Master the sovereign authority of Creator over all orders of being, the headship over all principality and power. He has declared, too, that from Christ's cross a magnetic influence streams out upwards as well as earthwards, binding all things together in the great reconciliation—and now he tells us that from that same cross shoot downwards darts of conquering power which subdue and despoil reluctant foes of other realms and regions than ours, in so far as they work among men.

That there are such seems plainly enough asserted in Christ's own words. However much discredit has been brought on the thought by monastic and Puritan exaggerations, it is clearly the teaching of Scripture; and however it may be ridiculed or set aside, it can never be disproved.

But the position which Christianity takes in reference to the whole matter is to maintain that Christ has conquered the banded kingdom of evil, and that no man owes it fear or obedience, if he will only hold fast by his Lord. In the cross is the judgment of this world, and by it is the prince of this world cast out. He has taken away the power of these Powers who were so mighty amongst men. They held men captive by temptations too strong to be overcome, but He has conquered the lesser temptations of the wilderness and the sorer of the cross, and therein has made us more than conquerors. They held men captive by ignorance of God, and the cross reveals Him; by the lie that sin was a trifle, but the cross teaches us its gravity and power; by the opposite lie that sin was unforgivable, but the cross brings pardon for every transgression and cleansing for every stain. By the cross the world is a redeemed world, and, as our Lord said in words which may have suggested the figure of our text, the strong man is bound, and his house *spoiled* of all his armour wherein he trusted. The prey is taken from the mighty and men are delivered from the dominion of evil. So that dark kingdom is robbed of its subjects and its rulers impoverished and restrained. The devout imagination of the monk-painter drew on the wall of the cell in his convent the conquering Christ with white banner bearing a blood-red cross, before whose glad coming the heavy doors of the prison-house fell from their hinges, crushing beneath their weight the demon jailer, while the long file of eager captives, from Adam onwards through ages of patriarchs and psalmists and prophets, hurried forward with outstretched hands to meet the Deliverer, who came bearing His own atmosphere of radiance and joy. Christ has conquered. His cross is His victory; and in that victory God has conquered. As the long files of the triumphal procession swept upwards to the temple with incense and music, before the gazing eyes of a gathered glad nation, while the conquered trooped chained behind the chariot, that all men might see their fierce eyes gleaming beneath their matted hair, and breathe more freely for the chains on their hostile wrists, so in the world-wide issues of the work of Christ, God triumphs before the universe, and enhances His glory in that He has rent the prey from the mighty and won men back to Himself.

So we learn to think of evil as conquered, and for ourselves in our own conflicts with the world, the flesh, and the devil, as well as for the whole race of man, to be of good cheer. True, the victory is but slowly being realised in all its consequences, and often it seems as if no territory had been won. But the main position has been carried, and though the struggle is still obstinate, it can end only in one way. The brute dies hard, but the naked heel of our Christ has bruised his head, and though still the dragon

> "Swinges the scaly horror of his folded tail,"

his death will come sooner or later. The regenerating power is lodged in the heart of humanity, and the centre from which it flows is the cross. The history of the world thenceforward is but the history of its more or less rapid assimilation of that power, and of its consequent deliverance from the bondage in which it has been held. The end can only be the entire and universal manifestation of the victory which was won when He bowed His head and died. Christ's cross is God's throne of triumph.

Let us see that we have our own personal part in that victory. Holding to Christ, and drawing from Him by faith a share in His new life, we shall no longer be under the yoke of law, but enfranchised into the obedience of love, which is liberty. We shall no longer be slaves of evil, but sons and servants of our conquering God, who woos and wins us by showing us all His love in Christ, and by giving us His own Son on the Cross, our peace-offering. If we let Him overcome, His victory will be life, not death. He will strip us of nothing but rags, and clothe us in garments of purity; He will so breathe beauty into us that He will show us openly to the universe as examples of His transforming power, and He will bind us glad captives to His chariot wheels, partakers of His victory as well as trophies of His all-conquering love. "Now thanks be unto God, which always triumphs over us in Jesus Christ."

XV
WARNINGS AGAINST TWIN CHIEF ERRORS, BASED UPON PREVIOUS POSITIVE TEACHING

"Let no man therefore judge you in meat, or in drink, or in respect of a feast day or a new moon or a sabbath day: which are a shadow of things to come; but the body is Christ's. Let no man rob you of your prize by a voluntary humility and worshipping of the angels, dwelling in the things which he hath seen, vainly puffed up by his fleshly mind, and not holding fast the Head, from whom all the body, being supplied and knit together through the joints and bands, increaseth with the increase of God." —Col. ii. 16–19 (Rev. Ver.).

"Let no man *therefore* judge you." That "therefore" sends us back to what the Apostle has been saying in the previous verses, in order to find there the ground of these earnest warnings. That ground is the whole of the foregoing exposition of the Christian relation to Christ as far back as verse 9, but especially the great truths contained in the immediately preceding verses, that the cross of Christ is the death of law, and God's triumph over all the powers of evil. Because it is so, the Colossian Christians are exhorted to claim and use their emancipation from both. Thus we have here the very heart and centre of the practical counsels of the Epistle—the double blasts of the trumpet warning against the two most pressing dangers besetting the Church. They are the same two which we have often met already—on the one hand, a narrow Judaising enforcement of ceremonial and punctilios of outward observance; on the other hand, a dreamy Oriental absorption in imaginations of a crowd of angelic mediators obscuring the one gracious presence of Christ our Intercessor.

I. Here then we have first, the claim for Christian liberty, with the great truth on which it is built.

The points in regard to which that liberty is to be exercised are specified. They are no doubt those, in addition to circumcision, which were principally in question then and there. "Meat and drink" refers to restrictions in diet, such as the prohibition of "unclean" things in the Mosaic law, and the question of the lawfulness of eating meat offered to idols; perhaps also, such as the Nazarite vow. There were few regulations as to "drink" in the Old Testament, so that probably other ascetic practices besides the Mosaic regulations were in question, but these must have been unimportant, else Paul could not have spoken of the whole as being a "shadow of things to come." The second point in regard to which liberty is here claimed is that of the sacred seasons of Judaism: the annual festivals, the monthly feast of the new moon, the weekly Sabbath.

The relation of the Gentile converts to these Jewish practices was an all-important question for the early Church. It was really the question whether Christianity was to be more than a Jewish sect—and the main force which, under God, settled the contest, was the vehemence and logic of the Apostle Paul.

Here he lays down the ground on which that whole question about diet and days, and all such matters, is to be settled. They "are a shadow of things to come" but the body is of Christ. "Coming events cast their shadows *before*." That great work of Divine love, the mission of Christ, Whose "goings forth have been from everlasting," may be thought of as having set out from the Throne as soon as time was, travelling in the greatness of its strength, like the beams of some far-off star that have not yet reached a dark world. The light from the Throne is behind Him as He advances across the centuries, and the shadow is thrown far in front.

Now that involves two thoughts about the Mosaic law and whole system. First, the purely prophetic and symbolic character of the Old Testament order, and especially of the Old Testament ritual. The absurd extravagance of many attempts to "spiritualize" the latter should not blind us to the truth which they caricature. Nor, on the other hand, should we be so taken with new attempts to reconstruct our notions of Jewish history and the dates of Old Testament books, as to forget that, though the New Testament is committed to no theory on these points, it is committed to the Divine origin and prophetic purpose of the Mosaic law and Levitical worship. We should thankfully accept all teaching which free criticism and scholarship can give us as to the process by which, and the time when, that great symbolic system of acted prophecy was built up; but we shall be further away than ever from understanding the Old Testament if we have gained critical knowledge of its genesis, and have lost the belief that its symbols were given by God to prophesy of His Son. That is the key to both Testaments; and I cannot but believe that the uncritical reader who reads his book of the law and the prophets with that conviction, has got nearer the very marrow of the book, than the critic, if he have parted with it, can ever come.

Sacrifice, altar, priest, temple spake of Him. The distinctions of meats were meant, among other purposes, to familiarize men with the conceptions of purity and impurity, and so, by stimulating conscience, to wake the sense of need of a Purifier. The yearly feasts set forth various aspects of the great work of Christ, and the sabbath showed in outward form the rest into which He leads those who cease from their own works and wear His yoke. All these observances, and the whole system to which they belong, are like outriders who precede a prince on his progress, and as they gallop through sleeping villages, rouse them with the cry, "The king is coming!"

And when the king *has* come, where are the heralds? and when the reality has come, who wants symbols? and if that which threw the shadow forward through the ages has arrived, how shall the shadow be visible too? Therefore the second principle here laid down, namely the cessation of all these observances, and their like, is really involved in the first, namely their prophetic character.

The practical conclusion drawn is very noteworthy, because it seems much narrower than the premises warrant. Paul does not say—therefore let no man observe any of these any more; but takes up the much more modest ground—let no man *judge* you about them. He claims a wide liberty of variation, and all that he repels is the right of anybody to dragoon Christian men into ceremonial observances on the ground that they are necessary. He does not quarrel with the rites, but with men insisting on the necessity of the rites.

In his own practice he gave the best commentary on his meaning. When they said to him, "You *must* circumcise Titus," he said, "Then I will *not*." When nobody tried to compel him, he took Timothy, and of his own accord circumcised him to avoid scandals. When it was needful as a protest, he rode right over all the prescriptions of the law, and "did eat with Gentiles." When it was advisable as a demonstration that he himself "walked orderly and kept the law," he performed the rites of purification and united in the temple worship.

In times of transition wise supporters of the new will not be in a hurry to break with the old. "I will lead on softly, according as the flock and the children be able to endure," said Jacob, and so says every good shepherd.

The brown sheaths remain on the twig after the tender green leaf has burst from within them, but there is no need to pull them off, for they will drop presently. "I will wear three surplices if they like," said Luther once. "Neither if we eat are we the better, neither if we eat not are we the worse," said Paul. Such is the spirit of the words here. It is a plea for Christian liberty. If not insisted on as necessary, the outward observances may be allowed. If they are regarded as helps, or as seemly adjuncts or the like, there is plenty of room for difference of opinion and for variety of practice, according to temperament and taste and usage. There are principles which should regulate even these diversities of practice, and Paul has set these forth, in the great chapter about meats in the Epistle to the Romans. But it is a different thing altogether when any external observances are insisted on as essential, either from the old Jewish or from the modern sacramentarian point of view. If a man comes saying, "Except ye be circumcised, ye cannot be saved," the only right answer is, Then I will not be circumcised, and if *you* are, because you believe that you cannot be saved without it, "Christ is become of none effect to you." Nothing is necessary but union to Him, and that comes through no outward observance, but through the faith which worketh by love. Therefore, let no man judge you, but repel all such attempts at thrusting any ceremonial ritual observances on you, on the plea of necessity, with the emancipating truth that the cross of Christ is the death of law.

A few words may be said here on the bearing of the principles laid down in these verses on the religious observance of Sunday. The obligation of the Jewish sabbath has passed away as much as sacrifices and circumcision. That seems unmistakably the teaching here. But the institution of a weekly day of rest is distinctly put in Scripture as independent of, and prior to, the special form and meaning given to the institution in the Mosaic law. That is the natural conclusion from the narrative of the creative rest in Genesis, and from our Lord's emphatic declaration that the sabbath was made for "man"—that is to say, for the race. Many traces of the pre-Mosaic sabbath have been adduced, and among others we may recall the fact that recent researches show it to have been observed by the Accadians, the early inhabitants of Assyria. It is a physical and moral necessity, and that is a sadly mistaken benevolence which on the plea of culture or amusement for the many, compels the labour of the few, and breaks down the distinction between the Sunday and the rest of the week.

The religious observance of the first day of the week rests on no recorded command, but has a higher origin, inasmuch as it is the outcome of a felt want. The early disciples naturally gathered together for worship on the day which had become so sacred to them. At first, no doubt, they observed the Jewish sabbath, and only gradually came to the practice which we almost see growing before our eyes in the Acts of the Apostles, in the mention of the disciples at Troas coming together on the first day of the week to break bread, and which we gather, from the Apostle's instructions as to weekly setting apart money for charitable purposes, to have existed in the Church at Corinth; as we know, that even in his lonely island prison far away from the company of his brethren, the Apostle John was in a condition of high religious contemplation on the Lord's day, ere yet he heard the solemn voice and saw "the things which are."

This gradual growing up of the practice is in accordance with the whole spirit of the New Covenant, which has next to nothing to say about the externals of worship, and leaves the new life to shape itself. Judaism gave prescriptions and minute regulations; Christianity, the religion of the spirit, gives principles. The necessity, for the nourishment of the Divine life, of the religious observance of the day of rest is certainly not less now than at first. In the hurry and drive of our modern life with the world forcing itself on us at every moment, we cannot keep up the warmth of devotion unless we use this day, not merely for physical rest, and family enjoyment, but for worship. They who know their own slothfulness of spirit, and are in earnest in seeking after a deeper, fuller Christian life, will thankfully own, "the week were dark but for its light." I distrust the spirituality which professes that all life is a sabbath, and therefore holds itself absolved from special seasons of worship. If the stream of devout communion is to flow through all our days, there must be frequent reservoirs along the road, or it will be lost in the sand, like the rivers of higher Asia. It is a poor thing to say, keep the day as a day of worship because it is a commandment. Better to think of it as a great gift for the highest purposes; and not let it be merely a day of rest for jaded bodies, but make it one of refreshment for cumbered spirits, and rekindle the smouldering flame of devotion, by drawing near to Christ in public and in private. So shall we gather stores that may help us to go in the strength of that meat for some more marches on the dusty road of life.

II. The Apostle passes on to his second peal of warning,—that against the teaching about angel mediators, which would rob the Colossian Christians of their prize,—and draws a rapid portrait of the teachers of whom they are to beware.

"Let no man rob you of your prize." The metaphor is the familiar one of the race or the wrestling ground; the umpire or judge is Christ; the reward is that incorruptible crown of glory, of righteousness, woven not of fading bay leaves, but of sprays from the "tree of life," which dower with undying blessedness the brows round which they are wreathed. Certain people are trying to rob them of their prize—not consciously, for that would be inconceivable, but such is the tendency of their teaching. No names will be mentioned, but he draws a portrait of the robber with swift firm hand, as if he had said, If you want to know whom I mean, here he is. Four clauses, like four rapid strokes of the pencil, do it, and are marked in the Greek by four participles, the first of which is obscured in the Authorised Version. "Delighting in humility and the worshipping of angels." So probably the first clause should be rendered. The first words are almost contradictory, and are meant to suggest that the humility has not the genuine ring about it. Self-conscious humility in which a man takes delight is not the real thing. A man who knows that he is humble, and is self-complacent about it, glancing out of the corners of his downcast eyes at any mirror where he can see himself, is not humble at all. "The devil's darling vice is the pride which apes humility."

So *very* humble were these people that they would not venture to pray to God! *There* was humility indeed. So far beneath did they feel themselves, that the utmost they could do was to lay hold of the lowest link of a long chain of angel mediators, in hope that the vibration might run upwards through all the links, and perhaps reach the throne at last. Such fantastic abasement which would not take God at His word, nor draw near to Him in His Son, was really the very height of pride.

Then follows a second descriptive clause, of which no altogether satisfactory interpretation has yet been given. Possibly, as has been suggested, we have here an early error in the text, which has affected all the manuscripts, and cannot now be corrected. Perhaps, on the whole, the translation adopted by the Revised Version presents the least difficulty — "dwelling in the things which he hath seen." In that case the seeing would be not by the senses, but by visions and pretended revelations, and the charge against the false teachers would be that they "walked in a vain show" of unreal imaginations and visionary hallucinations, whose many-coloured misleading lights they followed rather than the plain sunshine of revealed facts in Jesus Christ.

"Vainly puffed up by his fleshly mind" is the next feature in the portrait. The self-conscious humility was only skin deep, and covered the utmost intellectual arrogance. The heretic teacher, like a blown bladder, was swollen with what after all was only wind; he was dropsical from conceit of "mind," or, as we should say, "intellectual ability," which after all was only the instrument and organ of the "flesh," the sinful self. And, of course, being all these things, he would have no firm grip of Christ, from whom such tempers and views were sure to detach him. Therefore the damning last clause of the indictment is "not holding the Head." How could he do so? And the slackness of his grasp of the Lord Jesus would make all these errors and faults ten times worse.

Now the special forms of these errors which are here dealt with are all gone past recall. But the tendencies which underlay these special forms are as rampant as ever, and work unceasingly to loosen our hold of our dear Lord. The worship of angels is dead, but we are still often tempted to think that we are too lowly and sinful to claim our portion of the faithful promises of God. The spurious humility is by no means out of date, which knows better than God does, whether He can forgive us our sins, and bend over us in love. We do not slip in angel mediators between ourselves and Him, but the tendency to put the sole work of Jesus Christ "into commission," is not dead. We are all tempted to grasp at others as well as at Him, for our love, and trust, and obedience, and we all need the reminder that to lay hold of any other props is to lose hold of Him, and that he who does not cleave to Christ alone, does not cleave to Christ at all.

We do not see visions and dream dreams any more, except here and there some one led astray by a so-called "spiritualism," but plenty of us attach more importance to our own subjective fancies or speculations about the obscurer parts of Christianity than to the clear revelation of God in Christ. The "unseen world" has for many minds an unwholesome attraction. The Gnostic spirit is still in full force among us, which despises the foundation facts and truths of the gospel as "milk for babes," and values its own baseless artificial speculations about subordinate matters, which are unrevealed because they are subordinate, and fascinating to some minds because unrevealed, far above the truths which are clear because they are vital, and insipid to such minds because they are clear. We need to be reminded that Christianity is not for speculation, but to make us good, and that "He who has fashioned their hearts alike," has made us all to live by the same air, to be nourished by the same bread from heaven, to be saved and purified by the same truth. That is the gospel which the little child can understand, of which the outcast and the barbarian can get some kind of hold, which the failing spirit groping in the darkness of death can dimly see as its light in the valley—that is the all-important part of the gospel. What needs special training and capacity to understand is no essential portion of the truth that is meant for the world.

And a swollen self-conceit is of all things the most certain to keep a man away from Christ. We must feel our utter helplessness and need, before we shall lay hold on Him, and if ever that wholesome lowly sense of our own emptiness is clouded over, that moment will our fingers relax their tension, and that moment will the flow of life into our deadness run slow and pause. Whatever slackens our hold of Christ tends to rob us of the final prize, that crown of life which He gives.

Hence the solemn earnestness of these warnings. It was not only a doctrine more or less that was at stake, but it was their eternal life. Certain truths believed would increase the firmness of their hold on their Lord, and thereby would secure the prize. Disbelieved, the disbelief would slacken their grasp of Him, and thereby would deprive them of it. We are often told that the gospel gives heaven for right belief, and that that is unjust. But if a man does not believe a thing, he cannot have in his character or feelings the influence which the belief of it would produce. If he does not believe that Christ died for his sins, and that all his hopes are built on that great Saviour, he will not cleave to Him in love and dependence. If he does not so cleave to Him he will not draw from Him the life which would mould his character and stir him to run the race. If he do not run the race he will never win nor wear the crown. That crown is the reward and issue of character and conduct, made possible by the communication of strength and new nature from Jesus, which again is made possible through our faith laying hold of Him as revealed in certain truths, and of these truths as revealing Him. Therefore, intellectual error may loose our hold on Christ, and if we slacken that, we shall forfeit the prize. Mere speculative interest about the less plainly revealed corners of Christian truth may, and often do, act in paralysing the limbs of the Christian athlete. "Ye did run well, what hath hindered you?" has to be asked of many whom a spirit akin to this described in our text has made languid in the race. To us all, knowing in some measure how the whole sum of influences around us work to detach us from our Lord, and so to rob us of the prize which is inseparable from His presence, the solemn exhortation which He speaks from heaven may well come, "Hold fast that thou hast; let no man take thy crown."

III. The source and manner of all true growth is next set forth, in order to enforce the warning, and to emphasize the need of holding the Head.

Christ is not merely represented supreme and sovereign, when He is called "the head." The metaphor goes much deeper, and points to Him as the source of a real spiritual life, from Him communicated to all the members of the true Church, and constituting it an organic whole. We have found the same expression twice already in the Epistle; once as applied to His relation to "the body, the Church" (i. 18), and once in reference to the "principalities and powers." The errors in the Colossian Church derogated from Christ's sole sovereign place as fountain of all life natural and spiritual for all orders of beings, and hence the emphasis of the Apostle's proclamation of the counter truth. That life which flows from the head is diffused through the whole body by the various and harmonious action of all the parts. The body is "supplied and knit together," or in other words, the functions of nutrition and compaction into a whole are performed by the "joints and bands," in which last word are included muscles, nerves, tendons, and any of the "connecting bands which strap the body together." Their action is the condition of growth; but the Head is the source of all which the action of the members transmits to the body. Christ is the source of all nourishment. From Him flows the life-blood which feeds the whole, and by which every form of supply is ministered whereby the body grows. Christ is the source of all unity. Churches have been bound together by other bonds, such as creeds, polity, or even nationality; but that external bond is only like a rope round a bundle of fagots, while the true, inward unity springing from common possession of the life of Christ, is as the unity of some great tree, through which the same sap circulates from massive bole to the tiniest leaf that dances at the tip of the farthest branch.

These blessed results of supply and unity are effected through the action of the various parts. If each organ is in healthy action, the body grows. There is diversity in offices; the same life is light in the eyes, beauty in the cheek, strength in the hand, thought in the brain. The more you rise in the scale of life the more the body is differentiated, from the simple sac that can be turned inside out and has no division of parts or offices, up to man. So in the Church. The effect of Christianity is to heighten individuality, and to give each man his own proper "gift from God," and therefore each man his office, "one after this manner and another after that." Therefore is there need for the freest possible unfolding of each man's idiosyncrasy, heightened and hallowed by an indwelling Christ, lest the body should be the poorer if any member's activity be suppressed, or any one man be warped from his own work wherein he is strong, to become a feeble copy of another's. The perfect light is the blending of all colours.

A community where each member thus holds firmly by the Head, and each ministers in his degree to the nourishment and compaction of the members, will, says Paul, increase with the increase of God. The increase will come from Him, will be pleasing to Him, will be essentially the growth of His own life in the body. There is an increase not of God. These heretical teachers were swollen with dropsical self-conceit; but this is wholesome, solid growth. For individuals and communities of professing Christians the lesson is always seasonable, that it is very easy to get an increase of the other kind. The individual may increase in apparent knowledge, in volubility, in visions and speculations, in so-called Christian work; the Church may increase in members, in wealth, in culture, in influence in the world, in apparent activities, in subscription lists, and the like—and it may all be not sound growth, but proud flesh, which needs the knife. One way only there is by which we may increase with the increase of God, and that is that we keep fast hold of Jesus Christ, and "let Him not go, for He is our life." The one exhortation which includes all that is needful, and which being obeyed, all ceremonies and all speculations will drop into their right place, and become helps, not snares, is the exhortation which Barnabas gave to the new Gentile converts at Antioch—that "with purpose of heart they should cleave unto the Lord."

XVI
TWO FINAL TESTS OF THE FALSE TEACHING

"If ye died with Christ from the rudiments of the world,
why, as though living in the world, do ye subject yourselves
to ordinances. Handle not, nor taste, nor touch (all which
things are to perish with the using), after the precepts and
doctrines of men? Which things have indeed a show of
wisdom in will-worship, and humility, and severity to the
body; *but are* not of any value against the indulgence of the
flesh."—Col. ii. 20–23 (Rev. Ver.).

The polemical part of the Epistle is now coming to an end. We pass in
the next chapter, after a transitional paragraph, to simple moral precepts
which, with personal details, fill up the remainder of the letter. The
antagonist errors appear for the last time in the words which we have now
to consider. In these the Apostle seems to gather up all his strength to strike
two straight, crashing, final blows, which pulverize and annihilate the
theoretical positions and practical precepts of the heretical teachers. First,
he puts in the form of an unanswerable demand for the reason for their
teachings, their radical inconsistency with the Christian's death with Christ,
which is the very secret of his life. Then, by a contemptuous concession of
their apparent value to people who will not look an inch below the surface,
he makes more emphatic their final condemnation as worthless—less than
nothing and vanity—for the suppression of "the flesh"—the only aim of
all moral and religious discipline. So we have here two great tests by their
conformity to which we may try all teachings which assume to regulate
life, and all Christian teaching about the place and necessity for ritual and
outward prescriptions of conduct. "Ye are dead with Christ." All must fit in
with that great fact. The restraint and conquest of "the flesh" is the purpose
of all religion and of all moral teaching—our systems must do that or they
are naught, however fascinating they may be.

I. We have then to consider the great fact of the Christian's death with
Christ, and to apply it as a touch-stone.

The language of the Apostle points to a definite time when the Colossian
Christians "died" with Christ. That carries us back to former words in the

chapter, where, as we found, the period of their baptism considered as the symbol and profession of their conversion, was regarded as the time of their burial. They died with Christ when they clave with penitent trust to the truth that Christ died for them. When a man unites himself by faith to the dying Christ as his Peace, Pardon, and Saviour, then he too in a very real sense dies with Jesus.

That thought that every Christian is dead with Christ, runs through the whole of Paul's teaching. It is no mere piece of mysticism on his lips, though it has often become so, when divorced from morality, as it has been by some Christian teachers. It is no mere piece of rhetoric, though it has often become so, when men have lost the true thought of what Christ's death is for the world. But to Paul the cross of Christ was, first and foremost, the altar of sacrifice on which the oblation had been offered that took away all his guilt and sin; and then, because it was that, it became the law of his own life, and the power that assimilated him to his Lord.

The plain English of it all is, that when a man becomes a Christian by putting his trust in Christ Who died, as the ground of his acceptance and salvation, such a change takes place upon his whole nature and relationship to externals as is fairly comparable to a death.

The same illustration is frequent in ordinary speech. What do we mean when we talk of an old man being dead to youthful passions or follies or ambitions? We mean that they have ceased to interest him, that he is *separated* from them and *insensible* to them. Death is the separator. What an awful gulf there is between that fixed white face beneath the sheet, and all the things about which the man was so eager an hour ago! How impossible for any cries of love to pass the chasm! "His sons come to honour, and he knoweth it not." The "business" which filled his thoughts, crumbles to pieces, and he cares not. Nothing reaches him or interests him any more. So, if we have got hold of Christ as our Saviour, and have found in His cross the anchor of souls, that experience will deaden us to all which was our life, and the measure in which we are joined to Jesus by our faith in His great sacrifice, will be the measure in which we are detached from our former selves, and from old objects of interest and pursuit. The change may either be called dying with Christ, or rising with Him. The one phrase takes hold of it at an earlier stage than the other; the one puts stress on our ceasing to be what we were, the other on our beginning to be what we were not. So our text is followed by a paragraph corresponding in form and substance, and beginning, "If ye then be risen with Christ," as this begins, "If ye died with Christ!"

Such detachment from externals and separation from a former self is not unknown in ordinary life. Strong emotion of any kind makes us insensible to things around, and even to physical pain. Many a man with the excitement of the battle-field boiling in his brain, "receives but recks not of a wound." Absorption of thought and interest leads to what is called "absence of mind," where the surroundings are entirely unfelt, as in the case of the saint who rode all day on the banks of the Swiss lake, plunged in theological converse, and at evening asked where the lake was, though its waves had been rippling for twenty miles at his mule's feet. Higher tastes drive out lower ones, as some great stream turned into a new channel will sweep it clear of mud and rubbish. So, if we are joined to Christ, He will fill our souls with strong emotions and interests which will deaden our sensitiveness to things around us, and will inspire new loves, tastes and desires, which will make us indifferent to much that we used to be eager about and hostile to much that we once cherished.

To what shall we die if we are Christians? The Apostle answers that question in various ways, which we may profitably group together. "Reckon ye also yourselves to be dead indeed unto *sin*" (Rom. vi. 11). "He died for all, that they which live should no longer live unto *themselves*" (2 Cor. v. 14, 15). "Ye are become dead to the *law*" (Rom. vii. 6). By the cross of Christ, "the world hath been crucified unto me, and I unto *the world*." So then, to the whole mass of outward material things, all this present order which surrounds us, to the unrenounced self which has ruled us so long, and to the sin which results from the appeals of outward things to that evil self—to these, and to the mere outward letter of a commandment which is impotent to enforce its own behests or deliver self from the snares of the world and the burden of sin, we cease to belong in the measure in which we are Christ's. The separation is not complete; but, if we are Christians at all, it is begun, and henceforward our life is to be a "dying daily." It must either be a dying life or a living death. We shall still belong in our outward being—and, alas! far too much in heart also—to the world and self and sin—but, if we are Christians at all, there will be a real separation from these in the inmost heart of our hearts, and the germ of entire deliverance from them all will be in us.

This day needs that truth to be strongly urged. The whole meaning of the death of Christ is not reached when it is regarded as the great propitiation for our sins. Is it the pattern for our lives? has it drawn us away from our love of the world, from our sinful self, from the temptations to sin, from cowering before duties which we hate but dare not neglect? has it changed the current of our lives, and lifted us into a new region where we find new interests, loves and aims, before which the twinkling lights, which once were stars to us, pale their ineffectual fires? If so, then, just in as much as it is so, and not one hair's breadth the more, may we call ourselves Christians. If not, it is of no use for us to talk about looking to the cross as the source of our salvation. Such a look, if it be true and genuine, will certainly change all a man's tastes, habits, aspirations, and relationships. If we know nothing of dying with Christ, it is to be feared we know as little of Christ's dying for us.

This great fact of the Christian's death with Christ comes into view here mainly as pointing the contradiction between the Christian's position, and his subjection to the prescriptions and prohibitions of a religion which consists chiefly in petty rules about conduct. We are "dead" says Paul, "to the rudiments of the world,"—a phrase which we have already heard in verse 8 of this chapter, where we found its meaning to be "precepts of an elementary character, fit for babes, not for men in Christ, and moving principally in the region of the material." It implies a condemnation of all such regulation religion on the two grounds, that it is an anachronism, seeking to perpetuate an earlier stage which has been left behind, and that it has to do with the outsides of things, with the material and visible only. To such rudiments we are dead with Christ. Then, queries Paul, with irresistible triumphant question—why, in the name of consistency, "do you subject yourself to ordinances" (of which we have already heard in verse 14 of the chapter) such as "handle not, nor taste, nor touch?" These three prohibitions are not Paul's, but are quoted by him as specimens of the kind of rules and regulations which he is protesting against. The ascetic teachers kept on vehemently reiterating their prohibitions, and as the correct rendering of the words shows, with a constantly increasing intolerance. "Handle not" is a less rigid prohibition than "touch not." The first says, Do not lay hold of; the last Do not even touch with the tip of your finger. So asceticism, like many another tendency and habit, grows by indulgence, and demands abstinence ever more rigid and separation ever more complete. And the whole thing is out of date, and a misapprehension of the genius of Christianity. Man's work in religion is ever to confine it to the surface, to throw it outward and make it a mere round of things done and things abstained from. Christ's work in religion is to drive it inwards, and to focus all its energy on "the hidden man of the heart," knowing that if that be right, the visible will come right. It is waste labour to try to stick figs on the prickles of a thorn bush—as is the tree, so will be the fruit. There are plenty of pedants and martinets in religion as well as on the parade ground. There must be so many buttons on the uniform, and the shoulder belts must be pipe-clayed, and the rifles on the shoulders sloped at just such an angle—and then all will be right. Perhaps so. Disciplined courage is better than courage undisciplined. But there is much danger of all the attention being given to drill, and then, when the parade ground is exchanged for the battle-field, disaster comes because there is plenty of etiquette and no dash. Men's lives are pestered out of them by a religion which tries to tie them down with as many tiny threads as those with which the Liliputians fastened down Gulliver. But Christianity in its true and highest forms is not a religion of prescriptions but of principles. It does not keep perpetually dinning a set of petty commandments and prohibitions into our ears. Its language is not a continual "Do this, forbear from that,"—but "Love, and thou fulfillest the law." It works from the centre outwards to the circumference; first making clean the inside of the platter, and so ensuring that the outside shall be clean also. The error with which Paul fought, and which perpetually crops up anew, having its roots deep in human nature, begins with the circumference and wastes effort in burnishing the outside.

The parenthesis which follows in the text, "all which things are to perish with the using," contains an incidental remark intended to show the mistake of attaching such importance to regulations about diet and the like, from the consideration of the perishableness of these meats and drinks about which so much was said by the false teachers. "They are all destined for corruption, for physical decomposition—in the very act of consumption." You cannot use them without using them up. They are destroyed in the very moment of being used. Is it fitting for men who have died with Christ to this fleeting world, to make so much of its perishable things?

May we not widen this thought beyond its specific application here, and say that death with Christ to the world should deliver us from the temptation of making much of the things which perish with the using, whether that temptation is presented in the form of attaching exaggerated religious importance to ascetic abstinence from them or in that of exaggerated regard and unbridled use of them? Asceticism and Sybaritic luxury have in common an over-estimate of the importance of the material things. The one is the other turned inside out. Dives in his purple and fine linen, and the ascetic in his hair shirt, both make too much of "what they shall put on." The one with his feasts and the other with his fasts both think too much of what they shall eat and drink. A man who lives on high with his Lord puts all these things in their right place. There are things which do *not* perish with the using, but grow with use, like the five loaves in Christ's hands. Truth, love, holiness, all Christlike graces and virtues increase with exercise, and the more we feed on the bread which comes down from heaven, the more shall we have for our own nourishment and for our brother's need. There is a treasure which faileth not, bags which wax not old, the durable riches and undecaying possessions of the soul that lives on Christ and grows like Him. These let us seek after; for if our religion be worth anything at all, it should carry us past all the fleeting wealth of earth straight into the heart of things, and give us for our portion that God whom we can never exhaust, nor outgrow, but possess the more as we use His sweetness for the solace, and His all-sufficient Being for the good, of our souls.

The final inconsistency between the Christian position and the practical errors in question is glanced at in the words "after the commandments and doctrines of men," which refer, of course, to the ordinances of which Paul is speaking. The expression is a quotation from Isaiah's (xxix. 13) denunciation of the Pharisees of his day, and as used here seems to suggest that our Lord's great discourse on the worthlessness of the Jewish punctilios about meats and drinks was in the Apostle's mind, since the same words of Isaiah occur there in a similar connection. It is not fitting that we, who are withdrawn from dependence on the outward visible order of things by our union with Christ in His death, should be under the authority of men. Here is the true democracy of the Christian society. "Ye were redeemed with a price. Be not the servants of men." Our union to Jesus Christ is a union of absolute authority and utter submission. We all have access to the one source of illumination, and we are bound to take our orders from the one Master. The protest against the imposition of human authority on the Christian soul is made not in the interests of self-will, but from reverence to the only voice that has the right to give autocratic commands and to receive unquestioning obedience. We are free in proportion as we are dead to the world with Christ. We are free from men not that we may please ourselves, but that we may please Him. "Hold your peace, I want to hear what my Master has to command me," is the language of the Christian freedman, who is free that he may serve, and because he serves.

II. We have to consider one great purpose of all teaching and external worship, by its power in attaining which any system is to be tried.

"Which things have indeed a show of wisdom in will-worship, and humility, and severity to the body, *but are* not of any value against the indulgence of the flesh." Here is the conclusion of the whole matter, the parting summary of the indictment against the whole irritating tangle of restrictions and prescriptions. From a moral point of view it is worthless, as having no coercive power over "the flesh." Therein lies its conclusive condemnation, for if religious observances do not help a man to subdue his sinful self, what, in the name of common sense, is the use of them?

The Apostle knows very well that the system which he was opposing had much which commended it to people, especially to those who did not look very deep. It had a "show of wisdom" very fascinating on a superficial glance, and that in three points, all of which caught the vulgar eye, and all of which turned into the opposite on closer examination.

It has the look of being exceeding devotion and zealous worship. These teachers with their abundant forms impose upon the popular imagination, as if they were altogether given up to devout contemplation and prayer. But if one looks a little more closely at them, one sees that their devotion is the indulgence of their own will and not surrender to God's. They are not worshipping Him as He has appointed, but as they have themselves chosen, and as they are rendering services which He has not required, they are in a very true sense worshipping their own wills, and not God at all. By "will-worship" seems to be meant self-imposed forms of religious service which are the outcome not of obedience, nor of the instincts of a devout heart, but of a man's own will. And the Apostle implies that such supererogatory and volunteered worship is no worship. Whether offered in a cathedral or a barn, whether the worshipper wear a cope or a fustian jacket, such service is not accepted. A prayer which is but the expression of the worshipper's own will, instead of being "not my will but Thine be done," reaches no higher than the lips that utter it. If we are subtly and half unconsciously obeying self even while we seem to be bowing before God; if we are seeming to pray, and are all the while burning incense to ourselves, instead of being drawn out of ourselves by the beauty and the glory of the God towards whom our spirits yearn, then our devotion is a mask, and our prayers will be dispersed in empty air.

The deceptive appearance of wisdom in these teachers and their doctrines is further manifest in the humility which felt so profoundly the gulf between man and God that it was fain to fill the void with its fantastic creations of angel mediators. Humility is a good thing, and it looked very humble to say, We cannot suppose that such insignificant flesh-encompassed creatures as we can come into contact and fellowship with God; but it was a great deal more humble to take God at His word, and to let Him lay down the possibilities and conditions of intercourse, and to tread the way of approach to Him which He has appointed. If a great king were to say to all the beggars and ragged losels of his capital, Come to the palace to-morrow; which would be the humbler, he who went, rags and leprosy and all, or he who hung back because he was so keenly conscious of his squalor? God says to men, "Come to My arms through My Son. Never mind the dirt, come." Which is the humbler: he who takes God at His word, and runs to hide his face on his Father's breast, having access to Him through Christ the Way, or he who will not venture near till he has found some other mediators besides Christ? A humility so profound that it cannot think God's promise and Christ's mediation enough for it, has gone so far West that it has reached the East, and from humility has become pride.

Further, this system has a show of wisdom in "severity to the body." Any asceticism is a great deal more to men's taste than abandoning self. They will rather stick hooks in their backs and do the "swinging poojah," than give up their sins or yield up their wills. It is easier to travel the whole distance from Cape Comorin to the shrine of Juggernaut, measuring every foot of it by the body laid prostrate in the dust, than to surrender the heart to the love of God. In the same manner the milder forms of putting oneself to pain, hair shirts, scourgings, abstinence from pleasant things with the notion that thereby merit is acquired, or sin atoned for, have a deep root in human nature, and hence "a show of wisdom." It is strange, and yet not strange, that people should think that, somehow or other, they recommend themselves to God by making themselves uncomfortable, but so it is that religion presents itself to many minds mainly as a system of restrictions and injunctions which forbids the agreeable and commands the unpleasant. So does our poor human nature vulgarise and travesty Christ's solemn command to deny ourselves and take up our cross after Him.

The conclusive condemnation of all the crowd of punctilious restrictions of which the Apostle has been speaking lies in the fact that, however they may correspond to men's mistaken notions, and so seem to be the dictate of wisdom, they "are not of any value against the indulgence of the flesh." This is one great end of all moral and spiritual discipline, and if practical regulations do not tend to secure it, they are worthless.

Of course by "flesh" here we are to understand, as usually in the Pauline Epistles, not merely the body but the whole unregenerate personality, the entire unrenewed self that thinks and feels and wills and desires apart from God. To indulge and satisfy it is to die, to slay and suppress it is to live. All these "ordinances" with which the heretical teachers were pestering the Colossians, have no power, Paul thinks, to keep that self down, and therefore they seem to him so much rubbish. He thus lifts the whole question up to a higher level and implies a standard for judging much formal outward Christianity which would make very short work of it.

A man may be keeping the whole round of them and seven devils may be in his heart. They distinctly tend to foster some of the "works of the flesh," such as self-righteousness, uncharitableness, censoriousness, and they as distinctly altogether fail to subdue any of them. A man may stand on a pillar like Simeon Stylites for years, and be none the better. Historically, the ascetic tendency has not been associated with the highest types of real saintliness except by accident, and has never been their productive cause. The bones rot as surely inside the sepulchre though the whitewash on its dome be ever so thick.

So the world and the flesh are very willing that Christianity should shrivel into a religion of prohibitions and ceremonials, because all manner of vices and meannesses may thrive and breed under these, like scorpions under stones. There is only one thing that will put the collar on the neck of the animal within us, and that is the power of the indwelling Christ. The evil that is in us all is too strong for every other fetter. Its cry to all these "commandments and ordinances of men" is, "Jesus I know, and Paul I know, but who are ye?" Not in obedience to such, but in the reception into our spirits of His own life, is our power of victory over self. "This I say, Walk in the Spirit, and ye shall not fulfil the lusts of the flesh."

XVII
THE PRESENT CHRISTIAN LIFE, A RISEN LIFE

"If then ye were raised together with Christ, seek the things that are above, where Christ is, seated on the right hand of God. Set your mind on the things that are above, not on the things that are upon the earth. For ye died, and your life is hid with Christ in God. When Christ, *Who is* our life, shall be manifested, then shall ye also with Him be manifested in glory."—Col. iii. 1–4 (Rev. Ver.).

We have now done with controversy. We hear no more about heretical teachers. The Apostle has cut his way through the tangled thickets of error, and has said his say as to the positive truths with which he would hew them down. For the remainder of the letter, we have principally plain practical exhortations, and a number of interesting personal details.

The paragraph which we have now to consider is the transition from the controversial to the ethical portion of the Epistle. It touches the former by its first words, "If ye then were raised together with Christ," which correspond in form and refer in meaning to the beginning of the previous paragraph, "If ye died with Christ." It touches the latter because it embodies the broad general precept, "Seek the things that are above," of which the following practical directions are but varying applications in different spheres of duty.

In considering these words we must begin by endeavouring to put clearly their connection and substance. As they flew from Paul's eager lips, motive and precept, symbol and fact, the present and future are blended together. It may conduce to clearness if we try to part these elements.

There are here two similar exhortations, side by side. "Seek the things that are above," and "Set your mind on the things that are above." The first is *preceded*, and the second is *followed* by its reason. So the two laws of conduct are, as it were, enclosed like a kernel in its shell, or a jewel in a gold setting, by encompassing motives. These considerations, in which the commandment are imbedded, are the double thought of union with Christ in His resurrection, and in His death, and as consequent thereon, participation in His present hidden life, and in His future glorious manifestation. So we have here the present budding life of the Christian in union with the risen, hidden Christ; the future consummate flower of the Christian life in union with the glorious manifested Christ; and the practical aim and direction which alone is consistent with either bud or flower.

I. The present budding life of the Christian in union with the risen, hidden Christ.

Two aspects of this life are set forth in verses 1 and 3—"raised with Christ," and "ye died, and your life is hid with Christ." A still profounder thought lies in the words of verse 4, "Christ *is* our life."

We have seen in former parts of this Epistle that Paul believed that, when a man puts His faith in Jesus Christ, he is joined to Him in such a way that he is separated from his former self and dead to the world. That great change may be considered either with reference to what the man has ceased to be, or with reference to what he becomes. In the one aspect, it is a death; in the other, it is a resurrection. It depends on the point of view whether a semicircle seems convex or concave. The two thoughts express substantially the same fact. That great change was brought about in these Colossian Christians, at a definite time, as the language shows; and by a definite means—namely, by union with Christ through faith, which grasps His death and resurrection as at once the ground of salvation, the pattern for life, and the prophecy of glory. So then, the great truths here are these; the impartation of life by union with Christ, which life is truly a resurrection life, and is, moreover, hidden with Christ in God.

Union with Christ by faith is the condition of a real communication of life. "In Him was life," says John's Gospel, meaning thereby to assert, in the language of our Epistle, that "in Him were all things created, and in Him all things consist." Life in all its forms is dependent on union in varying manner with the Divine, and upheld only by His continual energy. The creature must touch God or perish. Of that energy the Uncreated Word of God is the channel—"with Thee is the fountain of life." As the life of the body, so the higher self-conscious life of the thinking, feeling, striving soul, is also fed and kept alight by the perpetual operation of a higher Divine energy, imparted in like manner by the Divine Word. Therefore, with deep truth, the psalm just quoted, goes on to say, "In Thy light shall we see light"—and therefore, too, John's Gospel continues: "And the life was the light of men."

But there is a still higher plane on which life may be manifested, and nobler energies which may accompany it. The body may live, and mind and heart be dead. Therefore Scripture speaks of a threefold life: that of the animal nature, that of the intellectual and emotional nature, and that of the spirit, which lives when it is conscious of God, and touches Him by aspiration, hope, and love. This is the loftiest life. Without it, a man is dead while he lives. With it, he lives though he dies. And like the others, it depends on union with the Divine life as it is stored in Jesus Christ—but in this case, the union is a conscious union by faith. If I trust to Him, and am thereby holding firmly by Him, my union with Him is so real, that, in the measure of my faith, His fulness passes over into my emptiness, His righteousness into my sinfulness, His life into my death, as surely as the electric shock thrills my nerves when I grasp the poles of the battery.

No man can breathe into another's nostrils the breath of life. But Christ can and does breathe His life into us; and this true miracle of a communication of spiritual life takes place in every man who humbly trusts himself to Him. So the question comes home to each of us—am I living by my union with Christ? do I draw from Him that better being which He is longing to pour into my withered, dead spirit? It is not enough to live the animal life; the more it is fed, the more are the higher lives starved and dwindled. It is not enough to live the life of intellect and feeling. That may be in brightest, keenest exercise, and yet we—our best selves—may be dead—separated from God in Christ, and therefore dead—and all our activity may be but as a galvanic twitching of the muscles in a corpse. Is Christ our life, its source, its strength, its aim, its motive? Do we live in Him, by Him, with Him, for Him? If not, we are dead while we live.

This life from Christ is a resurrection life. "The power of Christ's resurrection" is threefold—as a seal of His mission and Messiahship, "declared to be the Son of God, by His resurrection from the dead;" as a prophecy and pledge of ours, "now is Christ risen from the dead, and become the first-fruits of them that slept;" and as a symbol and pattern of our new life of Christian consecration, "likewise reckon ye also yourselves to be indeed dead unto sin." This last use of the resurrection of Christ is a plain witness of the firm, universal and uncontested belief in the historical fact, throughout the Churches which Paul addressed. The fact must have been long familiar and known as undoubted, before it could have been thus moulded into a symbol. But, passing from that, consider that our union to Christ produces a moral and spiritual change analogous to His resurrection. After all, it is the moral and not the mystical side which is the main thing in Paul's use of this thought. He would insist, that all true Christianity operates a death to the old self, to sin and to the whole present order of things, and endows a man with new tastes, desires and capacities, like a resurrection to a new being. These heathen converts—picked from the filthy cesspools in which many of them had been living, and set on a pure path, with the astounding light of a Divine love flooding it, and a bright hope painted on the infinite blackness ahead—had surely passed into a new life.

Many a man in this day, long familiar with Christian teaching, has found himself made over again in mature life, when his heart has grasped Christ. Drunkards, profligates, outcasts, have found it life from the dead; and even where there has not been such complete visible revolution as in them, there has been such deep-seated central alteration that it is no exaggeration to call it resurrection. The plain fact is that real Christianity in a man will produce in him a radical moral change. If our religion does not do that in us, it is nothing. Ceremonial and doctrine are but means to an end—making us better men. The highest purpose of Christ's work, for which He both "died and rose and revived," is to change us into the likeness of His own beauty of perfect purity. That risen life is no mere exaggeration of mystical rhetoric, but an imperative demand of the highest morality, and the plain issue of it is: "Let not sin therefore reign in your mortal body." Do I say that I am a Christian? The test by which my claim must be tried is the likeness of my life here to Him who has died unto sin, and liveth unto God.

But the believing soul is risen with Christ also, inasmuch as our union with Him makes us partakers of His resurrection as our victory over death. The water in the reservoir and in the fountain is the same; the sunbeam in the chamber and in the sky are one. The life which flows into our spirits from Christ is a life that has conquered death, and makes us victors in that last conflict, even though we have to go down into the darkness. If Christ live in us, we can never die. "It is not possible that *we* should be holden of *it*." The bands which He broke can never be fastened on our limbs. The gates of death were so warped and the locks so spoiled when He burst them asunder, that they can never be closed again. There are many arguments for a future life beyond the grave, but there is only one proof of it—the Resurrection of Jesus Christ. So, trusting in Him, and with our souls bound in the bundle of life with our Lord the King, we can cherish quiet thankfulness of heart, and bless the God and Father of our Lord who hath begotten us again into a lively hope by the resurrection of Jesus Christ from the dead.

This risen life is a hidden life. Its roots are in Him. He has passed in His ascension into the light which is inaccessible, and is hidden in its blaze, bearing with Him our life, concealed there with Him in God. Faith stands gazing into heaven, as the cloud, the visible manifestation from of old of the Divine presence, hides Him from sight, and turns away feeling that the best part of its true self is gone with Him. So here Paul points his finger upwards to where "Christ is, sitting at the right hand of God," and says—We are here in outward seeming, but our true life is there, if we are His. And what majestic, pregnant words these are! How full, and yet how empty for a prurient curiosity, and how reverently reticent even while they are triumphantly confident! How gently they suggest repose—deep and unbroken, and yet full of active energy! For if the attitude imply rest, the locality—"at the right hand of God"—expresses not only the most intimate approach to, but also the wielding of the Divine omnipotence. What is the right hand of God but the activity of His power? and what less can be ascribed to Christ here, than His being enthroned in closest union with the Father, exercising Divine dominion, and putting forth Divine power. No doubt the ascended and glorified bodily manhood of Jesus Christ has a local habitation, but the old psalm might teach us that wherever space is, even there "Thy right hand upholds," and there is our ascended Lord, sitting as in deepest rest, but working all the work of God. And it is just because He is at the right hand of God that He is hid. The light hides. He has been lost to sight in the glory.

He has gone in thither, bearing with Him the true source and root of our lives into the secret place of the Most High. Therefore we no longer belong to this visible order of things in the midst of which we tarry for a while. The true spring that feeds our lives lies deep beneath all the surface waters. These may dry up, but it will flow. These may be muddied with rain, but it will be limpid as ever. The things seen do not go deep enough to touch our real life. They are but as the winds that fret, and the currents that sway the surface and shallower levels of the ocean, while the great depths are still. The circumference is all a whirl; the centre is at rest.

Nor need we leave out of sight, though it be not the main thought here, that the Christian life is hidden, inasmuch as here on earth action ever falls short of thought, and the love and faith by which a good man lives can never be fully revealed in his conduct and character. You cannot carry electricity from the generator to the point where it is to work without losing two-thirds of it by the way. Neither word nor deed can adequately set forth a soul; and the profounder and nobler the emotion, the more inadequate are the narrow gates of tongue and hand to give it passage. The deepest love can often only "love and be silent." So, while every man is truly a mystery to his neighbour, a life which is rooted in Christ is more mysterious to the ordinary eye than any other. It is fed by hidden manna. It is replenished from a hidden source. It is guided by other than the world's motives, and follows unseen aims. "Therefore the world knoweth us not, because it knew Him not."

II. We have the future consummate flower of the Christian life in union with the manifested, glorious Christ.

The future personal manifestation of Jesus Christ in visible glory is, in the teaching of all the New Testament writers, the last stage in the series of His Divine human conditions. As surely as the Incarnation led to the cross, and the cross to the empty grave, and the empty grave to the throne, so surely does the throne lead to the coming again in glory. And as with Christ, so with His servants, the manifestation in glory is the certain end of all the preceding, as surely as the flower is of the tiny green leaves that peep above the frost-bound earth in bleak March days. Nothing in that future, however glorious and wonderful, but has its germ and vital beginning in our union with Christ here by humble faith. The great hopes which we may cherish are gathered up here into these words—"shall be manifested with Him." That is far more than was conveyed by the old translation—"shall appear." The roots of our being shall be disclosed, for He shall come, "and every eye shall see Him." We shall be seen for what we are. The outward life shall correspond to the inward. The faith and love which often struggled in vain for expression and were thwarted by the obstinate flesh, as a sculptor trying to embody his dream might be by a block of marble with many a flaw and speck, shall then be able to reveal themselves completely. Whatever is in the heart shall be fully visible in the life. Stammering words and imperfect deeds shall vex us no more. "His name shall be in their foreheads"—no longer only written in fleshly tables of the heart and partially visible in the character, but stamped legibly and completely on life and nature. They shall walk in the light, and so shall be seen of all. Here the truest followers of Christ shine like an intermittent star, seen through mist and driving cloud: "Then shall the righteous *blaze forth* like the sun in the kingdom of My Father."

But this is not all. The manifestation is to be "with Him." The union which was here effected by faith, and marred by many an interposing obstacle of sin and selfishness, of flesh and sense, is to be perfected then. No film of separation is any more to break its completeness. Here we often lose our hold of Him amidst the distractions of work, even when done for His sake; and our life is at best but an imperfect compromise between contemplation and action; but then, according to that great saying, "His servants shall serve Him, and see His face," the utmost activity of consecrated service, though it be far more intense and on a nobler scale than anything here, will not interfere with the fixed gaze on His countenance. We shall serve like Martha, and yet never remove from sitting with Mary, rapt and blessed at His feet.

This is the one thought of that solemn future worth cherishing. Other hopes may feed sentiment, and be precious sometimes to aching hearts. A reverent longing or an irreverent curiosity, may seek to discern something more in the far-off light. But it is enough for the heart to know that "we shall ever be with the Lord;" and the more we have that one hope in its solitary grandeur, the better. We shall be with Him in "in glory." That is the climax of all that Paul would have us hope. "Glory" is the splendour and light of the self-revealing God. In the heart of the blaze stands Christ; the bright cloud enwraps Him, as it did on the mountain of transfiguration, and into the dazzling radiance His disciples will pass as His companions did then, nor "fear as they enter into the cloud." They walk unshrinking in that beneficent fire, because with them is one like unto a Son of man, through whom they dwell, as in their own calm home, amidst "the everlasting burning," which shall not destroy them, but kindle them into the likeness of its own flashing glory.

Then shall the life which here was but in bud, often unkindly nipt and struggling, burst into the consummate beauty of the perfect flower "which fadeth not away."

III. We have the practical aim and direction which alone is consistent with either stage of the Christian life.

Two injunctions are based upon these considerations—"seek," and "set your mind upon," the things that are above. The one points to the outward life of effort and aim; the other to the inward life of thought and longing. Let the things above then, be the constant mark at which you aim. There is a vast realm of real existence of which your risen Lord is the centre and the life. Make it the point to which you strive. That will not lead to despising earth and nearer objects. These, so far as they are really good and worthy, stand right in the line of direction which our efforts will take if we are seeking the things that are above, and may all be stages on our journey Christwards. The lower objects are best secured by those who live for the higher. No man is so well able to do the smallest duties here, or to bear the passing troubles of this world of illusion and change, or to wring the last drop of sweetness out of swiftly fleeting joys, as he to whom everything on earth is dwarfed by the eternity beyond, as some hut beside a palace, and is great because it is like a little window a foot square through which infinite depths of sky with all their stars shine in upon him. The true meaning and greatness of the present is that it is the vestibule of the august future. The staircase leading to the presence chamber of the king may be of poor deal, narrow, crooked, and stowed away in a dark turret, but it has dignity by reason of that to which it gives access. So let our aims pass through the earthly and find in them helps to the things that are above. We should not fire all our bullets at the short range. Seek ye first the kingdom of God—the things which are above.

"Set your mind on" these things, says the Apostle further. Let them occupy mind and heart—and this in order that we may seek them. The direction of the aims will follow the set and current of the thoughts. "As a man thinketh in his heart, so is he." How can we be shaping our efforts to reach a good which we have not clearly before our imaginations as desirable? How should the life of so many professing Christians be other than a lame creeping along the low levels of earth, seeing that so seldom do they look up to "see the King in His beauty and the land that is very far off"? John Bunyan's "man with the muckrake" grubbed away so eagerly among the rubbish, because he never lifted his eyes to the crown that hung above his head. In many a silent, solitary hour of contemplation, with the world shut out and Christ brought very near, we must find the counterpoise to the pressure of earthly aims, or our efforts after the things that are above will be feeble and broken. Life goes at such a pace to-day, and the present is so exacting with most of us, that quiet meditation is, I fear me, almost out of fashion with Christian people. We must become more familiar with the secret place of the most High, and more often enter into our chambers and shut our doors about us, if in the bustle of our busy days we are to aim truly and strongly at the only object which saves life from being a waste and a sin, a madness and a misery — "the things which are above, where Christ is."

"Where Christ is." Yes, that is the only thought which gives definiteness and solidity to that else vague and nebulous unseen universe; the only thought which draws our affections thither. Without Him, there is no footing for us there. Rolling mists of doubt and dim hopes warring with fears, strangeness and terrors wrap it all. But if He be there, it becomes a home for our hearts. "I go to prepare a place for you" — a place where desire and thought may walk unterrified and undoubting even now, and where we ourselves may abide when our time comes, nor shrink from the light nor be oppressed by the glory.

> "My knowledge of that life is small,
> The eye of faith is dim,
> But 'tis enough that Christ knows all,
> And I shall be with Him."

Into that solemn world we shall all pass. We can choose whether we shall go to it as to our long-sought home, to find in it Him who is our life; or whether we shall go reluctant and afraid, leaving all for which we have cared, and going to Him whom we have neglected and that which we have feared. Christ will be manifested, and we shall see Him. We can choose whether it will be to us the joy of beholding the soul of our soul, the friend long-loved when dimly seen from afar; or whether it shall be the vision of a face that will stiffen us to stone and stab us with its light. We must make our choice. If we give our hearts to Him, and by faith unite ourselves with Him, then, "when He shall appear, we shall have boldness, and not be ashamed before Him at His coming."

XVIII
SLAYING SELF THE FOUNDATION PRECEPT OF PRACTICAL CHRISTIANITY

"Mortify therefore your members which are upon the earth; fornication, uncleanness, passion, evil desire, and covetousness, the which is idolatry; for which things' sake cometh the wrath of God upon the sons of disobedience; in the which ye also walked aforetime, when ye lived in these things. But now put ye also away all these; anger, wrath, malice, railing, shameful speaking out of your mouth: lie not one to another." —Col. iii. 5–9 (Rev. Ver.).

"Mortify *therefore*" —wherefore? The previous words give the reason. Because "ye died" with Christ, and because ye "were raised together with Him." In other words, the plainest, homeliest moral teaching of this Epistle, such as that which immediately follows, is built upon its "mystical" theology. Paul thinks that the deep things which he has been saying about union with Christ in His death and resurrection have the most intimate connection with common life. These profound truths have the keenest edge, and are as a sacrificial knife, to slay the life of self. Creed is meant to tell on conduct. Character is the last outcome and test of doctrine. But too many people deal with their theological beliefs as they do with their hassocks and prayer books and hymn books in their pews—use them for formal worship once a week, and leave them for the dust to settle on them till Sunday comes round again. So it is very necessary to put the practical inferences very plainly, to reiterate the most commonplace and threadbare precepts as the issue of the most recondite teaching, and to bind the burden of duty on men's backs with the cords of principles and doctrines.

Accordingly the section of the Epistle which deals with Christian character now begins, and this "therefore" knits the two halves together. That word protests against opposite errors. On the one hand, some good people are to be found impatient of exhortations to duties, and ready to say, Preach the gospel, and the duties will spring up spontaneously where it is received; on the other hand, some people are to be found who see no connection between the practice of common morality and the belief of Christian truths, and are ready to say, Put away your theology; it is useless lumber, the machine will work as well without it. But Paul believed that the firmest basis for moral teaching and the most powerful motive for moral conduct is "the truth as it is in Jesus."

I. We have here put very plainly the paradox of continual self-slaying as the all-embracing duty of a Christian.

It is a pity that the R. V. has retained "mortify" here, as that Latinized word says to an ordinary reader much less than is meant, and hides the allusion to the preceding contest. The marginal alternative "make dead" is, to say the least, not idiomatic English. The suggestion of the American revisers, which is printed at the end of the R. V., "put to death," is much better, and perhaps a single word, such as "slay" or "kill" might have been better still.

"Slay your members which are upon the earth." It is a vehement and paradoxical injunction, though it be but the echo of still more solemn and stringent words—"pluck it out, cut it off, and cast it from thee." The possibility of misunderstanding it and bringing it down to the level of that spurious asceticism and "severity to the body" against which he has just been thundering, seems to occur to the Apostle, and therefore he hastens to explain that he does not mean the maiming of selves, or hacking away limbs, but the slaying of the passions and desires which root themselves in our bodily constitution. The eager haste of the explanation destroys the congruity of the sentence, but he does not mind that. And then follows a grim catalogue of the evil-doers on whom sentence of death is passed.

Before dealing with that list, two points of some importance may be observed. The first is that the practical exhortations of this letter begin with this command to put off certain characteristics which are assumed to belong to the Colossian Christians in their natural state, and that only afterwards comes the precept to put on (ver. 12) the fairer robes of Christlike purity, clasped about by the girdle of perfectness. That is to say, Paul's anthropology regards men as wrong and having to get right. A great deal of the moral teaching which is outside of Christianity, and which does not sufficiently recognise that the first thing to be done is to cure and alter, but talks as if men were, on the whole, rather inclined to be good, is for that very reason perfectly useless. Its fine precepts and lofty sentiments go clean over people's heads, and are ludicrously inappropriate to the facts of the case. The serpent has twined itself round my limbs, and unless you can give me a knife, sharp and strong enough to cut its loathsome coils asunder, it is cruel to bid me walk. All men on the face of the earth need, for moral progress, to be shown and helped first how *not* to be what they have been, and only after that is it of the slightest use to tell them what they ought to be. The only thing that reaches the universal need is a power that will make us different from what we are. If we are to grow into goodness and beauty, we must begin by a complete reversal of tastes and tendencies. The thing we want first is not progress, the going on in the direction in which our faces are turned, but a power which can lay a mastering hand upon our shoulders, turn us right round, and make us go in the way opposite to that. Culture, the development of what is in us in germ, is not the beginning of good husbandry on human nature as it is. The thorns have to be stubbed up first, and the poisonous seeds sifted out, and new soil laid down, and then culture will bring forth something better than wild grapes. First—"mortify;" then—"put on."

Another point to be carefully noted is that, according to the Apostle's teaching, the root and beginning of all such slaying of the evil which is in us all, lies in our being dead with Christ to the world. In the former chapter we found that the Apostle's final condemnation of the false asceticism which was beginning to infect the Colossian Church, was that it was of no value as a counteractive of fleshly indulgence. But here he proclaims that what asceticism could not do, in that it was weak through the flesh, union with Jesus Christ in His death and risen life will do; it will subdue sin in the flesh. That slaying here enjoined as fundamental to all Christian holiness, is but the working out in life and character of the revolution in the inmost self which has been effected, if by faith we are joined to the living Lord, who was dead and is alive for evermore.

There must, however, be a very vigorous act of personal determination if the power of that union is to be manifested in us. The act of "slaying" can never be pleasant or easy. The vehemence of the command and the form of the metaphor express the strenuousness of the effort and the painfulness of the process, in the same way as Paul's other saying, "crucify the flesh," does. Suppose a man working at some machine. His fingers get drawn between the rollers or caught in some belting. Another minute and he will be flattened to a shapeless bloody mass. He catches up an axe lying by and with his own arm hacks off his own hand at the wrist. It takes some nerve to do that. It is not easy nor pleasant, but it is the only alternative to a horrible death. I know of no stimulus that will string a man up to the analogous spiritual act here enjoined, and enjoined by conscience also, except participation in the death of Christ and in the resulting life.

"Slay your members which are upon the earth" means tears and blood and more than blood. It is easier far to cut off the hand, which after all is not me, than to sacrifice passions and desires which, though they be my worst self, are myself. It is useless to blink the fact that the only road to holiness is through self-suppression, self-annihilation; and nothing can make that easy and pleasant. True, the paths of religion are ways of pleasantness and paths of peace, but they are steep, and climbing is never easy. The upper air is bracing and exhilarating indeed, but trying to lungs accustomed to the low levels. Religion is delightsome, but self-denial is always against the grain of the self which is denied, and there is no religion without it. Holiness is not to be won in a moment. It is not a matter of consciousness, possessed when we know that we possess it. But it has to be attained by effort. The way to heaven is not by "the primrose path." That leads to "the everlasting bonfire." For ever it remains true that men *obtain* forgiveness and eternal life as a gift for which the only requisite is faith, but they *achieve* holiness, which is the permeating of their characters with that eternal life, by patient, believing, continuous effort. An essential part of that effort is directed towards the conquest and casting out of the old self in its earthward-looking lusts and passions. The love of Jesus Christ and the indwelling of His renewing spirit make that conquest possible, by supplying an all-constraining motive and an all-conquering power. But even they do not make it easy, nor deaden the flesh to the cut of the sacrificial knife.

II. We have here a grim catalogue of the condemned to death.

The Apostle stands like a jailer at the prison door, with the fatal roll in his hand, and reads out the names of the evil doers for whom the tumbril waits to carry them to the guillotine. It is an ugly list but we need plain speaking that there may be no mistake as to the identity of the culprits. He enumerates evils which honeycombed society with rottenness then, and are rampant now. The series recounts various forms of evil love, and is so arranged as that it starts with the coarse, gross act, and goes on to more subtle and inward forms. It goes up the stream as it were, to the fountain head, passing inward from deed to desire. First stands "fornication," which covers the whole ground of immoral sexual relations, then "all uncleanness," which embraces every manifestation in word or look or deed of the impure spirit, and so is at once wider and subtler than the gross physical act. Then follow "passion" and "evil desire"; the sources of the evil deeds. These again are at once more inward and more general than the preceding. They include not only the lusts and longings which give rise to the special sins just denounced, but all forms of hungry appetite and desire after "the things that are upon the earth." If we are to try to draw a distinction between the two, probably "passion" is somewhat less wide than "desire," and the former represents the evil emotion as an affection which the mind suffers, while the latter represents it as a longing which it actively puts forth. The "lusts of the flesh" are in the one aspect kindled by outward temptations which come with terrible force and carry men captive, acting almost irresistibly on the animal nature. In the other aspect they are excited by the voluntary action of the man himself. In the one the evil comes into the heart; in the other the heart goes out to the evil.

Then follows covetousness. The juxtaposition of that vice with the grosser forms of sensuality is profoundly significant. It is closely allied with these. It has the same root, and is but another form of evil desire going out to the "things which are on the earth." The ordinary worldly nature flies for solace either to the pleasures of appetite or to the passion of acquiring. And not only are they closely connected in root, but covetousness often follows lust in the history of a life just as it does in this catalogue. When the former evil spirit loses its hold, the latter often takes its place. How many respectable middle-aged gentlemen are now mainly devoted to making money, whose youth was foul with sensual indulgence? When that palled, this came to titillate the jaded desires with a new form of gratification. Covetousness is "promoted *vice*, lust superannuated."

A reason for this warning against covetousness is appended, "inasmuch as (for such is the force of the word rendered 'the which') it is idolatry." If we say of anything, no matter what, "If I have only enough of this, I shall be satisfied; it is my real aim, my sufficient good," that thing is a god to me, and my real worship is paid to it, whatever may be my nominal religion. The lowest form of idolatry is the giving of supreme trust to a material thing, and making that a god. There is no lower form of fetish-worship than this, which is the real working religion to-day of thousands of Englishmen who go masquerading as Christians.

III. The exhortation is enforced by a solemn note of warning: "For which things' sake the wrath of God cometh upon the children of disobedience." Some authorities omit the words "upon the children of disobedience," which are supposed to have crept in here from the parallel passage, Eph. v. 6. But even the advocates of the omission allow that the clause has "preponderating support," and the sentence is painfully incomplete and abrupt without it. The R. V. has exercised a wise discretion in retaining it.

In the previous chapter the Apostle included "warning" in his statement of the various branches into which his Apostolic activity was divided. His duty seemed to him to embrace the plain stern setting forth of that terrible reality, the wrath of God. Here we have it urged as a reason for shaking off these evil habits.

That thought of wrath as an element in the Divine nature has become very unwelcome to this generation. The great revelation of God in Jesus Christ has taught the world His love, as it never knew it before, and knows it now by no other means. So profoundly has that truth that God is love penetrated the consciousness of the European world, that many people will not hear of the wrath of God because they think it inconsistent with His love—and sometimes reject the very gospel to which they owe their lofty conceptions of the Divine heart, because it speaks solemn words about His anger and its issues.

But surely these two thoughts of God's love and God's wrath are not inconsistent, for His wrath is His love, pained, wounded, thrown back upon itself, rejected and compelled to assume the form of aversion and to do its "strange work"—that which is not its natural operation—of punishment. When we ascribe wrath to God, we must take care of lowering the conception of it to the level of human wrath, which is shaken with passion and often tinged with malice, whereas in that affection of the Divine nature which corresponds to anger in us, there is neither passion nor wish to harm. Nor does it exclude the co-existence of love, as Paul witnesses in his Epistle to the Ephesians, in one verse declaring that "we were the children of wrath," and in the next that God "loved us with a great love even when we were dead in sins."

God would not be a holy God if it were all the same to Him whether a man were good or bad. As a matter of fact, the modern revulsion against the representation of the wrath of God is usually accompanied with weakened conceptions of His holiness, and of His moral government of the world. Instead of exalting, it degrades His love to free it from the admixture of wrath, which is like alloy with gold, giving firmness to what were else too soft for use. Such a God is not love, but impotent good nature. If there be no wrath, there is no love; if there were no love, there would be no wrath. It is more blessed and hopeful for sinful men to believe in a God who is angry with the wicked, whom yet He loves, every day, and who cannot look upon sin, than in one who does not love righteousness enough to hate iniquity, and from whose too indulgent hand the rod has dropped, to the spoiling of His children. "With the froward Thou wilt show Thyself froward." The mists of our sins intercept the gracious beams and turn the blessed sun into a ball of fire.

The wrath "*cometh.*" That majestic present tense may express either the continuous present incidence of the wrath as exemplified in the moral government of the world, in which, notwithstanding anomalies, such sins as have been enumerated drag after themselves their own punishment and are "avenged in kind," or it may be the present tense expressive of prophetic certainty, which is so sure of what shall come, that it speaks of it as already on its road. It is eminently true of those sins of lust and passion, that the men who do them reap as they have sown. How many young men come up into our great cities, innocent and strong, with a mother's kiss upon their lips, and a father's blessing hovering over their heads! They fall among bad companions in college or warehouse, and after a little while they disappear. Broken in health, tainted in body and soul, they crawl home to break their mothers' hearts—and to die. "His bones are full of the sins of his youth, which shall lie down with him in the dust." Whether in such extreme forms or no, that wrath comes even now, in plain and bitter consequences on men, and still more on women who sin in such ways.

And the present retribution may well be taken as the herald and prophet of a still more solemn manifestation of the Divine displeasure, which is already as it were on the road, has set out from the throne of God, and will certainly arrive here one day. These consequences of sin already realised serve to show the set and drift of things, and to suggest what will happen when retribution and the harvest of our present life of sowing come. The first fiery drops that fell on Lot's path as he fled from Sodom were not more surely precursors of an overwhelming rain, nor bade him flee for his life more urgently, than the present punishment of sin proclaims its sorer future punishment, and exhorts us all to come out of the storm into the refuge, even Jesus, who is ever even now "delivering us from the wrath which is" ever even now "coming" on the sons of disobedience.

IV. A further motive enforcing the main precept of self-slaying is the remembrance of a sinful past, which remembrance is at once penitent and grateful. "In the which ye also walked aforetime, when ye lived in them."

What is the difference between "walking" and "living" in these things? The two phrases seem synonymous, and might often be used indifferently; but here there is evidently a well marked diversity of meaning. The former is an expression frequent in the Pauline Epistles as well as in John's; as for instance, "to walk in love" or "in truth." That in which men walk is conceived of as an atmosphere encompassing them; or, without a metaphor, to walk in anything is to have the active life or conduct guided or occupied by it. These Colossian Christians, then, had in the past trodden that evil path, or their active life had been spent in that poisonous atmosphere— which is equivalent to saying that they had committed these sins. At what time? "When you lived in them." That does not mean merely "when your natural life was passed among them." That would be a trivial thing to say, and it would imply that their outward life now was not so passed, which would not be true. In that sense they still lived in the poisonous atmosphere. In such an age of unnameable moral corruption no man could live out of the foul stench which filled his nostrils whenever he walked abroad or opened his window. But the Apostle has just said that they were now "living in Christ," and their lives "hid with Him in God." So this phrase describes the condition which is the opposite of their present, and may be paraphrased, "When the roots of your life, tastes, affections, thoughts, desires were immersed, as in some feculent bog, in these and kindred evils." And the meaning of the whole is substantially—Your active life was occupied and guided by these sins in that past time when your inward being was knit to and nourished by them. Or to put it plainly, conduct followed and was shaped by inclinations and desires.

This retrospect enforces the main exhortation. It is meant to awaken penitence, and the thought that time enough has been wasted and incense enough offered on these foul altars. It is also meant to kindle thankfulness for the strong, loving hand which has drawn them from that pit of filth, and by both emotions to stimulate the resolute casting aside of that evil in which they once, like others, wallowed. Their joy on the one hand and their contrition on the other should lead them to discern the inconsistency of professing to be Christians and yet keeping terms with these old sins. They could not have the roots of half their lives above and of the other half down here. The gulf between the present and past of a regenerate man is too wide and deep to be bridged by flimsy compromises. "A man who is perverse in his two ways," that is, in double ways, "shall fall in one of them," as the Book of Proverbs has it. The attempt to combine incompatibles is sure to fail. It is impossible to walk firmly if one foot be down in the gutter and the other up on the curb-stone. We have to settle which level we shall choose, and then to plant both feet there.

V. We have, as conclusion, a still wider exhortation to an entire stripping off of the sins of the old state.

The whole force of the contrast and contrariety between the Colossian Christians' past and present lies in that emphatic "now." They as well as other heathen had been walking, because they had been living, in these muddy ways. But now that their life was hid with Christ in God; now that they had been made partakers of His death and resurrection, and of all the new loves and affinities which therein became theirs; now they must take heed that they bring not that dead and foul past into this bright and pure present, nor prolong winter and its frosts into the summer of the soul.

"Ye also." There is another "ye also" in the previous verse—"ye also walked," that is, you in company with other Gentiles followed a certain course of life. Here, by contrast, the expression means "you, in common with other Christians." A motive enforcing the subsequent exhortation is in it hinted rather than fully spoken. The Christians at Colossæ had belonged to a community which they have now left in order to join another. Let them behave as their company behaves. Let them keep step with their new comrades. Let them strip themselves, as their new associates do, of the uniform which they wore in that other regiment.

The metaphor of putting clothing on or off is very frequent in this Epistle. The precept here is substantially equivalent to the previous command to "slay," with the difference that the conception of vices as the garments of the soul is somewhat less vehement than that which regards them as members of the very self. "All these" are to be put off. That phrase points back to the things previously spoken of. It includes the whole of the unnamed members of the class, of which a few have been already named, and a handful more are about to be plucked like poison flowers, and suggests that there are many more as baleful growing by the side of this devil's bouquet which is next presented.

As to this second catalogue of vices, they may be summarised as, on the whole, being various forms of wicked hatred, in contrast with the former list, which consisted of various forms of wicked love. They have less to do with bodily appetites. But perhaps it is not without profound meaning that the fierce rush of unhallowed passion over the soul is put first, and the contrary flow of chill malignity comes second; for in the spiritual world, as in the physical, a storm blowing from one quarter is usually followed by violent gales from the opposite. Lust ever passes into cruelty, and dwells "hard by hate." A licentious epoch or man is generally a cruel epoch or man. Nero made torches of the Christians. Malice is evil desire iced.

This second list goes in the opposite direction to the former. That began with actions and went up the stream to desire; this begins with the sources, which are emotions, and comes down stream to their manifestations in action.

First we have anger. There is a just and righteous anger, which is part of the new man, and essential to his completeness, even as it is part of the image after which he is created. But here of course the anger which is to be put off is the inverted reflection of the earthly and passionate lust after the flesh; it is, then, of an earthly, passionate and selfish kind. "Wrath" differs from "anger" in so far as it may be called anger boiling over. If anger rises keep the lid on, do not let it get the length of wrath, nor effervesce into the brief madness of passion. But on the other hand, do not think that you have done enough when you have suppressed the wrath which is the expression of your anger, nor be content with saying, "Well, at all events I did not show it," but take the cure a step further back, and strip off anger as well as wrath, the emotion as well as the manifestation.

Christian people do not sufficiently bring the greatest forces of their religion and of God's Spirit to bear upon the homely task of curing small hastinesses of temper, and sometimes seem to think it a sufficient excuse to say, "I have naturally a hot disposition." But Christianity was sent to subdue and change natural dispositions. An angry man cannot have communion with God, any more than the sky can be reflected in the storm-swept tide; and a man in communion with God cannot be angry with a passionate and evil anger any more than a dove can croak like a raven or strike like a hawk. Such anger disturbs our insight into everything; eyes suffused with it cannot see; and it weakens all good in the soul, and degrades it before its own conscience.

"Malice" designates another step in the process. The anger boils over in wrath, and then cools down into malignity—the disposition which means mischief, and plans or rejoices in evil falling on the hated head. That malice, as cold, as clear, as colourless as sulphuric acid, and burning like it, is worse than the boiling rage already spoken of. There are many degrees of this cold drawn, double distilled rejoicing in evil, and the beginnings of it in a certain faint satisfaction in the misfortunes of those whom we dislike is by no means unusual.

An advance is now made in the direction of outward manifestation. It is significant that while the expressions of wicked love were deeds, those of wicked hate are words. The "blasphemy" of the Authorised Version is better taken, with the Revised, as "railing." The word means "speech that injures," and such speech may be directed either against God, which is blasphemy in the usual sense of the word, or against man. The hate blossoms into hurtful speech. The heated metal of anger is forged into poisoned arrows of the tongue. Then follows "shameful speaking out of your mouth," which is probably to be understood not so much of obscenities, which would more properly belong to the former catalogue, as of foul-mouthed abuse of the hated persons, that copiousness of vituperation and those volcanic explosions of mud, which are so natural to the angry Eastern.

Finally, we have a dehortation from lying, especially to those within the circle of the Church, as if that sin too were the child of hatred and anger. It comes from a deficiency of love, or a predominance of selfishness, which is the same thing. A lie ignores my brother's claims on me, and my union with him. "Ye are members one of another," is the great obligation to love which is denied and sinned against by hatred in all its forms and manifestations, and not least by giving my brother the poisoned bread of lies instead of the heavenly manna of pure truth, so far as it has been given to me.

On the whole, this catalogue brings out the importance to be attached to sins of speech, which are ranked here as in parallel lines with the grossest forms of animal passion. Men's words ought to be fountains of consolation and sources of illumination, encouragement, revelations of love and pity. And what are they? What floods of idle words, foul words, words that wound like knives and sting and bite like serpents, deluge the world! If all the talk that has its sources in these evils rebuked here, were to be suddenly made inaudible, what a dead silence would fall on many brilliant circles, and how many of us would stand making mouths but saying nothing.

All the practical exhortations of this section concern common homely duties which everybody knows to be such. It may be asked—does Christianity then only lay down such plain precepts? What need was there of all that prelude of mysterious doctrines, if we are only to be landed at last in such elementary and obvious moralities? No doubt they are elementary and obvious, but the main matter is—how to get them kept. And in respect to that, Christianity does two things which nothing else does. It breaks the entail of evil habits by the great gift of pardon for the past, and by the greater gift of a new spirit and life principle within, which is foreign to all evil, being the effluence of the spirit of life in Christ Jesus.

Therefore the gospel of Jesus Christ makes it possible that men should slay themselves, and put on the new life, which will expel the old as the new shoots on some trees push the last year's lingering leaves, brown and sere, from their places. All moral teachers from the beginning have agreed, on the whole, in their reading of the commandments which are printed on conscience in the largest capitals. Everybody who is not blind can read them. But reading is easy, keeping is hard. How to fulfil has been wanting. It is given us in the gospel, which is not merely a republication of old precepts, but the communication of new power. If we yield ourselves to Christ He will nerve our arms to wield the knife that will slay our dearest tastes, though beloved as Isaac by Abraham. If a man knows and feels that Christ has died for him, and that he lives in and by Christ, then, and not else, will he be able to crucify self. If he knows and feels that by His pardoning mercy and atoning death, Christ has taken off his foul raiment and clothed him in clean garments, then, and not else, will he be able, by daily effort after repression of self and appropriation of Christ, to put off the old man and to put on the new, which is daily being renewed into closer resemblance to the image of Him who created him.

XIX

THE NEW NATURE WROUGHT OUT IN NEW LIFE

"Seeing that ye have put off the old man with his doings, and have put on the new man, which is being renewed unto knowledge after the image of Him that created him: where there cannot be Greek and Jew, circumcision and uncircumcision, barbarian, Scythian, bondman, freeman; but Christ is all, and in all."—Col. iii. 9–11 (Rev. Ver.).

In previous section we were obliged to break the close connection between these words and the preceding. They adduce a reason for the moral exhortation going before, which at first sight may appear very illogical. "Put off these vices of the old nature because you have put off the old nature with its vices," sounds like, Do a thing because you have done it. But the apparent looseness of reasoning covers very accurate thought which a little consideration brings to light, and introduces a really cogent argument for the conduct it recommends. Nor do the principles contained in the verses now under examination look backward only to enforce the exhortation to put aside these evils. They also look forward, and are taken as the basis of the following exhortation, to put on the white robes of Christlikeness—which is coupled with this section by "therefore."

I. The first thing to be observed is the change of the spirit's dress, which is taken for granted as having occurred in the experience of all Christians.

We have already found the same idea presented under the forms of death and resurrection. The "death" is equivalent to the "putting off of the old," and the "resurrection" to "the putting on of the new man." That figure of a change of dress to express a change of moral character is very obvious, and is frequent in Scripture. Many a psalm breathes such prayers as, "Let Thy priests be clothed with righteousness." Zechariah in vision saw the high-priestly representative of the nation standing before the Lord "in filthy garments," and heard the command to strip them off him, and clothe him in festival robes, in token that God had "caused his iniquity to pass from him." Christ spoke His parable of the man at the wedding feast without the wedding garment, and of the prodigal, who was stripped of his rags stained with the filth of the swine troughs, and clothed with the best robe. Paul in many places touches the same image, as in his ringing exhortation—clear and rousing in its notes like the morning bugle—to Christ's soldiers, to put off their night gear, "the works of darkness," and to brace on the armour of light, which sparkles in the morning sunrise. Every reformatory and orphanage yields an illustration of the image, where the first thing done is to strip off and burn the rags of the new comers, then to give them a bath and dress them in clean, sweet, new clothes. Most naturally dress is taken as the emblem of character, which is indeed the garb of the soul. Most naturally *habit* means both *costume* and *custom*.

But here we have a strange paradox introduced, to the ruining of the rhetorical propriety of the figure. It is a "new man" that is put on. The Apostle does not mind hazarding a mixed metaphor, if it adds to the force of his speech, and he introduces this thought of the new *man*, though it somewhat jars, in order to impress on his readers that what they have to put off and on is much more truly part of themselves than an article of dress is. The "old man" is the unregenerate self; the new man is, of course, the regenerate self, the new Christian moral nature personified. There is a deeper self which remains the same throughout the change, the true man, the centre of personality; which is, as it were, draped in the moral nature, and can put it off and on. I myself change myself. The figure is vehement, and, if you will, paradoxical, but it expresses accurately and forcibly at once the depth of the change which passes on him who becomes a Christian, and the identity of the person through all change. If I am a Christian, there has passed on me a change so thorough that it is in one aspect a death, and in another a resurrection; in one aspect it is a putting off not merely of some garb of action, but of the old *man*, and in another a putting on not merely of some surface renovation, but of a new *man*—which is yet the same old self.

This entire change is taken for granted by Paul as having been realised in every Christian. It is here treated as having taken place at a certain point of time, namely when these Colossians began to put their trust in Jesus Christ, and in profession of that trust, and as a symbol of that change, were baptized.

Of course the contrast between the character before and after faith in Christ is strongest when, like the Christians at Colossæ, converts have been brought out of heathenism. With us, where some knowledge of Christianity is widely diffused, and its indirect influence has shaped the characters even of those who reject it, there is less room for a marked revolution in character and conduct. There will be many true saints who can point to no sudden change as their conversion; but have grown up, sometimes from childhood, under Christian influences, or who, if they have distinctly been conscious of a change, have passed through it as gradually as night passes into day. Be it so. In many respects that will be the highest form of experience. Yet even such souls will be aware of a "new man" formed in them which is at variance with their own old selves, and will not escape the necessity of the conflict with their lower nature, the immolation and casting off of the unregenerate self. But there are also many people who have grown up without God or Christ, who must become Christians by the way of sudden conversion, if they are ever to become Christians at all.

Why should such sudden change be regarded as impossible? Is it not a matter of every-day experience that some long ignored principle may suddenly come, like a meteor into the atmosphere, into a man's mind and will, may catch fire as it travels, and may explode and blow to pieces the solid habits of a lifetime? And why should not the truth concerning God's great love in Christ, which in too sad certainty is ignored by many, flame in upon blind eyes, and change the look of everything? The New Testament doctrine of conversion asserts that it may and does. It does not insist that everybody must become a Christian in the same fashion. Sometimes there will be a dividing line between the two states, as sharp as the boundary of adjoining kingdoms; sometimes the one will melt imperceptibly into the other. Sometimes the revolution will be as swift as that of the wheel of a locomotive, sometimes slow and silent as the movement of a planet in the sky. The main thing is that whether suddenly or slowly the face shall be turned to God.

But however brought about, this putting off of the old sinful self, is a certain mark of a Christian man. It can be assumed as true universally, and appealed to as the basis of exhortations such as those of the context. Believing certain truths does not make a Christian. If there have been any reality in the act by which we have laid hold of Christ as our Saviour, our whole being will be revolutionized; old things will have passed away— tastes, desires, ways of looking at the world, memories, habits, pricks of conscience and all cords that bound us to our God-forgetting past—and all things will have become new, because we ourselves move in the midst of the old things as new creatures with new love burning in our hearts and new motives changing all our lives, and a new aim shining before us, and a new hope illuminating the blackness beyond, and a new song on our lips, and a new power in our hands, and a new Friend by our sides.

This is a wholesome and most needful test for all who call themselves Christians, and who are often tempted to put too much stress on believing and feeling, and to forget the supreme importance of the moral change which true Christianity effects. Nor is it less needful to remember that this resolute casting off of the garment spotted by the flesh, and putting on of the new man, is a consequence of faith in Christ and is only possible as a consequence. Nothing else will strip the foul robes from a man. The moral change comes second, the union with Jesus Christ by faith must come first. To try to begin with the second stage, is like trying to begin to build a house at the second story.

But there is a practical conclusion drawn from this taken-for-granted change. Our text is introduced by "seeing that;" and though some doubts may be raised as to that translation and the logical connection of the paragraph, it appears on the whole most congruous with both the preceding and the following context, to retain it and to see here the reason for the exhortation which goes before — "Put off all these," and for that which follows — "Put on, therefore," the beautiful garment of love and compassion.

That great change, though taking place in the inmost nature whensoever a heart turns to Christ, needs to be wrought into character, and to be wrought out in conduct. The leaven is in the dough, but to knead it thoroughly into the mass is a lifelong task, which is only accomplished by our own continually repeated efforts. The old garment clings to the limbs like the wet clothes of a half-drowned man, and it takes the work of a lifetime to get quite rid of it. The "old man" dies hard, and we have to repeat the sacrifice hour by hour. The new man has to be put on afresh day by day.

So the apparently illogical exhortation, Put off what you have put off, and put on what you have put on, is fully vindicated. It means, Be consistent with your deepest selves. Carry out in detail what you have already done in bulk. Cast out the enemy, already ejected from the central fortress, from the isolated positions which he still occupies. You *may* put off the old man, for he is put off already; and the confidence that he is will give you strength for the struggle that still remains. You *must* put off the old man, for there is still danger of his again wrapping his poisonous rags about your limbs.

II. We have here, the continuous growth of the new man, its aim and pattern.

The thought of the garment passes for the moment out of sight, and the Apostle enlarges on the greatness and glory of this "new man," partly as a stimulus to obeying the exhortation, partly, with allusion to some of the errors which he had been combating, and partly because his fervid spirit kindles at the mention of the mighty transformation.

The new man, says he, is "being renewed." This is one of the instances where minute accuracy in translation is not pedantic, but clear gain. When we say, with the Authorised Version, "is renewed," we speak of a completed act; when we say with the Revised Version, "is being renewed," we speak of a continuous process; and there can be no question that the latter is the true idea intended here. The growth of the new man is constant, perhaps slow and difficult to discern, if the intervals of comparison be short. But like all habits and powers it steadily increases. On the other hand, a similar process works to opposite results in the "old man," which, as Paul says in the instructive parallel passage in the Epistle to the Ephesians (iv. 22), "waxeth corrupt, after the lusts of deceit." Both grow according to their inmost nature, the one steadily upwards; the other with accelerating speed downwards, till they are parted by the whole distance between the highest heaven and the lowest abyss. So mystic and awful is that solemn law of the persistent increase of the true ruling tendency of a man's nature, and its certain subjugation of the whole man to itself!

It is to be observed that this renewing is represented in this clause, as done *on* the new man, not by him. We have heard the exhortation to a continuous appropriation and increase of the new life by our own efforts. But there is a Divine side too, and the renewing is not merely effected by us, nor due only to the vital power of the new man, though growth is the sign of life there as everywhere, but is "the renewing by the Holy Ghost," whose touch quickens and whose indwelling renovates the inward man day by day. So there is hope for us in our striving, for He helps us; and the thought of that Divine renewal is not a pillow for indolence, but a spur to intenser energy, as Paul well knew when he wove the apparent paradox, "work out your own salvation, for it is God that worketh in you."

The new man is being renewed "*unto* knowledge." An advanced knowledge of God and Divine realities is the result of the progressive renewal. Possibly there may be a passing reference to the pretensions of the false teachers, who had so much to say about a higher wisdom open to the initiated, and to be won by ceremonial and asceticism. Their claims, hints Paul, are baseless; their pretended secrets a delusion; their method of attaining them a snare. There is but one way to press into the depths of the knowledge of God—namely growth into His likeness. We understand one another best by sympathy. We know God only on condition of resemblance. "If the eye were not sunlike how could it see the sun?" says Goethe. "If thou beest this, thou seest this," said Plotinus. Ever, as we grow in resemblance, shall we grow in knowledge, and ever as we grow in knowledge, shall we grow in resemblance. So in perpetual action and reaction of being and knowing, shall we draw nearer and nearer the unapproachable light, and receiving it full on our faces, shall be changed into the same image, as the moonbeams that touch the dark ocean transfigure its waves into silver radiance like their own. For all simple souls, bewildered by the strife of tongues and unapt for speculation, this is a message of gladness, that the way to know God is to be like Him, and the way to be like Him is to be renewed in the inward man, and the way to be renewed in the inward man is to put on Christ. They may wrangle and philosophize who will, but the path to God leads far away from all that. It may be trodden by a child's foot, and the wayfaring man though a fool shall not err therein, for all that is needed is a heart that desires to know Him, and is made like Him by love. Half the secret lies in the great word which tells us that "we shall be like Him, for we shall see Him as He is," and knowledge will work likeness. The other half lies in the great word which tells us that "blessed are the pure in heart, for they shall see God," and likeness will work a more perfect knowledge.

This new man is being renewed *after the image of Him that created him.* As in the first creation man was made in the image of God, so in the new creation. From the first moment in which the supernatural life is derived from Christ into the regenerated spirit, that new life is like its source. It is kindred, therefore it is like, as all derived life is. The child's life is like the father's. But the image of God which the new man bears is more than that which was stamped on man in his creation. That consisted mainly, if not wholly, in the reasonable soul, and the self-conscious personality, the broad distinctions which separate man from other animals. The image of God is often said to have been lost by sin, but Scripture seems rather to consider it as inseparable from humanity, even when stained by transgression. Men are still images of God, though darkened and "carved in ebony." The coin bears His image and superscription, though rusty and defaced. But the image of God, which the new man bears from the beginning in a rudimentary form, and which is continually imprinting itself more deeply upon him, has for its principal feature holiness. Though the majestic infinitudes of God can have no likeness in man, however exalted, and our feebleness cannot copy His strength, nor our poor blind knowledge, with its vast circumference of ignorance, be like His ungrowing and unerring knowledge, we may be "holy *as* He is holy"; we may be "imitators of God as beloved children, and walk in love as He hath loved us"; we may *"walk* in the light as He *is* in the light," with only the difference between His calm, eternal being, and our changeful and progressive motion therein; we may even "be perfect as our Father is perfect." This is the end of all our putting off the old and putting on the new. This is the ultimate purpose of God, in all His self-revelation. For this Christ has come and died and lives. For this the Spirit of God dwells in us. This is the immortal hope with which we may re-create and encourage our souls in our often weary struggles. Even our poor sinful natures may be transformed into that wondrous likeness. Coal and diamond are but varying forms of carbon, and the blackest lump dug from the deepest mine, may be transmuted by the alchemy of that wondrous transforming union with Christ, into a brightness that shall flash back all the glory of the sunlight, and gleam for ever, set in one of His many crowns.

III. We have here finally the grand unity of this new creation.

We may reverse the order of the words as they stand here, and consider the last clause first, inasmuch as it is the reason for the doing away of all distinctions of race, or ceremony, or culture, or social condition.

"Christ is all." Wherever that new nature is found, it lives by the life of Christ. He dwells in all who possess it. The Spirit of life in Christ is in them. His blood passes into their veins. The holy desires, the new tastes, the kindling love, the clearer vision, the gentleness and the strength, and whatsoever things beside are lovely and of good report, are all His—nay, we may say, are all Himself.

And, of course, all who are His are partakers of that common gift, and He is *in* all. There is no privileged class in Christ's Church, as these false teachers in Colossæ had taught. Against every attempt to limit the universality of the gospel, whether it came from Jewish Pharisees or Eastern philosophers, Paul protested with his whole soul. He has done so already in this Epistle, and does so here in his emphatic assertion that Christ was not the possession of an aristocracy of "intelligence," but belonged to every soul that trusted Him.

Necessarily, therefore, surface distinctions disappear. There is triumph in the roll of his rapid enumeration of these clefts that have so long kept brothers apart, and are now being filled up. He looks round on a world, the antagonisms of which we can but faintly imagine, and his eye kindles and his voice rises into vibrating emotion, as he thinks of the mighty magnetism that is drawing enemies towards the one centre in Christ. His catalogue here may profitably be compared with his other in the Epistle to the Galatians (iii. 28). There he enumerates the three great distinctions which parted the old world: race (Jew and Greek), social condition (bond and free), and sex (male and female.) These, he says, as separating powers, are done away in Christ. Here the list is modified, probably with reference to the errors in the Colossian Church.

"There cannot be Greek and Jew." The cleft of national distinctions, which certainly never yawned more widely than between the Jew and every other people, ceases to separate, and the teachers who had been trying to perpetuate that distinction in the Church were blind to the very meaning of the gospel. "Circumcision and uncircumcision" separated. Nothing makes deeper and bitterer antagonisms than differences in religious forms, and people who have not been born into them are usually the most passionate in adherence to them, so that cleft did not entirely coincide with the former. "Barbarian, Scythian," is not an antithesis, but a climax—the Scythians were looked upon as the most savage of barbarians. The Greek contempt for the outside races, which is reflected in this clause, was largely the contempt for a supposed lower stage of culture. As we have seen, Colossæ especially needed the lesson that differences in culture disappeared in the unity of Christ, for the heretical teachers attached great importance to the wisdom which they professed to impart. A cultivated class is always tempted to superciliousness, and a half cultivated class is even more so. There is abundance of that arrogance born of education among us to-day, and sorely needing and quite disbelieving the teaching that there are things which can make up for the want of what it possesses. It is in the interest of the humble virtues of the uneducated godly as well as of the nations called uncivilized, that Christianity wars against that most heartless and ruinous of all prides, the pride of culture, by its proclamation that in Christ, barbarian, Scythian and the most polished thinker or scholar are one.

"Bondman, freeman" is again an antithesis. That gulf between master and slave was indeed wide and deep; too wide for compassion to cross, though not for hatred to stride over. The untold miseries of slavery in the old world are but dimly known; but it and war and the degradation of women made an infernal trio which crushed more than half the race into a hell of horrors. Perhaps Paul may have been the more ready to add this clause to his catalogue because his thoughts had been occupied with the relation of master and slave on the occasion of the letter to Philemon which was sent along with this to Colossæ.

Christianity waged no direct war against these social evils of antiquity, but it killed them much more effectually by breathing into the conscience of the world truths which made their continuance impossible. It girdled the tree, and left it to die—a much better and more thorough plan than dragging it out of the ground by main force. Revolution cures nothing. The only way to get rid of evils engrained in the constitution of society is to elevate and change the tone of thought and feeling, and then they die of atrophy. Change the climate, and you change the vegetation. Until you do, neither mowing nor uprooting will get rid of the foul growths.

So the gospel does with all these lines of demarcation between men. What becomes of them? What becomes of the ridges of sand that separate pool from pool at low water? The tide comes up over them and makes them all one, gathered into the oneness of the great sea. They may remain, but they are seen no more, and the roll of the wave is not interrupted by them. The powers and blessings of the Christ pass freely from heart to heart, hindered by no barriers. Christ founds a deeper unity independent of all these superficial distinctions, for the very conception of humanity is the product of Christianity, and the true foundation for the brotherhood of mankind is the revelation in Christ of the fatherhood of God. Christ is the brother of us all; His death is for every man; the blessing of His gospel is offered to each; He will dwell in the heart of any. Therefore all distinctions, national, ceremonial, intellectual or social, fade into nothingness. Love is of no nation, and Christ is the property of no aristocracy in the Church. That great truth was a miraculous new thing in that old world, all torn apart by deep clefts like the grim cañons of American rivers. Strange it must have seemed to find slaves and their masters, Jew and Greek, sitting at one table and bound in fraternal ties. The world has not yet fully grasped that truth, and the Church has woefully failed in showing it to be a reality. But it arches above all our wars, and schisms, and wretched class distinctions, like a rainbow of promise, beneath whose open portal the world shall one day pass into that bright land where the wandering peoples shall gather together in peace round the feet of Jesus, and there shall be one fold because there is one Shepherd.

XX
THE GARMENTS OF THE RENEWED SOUL

"Put on therefore, as God's elect, holy and beloved, a heart of compassion, kindness, humility, meekness, longsuffering; forbearing one another, and forgiving each other, if any man have a complaint against any; even as the Lord forgave you, so also do ye: and above all these things put on love, which is the bond of perfectness."—Col. iii.12–14 (Rev. Ver.).

We need not repeat what has been already said as to the logic of the inference, You have put off the "old man," therefore put off the vices which belong to him. Here we have the same argument in reference to the "new man" who is to be "put on" because he has been put on. This "therefore" rests the exhortation both on that thought, and on the nearer words, "Christ is all and in all." Because the new nature has been assumed in the very act of conversion, therefore array your souls in vesture corresponding. Because Christ is all and in all, therefore clothe yourselves with all brotherly graces, corresponding to the great unity into which all Christians are brought by their common possession of Christ. The whole field of Christian morality is not traversed here, but only so much of it as concerns the social duties which result from that unity.

But besides the foundation for the exhortations which is laid in the possession of the "New Man," consequent on participation in Christ, another ground for them is added in the words, "as God's elect, holy and beloved." Those who are in Christ and are thus regenerated in Him, are of the chosen race, are consecrated as belonging especially to God, and receive the warm beams of the special paternal love with which He regards the men who are in some measure conformed to His likeness and moulded after His will. That relation to God should draw after it a life congruous with itself—a life of active goodness and brotherly gentleness. The outcome of it should be not mere glad emotion, nor a hugging of one's self in one's happiness, but practical efforts to turn to men a face lit by the same dispositions with which God has looked on us, or as the parallel passage in Ephesians has it, "Be imitators of God, as beloved children." That is a wide and fruitful principle—the relation to men will follow the relation to God. As we think

God has been to us, so let us try to be to others. The poorest little fishing cobble is best guided by celestial observations, and dead reckoning without sun or stars is but second best. Independent morality cut loose from religion will be feeble morality. On the other hand, religion which does not issue in morality is a ghost without substance. Religion is the soul of morality. Morality is the body of religion, more than ceremonial worship is. The virtues which all men know, are the fitting garments of the elect of God.

I. We have here then an enumeration of the fair garments of the new man.

Let us go over the items of this list of the wardrobe of the consecrated soul.

"A heart of compassion." So the Revised Version renders the words given literally in the Authorised as "bowels of mercies," an expression which that very strange thing called conventional propriety regards as coarse, simply because Jews chose one part of the body and we another as the supposed seat of the emotions. Either phrase expresses substantially the Apostle's meaning.

Is it not beautiful that the series should begin with *pity*? It is the most often needed, for the sea of sorrow stretches so widely that nothing less than a universal compassion can arch it over as with the blue of heaven. Every man would seem in some respect deserving of and needing sympathy, if his whole heart and history could be laid bare. Such compassion is difficult to achieve, for its healing streams are dammed back by many obstructions of inattention and occupation, and dried up by the fierce heat of selfishness. Custom, with its deadening influence, comes in to make us feel least the sorrows which are most common in the society around us. As a man might live so long in an asylum that lunacy would seem to him almost the normal condition, so the most widely diffused griefs are those least observed and least compassionated; and good, tender-hearted men and women walk the streets of our great cities and see sights—children growing up for the gallows and the devil, gin-shops at every corner—which might make angels weep, and suppose them to be as inseparable from our "civilization" as the noise of wheels from a carriage or bilge water from a ship. Therefore we have to make conscious efforts to "put on" that sympathetic disposition, and to fight against the faults which hinder its free play. Without it, no help will be of much use to the receiver, nor of any to the giver. Benefits bestowed on the needy and sorrowful, if bestowed without sympathy, will hurt like a blow. Much is said about ingratitude, but very often it is but the instinctive recoil of the heart from the unkind doer of a kindness. Aid flung to a man as a bone is to a dog usually gets as much gratitude as the sympathy which it expresses deserves. But if we really make another's sorrows ours, that teaches us tact and gentleness, and makes our clumsy hands light and deft to bind up sore hearts.

Above all things, the practical discipline which cultivates pity will beware of letting it be excited and then not allowing the emotion to act. To stimulate feeling and do nothing in consequence is a short road to destroy the feeling. Pity is meant to be the impulse toward help, and if it is checked and suffered to pass away idly, it is weakened, as certainly as a plant is weakened by being kept close nipped and hindered from bringing its buds to flower and fruit.

"Kindness" comes next—a wider benignity, not only exercised where there is manifest room for pity, but turning a face of goodwill to all. Some souls are so dowered that they have this grace without effort, and come like the sunshine with welcome and cheer for all the world. But even less happily endowed natures can cultivate the disposition, and the best way to cultivate it is to be much in communion with God. When Moses came down from the mount, his face shone. When we come out from the secret place of the Most High we shall bear some reflection of His great kindness whose "tender mercies are over all His works." This "kindness" is the opposite of that worldly wisdom, on which many men pride themselves as the ripe fruit of their knowledge of men and things, and which keeps up vigilant suspicion of everybody, as in the savage state, where "stranger" and "enemy" had only one word between them. It does not require us to be blind to facts or to live in fancies, but it does require us to cherish a habit of goodwill, ready to become pity if sorrow appears, and slow to turn away even if hostility appears. Meet your brother with kindness, and you will generally find it returned. The prudent hypocrites who get on in the world, as ships are launched, by "greasing the ways" with flattery, and smiles, teach us the value of the true thing, since even a coarse caricature of it wins hearts and disarms foes. This "kindness" is the most powerful solvent of illwill and indifference.

Then follows "humility." That seems to break the current of thought by bringing a virtue entirely occupied with self into the middle of a series referring exclusively to others. But it does not really do so. From this point onwards all the graces named have reference to our demeanour under slights and injuries—and humility comes into view here only as constituting the foundation for the right bearing of these. Meekness and longsuffering must stand on a basis of humility. The proud man, who thinks highly of himself and of his own claims, will be the touchy man, if any one derogates from these.

"Humility," or lowly-mindedness, a lowly estimate of ourselves, is not necessarily blindness to our strong points. If a man can do certain things better than his neighbours, he can hardly help knowing it, and Christian humility does not require him to be ignorant of it. I suppose Milton would be none the less humble, though he was quite sure that his work was better than that of Sternhold and Hopkins. The consciousness of power usually accompanies power. But though it may be quite right to "know myself" in the strong points, as well as in the weak, there are two considerations which should act as dampers to any unchristian fire of pride which the devil's breath may blow up from that fuel. The one is, "What hast thou that thou hast not received?" the other is, "Who is pure before God's judgment-seat?" Your strong points are nothing so very wonderful, after all. If you have better brains than some of your neighbours, well, that is not a thing to give yourself such airs about. Besides, where did you get the faculties you plume yourself on? However cultivated by yourself, how came they yours at first? And, furthermore, whatever superiorities may lift you above any men, and however high you may be elevated, it is a long way from the top of the highest molehill to the sun, and not much longer to the top of the lowest. And, besides all that, you may be very clever and brilliant, may have made books or pictures, may have stamped your name on some invention, may have won a place in public life, or made a fortune—and yet you and the beggar who cannot write his name are both guilty before God. Pride seems out of place in creatures like us, who have all to bow our heads in the presence of His perfect judgment, and cry, "God be merciful to me a sinner!"

Then follow "meekness, long-suffering." The distinction between these two is slight. According to the most thorough investigators, the former is the temper which accepts God's dealings, or evil inflicted by men as His instruments, without resistance, while the latter is the long holding out of the mind before it gives way to a temptation to action, or passion, especially the latter. The opposite of meekness is rudeness or harshness; the opposite of long-suffering, swift resentment or revenge. Perhaps there may be something in the distinction, that while long-suffering does not get angry soon, meekness does not get angry at all. Possibly, too, meekness implies a lowlier position than long-suffering does. The meek man puts himself below the offender; the long-suffering man does not. God is long-suffering, but the incarnate God alone can be "meek and lowly."

The general meaning is plain enough. The "hate of hate," the "scorn of scorn," is not the Christian ideal. I am not to allow my enemy always to settle the terms on which we are to be. Why should I scowl back at him, though he frowns at me? It is hard work, as we all know, to repress the retort that would wound and be so neat. It is hard not to repay slights and offences in kind. But, if the basis of our dispositions to others be laid in a wise and lowly estimate of ourselves, such graces of conduct will be possible, and they will give beauty to our characters.

"Forbearing and forgiving" are not new virtues. They are meekness and long-suffering in exercise, and if we were right in saying that "long-suffering" was not *soon* angry, and "meekness" was not angry at all, then "forbearance" would correspond to the former and "forgiveness" to the latter; for a man may exercise forbearance, and bite his lips till the blood come rather than speak, and violently constrain himself to keep calm and do nothing unkind, and yet all the while seven devils may be in his spirit; while forgiveness, on the other hand, is an entire wiping of all enmity and irritation clean out of the heart.

Such is the Apostle's outline sketch of the Christian character in its social aspect, all rooted in pity, and full of soft compassion; quick to apprehend, to feel, and to succour sorrow; a kindliness, equable and widespread, illuminating all who come within its reach; a patient acceptance of wrongs without resentment or revenge, because a lowly judgment of self and its claims, a spirit schooled to calmness under all provocations, disdaining to requite wrong by wrong, and quick to forgive.

The question may well be asked—is that a type of character which the world generally admires? Is it not uncommonly like what most people would call "a poor spiritless creature." It was "a new man," most emphatically, when Paul drew that sketch, for the heathen world had never seen anything like it. It is a "new man" still; for although the modern world has had some kind of Christianity—at least has had a Church—for all these centuries, that is not the kind of character which is its ideal. Look at the heroes of history and of literature. Look at the tone of so much contemporary biography and criticism of public actions. Think of the ridicule which is poured on the attempt to regulate politics by Christian principles, or, as a distinguished soldier called them in public recently, "puling principles." It may be true that Christianity has not added any new virtues to those which are prescribed by natural conscience, but it has most certainly altered the perspective of the whole, and created a type of excellence, in which the gentler virtues predominate, and the novelty of which is proved by the reluctance of the so-called Christian world to recognise it even yet.

By the side of its serene and lofty beauty, the "heroic virtues" embodied in the world's type of excellence show vulgar and glaring, like some daub representing a soldier, the sign-post of a public-house, by the side of Angelico's white-robed visions on the still convent walls. The highest exercise of these more gaudy and conspicuous qualities is to produce the pity and meekness of the Christian ideal. More self-command, more heroic firmness, more contempt for the popular estimate, more of everything strong and manly, will find a nobler field in subduing passion and cherishing forgiveness, which the world thinks folly and spiritless, than anywhere else. Better is he that ruleth his spirit than he that taketh a city.

The great pattern and motive of forgiveness is next set forth. We are to forgive as Christ has forgiven us; and that "as" may be applied either as meaning "in like manner," or as meaning "because." The Revised Version, with many others, adopts the various reading of "the Lord," instead of "Christ," which has the advantage of recalling the parable that was no doubt in Paul's mind, about the servant who, having been forgiven by his "*Lord*" all his great debt, took his fellow-servant by the throat and squeezed the last farthing out of him.

The great transcendent act of God's mercy brought to us by Christ's cross is sometimes, as in the parallel passage in Ephesians, spoken of as "God for Christ's sake forgiving us," and sometimes as here, Christ is represented as forgiving. We need not pause to do more than point to that interchange of Divine office and attributes, and ask what notion of Christ's person underlies it.

We have already had the death of Christ set forth as in a very profound sense our pattern. Here we have one special case of the general law that the life and death of our Lord are the embodied ideal of human character and conduct. His forgiveness is not merely revealed to us that trembling hearts may be calm, and that a fearful looking for of judgment may no more trouble a foreboding conscience. For whilst we must ever begin with cleaving to it as our hope, we must never stop there. A heart touched and softened by pardon will be a heart apt to pardon, and the miracle of forgiveness which has been wrought for it will constitute the law of its life as well as the ground of its joyful security.

This new pattern and new motive, both in one, make the true novelty and specific difference of Christian morality. "As I have loved you," makes the commandment "love one another" a new commandment. And all that is difficult in obedience becomes easier by the power of that motive. Imitation of one whom we love is instinctive. Obedience to one whom we love is delightful. The far off ideal becomes near and real in the person of our best friend. Bound to him by obligations so immense, and a forgiveness so costly and complete, we shall joyfully yield to "the cords of love" which draw us after Him. We have each to choose what shall be the pattern for us. The world takes Cæsar, the hero; the Christian takes Christ, in whose meekness is power, and whose gentle long-suffering has been victor in a sterner conflict than any battle of the warrior with garments rolled in blood.

Paul says, "Even as the Lord forgave you, so also do ye." The Lord's prayer teaches us to ask, Forgive us our trespasses, as we also forgive. In the one case Christ's forgiveness is the example and the motive for ours. In the other, our forgiveness is the condition of God's. Both are true. We shall find the strongest impulse to pardon others in the consciousness that we have been pardoned by Him. And if we have grudgings against our offending brother in our hearts, we shall not be conscious of the tender forgiveness of our Father in heaven. That is no arbitrary limitation, but inherent in the very nature of the case.

II. We have here the girdle which keeps all the garments in their places.

"Above all these things, put on love, which is the bond of perfectness."

"Above all these" does not mean "besides," or "more important than," but is clearly used in its simplest local sense, as equivalent to "over," and thus carries on the metaphor of the dress. Over the other garments is to be put the silken sash or girdle of love, which will brace and confine all the rest into a unity. It is "the girdle of perfectness," by which is not meant, as is often supposed, the perfect principle of union among men. Perfectness is not the quality of the girdle, but the thing which it girds, and is a collective expression for "the various graces and virtues, which together make up perfection." So the metaphor expresses the thought that love knits into a harmonious whole, the graces which without it would be fragmentary and incomplete.

We can conceive of all the dispositions already named as existing in some fashion without love. There might be pity which was not love, though we know it is akin to it. The feeling with which one looks upon some poor outcast, or on some stranger in sorrow, or even on an enemy in misery, may be very genuine compassion, and yet clearly separate from love. So with all the others. There may be kindness most real without any of the diviner emotion, and there may even be forbearance reaching up to forgiveness, and yet leaving the heart untouched in its deepest recesses. But if these virtues were thus exercised, in the absence of love they would be fragmentary, shallow, and would have no guarantee for their own continuance. Let love come into the heart and knit a man to the poor creature whom he had only pitied before, or to the enemy whom he had at the most been able with an effort to forgive; and it lifts these other emotions into a nobler life. He who pities may not love, but he who loves cannot but pity; and that compassion will flow with a deeper current and be of a purer quality than the shrunken stream which does not rise from that higher source.

Nor is it only the virtues enumerated here for which love performs this office; but all the else isolated graces of character, it binds or welds into a harmonious whole. As the broad Eastern girdle holds the flowing robes in position, and gives needed firmness to the figure as well as composed order to the attire; so this broad band, woven of softest fabric, keeps all emotions in their due place and makes the attire of the Christian soul beautiful in harmonious completeness.

Perhaps it is a yet deeper truth that love produces all these graces. Whatsoever things men call virtues, are best cultivated by cultivating it. So with a somewhat similar meaning to that of our text, but if anything, going deeper down, Paul in another place calls love the fulfilling of the law, even as his Master had taught him that all the complex of duties incumbent upon us were summed up in love to God, and love to men. Whatever I owe to my brother will be discharged if I love God, and live my love. Nothing of it, not even the smallest mite of the debt will be discharged, however vast my sacrifices and services, if I do not.

So end the frequent references in this letter to putting off the old and putting on the new. The sum of them all is, that we must first put on Christ by faith, and then by daily effort clothe our spirits in the graces of character which He gives us, and by which we shall be like Him.

We have said that this dress of the Christian soul which we have been now considering does not include the whole of Christian duty. We may recall the other application of the same figure which occurs in the parallel Epistle to the Ephesians, where Paul sketches for us in a few rapid touches the armed Christian soldier. The two pictures may profitably be set side by side. Here he dresses the Christian soul in the robes of peace, bidding him put on pity and meekness, and above all, the silken girdle of love.

> "In peace, there's nothing so becomes a man
> As modest stillness and humility;
> But when the blast of war blows in our ears,"

then "put on the whole armour of God," the leathern girdle of truth, the shining breastplate of righteousness, and above all, the shield of faith—and so stand a flashing pillar of steel. Are the two pictures inconsistent? must we doff the robes of peace to don the armour, or put off the armour to resume the robes of peace? Not so; both must be worn together, for neither is found in its completeness without the other. Beneath the armour must be the fine linen, clean and white—and at one and the same time, our souls may be clad in all pity, mercifulness and love, and in all the sparkling panoply of courage and strength for battle.

But both the armour and the dress of peace presuppose that we have listened to Christ's pleading counsel to buy of Him "white raiment that we may be clothed, and that the shame of our nakedness do not appear." The garment for the soul, which is to hide its deformities and to replace our own filthy rags, is woven in no earthly looms, and no efforts of ours will bring us into possession of it. We must be content to owe it wholly to Christ's gift, or else we shall have to go without it altogether. The first step in the Christian life is by simple faith to receive from Him the forgiveness of all our sins, and that new nature which He alone can impart, and which we can neither create nor win, but must simply accept. Then, after that, come the field and the time for efforts put forth in His strength, to array our souls in His likeness, and day by day to put on the beautiful garments which He bestows. It is a lifelong work thus to strip ourselves of the rags of our old vices, and to gird on the robe of righteousness. Lofty encouragements, tender motives, solemn warnings, all point to this as our continual task. We should set ourselves to it in His strength, if so be that being clothed, we may not be found naked—and then, when we lay aside the garment of flesh and the armour needed for the battle, we shall hear His voice welcoming us to the land of peace, and shall walk with Him in victor's robes, glistening "so as no fuller on earth could white them."

XXI

THE PRACTICAL EFFECTS OF THE PEACE OF CHRIST, THE WORD OF CHRIST, AND THE NAME OF CHRIST

"And let the peace of Christ rule in your hearts, to the which also ye were called in one body; and be ye thankful. Let the word of Christ dwell in you richly in all wisdom; teaching and admonishing one another with psalms *and* hymns *and* spiritual songs, singing with grace in your hearts unto God. And whatsoever ye do in word or in deed, *do* all in the name of the Lord Jesus, giving thanks to God the Father through Him."—Col. iii. 15–17 (Rev. Vers.).

There are here three precepts somewhat loosely connected, of which the first belongs properly to the series considered in our last section, from which it is only separated as not sharing in the metaphor under which the virtues contained in the former verses were set forth. In substance it is closely connected with them, though in form it is different, and in sweep is more comprehensive. The second refers mainly to Christian intercourse, especially to social worship; and the third covers the whole field of conduct, and fitly closes the series, which in it reaches the utmost possible generality, and from it drops to the inculcation of very special domestic duties. The three verses have each a dominant phrase round which we may group their teaching. These three are, the peace of Christ, the word of Christ, the name of the Lord Jesus.

I. The Ruling Peace of Christ.

The various reading "peace of Christ," for "peace of God," is not only recommended by manuscript authority, but has the advantage of bringing the expression into connection with the great words of the Lord, "Peace I leave with you, My peace I give unto you." A strange legacy to leave, and a strange moment at which to speak of His peace! It was but an hour or so since He had been "troubled in spirit," as He thought of the betrayer—and in an hour more He would be beneath the olives of Gethsemane; and yet, even at such a time, He bestows on His friends some share in His own deep repose of spirit. Surely "the peace of Christ" must mean what "My peace" meant; not only the peace which He gives, but the peace which lay, like a great calm on the sea, on His own deep heart; and surely we cannot restrict so solemn an expression to the meaning of mutual concord among brethren. That, no doubt, is included in it, but there is much more than that. Whatever made the strange calm which leaves such unmistakable traces in the picture of Christ drawn in the Gospels, may be ours. When He gave us His peace, He gave us some share in that meek submission of will to His Father's will, and in that stainless purity, which were its chief elements. The hearts and lives of men are made troubled, not by circumstances, but by themselves. Whoever can keep his own will in harmony with God's enters into rest, though many trials and sorrows may be his. Even if within and without are fightings, there may be a central "peace subsisting at the heart of endless agitation." We are our own disturbers. The eager swift motions of our own wills keep us restless. Forsake these, and quiet comes. Christ's peace was the result of the perfect harmony of all His nature. All was co-operant to one great purpose; desires and passions did not war with conscience and reason, nor did the flesh lust against the Spirit. Though that complete uniting of all our inner selves in the sweet concord of perfect obedience is not attained on earth, yet its beginnings are given to us by Christ, and in Him we may be at peace with ourselves, and have one great ruling power binding all our conflicting desires in one, as the moon draws after her the heaped waters of the sea.

We are summoned to improve that gift—to "*let* the peace of Christ" have its way in our hearts. The surest way to increase our possession of it is to decrease our separation from Him. The fulness of our possession of His gift of peace depends altogether on our proximity to the Giver. It evaporates in carrying. It "diminishes as the square of the distance" from the source. So the exhortation to let it rule in us will be best fulfilled by keeping thought and affection in close union with our Lord.

This peace is to "rule" in our hearts. The figure contained in the word here translated *rule* is that of the umpire or arbitrator at the games, who, looking down on the arena, watches that the combatants strive lawfully, and adjudges the prize. Possibly the force of the figure may have been washed out of the word by use, and the "rule" of our rendering may be all that it means. But there seems no reason against keeping the full force of the expression, which adds picturesqueness and point to the precept. The peace of Christ, then, is to sit enthroned as umpire in the heart; or, if we might give a mediæval instead of a classical shape to the figure, that fair sovereign, Peace, is to be Queen of the Tournament, and her "eyes rain influence and adjudge the prize." When contending impulses and reasons distract and seem to pull us in opposite directions, let her settle which is to prevail. How can the peace of Christ do that for us? We may make a rude test of good and evil by their effects on our inward repose. Whatever mars our tranquillity, ruffling the surface so that Christ's image is no longer visible, is to be avoided. That stillness of spirit is very sensitive and shrinks away at the presence of an evil thing. Let it be for us what the barometer is to a sailor, and if it sinks, let us be sure a storm is at hand. If we find that a given course of action tends to break our peace, we may be certain that there is poison in the draught which as in the old stories, has been detected by the shivered cup, and we should not drink any more. There is nothing so precious that it is worth while to lose the peace of Christ for the sake of it. Whenever we find it in peril, we must retrace our steps.

Then follows appended a reason for cultivating the peace of Christ "to which also ye were called in one body." The very purpose of God's merciful summons and invitation to them in the gospel was that they might share in this peace. There are many ways of putting God's design in His call by the gospel—it may be represented under many angles and from many points of view, and is glorious from all and each. No one word can state all the fulness to which we are called by His wonderful love, but none can be tenderer and more blessed than this thought, that God's great voice has summoned us to a share in Christ's peace. Being so called, all who share in it of course find themselves knit to each other by possession of a common gift. What a contradiction then, to be summoned in order to so blessed a possession, and not to allow it sovereign sway in moulding heart and life! What a contradiction, further, to have been gathered into one body by the common possession of the peace of Christ, and yet not to allow it to bind all the members in its sweet fetters with cords of love! The sway of the "peace of Christ" in our hearts will ensure the perfect exercise of all the other graces of which we have been hearing, and therefore this precept fitly closes the series of exhortations to brotherly affections, and seals all with the thought of the "one body" of which all these "new men" are members.

The very abruptness of the introduction of the next precept gives it force, "and be ye thankful," or, as we might translate with an accuracy which perhaps is not too minute, "become thankful," striving towards deeper gratitude than you have yet attained. Paul is ever apt to catch fire as often as his thought brings him in sight of God's great love in drawing men to Himself, and in giving them such rich gifts. It is quite a feature of his style to break into sudden bursts of praise as often as his path leads him to a summit from which he catches a glimpse of that great miracle of love. This interjected precept is precisely like these sudden jets of praise. It is as if he had broken off for a moment from the line of his thought, and had said to his hearers—Think of that wonderful love of your Father God. He has called you from the midst of your heathenism, He has called you from a world of tumult and a life of troubled unrest to possess the peace which brooded ever, like the mystic dove, over Christ's head; He has called you in one body, having knit in a grand unity us, Jews and Gentiles, so widely parted before. Let us pause and lift up our voices in praise to Him. True thankfulness will well up at all moments, and will underlie and blend with all duties. There are frequent injunctions to thankfulness in this letter, and we have it again enjoined in the closing words of the verses which we are now considering, so that we may defer any further remarks till we come to deal with these.

II. The Indwelling Word of Christ.

The main reference of this verse seems to be to the worship of the Church—the highest expression of its oneness. There are three points enforced in its three clauses, of which the first is the dwelling in the hearts of the Colossian Christians of the "word of Christ," by which is meant, as I conceive, not simply "the presence of Christ in the heart, as an inward monitor,"[3] but the indwelling of the definite body of truths contained in the gospel which had been preached to them. That gospel is the word of Christ, inasmuch as He is its subject. These early Christians received that body of truth by oral teaching. To us it comes in the history of Christ's life and death, and in the exposition of the significance and far-reaching depth and power of these, which are contained in the rest of the New Testament—a very definite body of teaching. How can it abide in the heart? or what is the dwelling of that word within us but the occupation of mind and heart and will with the truth concerning Jesus revealed to us in Scripture? This indwelling is in our own power, for it is matter of precept and not of promise—and if we want to have it we must do with religious truth just what we do with other truths that we want to keep in our minds—ponder them, use our faculties on them, be perpetually recurring to them, fix them in our memories, like nails fastened in a sure place, and, that we may remember them, "get them by heart," as the children say. Few things are more wanting to-day than this. The popular Christianity of the day is strong in philanthropic service, and some phases of it are full of "evangelistic" activity, but it is wofully lacking in intelligent grasp of the great principles involved and revealed in the gospel. Some Christians have yielded to the popular prejudice against "dogma," and have come to dislike and neglect the doctrinal side of religion, and others are so busy in good works of various kinds that they have no time nor inclination to reflect nor to learn, and for others "the cares of this world and the lusts of other things, entering in, choke the word." A merely intellectual Christianity is a very poor thing, no doubt; but that has been dinned into our ears so long and loudly for a generation now, that there is much need for a clear preaching of the other side—namely, that a merely emotional Christianity is a still poorer, and that if feeling on the one hand and conduct on the other are to be worthy of men with heads on their shoulders and brains in their heads, both feeling and conduct must be built on a foundation of truth believed and pondered. In the ordered monarchy of human nature, reason is meant to govern, but she is also meant to submit, and for her the law holds good, she must learn to obey that she may be able to rule. She must bow to the word of Christ, and then she will sway aright the kingdom of the soul. It becomes us to make conscience of seeking to get a firm and intelligent grasp of Christian truth as a whole, and not to be always living on milk meant for babes, nor to expect that teachers and preachers should only repeat for ever the things which we know already.

That word is to dwell in Christian men *richly*. It is their own fault if they possess it, as so many do, in scant measure. It might be a full tide. Why in so many is it a mere trickle, like an Australian river in the heat, a line of shallow ponds with no life or motion, scarcely connected by a thread of moisture, and surrounded by great stretches of blinding shingle, when it might be a broad water—"waters to swim in"? Why, but because they do not do with this word, what all students do with the studies which they love?

The word should manifest the rich abundance of its dwelling in men by opening out in their minds into "every kind of wisdom." Where the gospel in its power dwells in a man's spirit, and is intelligently meditated on and studied, it will effloresce into principles of thought and action applicable to all subjects, and touching the whole round horizon of human life. All, and more than all, the wisdom which these false teachers promised in their mysteries, is given to the babes and the simple ones who treasure the word of Christ in their hearts, and the least among them may say, "I have more understanding than all my teachers, for Thy testimonies are my meditation." That gospel which the child may receive, has "infinite riches in a narrow room," and, like some tiny black seed, for all its humble form, has hidden in it the promise and potency of wondrous beauty of flower, and nourishment of fruit. Cultured and cared for in the heart where it is sown, it will unfold into all truth which a man can receive or God can give, concerning God and man, our nature, duties, hopes and destinies, the tasks of the moment, and the glories of eternity. He who has it and lets it dwell richly in his heart is wise; he who has it not, "at his latter end shall be a fool."

The second clause of this verse deals with the manifestations of the indwelling word in the worship of the Church. The individual possession of the word in one's own heart does not make us independent of brotherly help. Rather, it is the very foundation of the duty of sharing our riches with our fellows, and of increasing ours by contributions from their stores. And so—"teaching and admonishing one another" is the outcome of it. The universal possession of Christ's word involves the equally universal right and duty of mutual instruction.

We have already heard the Apostle declaring it to be his work to "admonish every man and to teach every man," and found that the former office pointed to practical ethical instruction, not without rebuke and warning, while the latter referred rather to doctrinal teaching. What he there claimed for himself, he here enjoins on the whole Christian community. We have here a glimpse of the perfectly simple, informal public services of the early Church, which seem to have partaken much more of the nature of a free conference than of any of the forms of worship at present in use in any Church. The evidence both of this passage and of the other Pauline Epistles, especially of the first Epistle to the Corinthians (xiv.) unmistakably shows this. The forms of worship in the apostolic Church are not meant for models, and we do not prove a usage as intended to be permanent because we prove it to be primitive; but the principles which underlie the usages are valid always and everywhere, and one of these principles is the universal though not equal inspiration of Christian men, which results in their universal calling to teach and admonish. In what forms that principle shall be expressed, how safeguarded and controlled, is of secondary importance. Different stages of culture and a hundred other circumstances will modify these, and nobody but a pedant or religious martinet will care about uniformity. But I cannot but believe that the present practice of confining the public teaching of the Church to an official class has done harm. Why should one man be for ever speaking, and hundreds of people who are able to teach, sitting dumb to listen or pretend to listen to him? Surely there is a wasteful expenditure there. I hate forcible revolution, and do not believe that any institutions, either political or ecclesiastical, which need violence to sweep them away, are ready to be removed; but I believe that if the level of spiritual life were raised among us, new forms would naturally be evolved, in which there should be a more adequate recognition of the great principle on which the democracy of Christianity is founded, namely, "I will pour out My Spirit on all flesh—and on My servants and on My handmaidens I will pour out in these days of My Spirit, and they shall prophesy." There are not wanting signs that many different classes of Christian worshippers have ceased to find edification in the present manner of teaching. The more cultured write books on "the decay of preaching;" the more earnest take to mission halls and a "freer service," and "lay preaching;" the more indifferent stay at home. When the tide rises, all the idle craft stranded on the mud are set in motion; such a time is surely coming for the Church, when the aspiration that has waited millenniums for its fulfilment, and received but a partial accomplishment at Pentecost, shall at last be a fact: "would God that all the Lord's people were prophets, and that the Lord would put His Spirit upon them!"

The teaching and admonishing is here regarded as being effected by means of song. That strikes one as singular, and tempts to another punctuation of the verse, by which "In all wisdom teaching and admonishing one another" should make a separate clause, and "in psalms and hymns and spiritual songs" should be attached to the following words. But probably the ordinary arrangement of clauses is best on the whole. The distinction between "psalms" and "hymns" appears to be that the former is a song with a musical accompaniment, and that the latter is vocal praise to God. No doubt the "psalms" meant were chiefly those of the Psalter, the Old Testament element in the early Christian worship, while the "hymns" were the new product of the spirit of devotion which had naturally broken into song, the first beginnings of the great treasure of Christian hymnody. "Spiritual songs" is a more general expression, including all varieties of Christian poesy, provided that they come from the Spirit moving in the heart. We know from many sources that song had a large part in the worship of the early Church. Indeed, whenever a great quickening of religious life comes, a great burst of Christian song comes with it. The onward march of the Church has ever been attended by music of praise; "as well the singers as the players on instruments" have been there. The mediæval Latin hymns cluster round the early pure days of the monastic orders; Luther's rough stormy hymns were as powerful as his treatises; the mystic tenderness and rapture of Charles Wesley's have become the possession of the whole Church. We hear from outside observers, that one of the practices of the early Christians which most attracted heathen notice was, that they assembled daily before it was light and "sang hymns of praise to one Christus as to a god."

These early hymns were of a dogmatic character. No doubt, just as in many a missionary Church a hymn is found to be the best vehicle for conveying the truth, so it was in these early Churches, which were made up largely of slaves and women—both uneducated. "Singing the gospel" is a very old invention, though the name be new. The picture which we get here of the meetings of the early Christians is very remarkable. Evidently their gatherings were free and social, with the minimum of form, and that most elastic. If a man had any word of exhortation for the people, he might say on. "Every one of you hath a psalm, a doctrine." If a man had some fragment of an old psalm, or some strain that had come fresh from the Christian heart, he might sing it, and his brethren would listen. We do not have that sort of psalmody now. But what a long way we have travelled from it to a modern congregation, standing with books that they scarcely look at, and "worshipping" in a hymn which half of them do not open their mouths to sing at all, and the other half do in a voice inaudible three pews off.

The best praise, however, is a heart song. So the Apostle adds "singing in your hearts unto God." And it is to be in "grace," that is to say, *in* it as the atmosphere and element in which the song moves, which is nearly equivalent to "by means of the Divine grace" which works in the heart, and impels to that perpetual music of silent praise. If we have the peace of Christ in our hearts, and the word of Christ dwelling in us richly in all wisdom, then an unspoken and perpetual music will dwell there too, "a noise like of a hidden brook" singing for ever its "quiet tune."

III. The all-hallowing Name of Jesus.

From worship the Apostle passes to life, and crowns the entire series of injunctions with an all-comprehensive precept, covering the whole ground of action. "*Whatsoever* ye do, in word or deed"—then, not merely worship, specially so called, but everything is to come under the influence of the same motive. That expresses emphatically the sanctity of common life, and extends the idea of worship to all deeds. "Whatsoever ye *do* in *word*"—then words are *doings*, and in many respects the most important of our doings. Some words, though they fade off the ear so quickly, outlast all contemporary deeds, and are more lasting than brass. Not only "the word of the Lord," but, in a very solemn sense, the word of man "endureth for ever."

Do all "in the name of the Lord Jesus." That means at least two things— in obedience to His authority, and in dependence on His help. These two are the twin talismans which change the whole character of our actions, and preserve us, in doing them, from every harm. That name hallows and ennobles all work. Nothing can be so small but this will make it great, nor so monotonous and tame but this will make it beautiful and fresh. The name now, as of old, casts out devils and stills storms. "For the name of the Lord Jesus" is the silken padding which makes our yokes easy. It brings the sudden strength which makes our burdens light. We may write it over all our actions. If there be any on which we dare not inscribe it, they are not for us.

Thus done in the name of Christ, all deeds will become thanksgiving, and so reach their highest consecration and their truest blessedness. "Giving thanks to God the Father through Him" is ever to accompany the work in the name of Jesus. The exhortation to thanksgiving, which is in a sense the Alpha and the Omega of the Christian life, is perpetually on the Apostle's lips, because thankfulness should be in perpetual operation in our hearts.

It is so important because it presupposes all-important things, and because it certainly leads to every Christian grace. For continual thankfulness there must be a continual direction of mind towards God and towards the great gifts of our salvation in Jesus Christ. There must be a continual going forth of our love and our desire to these, that is to say—thankfulness rests on the reception and the joyful appropriation of the mercies of God, brought to us by our Lord. And it underlies all acceptable service and all happy obedience. The servant who thinks of God as a harsh exactor is slothful; the servant who thinks of Him as the "giving God" rejoices in toil. He who brings his work in order to be paid for it, will get no wages, and turn out no work worth any. He who brings it because he feels that he has been paid plentiful wages beforehand, of which he will never earn the least mite, will present service well pleasing to the Master.

So we should keep thoughts of Jesus Christ, and of all we owe to Him, ever before us in our common work, in shop and mill and counting-house, in study and street and home. We should try to bring all our actions more under their influence, and, moved by the mercies of God, should yield ourselves living thank-offerings to Him, who is the sin-offering for us. If, as every fresh duty arises, we hear Christ saying, "This do in remembrance of Me," all life will become a true communion with Him, and every common vessel will be as a sacramental chalice, and the bells of the horses will bear the same inscription as the high priest's mitre—"Holiness to the Lord." To lay work on that altar sanctifies both the giver and the gift. Presented through Him, by whom all blessings come to man and all thanks go to God, and kindled by the flame of gratitude, our poor deeds, for all their grossness and earthliness, shall go up in curling wreaths of incense, an odour of a sweet smell acceptable to God by Jesus Christ.

FOOTNOTES:

[3] Lightfoot.

XXII
THE CHRISTIAN FAMILY

"Wives, be in subjection to your husbands, as is fitting in the Lord. Husbands, love your wives, and be not bitter against them.

"Children, obey your parents in all things, for this is well-pleasing in the Lord. Fathers, provoke not your children, that they be not discouraged.

"Servants, obey in all things them that are your masters according to the flesh; not with eyeservice, as men-pleasers; but in singleness of heart, fearing the Lord: whatsoever ye do, work heartily, as unto the Lord, and not unto men; knowing that from the Lord ye shall receive the recompense of the inheritance: ye serve the Lord Christ. For he that doeth wrong shall receive again for the wrong that he hath done: and there is no respect of persons.

"Masters, render unto your servants that which is just and equal; knowing that ye also have a Master in Heaven." — Col. iii. 18–iv. 1 (Rev. Ver.).

This section deals with the Christian family, as made up of husband and wife, children, and servants. In the family, Christianity has most signally displayed its power of refining, ennobling, and sanctifying earthly relationships. Indeed, one may say that domestic life, as seen in thousands of Christian homes, is purely a Christian creation, and would have been a new revelation to the heathenism of Colossæ, as it is to-day in many a mission field.

We do not know what may have led Paul to dwell with special emphasis on the domestic duties, in this letter, and in the contemporaneous Epistle of the Ephesians. He does so, and the parallel section there should be carefully compared throughout with this paragraph. The former is considerably more expanded, and may have been written after the verses before us; but, however that may be, the verbal coincidences and variations in the two sections are very interesting as illustrations of the way in which a mind fully charged with a theme will freely repeat itself, and use the same words in different combinations and with infinite shades of modification.

The precepts given are extremely simple and obvious. Domestic happiness and family Christianity are made up of very homely elements. One duty is prescribed for the one member of each of the three family groups, and varying forms of another for the other. The wife, the child, the servant are bid to obey; the husband to love, the father to show his love in gentle considerateness; the master to yield his servants their dues. Like some perfume distilled from common flowers that grow on every bank, the domestic piety which makes home a house of God, and a gate of heaven, is prepared from these two simples—obedience and love. These are all.

We have here then the ideal Christian household in the three ordinary relationships which make up the family; wife and husband, children and father, servant and master.

I. The Reciprocal Duties of wife and husband—subjection and love.

The duty of the wife is "subjection," and it is enforced on the ground that it is "fitting in the Lord"—that is, "it is," or perhaps "it became" at the time of conversion, "the conduct corresponding to or befitting the condition of being in the Lord." In more modern language—the Christian ideal of the wife's duty has for its very centre—subjection.

Some of us will smile at that; some of us will think it an old-fashioned notion, a survival of a more barbarous theory of marriage than this century recognises. But, before we decide upon the correctness of the apostolic precept, let us make quite sure of its meaning. Now, if we turn to the corresponding passage in Ephesians, we find that marriage is regarded from a high and sacred point of view, as being an earthly shadow and faint adumbration of the union between Christ and the Church.

To Paul, all human and earthly relationships were moulded after the patterns of things in the heavens, and the whole fleeting visible life of man was a parable of the "things which are" in the spiritual realm. Most chiefly, the holy and mysterious union of man and woman in marriage is fashioned in the likeness of the only union which is closer and more mysterious than itself, namely that between Christ and His Church.

Such then as are the nature and the spring of the Church's "subjection" to Christ, such will be the nature and the spring of the wife's "subjection" to the husband. That is to say, it is a subjection of which love is the very soul and animating principle. In a true marriage, as in the loving obedience of a believing soul to Christ, the wife submits not because she has found a master, but because her heart has found its rest. Everything harsh or degrading melts away from the requirement when thus looked at. It is a joy to serve where the heart is engaged, and that is eminently true of the feminine nature. For its full satisfaction, a woman's heart needs to look up where it loves. She has certainly the fullest wedded life who can "reverence" her husband. For its full satisfaction, a woman's heart needs to serve where it loves. That is the same as saying that a woman's love is, in the general, nobler, purer, more unselfish than a man's, and therein, quite as much as in physical constitution, is laid the foundation of that Divine ideal of marriage, which places the wife's delight and dignity in sweet loving subjection.

Of course the subjection has its limitations. "We must obey God rather than man" bounds the field of all human authority and control. Then there are cases in which, on the principle of "the tools to the hands that can use them," the rule falls naturally to the wife as the stronger character. Popular sarcasm, however, shows that such instances are felt to be contrary to the true ideal, and such a wife lacks something of repose for her heart.

No doubt, too, since Paul wrote, and very largely by Christian influences, women have been educated and elevated, so as to make mere subjection impossible now, if ever it were so. Woman's quick instinct as to persons, her finer wisdom, her purer discernment as to moral questions, make it in a thousand cases the wisest thing a man can do to listen to the "subtle flow of silver-paced counsel" which his wife gives him. All such considerations are fully consistent with this apostolic teaching, and it remains true that the wife who does not reverence and lovingly obey is to be pitied if she cannot, and to be condemned if she will not.

And what of the husband's duty? He is to love, and because he loves, not to be harsh or bitter, in word, look or act. The parallel in Ephesians adds the solemn elevating thought, that a man's love to the woman, whom he has made his own, is to be like Christ's to the Church. Patient and generous, utterly self-forgetting and self-sacrificing, demanding nothing, grudging nothing, giving all, not shrinking from the extreme of suffering and pain and death itself—that he may bless and help—such was the Lord's love to His bride, such is to be a Christian husband's love to his wife. That solemn example, which lifts the whole emotion high above mere passion or selfish affection, carries a great lesson too as to the connection between man's love and woman's "subjection." The former is to evoke the latter, just as in the heavenly pattern, Christ's love melts and moves human wills to glad obedience, which is liberty. We do not say that a wife is utterly absolved from obedience where a husband fails in self-forgetting love, though certainly it does not lie in *his* mouth to accuse, whose fault is graver than and the origin of hers. But, without going so far as that, we may recognise the true order to be that the husband's love, self-sacrificing and all-bestowing, is meant to evoke the wife's love, delighting in service, and proud to crown him her king.

Where there is such love, there will be no question of mere command and obedience, no tenacious adherence to rights, or jealous defence of independence. Law will be transformed into choice. To obey will be joy; to serve, the natural expression of the heart. Love uttering a wish speaks music to love listening; and love obeying the wish is free and a queen. Such sacred beauty may light up wedded life, if it catches a gleam from the fountain of all light, and shines by reflection from the love that binds Christ to His Church as the links of the golden beams bind the sun to the planet. Husbands and wives are to see to it that this supreme consecration purifies and raises their love. Young men and maidens are to remember that the nobleness and heart-repose of their whole life may be made or marred by marriage, and to take heed where they fix their affections. If there be not unity in the deepest thing of all, love to Christ, the sacredness and completeness will fade away from any love. But if a man and woman love and marry "in the Lord," He will be "in the midst," walking between them, a third who will make them one, and that threefold cord will not be quickly broken.

II. The Reciprocal Duties of children and parents—obedience and gentle loving authority.

The injunction to children is laconic, decisive, universal. "Obey your parents in all things." Of course, there is one limitation to that. If God's command looks one way, and a parent's the opposite, disobedience is duty—but such extreme case is probably the only one which Christian ethics admit as an exception to the rule. The Spartan brevity of the command is enforced by one consideration, "for this is well-pleasing *in* the Lord," as the Revised Version rightly reads, instead of "to the Lord," as in the Authorised, thus making an exact parallel to the former "fitting in the Lord." Not only to Christ, but to all who can appreciate the beauty of goodness, is filial obedience beautiful. The parallel in Ephesians substitutes "for this is right," appealing to the natural conscience. Right and fair in itself, it is accordant with the law stamped on the very relationship, and it is witnessed as such by the instinctive approbation which it evokes.

No doubt, the moral sentiment of Paul's age stretched parental authority to an extreme, and we need not hesitate to admit that the Christian idea of a father's power and a child's obedience has been much softened by Christianity; but the softening has come from the greater prominence given to love, rather than from the limitation given to obedience.

Our present domestic life seems to me to stand sorely in need of Paul's injunction. One cannot but see that there is great laxity in this matter in many Christian households, in reaction perhaps from the too great severity of past times. Many causes lead to this unwholesome relaxation of parental authority. In our great cities, especially among the commercial classes, children are generally better educated than their fathers and mothers, they know less of early struggles, and one often sees a sense of inferiority making a parent hesitate to command, as well as a misplaced tenderness making him hesitate to forbid. A very misplaced and cruel tenderness it is to say "would you like?" when he ought to say "I wish." It is unkind to lay on young shoulders "the weight of too much liberty," and to introduce young hearts too soon to the sad responsibility of choosing between good and evil. It were better and more loving by far to put off that day, and to let the children feel that in the safe nest of home, their feeble and ignorant goodness is sheltered behind a strong barrier of command, and their lives simplified by having the one duty of obedience. By many parents the advice is needed—consult your children less, command them more.

And as for children, here is the one thing which God would have them do: "Obey your parents in all things." As fathers used to say when I was a boy—"not only obedience, but prompt obedience." It is right. That should be enough. But children may also remember that it is "pleasing"—fair and good to see, making them agreeable in the eyes of all whose approbation is worth having, and pleasing to themselves, saving them from many a bitter thought in after days, when the grave has closed over father and mother. One remembers the story of how Dr. Johnson, when a man, stood in the market place at Lichfield, bareheaded, with the rain pouring on him, in remorseful remembrance of boyish disobedience to his dead father. There is nothing bitterer than the too late tears for wrongs done to those who are gone beyond the reach of our penitence. "Children obey your parents in all things," that you may be spared the sting of conscience for childish faults, which may be set tingling and smarting again even in old age.

The law for parents is addressed to "fathers," partly because a mother's tenderness has less need of the warning "provoke not your children," than a father's more rigorous rule usually has, and partly because the father is regarded as the head of the household. The advice is full of practical sagacity. How do parents provoke their children? By unreasonable commands, by perpetual restrictions, by capricious jerks at the bridle, alternating with as capricious dropping of the reins altogether, by not governing their own tempers, by shrill or stern tones where quiet, soft ones would do, by frequent checks and rebukes, and sparing praise. And what is sure to follow such mistreatment by father or mother? First, as the parallel passage in Ephesians has it; "wrath"—bursts of temper, for which probably the child is punished and the parent is guilty—and then spiritless listlessness and apathy. "I cannot please him whatever I do," leads to a rankling sense of injustice, and then to recklessness—"it is useless to try any more." And when a child or a man loses heart, there will be no more obedience. Paul's theory of the training of children is closely connected with his central doctrine, that love is the life of service, and faith the parent of righteousness. To him hope and gladness and confident love underlie all obedience. When a child loves and trusts, he will obey. When he fears and has to think of his father as capricious, exacting or stern, he will do like the man in the parable, who was afraid because he thought of his master as austere, reaping where he did not sow, and therefore went and hid his talent. Children's obedience must be fed on love and praise. Fear paralyses activity, and kills service, whether it cowers in the heart of a boy to his father, or of a man to his Father in heaven.

So parents are to let the sunshine of their smile ripen their children's love to fruit of obedience, and remember that frost in spring scatters the blossoms on the grass. Many a parent, especially many a father, drives his child into evil by keeping him at a distance. He should make his boy a companion and playmate, teach him to think of his father as his confidant, try to keep his child nearer to himself than to anybody beside, and then his authority will be absolute, his opinions an oracle, and his lightest wish a law. Is not the kingdom of Jesus Christ based on His becoming a brother and one of ourselves, and is it not wielded in gentleness and enforced by love? Is it not the most absolute of rules? and should not the parental authority be like it—having a reed for a sceptre, lowliness and gentleness being stronger to rule and to sway than the "rods of iron" or of gold which earthly monarchs wield?

There is added to this precept, in Ephesians, an injunction on the positive side of parental duty: "Bring them up in the nurture and admonition of the Lord." I fear that is a duty fallen wofully into disuse in many Christian households. Many parents think it wise to send their children away from home for their education, and so hand over their moral and religious training to teachers. That may be right, but it makes the fulfilment of this precept all but impossible. Others, who have their children beside them, are too busy all the week, and too fond of "rest" on Sunday. Many send their children to a Sunday school chiefly that they themselves may have a quiet house and a sound sleep in the afternoon. Every Christian minister, if he keeps his eyes open, must see that there is no religious instruction worth calling by the name in a very large number of professedly Christian households; and he is bound to press very earnestly on his hearers the question, whether the Christian fathers and mothers among them do their duty in this matter.

Many of them, I fear, have never opened their lips to their children on religious subjects. Is it not a grief and a shame that men and women with some religion in them, and loving their little ones dearly, should be tongue-tied before them on the most important of all things? What can come of it but what does come of it so often that it saddens one to see how frequently it occurs—that the children drift away from a faith which their parents did not care enough about to teach it to them? A silent father makes prodigal sons, and many a grey head has been brought down with sorrow to the grave, and many a mother's heart broken, because he and she neglected their plain duty, which can be handed over to no schools or masters—the duty of religious instruction. "These words which I command thee, shall be in thine heart; and thou shalt teach them diligently to thy children, and shalt talk of them when thou sittest in thine house."

III. The Reciprocal Duties of servants and masters—obedience and justice.

The first thing to observe here is, that these "servants" are slaves, not persons who have voluntarily given their work for wages. The relation of Christianity to slavery is too wide a subject to be touched here. It must be enough to point out that Paul recognises that "sum of all villanies," gives instructions to both parties in it, never says one word in condemnation of it. More remarkable still; the messenger who carried this letter to Colossæ carried in the same bag the Epistle to Philemon, and was accompanied by the fugitive slave Onesimus, on whose neck Paul bound again the chain, so to speak, with his own hands. And yet the gospel which Paul preached has in it principles which cut up slavery by the roots; as we read in this very letter, "In Christ Jesus there is neither bond nor free." Why then did not Christ and His apostles make war against slavery? For the same reason for which they did not make war against *any* political or social institutions. "First make the tree good and his fruit good." The only way to reform institutions is to elevate and quicken the general conscience, and then the evil will be outgrown, left behind, or thrown aside. Mould men and the men will mould institutions. So Christianity did not set itself to fell this upas tree, which would have been a long and dangerous task; but girdled it, as we may say, stripped the bark off it, and left it to die—and it *has* died in all Christian lands now.

But the principles laid down here are quite as applicable to our form of domestic and other service as to the slaves and masters of Colossæ.

Note then the extent of the servant's obedience—"in all things." Here, of course, as in former cases, is there presupposed the limit of supreme obedience to God's commands; that being safe, all else is to give way to the duty of submission. It is a stern command, that seems all on the side of the masters. It might strike a chill into many a slave, who had been drawn to the gospel by the hope of finding some little lightening of the yoke that pressed so heavily on his poor galled neck, and of hearing some voice speaking in tenderer tones than those of harsh command. Still more emphatically, and, as it might seem, still more harshly, the Apostle goes on to insist on the inward completeness of the obedience—"not with eyeservice (a word of Paul's own coining) as men-pleasers." We have a proverb about the worth of the master's eye, which bears witness that the same fault still clings to hired service. One has only to look at the next set of bricklayers one sees on a scaffold, or of haymakers one comes across in a field, to see it. The vice was venial in slaves; it is inexcusable, because it darkens into theft, in paid servants—and it spreads far and wide. All scamped work, all productions of man's hand or brain which are got up to look better than they are, all fussy parade of diligence when under inspection and slackness afterwards—and all their like which infect and infest every trade and profession, are transfixed by the sharp point of this precept.

"But in singleness of heart," that is, with undivided motive, which is the antithesis and the cure for "eyeservice"—and "fearing God," which is opposed to "pleasing men." Then follows the positive injunction, covering the whole ground of action and lifting the constrained obedience to the earthly master up into the sacred and serene loftiness of religious duty, "whatsoever ye do, work heartily," or from the soul. The word for *work* is stronger than that for *do*, and implies effort and toil. They are to put all their power into their work, and not be afraid of hard toil. And they are not only to bend their backs but their wills, and to labour "from the soul," that is, cheerfully and with interest—a hard lesson for a slave and asking more than could be expected from human nature, as many of them would, no doubt, think. Paul goes on to transfigure the squalor and misery of the slave's lot by a sudden beam of light—"as to the Lord"—your true "Master," for it is the same word as in the previous verse—"and not unto men." Do not think of your tasks as only enjoined by harsh, capricious, selfish men, but lift your thoughts to Christ, who is your Lord, and glorify all these sordid duties by seeing *His* will in them. He only who works as "to the Lord," will work "heartily." The thought of Christ's command, and of my poor toil as done for His sake, will change constraint into cheerfulness, and make unwelcome tasks pleasant, and monotonous ones fresh, and trivial ones great. It will evoke new powers, and renewed consecration. In that atmosphere, the dim flame of servile obedience will burn more brightly, as a lamp plunged into a jar of pure oxygen.

The stimulus of a great hope for the ill-used, unpaid slave, is added. Whatever their earthly masters might fail to give them, the true Master whom they really served would accept no work for which He did not return more than sufficient wages. "From the Lord ye shall receive the recompense of the inheritance." Blows and scanty food and poor lodging may be all that they get from their owners for all their sweat and toil, but if they are Christ's slaves, they will be treated no more as slaves, but as sons, and receive a son's portion, the exact recompense which consists of the "inheritance." The juxtaposition of the two ideas of the slave and the inheritance evidently hints at the unspoken thought, that they are heirs because they are sons—a thought which might well lift up bowed backs and brighten dull faces. The hope of that reward came like an angel into the smoky huts and hopeless lives of these poor slaves. It shone athwart all the gloom and squalor, and taught patience beneath "the oppressor's wrong, the proud man's contumely." Through long, weary generations it has lived in the hearts of men driven to God by man's tyranny, and forced to clutch at heaven's brightness to keep them from being made mad by earth's blackness. It may irradiate our poor lives, especially when we fail, as we all do sometimes, to get recognition of our work, or fruit from it. If we labour for man's appreciation or gratitude, we shall certainly be disappointed; but if for Christ, we have abundant wages beforehand, and we shall have an overabundant requital, the munificence of which will make us more ashamed of our unworthy service than anything else could do. Christ remains in no man's debt. "Who hath first given, and it shall be recompensed to him again?"

The last word to the slave is a warning against neglect of duty. There is to be a double recompense—to the slave of Christ the portion of a son; to the wrong doer retribution "for the wrong that he has done." Then, though slavery was itself a wrong, though the master who held a man in bondage was himself inflicting the greatest of all wrongs, yet Paul will have the slave think that he still has duties to his master. That is part of Paul's general position as to slavery. He will not wage war against it, but for the present accept it. Whether he saw the full bearing of the gospel on that and other infamous institutions may be questioned. He has given us the principles which will destroy them, but he is no revolutionist, and so his present counsel is to remember the master's rights, even though they be founded on wrong, and he has no hesitation in condemning and predicting retribution for evil things done by a slave to his master. A superior's injustice does not warrant an inferior's breach of moral law, though it may excuse it. Two blacks do not make a white. Herein lies the condemnation of all the crimes which enslaved nations and classes have done, of many a deed which has been honoured and sung, of the sanguinary cruelties of servile revolts, as well as of the questionable means to which labour often resorts in modern industrial warfare. The homely, plain principle, that a man does not receive the right to break God's laws because he is ill-treated, would clear away much fog from some people's notions of how to advance the cause of the oppressed.

But, on the other hand, this warning may look towards the masters also; and probably the same double reference is also to be discerned in the closing words to the slaves, "and there is no respect of persons." The servants were naturally tempted to think that God was on their side, as indeed He was, but also to think that the great coming day of judgment was mostly meant to be terrible to tyrants and oppressors, and so to look forward to it with a fierce un-Christian joy, as well as with a false confidence built only on their present misery. They would be apt to think that God did "respect persons," in the opposite fashion from that of a partial judge—namely, that He would incline the scale in favour of the ill-used, the poor, the down-trodden; that they would have an easy test and a light sentence, while His frowns and His severity would be kept for the powerful and the rich who had ground the faces of the poor and kept back the hire of the labourer. It was therefore a needful reminder for them, and for us all, that that judgment has nothing to do with earthly conditions, but only with conduct and character; that sorrow and calamity here do not open heaven's gates hereafter, and that the slave and master are tried by the same law.

The series of precepts closes with a brief but most pregnant word to masters. They are bid to give to their slaves "that which is just and equal," that is to say, "equitable." A startling criterion for a master's duty to the slave who was denied to have any rights at all. They were chattels, not persons. A master might, in regard to them, do what he liked with his own; he might crucify or torture, or commit any crime against manhood either in body or soul, and no voice would question or forbid. How astonished Roman lawgivers would have been if they could have heard Paul talking about justice and equity as applied to a slave! What a strange new dialect it must have sounded to the slave-owners in the Colossian Church! They would not see how far the principle, thus quietly introduced, was to carry succeeding ages; they could not dream of the great tree that was to spring from this tiny seed-precept; but no doubt the instinct which seldom fails an unjustly privileged class, would make them blindly dislike the exhortation, and feel as if they were getting out of their depth when they were bid to consider what was "right" and "equitable" in their dealings with their slaves.

The Apostle does not define what *is* "right and equal." That will come. The main thing is to drive home the conviction that there are duties owing to slaves, inferiors, employés. We are far enough from a satisfactory discharge of these yet; but, at any rate, everybody now admits the principle—and we have mainly to thank Christianity for that. Slowly the general conscience is coming to recognise that simple truth more and more clearly, and its application is becoming more decisive with each generation. There is much to be done before society is organized on that principle, but the time is coming—and till it is come, there will be no peace. All masters and employers of labour, in their mills and warehouses, are bid to base their relations to "hands" and servants on the one firm foundation of "justice." Paul does not say, Give your servants what is kind and patronising. He wants a great deal more than that. Charity likes to come in and supply the wants which would never have been felt had there been equity. An ounce of justice is sometimes worth a ton of charity.

This duty of the masters is enforced by the same thought which was to stimulate the servants to their tasks: "ye also have a Master in heaven." That is not only stimulus, but it is pattern. I said that Paul did not specify what was just and right, and that his precept might therefore be objected to as vague. Does the introduction of this thought of the master's Master in heaven, take away any of the vagueness? If Christ is our Master, then we are to look to Him to see what a master ought to be, and to try to be masters like that. That is precise enough, is it not? That grips tight enough, does it not? Give your servants what you expect and need to get from Christ. If we try to live that commandment for twenty-four hours, it will probably not be its vagueness of which we complain.

"Ye have a Master in heaven" is the great principle on which all Christian duty reposes. Christ's command is my law, His will is supreme, His authority absolute, His example all-sufficient. My soul, my life, my all are His. My will is not my own. My possessions are not my own. My being is not my own. All duty is elevated into obedience to Him, and obedience to Him, utter and absolute, is dignity and freedom. We are Christ's slaves, for He has bought us for Himself, by giving Himself for us. Let that great sacrifice win our heart's love and our perfect submission. "O Lord, truly I am Thy servant, Thou hast loosed my bonds." Then all earthly relationships will be fulfilled by us; and we shall move among men, breathing blessing and raying out brightness, when in all, we remember that we have a Master in heaven, and do all our work from the soul as to Him and not to men.

XXIII
PRECEPTS FOR THE INNERMOST
AND OUTERMOST LIFE

"Continue stedfastly in prayer, watching therein with thanksgiving; withal praying for us also, that God may open unto us a door for the word, to speak the mystery of Christ, for which I am also in bonds; that I may make it manifest, as I ought to speak. Walk in wisdom toward them that are without, redeeming the time. Let your speech be always with grace, seasoned with salt, that ye may know how ye ought to answer each one." —Col. iv. 2–6 (Rev. Ver.).

So ends the ethical portion of the Epistle. A glance over the series of practical exhortations, from the beginning of the preceding chapter onwards, will show that, in general terms we may say that they deal successively with a Christian's duties to himself, the Church, and the family. And now, these last advices touch the two extremes of life, the first of them having reference to the hidden life of prayer, and the second and third to the outward, busy life of the market-place and the street. That bringing together of the extremes seems to be the link of connection here. The Christian life is first regarded as gathered into itself—coiled as it were on its centre, like some strong spring. Next, it is regarded as it operates in the world, and, like the uncoiling spring, gives motion to wheels and pinions. These two sides of experience and duty are often hard to blend harmoniously. The conflict between busy Martha, who serves, and quiet Mary, who only sits and gazes, goes on in every age and in every heart. Here we may find, in some measure, the principle of reconciliation between their antagonistic claims. Here is, at all events, the protest against allowing either to oust the other. Continual prayer is to blend with unwearied action. We are so to walk the dusty ways of life as to be ever in the secret place of the Most High. "Continue stedfastly in prayer," and withal let there be no unwholesome withdrawal from the duties and relationships of the outer world, but let the prayer pass into, first, a wise walk, and second, an ever-gracious speech.

I. So we have here, first, an exhortation to a hidden life of constant prayer.

The word rendered "continue" in the Authorised Version, and more fully in the Revised Version by "continue stedfastly," is frequently found in reference to prayer, as well as in other connections. A mere enumeration of some of these instances may help to illustrate its full meaning. "We *will give ourselves* to prayer," said the apostles in proposing the creation of the office of deacon. "*Continuing instant* in prayer" says Paul to the Roman Church. "They *continuing* daily with one accord in the Temple" is the description of the early believers after Pentecost. Simon Magus is said to have "continued with Philip," where there is evidently the idea of close adherence as well as of uninterrupted companionship. These examples seem to show that the word implies both earnestness and continuity; so that this injunction not only covers the ground of Paul's other exhortation, "Pray without ceasing," but includes fervour also.

The Christian life, then, ought to be one of unbroken prayer.

What manner of prayer can that be which is to be continuous through a life that must needs be full of toil on outward things? How can such a precept be obeyed? Surely there is no need for paring down its comprehensiveness, and saying that it merely means—a very frequent recurrence to devout exercises, as often as the pressure of daily duties will permit. That is not the direction in which the harmonising of such a precept with the obvious necessities of our position is to be sought. We must seek it in a more inward and spiritual notion of prayer. We must separate between the form and the substance, the treasure and the earthen vessel which carries it. What is prayer? Not the utterance of words—they are but the vehicle; but the attitude of the spirit. Communion, aspiration, and submission, these three are the elements of prayer—and these three may be diffused through a life. It is possible, though difficult. There may be unbroken communion, a constant consciousness of God's presence, and of our contact with Him, thrilling through our souls and freshening them, like some breath of spring reaching the toilers in choky factories and busy streets; or even if the communion do not run like an absolutely unbroken line of light through our lives, the points may be so near together as all but to touch. In such communion words are needless. When spirits draw closest together there is no need for speech. Silently the heart may be kept fragrant with God's felt presence, and sunny with the light of His face. There are towns nestling beneath the Alps, every narrow filthy alley of which looks to the great solemn snow-peaks, and the inhabitants, amid all the squalor of their surroundings, have that apocalypse of wonder ever before them, if they would only lift their eyes. So we, if we will, may live with the majesties and beauties of the great white throne and of Him that sat on it closing every vista and filling the end of every commonplace passage in our lives.

In like manner, there may be a continual, unspoken and unbroken presence of the second element of prayer, which is aspiration, or desire after God. All circumstances, whether duty, sorrow or joy, should and may be used to stamp more deeply on my consciousness the sense of my weakness and need; and every moment, with its experience of God's swift and punctual grace, and all my communion with Him which unveils to me His beauty—should combine to move longings for Him, for more of Him. The very deepest cry of the heart which understands its own yearnings, is for the living God; and perpetual as the hunger of the spirit for the food which will stay its profound desires, will be the prayer, though it may often be voiceless, of the soul which knows where alone that food is.

Continual too may be our submission to His will, which is an essential of all prayer. Many people's notion is that our prayer is urging our wishes on God, and that His answer is giving us what we desire. But true prayer is the meeting in harmony of God's will and man's, and its deepest expression is not, Do this, because I desire it, O Lord; but, I do this because Thou desirest it, O Lord. That submission may be the very spring of all life, and whatsoever work is done in such spirit, however "secular" and however small it be, were it making buttons, is truly prayer.

So there should run all through our lives the music of that continual prayer, heard beneath all our varying occupations like some prolonged deep bass note, that bears up and gives dignity to the lighter melody that rises and falls and changes above it, like the spray on the crest of a great wave. Our lives will then be noble and grave, and woven into a harmonious unity, when they are based upon continual communion with, continual desire after, and continual submission to, God. If they are not, they will be worth nothing and will come to nothing.

But such continuity of prayer is not to be attained without effort; therefore Paul goes on to say, "Watching therein." We are apt to do drowsily whatever we do constantly. Men fall asleep at any continuous work. There is also the constant influence of externals, drawing our thoughts away from their true home in God, so that if we are to keep up continuous devotion, we shall have to rouse ourselves often when in the very act of dropping off to sleep. "Awake up, my glory!" we shall often have to say to our souls. Do we not all know that subtly approaching languor? and have we not often caught ourselves in the very act of falling asleep at our prayers? We must make distinct and resolute efforts to rouse ourselves—we must concentrate our attention and apply the needed stimulants, and bring the interest and activity of our whole nature to bear on this work of continual prayer, else it will become drowsy mumbling as of a man but half awake. The world has strong opiates for the soul, and we must stedfastly resist their influence, if we are to "continue in prayer."

One way of so watching is to have and to observe definite times of spoken prayer. We hear much now-a-days about the small value of times and forms of prayer, and how, as I have been saying, true prayer is independent of these, and needs no words. All that, of course, is true; but when the practical conclusion is drawn that therefore we can do without the outward form, a grave mistake, full of mischief, is committed. I do not, for my part, believe in a devotion diffused through a life and never concentrated and coming to the surface in visible outward acts or audible words; and, as far as I have seen, the men whose religion is spread all through their lives most really are the men who keep the central reservoir full, if I may so say, by regular and frequent hours and words of prayer. The Christ, whose whole life was devotion and communion with the Father, had His nights on the mountains, and rising up a great while before day, He watched unto prayer. We must do the like.

One more word has still to be said. This continual prayer is to be "with thanksgiving"—again the injunction so frequent in this letter, in such various connections. Every prayer should be blended with gratitude, without the perfume of which, the incense of devotion lacks one element of fragrance. The sense of need, or the consciousness of sin, may evoke "strong crying and tears," but the completest prayer rises confident from a grateful heart, which weaves memory into hope, and asks much because it has received much. A true recognition of the lovingkindness of the past has much to do with making our communion sweet, our desires believing, our submission cheerful. Thankfulness is the feather that wings the arrow of prayer—the height from which our souls rise most easily to the sky.

And now the Apostle's tone softens from exhortation to entreaty, and with very sweet and touching humility he begs a supplemental corner in their prayers. "Withal praying also for us." The "withal" and "also" have a tone of lowliness in them, while the "us," including as it does Timothy, who is associated with him in the superscription of the letter, and possibly others also, increases the impression of modesty. The subject of their prayers for Paul and the others is to be that "God may open unto us a door for the word." That phrase apparently means an unhindered opportunity of preaching the gospel, for the consequence of the door's being opened is added—"to speak (so that I may speak) the mystery of Christ." The special reason for this prayer is, "for which I am also (in addition to my other sufferings) in bonds."

He was a prisoner. He cared little about that or about the fetters on his wrists, so far as his own comfort was concerned; but his spirit chafed at the restraint laid upon him in spreading the good news of Christ, though he had been able to do much in his prison, both among the Prætorian guard, and throughout the whole population of Rome. Therefore he would engage his friends to ask God to open the prison doors, as He had done for Peter, not that Paul might come out, but that the gospel might. The personal was swallowed up; all that he cared for was to do his work.

But he wants their prayers for more than that—"that I may make it manifest as I ought to speak." This is probably explained most naturally as meaning his endowment with power to set forth the message in a manner adequate to its greatness. When he thought of what it was that he, unworthy, had to preach, its majesty and wonderfulness brought a kind of awe over his spirit; and endowed, as he was, with apostolic functions and apostolic grace; conscious, as he was, of being anointed and inspired by God, he yet felt that the richness of the treasure made the earthen vessel seem terribly unworthy to bear it. His utterances seemed to himself poor and unmelodious beside the majestic harmonies of the gospel. He could not soften his voice to breathe tenderly enough a message of such love, nor give it strength enough to peal forth a message of such tremendous import and world-wide destination.

If Paul felt his conception of the greatness of the gospel dwarfing into nothing *his* words when he tried to preach it, what must every other true minister of Christ feel? If he, in the fulness of his inspiration, besought a place in his brethren's prayers, how much more must they need it, who try with stammering tongues to preach the truth that made his fiery words seem ice? Every such man must turn to those who love him and listen to his poor presentment of the riches of Christ, with Paul's entreaty. His friends cannot do a kinder thing to him than to bear him on their hearts in their prayers to God.

II. We have here next, a couple of precepts, which spring at a bound from the inmost secret of the Christian life to its circumference, and refer to the outward life in regard to the non-Christian world, enjoining, in view of it, a wise walk and gracious speech.

"Walk in wisdom towards them that are without." Those that are within are those who have "fled for refuge" to Christ, and are within the fold, the fortress, the ark. Men who sit safe within while the storm howls, may simply think with selfish complacency of the poor wretches exposed to its fierceness. The phrase may express spiritual pride and even contempt. All close corporations tend to generate dislike and scorn of outsiders, and the Church has had its own share of such feeling; but there is no trace of anything of the sort here. Rather is there pathos and pity in the word, and a recognition that their sad condition gives these outsiders a claim on Christian men, who are bound to go out to their help and bring them in.

Precisely because they are "without" do those within owe them a wise walk, that "if any will not hear the word, they may without the word be won." The thought is in some measure parallel to our Lord's words, of which perhaps it is a reminiscence. "Behold I send you forth"—a strange thing for a careful shepherd to do—"as sheep in the midst of wolves; be ye therefore wise as serpents." Think of that picture—the handful of cowering frightened creatures huddled against each other, and ringed round by that yelping, white-toothed crowd, ready to tear them to pieces! So are Christ's followers in the world. Of course, things have changed in many respects since those days; partly because persecution has gone out of fashion, and partly because "the world" has been largely influenced by Christian morality, and partly because the Church has been largely secularized. The temperature of the two has become nearly equalized over a large tract of professing Christendom. So a tolerably good understanding and a brisk trade has sprung up between the sheep and the wolves. But for all that, there is fundamental discord, however changed may be its exhibition, and if we are true to our Master and insist on shaping our lives by His rules, we shall find out that there is.

We need, therefore, to "walk in wisdom" towards the non-Christian world; that is, to let practical prudence shape all our conduct. If we are Christians, we have to live under the eyes of vigilant and not altogether friendly observers, who derive satisfaction and harm from any inconsistency of ours. A plainly Christian life that needs no commentary to exhibit its harmony with Christ's commandments is the first duty we owe to them.

And the wisdom which is to mould our lives in view of these outsiders will "discern both time and judgment," will try to take the measure of men and act accordingly. Common sense and practical sagacity are important accompaniments of Christian zeal. What a singularly complex character, in this respect, was Paul's—enthusiastic and yet capable of such diplomatic adaptation; and withal never dropping to cunning, nor sacrificing truth! Enthusiasts who despise worldly wisdom, and therefore often dash themselves against stone walls, are not rare; cool calculators who abhor all generous glow of feeling and have ever a pailful of cold water for any project which shows it, are only too common—but fire and ice together, like a volcano with glaciers streaming down its cone, are rare. Fervour married to tact, common sense which keeps close to earth and enthusiasm which flames heaven high, are a rare combination. It is not often that the same voice can say, "I count not my life dear to myself," and "I became all things to all men."

A dangerous principle that last, a very slippery piece of ground to get upon!—say people, and quite truly. It *is* dangerous, and one thing only will keep a man's feet when on it, and that is, that his wise adaptation shall be perfectly unselfish, and that he shall ever keep clear before him the great object to be gained, which is nothing personal, but "that I might by all means save some." If that end is held in view, we shall be saved from the temptation of hiding or maiming the very truth which we desire should be received, and our wise adaptation of ourselves and of our message to the needs and weaknesses and peculiarities of those "who are without," will not degenerate into handling the word of God deceitfully. Paul advised "walking in wisdom;" he abhorred "walking in craftiness."

We owe them that are without such a walk as may tend to bring them in. Our life is to a large extent their Bible. They know a great deal more about Christianity, as they see it in us, than as it is revealed in Christ, or recorded in Scripture—and if, as seen in us, it does not strike them as very attractive, small wonder if they still prefer to remain where they are. Let us take care lest instead of being doorkeepers to the house of the Lord, to beckon passers-by and draw them in, we block the doorway, and keep them from seeing the wonders within.

The Apostle adds a special way in which this wisdom shows itself— namely, "redeeming the time." The last word here does not denote time in general, but a definite season, or *opportunity*. The lesson, then, is not that of making the best use of all the moments as they fly, precious as that lesson is, but that of discerning and eagerly using appropriate opportunities for Christian service. The figure is simple enough; to "buy up" means to make one's own. "Make much of time, let not advantage slip," is an advice in exactly the same spirit. Two things are included in it; the watchful study of characters, so as to know the right times to bring influences to bear on them, and an earnest diligence in utilizing these for the highest purposes. We have not acted wisely towards those who are without unless we have used every opportunity to draw them in.

But besides a wise walk, there is to be "gracious speech." "Let your speech be always with grace." A similar juxtaposition of "wisdom" and "grace" occurred in chapter iii. 16. "Let the word of Christ dwell in you richly in all wisdom ... singing with grace in your hearts"; and there as here, "grace" may be taken either in its lower æsthetic sense, or in its higher spiritual. It may mean either favour, agreeableness, or the Divine gift, bestowed by the indwelling Spirit. The former is supposed by many good expositors to be the meaning here. But is it a Christian's duty to make his speech always agreeable? Sometimes it is his plain duty to make it very disagreeable indeed. If our speech is to be true, and wholesome, it must sometimes rasp and go against the grain. Its pleasantness depends on the inclinations of the hearers rather than on the will of the honest speaker. If he is to "redeem the time" and "walk wisely to them that are without," his speech cannot be always with such grace. The advice to make our words always pleasing may be a very good maxim for worldly success, but it smacks of Chesterfield's Letters rather than of Paul's Epistles.

We must go much deeper for the true import of this exhortation. It is substantially this—whether you can speak smooth things or no, and whether your talk is always directly religious or no—and it need not and cannot always be that—let there ever be in it the manifest influence of God's Spirit, Who dwells in the Christian heart, and will mould and sanctify your speech. Of you, as of your Master, let it be true, "Grace is poured into thy lips." He in whose spirit the Divine Spirit abides will be truly "Golden-mouthed"; his speech shall distil as the dew, and whether his grave and lofty words please frivolous and prurient ears or no, they will be beautiful in the truest sense, and show the Divine life pulsing through them, as some transparent skin shows the throbbing of the blue veins. Men who feed their souls on great authors catch their style, as some of our great living orators, who are eager students of English poetry. So if we converse much with God, listening to His voice in our hearts, our speech will have in it a tone that will echo that deep music. Our accent will betray our country. Then our speech will be with grace in the lower sense of pleasingness. The truest gracefulness, both of words and conduct, comes from heavenly grace. The beauty caught from God, the fountain of all things lovely, is the highest.

The speech is to be "seasoned with salt." That does not mean the "Attic salt" of wit. There is nothing more wearisome than the talk of men who are always trying to be piquant and brilliant. Such speech is like a "pillar of salt"—it sparkles, but is cold, and has points that wound, and it tastes bitter. That is not what Paul recommends. Salt was used in sacrifice—let the sacrificial salt be applied to all our words; that is, let all we say be offered up to God, "a sacrifice of praise to God continually." Salt preserves. Put into your speech what will keep it from rotting, or, as the parallel passage in Ephesians has it, "let no *corrupt* communication proceed out of your mouth." Frivolous talk, dreary gossip, ill-natured talk, idle talk, to say nothing of foul and wicked words, will be silenced when your speech is seasoned with salt.

The following words make it probable that salt here is used also with some allusion to its power of giving savour to food. Do not deal in insipid generalities, but suit your words to your hearers, "that ye may know how ye ought to answer each one." Speech that fits close to the characteristics and wants of the people to whom it is spoken is sure to be interesting, and that which does not will for them be insipid. Commonplaces that hit full against the hearer will be no commonplaces to him, and the most brilliant words that do not meet his mind or needs will to him be tasteless "as the white of an egg."

Individual peculiarities, then, must determine the wise way of approach to each man, and there will be wide variety in the methods. Paul's language to the wild hill tribes of Lycaonia was not the same as to the cultivated, curious crowd on Mars' Hill, and his sermons in the synagogues have a different tone from his reasonings of judgment to come before Felix.

All that is too plain to need illustration. But one word may be added. The Apostle here regards it as the task of every Christian man to speak for Christ. Further, he recommends dealing with individuals rather than masses, as being within the scope of each Christian, and as being much more efficacious. Salt has to be rubbed in, if it is to do any good. It is better for most of us to fish with the rod than with the net, to angle for single souls, rather than to try and enclose a multitude at once. Preaching to a congregation has its own place and value; but private and personal talk, honestly and wisely done, will effect more than the most eloquent preaching. Better to drill in the seeds, dropping them one by one into the little pits made for their reception, than to sow them broadcast.

And what shall we say of Christian men and women, who can talk animatedly and interestingly of anything but of their Saviour and His kingdom? Timidity, misplaced reverence, a dread of seeming to be self-righteous, a regard for conventional proprieties, and the national reserve account for much of the lamentable fact that there are so many such. But all these barriers would be floated away like straws, if a great stream of Christian feeling were pouring from the heart. What fills the heart will overflow by the floodgates of speech. So that the real reason for the unbroken silence in which many Christian people conceal their faith is mainly the small quantity of it which there is to conceal.

A solemn ideal is set before us in these parting injunctions—a higher righteousness than was thundered from Sinai. When we think of our hurried, formal devotion, our prayers forced from us sometimes by the pressure of calamity, and so often suspended when the weight is lifted; of the occasional glimpses that we get of God—as sailors may catch sight of a guiding star for a moment through driving fog, and of the long tracts of life which would be precisely the same, as far as our thoughts are concerned, if there were no God at all, or He had nothing to do with us—what an awful command that seems, "Continue stedfastly in prayer"!

When we think of our selfish disregard of the woes and dangers of the poor wanderers without, exposed to the storm, while we think ourselves safe in the fold, and of how little we have meditated on and still less discharged our obligations to them, and of how we have let precious opportunities slip through our slack hands, we may well bow rebuked before the exhortation, "Walk in wisdom toward them that are without."

When we think of the stream of words ever flowing from our lips, and how few grains of gold that stream has brought down amid all its sand, and how seldom Christ's name has been spoken by us to hearts that heed Him not nor know Him, the exhortation, "Let your speech be always with grace," becomes an indictment as truly as a command.

There is but one place for us, the foot of the cross, that there we may obtain forgiveness for all the faulty past and thence may draw consecration and strength for the future, to enable us to keep that lofty law of Christian morality, which is high and hard if we think only of its precepts, but becomes light and easy when we open our hearts to receive the power for obedience, "which," as this great Epistle manifoldly teaches, "is Christ in you, the hope of glory."

XXIV
TYCHICUS AND ONESIMUS,
THE LETTER-BEARERS

"All my affairs shall Tychicus make known unto you, the beloved brother and faithful minister and fellow-servant in the Lord: whom I have sent unto you for this very purpose, that ye may know our estate, and that he may comfort your hearts; together with Onesimus, the faithful and beloved brother, who is one of you. They shall make known unto you all things that *are done* here." —Col. iv. 7–9 (Rev. Ver.).

In Paul's days it was perhaps more difficult to get letters delivered than to write them. It was a long, weary journey from Rome to Colossæ, — across Italy, then by sea to Greece, across Greece, then by sea to the port of Ephesus, and thence by rough ways to the upland valley where lay Colossæ, with its neighbouring towns of Laodicea and Hierapolis. So one thing which the Apostle has to think about is to find messengers to carry his letter. He pitches upon these two, Tychicus and Onesimus. The former is one of his personal attendants, told off for this duty; the other, who has been in Rome under very peculiar circumstances, is going home to Colossæ, on a strange errand, in which he may be helped by having a message from Paul to carry.

We shall not now deal with the words before us, so much as with these two figures, whom we may regard as representing certain principles, and embodying some useful lessons.

I. Tychicus may stand as representing the greatness and sacredness of small and secular service done for Christ.

We must first try, in as few words as may be, to change the name into a man. There is something very solemn and pathetic in these shadowy names which appear for a moment on the page of Scripture, and are swallowed up of black night, like stars that suddenly blaze out for a week or two, and then dwindle and at last disappear altogether. They too lived, and loved, and strove, and suffered, and enjoyed: and now—all is gone, gone; the hot fire burned down to such a little handful of white ashes. Tychicus and Onesimus! two shadows that once were men! and as they are, so we shall be.

As to Tychicus, there are several fragmentary notices about him in the Acts of the Apostles and in Paul's letters, and although they do not amount to much, still by piecing them together, and looking at them with some sympathy, we can get a notion of the man.

He does not appear till near the end of Paul's missionary work, and was probably one of the fruits of the Apostle's long residence in Ephesus on his last missionary tour, as we do not hear of him till after that period. That stay in Ephesus was cut short by the silversmiths' riot—the earliest example of trades' unions—when they wanted to silence the preaching of the gospel because it damaged the market for "shrines," and "*also*" was an insult to the great goddess! Thereupon Paul retired to Europe, and after some months there, decided on his last fateful journey to Jerusalem. On the way he was joined by a remarkable group of friends seven in number, and apparently carefully selected so as to represent the principal fields of the Apostle's labours. There were three Europeans, two from "Asia"—meaning by that name, of course, only the Roman province, which included mainly the western seaboard—and two from the wilder inland country of Lycaonia. Tychicus was one of the two from Asia; the other was Trophimus, whom we know to have been an Ephesian (Acts xxi. 29), as Tychicus may not improbably have also been.

We do not know that all the seven accompanied Paul to Jerusalem. Trophimus we know did, and another of them, Aristarchus, is mentioned as having sailed with him on the return voyage from Palestine (Acts xxvii. 2). But if they were not intended to go to Jerusalem, why did they meet him at all? The sacredness of the number seven, the apparent care to secure a representation of the whole field of apostolic activity, and the long distances that some of them must have travelled, make it extremely unlikely that these men should have met him at a little port in Asia Minor for the mere sake of being with him for a few days. It certainly seems much more probable that they joined his company and went on to Jerusalem. What for? Probably as bearers of money contributions from the whole area of the Gentile Churches, to the "poor saints" there—a purpose which would explain the composition of the delegation. Paul was too sensitive and too sagacious to have more to do with money matters than he could help. We learn from his letter to the Church at Corinth that he insisted on another brother being associated with him in the administration of their alms, so that no man could raise suspicions against him. Paul's principle was that which ought to guide every man entrusted with other people's money to spend for religious or charitable purposes—"I shall not be your almoner unless some one appointed by you stands by me to see that I spend your money rightly"—a good example which, it is much to be desired, were followed by all workers, and required to be followed as a condition of all giving.

These seven, at all events, began the long journey with Paul. Among them is our friend Tychicus, who may have learned to know the Apostle more intimately during it, and perhaps developed qualities in travel which marked him out as fit for the errand on which we here find him.

This voyage was about the year 58 a.d. Then comes an interval of some three or four years, in which occur Paul's arrest and imprisonment at Cæsarea, his appearance before governors and kings, his voyage to Italy and shipwreck, with his residence in Rome. Whether Tychicus was with him during all this period, as Luke seems to have been, we do not know, nor at what point he joined the Apostle, if he was not his companion throughout. But the verses before us show that he was with Paul during part of his first Roman captivity, probably about a.d. 62 or 63; and their commendation of him as "a faithful minister," or helper of Paul, implies that for a considerable period before this he had been rendering services to the Apostle.

He is now despatched all the long way to Colossæ to carry this letter, and to tell the Church by word of mouth all that had happened in Rome. No information of that kind is in the letter itself. That silence forms a remarkable contrast to the affectionate abundance of personal details in another prison letter, that to the Philippians, and probably marks this Epistle as addressed to a Church never visited by Paul. Tychicus is sent, according to the most probable reading, that "ye may know our estate, and that he may comfort your hearts"—encouraging the brethren to Christian stedfastness, not only by his news of Paul, but by his own company and exhortations.

The very same words are employed about him in the contemporaneous letter to the Ephesians. Evidently, then, he carried both epistles on the same journey; and one reason for selecting him as messenger is plainly that he was a native of the province, and probably of Ephesus. When Paul looked round his little circle of attendant friends, his eye fell on Tychicus, as the very man for such an errand. "You go, Tychicus. It is your home; they all know you."

The most careful students now think that the Epistle to the Ephesians was meant to go the round of the Churches of Asia Minor, beginning, no doubt, with that in the great city of Ephesus. If that be so, and Tychicus had to carry it to these Churches in turn, he would necessarily come, in the course of his duty, to Laodicea, which was only a few miles from Colossæ, and so could most conveniently deliver this Epistle. The wider and the narrower mission fitted into each other.

No doubt he went, and did his work. We can fancy the eager groups, perhaps in some upper room, perhaps in some quiet place of prayer by the river side; in their midst the two messengers, with a little knot of listeners and questioners round each. How they would have to tell the story a dozen times over! how every detail would be precious! how tears would come and hearts would glow! how deep into the night they would talk! and how many a heart that had begun to waver would be confirmed in cleaving to Christ by the exhortations of Tychicus, by the very sight of Onesimus, and by Paul's words of fire!

What became of Tychicus after that journey we do not know. Perhaps he settled down at Ephesus for a time, perhaps he returned to Paul. At any rate, we get two more glimpses of him at a later period—one in the Epistle to Titus, in which we hear of the Apostle's intention to despatch him on another journey to Crete, and the last in the close of the second Epistle to Timothy, written from Rome probably about a.d. 67. The Apostle believes that his death is near, and seems to have sent away most of his staff. Among the notices of their various appointments we read, "Tychicus have I sent to Ephesus." He is not said to have been sent on any mission connected with the Churches. It may be that he was simply sent away because, by reason of his impending martyrdom, Paul had no more need of him. True, he still has Luke by him, and he wishes Timothy to come and bring his first "minister," Mark, with him. But he has sent away Tychicus, as if he had said, Now, go back to your home, my friend! You have been a faithful servant for ten years. I need you no more. Go to your own people, and take my blessing. God be with you! So they parted, he that was for death, to die! and he that was for life, to live and to treasure the memory of Paul in his heart for the rest of his days. These are the facts; ten years of faithful service to the Apostle, partly during his detention in Rome, and much of it spent in wearisome and dangerous travelling undertaken to carry a couple of letters.

As for his character, Paul has given us something of it in these few words, which have commended him to a wider circle than the handful of Christians at Colossæ. As for his personal godliness and goodness, he is "a beloved brother," as are all who love Christ; but he is also a "faithful minister," or personal attendant upon the Apostle. Paul always seems to have had one or two such about him, from the time of his first journey, when John Mark filled the post, to the end of his career. Probably he was no great hand at managing affairs, and needed some plain common-sense nature beside him, who would be secretary or amanuensis sometimes, and general helper and factotum. Men of genius and men devoted to some great cause which tyrannously absorbs attention, want some person to fill such a homely office. The person who filled it would be likely to be a plain man, not gifted in any special degree for higher service. Common sense, willingness to be troubled with small details of purely secular arrangements, and a hearty love for the chief, and desire to spare him annoyance and work, were the qualifications. Such probably was Tychicus—no orator, no organiser, no thinker, but simply an honest, loving soul, who did not shrink from rough outward work, if only it might help the cause. We do not read that he was a teacher or preacher, or miracle worker. His gift was—ministry, and he gave himself to his ministry. His business was to run Paul's errands, and, like a true man, he ran them "faithfully."

So then, he is fairly taken as representing the greatness and sacredness of small and secular service for Christ. For the Apostle goes on to add something to his eulogium as a "faithful minister"—when he calls him "a fellow-servant," or slave, "in the Lord." As if he had said, Do not suppose that because I write this letter, and Tychicus carries it, there is much difference between us. We are both slaves of the same Lord who has set each of us his tasks; and though the tasks be different, the obedience is the same, and the doers stand on one level. I am not Tychicus' master, though he be my minister. We have both, as I have been reminding you that you all have, an owner in heaven. The delicacy of the turn thus given to the commendation is a beautiful indication of Paul's generous, chivalrous nature. No wonder that such a soul bound men like Tychicus to him!

But there is more than merely a revelation of a beautiful character in the words; there are great truths in them. We may draw them out in two or three thoughts.

Small things done for Christ are great. Trifles that contribute and are indispensable to a great result are great; or perhaps, more properly, both words are out of place. In some powerful engine there is a little screw, and if it drop out, the great piston cannot rise nor the huge crank turn. What have big and little to do with things which are equally indispensable? There is a great rudder that steers an ironclad. It moves on a "pintle" a few inches long. If that bit of iron were gone, what would become of the rudder, and what would be the use of the ship with all her guns? There is an old jingling rhyme about losing a shoe for want of a nail, and a horse for want of a shoe, and a man for want of a horse, and a battle for want of a man, and a kingdom for loss of a battle. The intervening links may be left out—and the nail and the kingdom brought together. In a similar spirit, we may say that the trifles done for Christ which help the great things are as important as these. What is the use of writing letters, if you cannot get them delivered? It takes both Paul and Tychicus to get the letter into the hands of the people at Colossæ.

Another thought suggested by the figure of Paul's minister, who was also his fellow-slave, is the sacredness of secular work done for Christ. When Tychicus is caring for Paul's comfort, and looking after common things for him, he is serving Christ, and his work is "in the Lord." That is equivalent to saying that the distinction between sacred and secular, religious and non-religious, like that of great and small, disappears from work done for and in Jesus. Whenever there is organization, there must be much work concerned with purely material things: and the most spiritual forces must have some organization. There must be men for "the outward business of the house of God" as well as white-robed priests at the altar, and the rapt gazer in the secret place of the Most High. There are a hundred matters of detail and of purely outward and mechanical sort which must be seen to by somebody. The alternative is to do them in a purely mechanical and secular manner and so to make the work utterly dreary and contemptible, or in a devout and earnest manner and so to hallow them all, and make worship of them all. The difference between two lives is not in the material on which, but in the motive from which, and in the end for which, they are respectively lived. All work done in obedience to the same Lord is the same in essence; for it is all obedience; and all work done for the same God is the same in essence, for it is all worship. The distinction between secular and sacred ought never to have found its way into Christian morals, and ought for evermore to be expelled from Christian life.

Another thought may be suggested—fleeting things done for Christ are eternal. How astonished Tychicus would have been if anybody had told him on that day when he got away from Rome, with the two precious letters in his scrip, that these bits of parchment would outlast all the ostentatious pomp of the city, and that his name, because written in them, would be known to the end of time all over the world! The eternal things are the things done for Christ. They are eternal in His memory who has said, "I will never forget any of their works," however they may fall from man's remembrance. They are perpetual in their consequences. True, no man's contribution to the mighty sum of things "that make for righteousness" can very long be traced as separate from the others, any more than the raindrop that refreshed the harebell on the moor can be traced in burn, and river, and sea. But for all that, it is there. So our influence for good blends with a thousand others, and may not be traceable beyond a short distance, still it is there: and no true work for Christ, abortive as it may seem, but goes to swell the great aggregate of forces which are working on through the ages to bring the perfect Order.

That Colossian Church seems a failure. Where is it now? Gone. Where are its sister Churches of Asia? Gone. Paul's work and Tychicus' seem to have vanished from the earth, and Mohammedanism to have taken its place. Yes! and here are we to-day in England, and Christian men all over the world in lands that were mere slaughterhouses of savagery then, learning our best lessons from Paul's words, and owing something for our knowledge of them to Tychicus' humble care. Paul meant to teach a handful of obscure believers—he has edified the world. Tychicus thought to carry the precious letter safely over the sea—he was helping to send it across the centuries, and to put it into our hands. So little do we know where our work will terminate. Our only concern is where it begins. Let us look after this end, the motive; and leave God to take care of the other, the consequences.

Such work will be perpetual in its consequences on ourselves. "Though Israel be not gathered, yet shall I be glorious." Whether our service for Christ does others any good or no, it will bless ourselves, by strengthening the motives from which it springs, by enlarging our own knowledge and enriching our own characters, and by a hundred other gracious influences which His work exerts upon the devout worker, and which become indissoluble parts of himself, and abide with him for ever, over and above the crown of glory that fadeth not away.

And, as the reward is given not to the outward deed, but to the motive which settles its value, all work done from the same motive is alike in reward, howsoever different in form. Paul in the front, and Tychicus obscure in the rear, the great teachers and path-openers whom Christ through the ages raises up for large spiritual work, and the little people whom Christ through the ages raises up to help and sympathize—shall share alike at last, if the Spirit that moved them has been the same, and if in different administrations they have served the same Lord. "He that receiveth a prophet in the name of a prophet"—though no prophecy come from his lips—"shall receive a prophet's reward."

II. We must now turn to a much briefer consideration of the second figure here, Onesimus, as representing the transforming and uniting power of Christian faith.

No doubt this is the same Onesimus as we read of in the Epistle to Philemon. His story is familiar and need not be dwelt on. He had been an "unprofitable servant," good-for-nothing, and apparently had robbed his master, and then fled. He had found his way to Rome, to which all the scum of the empire seemed to drift. There he had burrowed in some hole, and found obscurity and security. Somehow or other he had come across Paul— surely not, as has been supposed, having sought the Apostle as a friend of his master's, which would rather have been a reason for avoiding him. However that may be, he had found Paul, and Paul's Master had found *him* by the gospel which Paul spoke. His heart had been touched. And now he is to go back to his owner. With beautiful considerateness the Apostle unites him with Tychicus in his mission, and refers the Church to him as an authority. That is most delicate and thoughtful. The same sensitive regard for his feelings marks the language in which he is commended to them. There is now no word about "a fellow-slave"—that might have been misunderstood and might have hurt. Paul will only say about him half of what he said about Tychicus. He cannot leave out the "faithful," because Onesimus had been eminently unfaithful, and so he attaches it to that half of his former commendation which he retains, and testifies to him as "a faithful and beloved brother." There are no references to his flight or to his peculations. Philemon is the person to be spoken to about these. The Church has nothing to do with them. The man's past was blotted out—enough that he is "faithful," exercising trust in Christ, and therefore to be trusted. His condition was of no moment—enough that he is "a brother," therefore to be beloved.

Does not then that figure stand forth a living illustration of the *transforming* power of Christianity? Slaves had well-known vices, largely the result of their position—idleness, heartlessness, lying, dishonesty. And this man had had his full share of the sins of his class. Think of him as he left Colossæ, slinking from his master, with stolen property in his bosom, madness and mutiny in his heart, an ignorant heathen, with vices and sensualities holding carnival in his soul. Think of him as he came back, Paul's trusted representative, with desires after holiness in his deepest nature, the light of the knowledge of a loving and pure God in his soul, a great hope before him, ready for all service and even to put on again the abhorred yoke! What had happened? Nothing but this—the message had come to him, "Onesimus! fugitive, rebel, thief as thou art, Jesus Christ has died for thee, and lives to cleanse and bless thee. Believest thou this?" And he believed, and leant his whole sinful self on that Saviour, and the corruption faded away from his heart, and out of the thief was made a trustworthy man, and out of the slave a beloved brother. The cross had touched his heart and will. That was all. It had changed his whole being. He is a living illustration of Paul's teaching in this very letter. He is dead with Christ to his old self; he lives with Christ a new life.

The gospel can do that. It can and does do so to-day and to us, if we will. Nothing else can; nothing else ever has done it; nothing else ever will. Culture may do much; social reformation may do much; but the radical transformation of the nature is only effected by the "love of God shed abroad in the heart," and by the new life which we receive through our faith in Christ.

That change can be produced on all sorts and conditions of men. The gospel despairs of none. It knows of no hopelessly irreclaimable classes. It can kindle a soul under the ribs of death. The filthiest rags can be cleaned and made into spotlessly white paper, which may have the name of God written upon it. None are beyond its power; neither the savages in other lands, nor the more hopeless heathens festering and rotting in our back slums, the opprobrium of our civilization and the indictment of our Christianity. Take the gospel that transformed this poor slave, to them, and some hearts will own it, and we shall pick out of the kennel souls blacker than his, and make them like him, brethren, faithful and beloved.

Further, here is a living illustration of the power which the gospel has of binding men into a true brotherhood. We can scarcely picture to ourselves the gulf which separated the master from his slave. "So many slaves, so many enemies," said Seneca. That great crack running through society was a chief weakness and peril of the ancient world. Christianity gathered master and slave into one family, and set them down at one table to commemorate the death of the Saviour who held them all in the embrace of His great love.

All true union among men must be based upon their oneness in Jesus Christ. The brotherhood of man is a consequence of the fatherhood of God, and Christ shows us the Father. If the dreams of men's being knit together in harmony are ever to be more than dreams, the power that makes them facts must flow from the cross. The world must recognise that "One is your master," before it comes to believe as anything more than the merest sentimentality that "all ye are brethren."

Much has to be done before the dawn of that day reddens in the east, "when, man to man, the wide world o'er, shall brothers be," and much in political and social life has to be swept away before society is organized on the basis of Christian fraternity. The vision tarries. But we may remember how certainly, though slowly, the curse of slavery has disappeared, and take courage to believe that all other evils will fade away in like manner, until the cords of love shall bind all hearts in fraternal unity, because they bind each to the cross of the Elder Brother, through whom we are no more slaves but sons, and if sons of God, then brethren of one another.

XXV
SALUTATIONS FROM THE PRISONER'S FRIENDS

"Aristarchus my fellow-prisoner saluteth you, and Mark, the cousin of Barnabas (touching whom ye received commandments; if he come unto you, receive him), and Jesus, which is called Justus, who are of the circumcision: these only *are my* fellow-workers unto the kingdom of God, men that have been a comfort unto me. Epaphras, who is one of you, a servant of Christ Jesus, saluteth you, always striving for you in his prayers, that ye may stand perfect and fully assured in all the will of God. For I bear him witness, that he hath much labour for you, and for them in Laodicea, and for them in Hierapolis. Luke, the beloved physician, and Demas salute you." —Col. iv. 10–14 (Rev. Ver.).

Here are men of different races, unknown to each other by face, clasping hands across the seas, and feeling that the repulsions of nationality, language, conflicting interests, have disappeared in the unity of faith. These greetings are a most striking, because unconscious, testimony to the reality and strength of the new bond that knit Christian souls together.

There are three sets of salutations here, sent from Rome to the little far-off Phrygian town in its secluded valley. The first is from three large-hearted Jewish Christians, whose greeting has a special meaning as coming from that wing of the Church which had least sympathy with Paul's work or converts. The second is from the Colossians' towns-man Epaphras; and the third is from two Gentiles like themselves, one well known as Paul's most faithful friend, one almost unknown, of whom Paul has nothing to say, and of whom nothing good can be said. All these may yield us matter for consideration. It is interesting to piece together what we know of the bearers of these shadowy names. It is profitable to regard them as exponents of certain tendencies and principles.

1. These three sympathetic Jewish Christians may stand as types of a progressive and non-ceremonial Christianity.

We need spend little time in outlining the figures of these three, for he in the centre is well known to every one, and his two supporters are little known to any one. Aristarchus was a Thessalonian (Acts xx. 4), and so perhaps one of Paul's early converts on his first journey to Europe. His purely Gentile name would not have led us to expect him to be a Jew. But we have many similar instances in the New Testament, such for instance, as the names of six of the seven deacons (Acts vii. 5), which show that the Jews of "the dispersion," who resided in foreign countries, often bore no trace of their nationality in their names. He was with Paul in Ephesus at the time of the riot, and was one of the two whom the excited mob, in their zeal for trade and religion, dragged into the theatre, to the peril of their lives. We next find him like Tychicus, a member of the deputation which joined Paul on his voyage to Jerusalem. Whatever was the case with the other, Aristarchus was in Palestine with Paul, for we learn that he sailed with him thence (Acts xxvii. 2). Whether he kept company with Paul during all the journey we do not know. But more probably he went home to Thessalonica, and afterwards rejoined Paul at some point in his Roman captivity. At any rate here he is, standing by Paul, having drunk in his spirit, and enthusiastically devoted to him and his work.

He receives here a remarkable and honourable title, "my fellow-prisoner." I suppose that it is to be taken literally, and that Aristarchus was, in some way, at the moment of writing, sharing Paul's imprisonment. Now it has been often noticed that, in the Epistle to Philemon, where almost all these names re-appear, it is not Aristarchus, but Epaphras, who is honoured with this epithet; and that interchange has been explained by an ingenious supposition that Paul's friends took it in turn to keep him company, and were allowed to live with him, on condition of submitting to the same restrictions, military guardianship, and so on. There is no positive evidence in favour of this, but it is not improbable, and, if accepted, helps to give an interesting glimpse of Paul's prison life, and of the loyal devotion which surrounded him.

Mark comes next. His story is well known—how twelve years before, he had joined the first missionary band from Antioch, of which his cousin Barnabas was the leader, and had done well enough as long as they were on known ground, in Barnabas' (and perhaps his own) native island of Cyprus, but had lost heart and run home to his mother as soon as they crossed into Asia Minor. He had long ago effaced the distrust of him which Paul naturally conceived on account of this collapse. How he came to be with Paul at Rome is unknown. It has been conjectured that Barnabas was dead, and that so, Mark was free to join the Apostle; but that is unsupported supposition. Apparently he is now purposing a journey to Asia Minor, in the course of which, if he should come to Colossæ (which was doubtful, perhaps on account of its insignificance), Paul repeats his previous injunction, that the church should give him a cordial welcome. Probably this commendation was given because the evil odour of his old fault might still hang about his name. The calculated emphasis of the exhortation, "receive him," seems to show that there was some reluctance to give him a hearty reception and take him to their hearts. So we have an "undesigned coincidence." The tone of the injunction here is naturally explained by the story in the Acts.

So faithful a friend did he prove, that the lonely old man, fronting death, longed to have his affectionate tending once more; and his last word about him, "Take Mark, and bring him with thee, for he is profitable to me for *the ministry*," condones the early fault, and restores him to the office which, in a moment of selfish weakness, he had abandoned. So it is possible to efface a faultful past, and to acquire strength and fitness for work, to which we are by nature most inapt and indisposed. Mark is an instance of early faults nobly atoned for, and a witness of the power of repentance and faith to overcome natural weakness. Many a ragged colt makes a noble horse.

The third man is utterly unknown—"Jesus, which is called Justus." How startling to come across that name, borne by this obscure Christian! How it helps us to feel the humble manhood of Christ, by showing us that many another Jewish boy bore the same name; common and undistinguished then, though too holy to be given to any since. His surname Justus may, perhaps, like the same name given to James, the first bishop of the Church in Jerusalem, hint his rigorous adherence to Judaism, and so may indicate that, like Paul himself, he came from the straitest sect of their religion into the large liberty in which he now rejoiced.

He seems to have been of no importance in the Church, for his name is the only one in this context which does not re-appear in Philemon, and we never hear of him again. A strange fate his! to be made immortal by three words—and because he wanted to send a loving message to the Church at Colossæ! Why, men have striven and schemed, and broken their hearts, and flung away their lives, to grasp the bubble of posthumous fame; and how easily this good "Jesus which is called Justus" has got it! He has his name written for ever on the world's memory, and he very likely never knew it, and does not know it, and was never a bit the better for it! What a satire on "the last infirmity of noble minds!"

These three men are united in this salutation, because they are all three, "of the circumcision;" that is to say, are Jews, and being so, have separated themselves from all the other Jewish Christians in Rome, and have flung themselves with ardour into Paul's missionary work among the Gentiles, and have been his fellow-workers for the advancement of the kingdom—aiding him, that is, in seeking to win willing subjects to the loving, kingly will of God. By this co-operation in the aim of his life, they have been a "comfort" to him. He uses a half medical term, which perhaps he had caught from the physician at his elbow, which we might perhaps parallel by saying they had been a "cordial" to him—like a refreshing draught to a weary man, or some whiff of pure air stealing into a close chamber and lifting the damp curls on some hot brow.

Now these three men, the only three Jewish Christians in Rome who had the least sympathy with Paul and his work, give us, in their isolation, a vivid illustration of the antagonism which he had to face from that portion of the early Church. The great question for the first generation of Christians was, not whether Gentiles might enter the Christian community, but whether they must do so by circumcision, and pass through Judaism on their road to Christianity. The bulk of the Palestinian Jewish Christians naturally held that they must; while the bulk of Jewish Christians who had been born in other countries as naturally held that they need not. As the champion of this latter decision, Paul was worried and counter-worked and hindered all his life by the other party. They had no missionary zeal, or next to none, but they followed in his wake and made mischief wherever they could. If we can fancy some modern sect that sends out no missionaries of its own, but delights to come in where better men have forced a passage, and to upset their work by preaching its own crotchets, we get precisely the kind of thing which dogged Paul all his life.

There was evidently a considerable body of these men in Rome; good men no doubt in a fashion, believing in Jesus as the Messiah, but unable to comprehend that he had antiquated Moses, as the dawning day makes useless the light in a dark place. Even when he was a prisoner, their unrelenting antagonism pursued the Apostle. They preached Christ of "envy and strife." Not one of them lifted a finger to help him, or spoke a word to cheer him. With none of them to say, God bless him! he toiled on. Only these three were large-hearted enough to take their stand by his side, and by this greeting to clasp the hands of their Gentile brethren in Colossæ and thereby to endorse the teaching of this letter as to the abrogation of Jewish rites.

It was a brave thing to do, and the exuberance of the eulogium shows how keenly Paul felt his countrymen's coldness, and how grateful he was to "the dauntless three." Only those who have lived in an atmosphere of misconstruction, surrounded by scowls and sneers, can understand what a cordial the clasp of a hand, or the word of sympathy is. These men were like the old soldier that stood on the street of Worms, as Luther passed in to the

Diet, and clapped him on the shoulder, with "Little monk! little monk! you are about to make a nobler stand to-day than we in all our battles have ever done. If your cause is just, and you are sure of it, go forward in God's name, and fear nothing." If we can do no more, we can give some one who is doing more a cup of cold water, by our sympathy and taking our place at his side, and *so* can be fellow-workers to the kingdom of God.

We note, too, that the best comfort Paul could have was help in his work. He did not go about the world whimpering for sympathy. He was much too strong a man for that. He wanted men to come down into the trench with him, and to shovel and wheel there till they had made in the wilderness some kind of a highway for the King. The true cordial for a true worker is that others get into the traces and pull by his side.

But we may further look at these men as representing for us progressive as opposed to reactionary, and spiritual as opposed to ceremonial Christianity. Jewish Christians looked backwards; Paul and his three sympathisers looked forward. There was much excuse for the former. No wonder that they shrank from the idea that things divinely appointed could be laid aside. Now there is a broad distinction between the divine in Christianity and the divine in Judaism. For Jesus Christ is God's last word, and abides for ever. His divinity, His perfect sacrifice, His present life in glory for us, His life within us, these and their related truths are the perennial possession of the Church. To Him we must look back, and every generation till the end of time will have to look back, as the full and final expression of the wisdom and will and mercy of God. "Last of all He sent unto them His Son."

That being distinctly understood, we need not hesitate to recognise the transitory nature of much of the embodiment of the eternal truth concerning the eternal Christ. To draw the line accurately between the permanent and the transient would be to anticipate history and read the future. But the clear recognition of the distinction between the Divine revelation and the vessels in which it is contained, between Christ and creed, between Churches, forms of worship, formularies of faith on the one hand, and the everlasting word of God spoken to us once for all in His Son, and recorded in Scripture, on the other, is needful at all times, and especially at such times of sifting and unsettlement as the present. It will save some of us from an obstinate conservatism which might read its fate in the decline and disappearance of Jewish Christianity. It will save us equally from needless fears, as if the stars were going out, when it is only men-made lamps that are paling. Men's hearts often tremble for the ark of God, when the only things in peril are the cart that carries it, or the oxen that draw it. "We have received a kingdom that cannot be moved," because we have received a King eternal, and therefore may calmly see the removal of things that can be shaken, assured that the things which cannot be shaken will but the more conspicuously assert their permanence. The existing embodiments of God's truth are not the highest, and if Churches and forms crumble and disintegrate, their disappearance will not be the abolition of Christianity, but its progress. These Jewish Christians would have found all that they strove to keep, in higher form and more real reality, in Christ; and what seemed to them the destruction of Judaism was really its coronation with undying life.

II. Epaphras is for us the type of the highest service which love can render.

All our knowledge of Epaphras is contained in these brief notices in this Epistle. We learn from the first chapter that he had introduced the gospel to Colossæ, and perhaps also to Laodicea and Hierapolis. He was "one of you," a member of the Colossian community, and a resident in, possibly a native of, Colossæ. He had come to Rome, apparently to consult the Apostle about the views which threatened to disturb the Church. He had told him, too, of their love, not painting the picture too black, and gladly giving full prominence to any bits of brightness. It was his report which led to the writing of this letter.

Perhaps some of the Colossians were not over pleased with his having gone to speak with Paul, and having brought down this thunderbolt on their heads; and such a feeling may account for the warmth of Paul's praises of him as his "fellow-slave," and for the emphasis of his testimony on his behalf. However they might doubt it, Epaphras' love for them was warm. It showed itself by continual fervent prayers that they might stand "perfect and fully persuaded in all the will of God," and by toil of body and mind for them. We can see the anxious Epaphras, far away from the Church of his solicitude, always burdened with the thought of their danger, and ever wrestling in prayer on their behalf.

So we may learn the noblest service which Christian love can do— prayer. There is a real power in Christian intercession. There are many difficulties and mysteries round that thought. The manner of the blessing is not revealed, but the fact that we help one another by prayer is plainly taught, and confirmed by many examples, from the day when God heard Abraham and delivered Lot, to the hour when the loving authoritative words were spoken, "Simon, Simon, I have prayed for thee that thy faith fail not." A spoonful of water sets a hydraulic press in motion, and brings into operation a force of tons' weight; so a drop of prayer at the one end may move an influence at the other which is omnipotent. It is a service which all can render. Epaphras could not have written this letter, but he could pray. Love has no higher way of utterance than prayer. A prayerless love may be very tender, and may speak murmured words of sweetest sound, but it lacks the deepest expression, and the noblest music of speech. We never help our dear ones so well as when we pray for them. Do we thus show and consecrate our family loves and our friendships?

We notice too the kind of prayer which love naturally presents. It is constant and earnest—"always striving," or as the word might be rendered, "agonizing." That word suggests first the familiar metaphor of the wrestling-ground. True prayer is the intensest energy of the spirit pleading for blessing with a great striving of faithful desire. But a more solemn memory gathers round the word, for it can scarcely fail to recall the hour beneath the olives of Gethsemane, when the clear paschal moon shone down on the suppliant who, "being in an agony, prayed the more earnestly." And both Paul's word here, and the evangelist's there, carry us back to that mysterious scene by the brook Jabbok, where Jacob "wrestled" with "a man" until the breaking of the day, and prevailed. Such is prayer; the wrestle in the arena, the agony in Gethsemane, the solitary grapple with the "traveller unknown"; and such is the highest expression of Christian love.

Here, too, we learn what love asks for its beloved. Not perishable blessings, not the prizes of earth—fame, fortune, friends; but that "ye may stand perfect and fully assured in all the will of God." The first petition is for stedfastness. To stand has for opposites—to fall, or totter, or give ground; so the prayer is that they may not yield to temptation, or opposition, nor waver in their fixed faith, nor go down in the struggle; but keep erect, their feet planted on the rock, and holding their own against every foe. The prayer is also for their maturity of Christian character, that they may stand firm, because perfect, having attained that condition which Paul in this Epistle tell us is the aim of all preaching and warning. As for ourselves, so for our dear ones, we are to be content with nothing short of entire conformity to the will of God. His merciful purpose for us all is to be the goal of our efforts for ourselves, and of our prayers for others. We are to widen our desires to coincide with His gift, and our prayers are to cover no narrower space than His promises enclose.

Epaphras' last desire for his friends, according to the true reading, is that they may be "fully assured" in all the will of God. There can be no higher blessing than that—to be quite sure of what God desires me to know and do and be—if the assurance comes from the clear light of His illumination, and not from hasty self-confidence in my own penetration. To be free from the misery of intellectual doubts and practical uncertainties, to walk in the sunshine—is the purest joy. And it is granted in needful measure to all who have silenced their own wills, that they may hear what God says,—"If any man wills to do His will, he shall know."

Does our love speak in prayer? and do our prayers for our dear ones plead chiefly for such gifts? Both our love and our desires need purifying if this is to be their natural language. How can we offer such prayers for them if, at the bottom of our hearts, we had rather see them well off in the world than stedfast, matured and assured Christians? How can we expect an answer to such prayers if the whole current of our lives shows that neither for them nor for ourselves do we "seek first the kingdom of God and His righteousness"?

III. The last salutation comes from a singularly contrasted couple—Luke and Demas, the types respectively of faithfulness and apostasy. These two unequally yoked together stand before us like the light and the dark figures that Ary Scheffer delights to paint, each bringing out the colouring of the other more vividly by contrast. They bear the same relation to Paul which John, the beloved disciple, and Judas did to Paul's master.

As for Luke, his long and faithful companionship of the Apostle is too well known to need repetition here. His first appearance in the Acts nearly coincides with an attack of Paul's constitutional malady, which gives probability to the suggestion that one reason for Luke's close attendance on the Apostle was the state of his health. Thus the form and warmth of the reference here would be explained—"Luke the physician, the beloved." We trace Luke as sharing the perils of the winter voyage to Italy, making his presence known only by the modest "we" of the narrative. We find him here sharing the Roman captivity, and, in the second imprisonment, he was Paul's only companion. All others had been sent away, or had fled; but Luke could not be spared, and would not desert him, and no doubt was by his side till the end, which soon came.

As for Demas, we know no more about him except the melancholy record, "Demas hath forsaken me, having loved this present world; and is departed unto Thessalonica." Perhaps he was a Thessalonian, and so went home. His love of the world, then, was his reason for abandoning Paul. Probably it was on the side of danger that the world tempted him. He was a coward, and preferred a whole skin to a clear conscience. In immediate connection with the record of his desertion we read, "At my first answer, no man stood with me, but all men forsook me." As the same word is used, probably Demas may have been one of those timid friends, whose courage was not equal to standing by Paul when, to use his own metaphor, he thrust his head into the lion's mouth. Let us not be too hard on the constancy that warped in so fierce a heat. All that Paul charges him with is, that he was a faithless friend, and too fond of the present world. Perhaps his crime did not reach the darker hue. He may not have been an apostate Christian, though he was a faithless friend. Perhaps, if there were departure from Christ as well as from Paul, he came back again, like Peter, whose sins against love and friendship were greater than his—and, like Peter, found pardon and a welcome. Perhaps, away in Thessalonica, he repented him of his evil, and perhaps Paul and Demas met again before the throne, and there clasped inseparable hands. Let us not judge a man of whom we know so little, but take to ourselves the lesson of humility and self-distrust!

How strikingly these two contrasted characters bring out the possibility of men being exposed to the same influences and yet ending far away from each other! These two set out from the same point, and travelled side by side, subject to the same training, in contact with the magnetic attraction of Paul's strong personality, and at the end they are wide as the poles asunder. Starting from the same level, one line inclines ever so little upwards, the other imperceptibly downwards. Pursue them far enough, and there is room for the whole solar system with all its orbits in the space between them. So two children trained at one mother's knee, subjects of the same prayers, with the same sunshine of love and rain of good influences upon them both, may grow up, one to break a mother's heart and disgrace a father's home, and the other to walk in the ways of godliness and serve the God of his fathers. Circumstances are mighty; but the use we make of circumstances lies with ourselves. As we trim our sails and set our rudder, the same breeze will take us in opposite directions. We are the architects and builders of our own characters, and may so use the most unfavourable influences as to strengthen and wholesomely harden our natures thereby, and may so misuse the most favourable as only thereby to increase our blameworthiness for wasted opportunities.

We are reminded, also, from these two men who stand before us like a double star—one bright and one dark—that no loftiness of Christian position, nor length of Christian profession is a guarantee against falling and apostasy. As we read in another book, for which also the Church has to thank a prison cell—the place where so many of its precious possessions have been written—there is a backway to the pit from the gate of the Celestial City. Demas had stood high in the Church, had been admitted to the close intimacy of the Apostle, was evidently no raw novice, and yet the world could drag him back from so eminent a place in which he had long stood. "Let him that thinketh he standeth take heed lest he fall."

The world that was too strong for Demas will be too strong for us if we front it in our own strength. It is ubiquitous, working on us everywhere and always, like the pressure of the atmosphere on our bodies. Its weight will crush us unless we can climb to and dwell on the heights of communion with God, where pressure is diminished. It acted on Demas through his fears. It acts on us through our ambitions, affections and desires. So, seeing that miserable wreck of Christian constancy, and considering ourselves lest we also be tempted, let us not judge another, but look at home. There is more than enough there to make profound self-distrust our truest wisdom, and to teach us to pray, "Hold Thou me up, and I shall be safe."

XXVI
CLOSING MESSAGES

"Salute the brethren that are in Laodicea, and Nymphas, and the Church that is in their house. And when this epistle hath been read among you, cause that it be read also in the Church of the Laodiceans; and that ye also read the epistle from Laodicea. And say to Archippus, Take heed to the ministry which thou hast received in the Lord, that thou fulfil it. The salutation of me Paul with mine own hand. Remember my bonds. Grace be with you."—Col. iv. 15–end (Rev. Ver.).

There is a marked love of triplets in these closing messages. There were three of the circumcision who desired to salute the Colossians; and there were three Gentiles whose greetings followed these. Now we have a triple message from the Apostle himself—his greeting to Laodicea, his message as to the interchange of letters with that Church, and his grave, stringent charge to Archippus. Finally, the letter closes with a few hurried words in his own handwriting, which also are threefold, and seem to have been added in extreme haste, and to be compressed to the utmost possible brevity.

I. We shall first look at the threefold greeting and warnings to Laodicea.

In the first part of this triple message we have a glimpse of the Christian life of that city, "Salute the brethren that are in Laodicea." These are, of course, the whole body of Christians in the neighbouring town, which was a much more important place than Colossæ. They are the same persons as "the Church of the Laodiceans." Then comes a special greeting to "Nymphas," who was obviously a brother of some importance and influence in the Laodicean Church, though to us he has sunk to be an empty name. With him Paul salutes "the Church that is in *their* house" (Rev. Ver.). Whose house? Probably that belonging to Nymphas and his family. Perhaps that belonging to Nymphas and the Church that met in it, if these were other than his family. The more difficult expression is adopted by preponderating textual authorities, and "*his* house" is regarded as a correction to make the sense easier. If so, then the expression is one of which in our ignorance we have lost the key, and which must be content to leave unexplained.

But what was this "Church in the house"? We read that Prisca and Aquila had such both in their house in Rome (Rom. xvi. 5) and in Ephesus (1 Cor. xvi. 19), and that Philemon had such in his house at Colossæ. It may be that only the household of Nymphas is meant, and that the words import no more than that it was a Christian household; or it may be, and more probably is, that in all these cases there was some gathering of a few of the Christians resident in each city, who were closely connected with the heads of the household, and met in their houses more or less regularly to worship and to help one another in the Christian life. We have no facts that decide which of these two suppositions is correct. The early Christians had, of course no buildings especially used for their meetings, and there may often have been difficulty in finding suitable places, particularly in cities where the Church was numerous. It may have been customary, therefore, for brethren who had large and convenient houses, to gather together portions of the whole community in these. In any case, the expression gives us a glimpse of the primitive elasticity of Church order, and of the early fluidity, so to speak, of ecclesiastical language. The word "Church" has not yet been hardened and fixed to its present technical sense. There was but one Church in Laodicea, and yet within it there was this little Church—an *imperium in imperio*—as if the word had not yet come to mean more than an assembly, and as if all arrangements of order and worship, and all the terminology of later days, were undreamed of yet. The life was there, but the forms which were to grow out of the life, and to protect it sometimes, and to stifle it often, were only beginning to show themselves, and were certainly not yet felt to be forms.

We may note, too, the beautiful glimpse we get here of domestic and social religion.

If the Church in the house of Nymphas consisted of his own family and dependants, it stands for us as a lesson of what every family, which has a Christian man or woman at its head, ought to be. Little knowledge of the ordering of so-called Christian households is needed to be sure that domestic religion is wofully neglected to-day. Family worship and family instruction are disused, one fears, in many homes, the heads of which can remember both in their father's houses; and the unspoken aroma and atmosphere of religion does not fill the house with its odour, as it ought to do. If a Christian householder have not "a Church in his house," the family union is tending to become "a synagogue of Satan." One or other it is sure to be. It is a solemn question for all parents and heads of households, What am I doing to make my house a Church, my family a family united by faith in Jesus Christ?

A like suggestion may be made if, as is possible, the Church in the house of Nymphas included more than relatives and dependants. It is a miserable thing when social intercourse plays freely round every other subject, and taboos all mention of religion. It is a miserable thing when Christian people choose and cultivate society for worldly advantages, business connections, family advancement, and for every reason under heaven—sometimes a long way under—except those of a common faith, and of the desire to increase it.

It is not needful to lay down extravagant, impracticable restrictions, by insisting either that we should limit our society to religious men, or our conversation to religious subjects. But it is a bad sign when our chosen associates are chosen for every other reason but their religion, and when our talk flows copiously on all other subjects, and becomes a constrained driblet when religion comes to be spoken of. Let us try to carry about with us an influence which shall permeate all our social intercourse, and make it, if not directly religious, yet never antagonistic to religion, and always capable of passing easily and naturally into the highest regions. Our godly forefathers used to carve texts over their house doors. Let us do the same in another fashion, so that all who cross the threshold may feel that they have come into a Christian household, where cheerful godliness sweetens and brightens the sanctities of home.

We have next a remarkable direction as to the interchange of Paul's letters to Colossæ and Laodicea. The present Epistle is to be sent over to the neighbouring Church of Laodicea—that is quite clear. But what is "the Epistle from Laodicea" which the Colossians are to be sure to get and to read? The connection forbids us to suppose that a letter written by the Laodicean Church is meant. Both letters are plainly Pauline epistles, and the latter is said to be "from Laodicea," simply because the Colossians were to procure it from that place. The "from" does not imply authorship, but transmission. What then has become of this letter? Is it lost? So say some commentators; but a more probable opinion is that it is no other than the Epistle which we know as that to the Ephesians. This is not the occasion to enter on a discussion of that view. It will be enough to notice that very weighty textual authorities omit the words "In Ephesus," in the first verse of that Epistle. The conjecture is a very reasonable one, that the letter was intended for a circle of Churches, and had originally no place named in the superscription, just as we might issue circulars "To the Church in— —," leaving a blank to be filled in with different names. This conjecture is strengthened by the marked absence of personal references in the letter, which in that respect forms a striking contrast to the Epistle to the Colossians, which it so strongly resembles in other particulars. Probably, therefore, Tychicus had both letters put into his hands for delivery. The circular would go first to Ephesus as the most important Church in Asia, and thence would be carried by him to one community after another, till he reached Laodicea, from which he would come further up the valley to Colossæ, bringing both letters with him. The Colossians are not told to *get* the letter from Laodicea, but to be sure that they *read* it. Tychicus would see that it came to them; their business was to see that they marked, learned, and inwardly digested it.

The urgency of these instructions that Paul's letters should be read, reminds us of a similar but still more stringent injunction in his earliest epistle (1 Thess. v. 27), "I charge you by the Lord that this epistle be read unto all the holy brethren." Is it possible that these Churches did not much care for Paul's words, and were more willing to admit that they were weighty and powerful, than to study them and lay them to heart? It looks almost like it. Perhaps they got the same treatment then as they often do now, and were more praised than read, even by those who professed to look upon him as their teacher in Christ!

But passing by that, we come to the last part of this threefold message, the solemn warning to a slothful servant.

"Say to Archippus, Take heed to the ministry which thou hast received in the Lord, that thou fulfil it." A sharp message that—and especially sharp, as being sent through others, and not spoken directly to the man himself. If this Archippus were a member of the Church at Colossæ, it is remarkable that Paul should not have spoken to him directly, as he did to Euodia and Syntyche, the two good women at Philippi, who had fallen out. But it is by no means certain that he was. We find him named again, indeed, at the beginning of the Epistle to Philemon, in such immediate connection with the latter, and with his wife Apphia, that he has been supposed to be their son. At all events, he was intimately associated with the Church in the house of Philemon, who, as we know, was a Colossian. The conclusion, therefore, seems at first sight most natural that Archippus too belonged to the Colossian Church. But on the other hand the difficulty already referred to seems to point in another direction; and if it be further remembered that this whole section is concerned with the Church at Laodicea, it will be seen to be a likely conclusion from all the facts that Archippus, though perhaps a native of Colossæ, or even a resident there, had his "ministry" in connection with that other neighbouring Church.

It may be worth notice, in passing, that all these messages to Laodicea occurring here, strongly favour the supposition that the epistle from that place cannot have been a letter especially meant for the Laodicean church, as, if it had been, these would have naturally been inserted in it. So far, therefore, they confirm the hypothesis that it was a circular.

Some may say, Well, what in the world does it matter where Archippus worked? Not very much perhaps; and yet one cannot but read this grave exhortation to a man who was evidently getting languid and negligent, without remembering what we hear about Laodicea and the angel of the Church there, when next we meet it in the page of Scripture. It is not impossible that Archippus was that very "angel," to whom the Lord Himself sent the message through His servant John, more awful than that which Paul had sent through his brethren at Colossæ, "Because thou art neither cold nor hot, I will spue thee out of My mouth."

Be that as it may, the message is for us all. Each of us has a "ministry," a sphere of service. We may either fill it full, with earnest devotion and patient heroism, as some expanding gas fills out the silken round of its containing vessel, or we may breathe into it only enough to occupy a little portion, while all the rest hangs empty and flaccid. We have to "fulfil our ministry."

A sacred motive enhances the obligation—we have received it "*in the Lord.*" In union with Him it has been laid on us. No human hand has imposed it, nor does it arise merely from earthly relationships, but our fellowship with Jesus Christ, and incorporation into the true Vine, has laid on us responsibilities, and exalted us by service.

There must be diligent watchfulness, in order to fulfil our ministry. We must take heed to our service, and we must take heed to ourselves. We have to reflect upon it, its extent, nature, imperativeness, upon the manner of discharging it, and the means of fitness for it. We have to keep our work ever before us. Unless we are absorbed in it, we shall not fulfil it. And we have to take heed to ourselves, ever feeling our weakness and the strong antagonisms in our own natures which hinder our discharge of the plainest, most imperative duties.

And let us remember, too, that if once we begin, like Archippus, to be a little languid and perfunctory in our work, we may end where the Church of Laodicea ended, whether he were its angel or no, with that nauseous lukewarmness which sickens even Christ's longsuffering love, and forces Him to reject it with loathing.

II. And now we come to the end of our task, and have to consider the hasty last words in Paul's own hand.

We can see him taking the reed from the amanuensis and adding the three brief sentences which close the letter. He first writes that which is equivalent to our modern usage of signing the letter—"the salutation of me Paul with mine own hand." This appears to have been his usual practice, or, as he says in 2 Thess. (iii. 17), it was "his token in every epistle"—the evidence that each was the genuine expression of his mind. Probably his weak eyesight, which appears certain, may have had something to do with his employing a secretary, as we may assume him to have done, even when there is no express mention of his autograph in the closing salutations. We find for example in the Epistle to the Romans no words corresponding to these, but the modest amanuensis steps for a moment into the light near the end: "I Tertius, who write the epistle, salute you in the Lord."

The endorsement with his name is followed by a request singularly pathetic in its abrupt brevity, "Remember my bonds." This is the one personal reference in the letter, unless we add as a second, his request for their prayers that he may speak the mystery of Christ, for which he is in bonds. There is a striking contrast in this respect with the abundant allusions to his circumstances in the Epistle to the Philippians, which also belongs to the period of his captivity. He had been swept far away from thoughts of self by the enthusiasm of his subject. The vision that opened before him of his Lord in His glory, the Lord of Creation, the Head of the Church, the throned helper of every trusting soul, had flooded his chamber with light, and swept guards and chains and restrictions out of his consciousness. But now the spell is broken, and common things re-assert their power. He stretches out his hand for the reed to write his last words, and as he does so, the chain which fastens him to the Prætorian guard at his side pulls and hinders him. He wakes to the consciousness of his prison. The seer, swept along by the storm wind of a Divine inspiration, is gone. The weak man remains. The exhaustion after such an hour of high communion makes him more than usually dependent; and all his subtle profound teachings, all his thunderings and lightnings, end in the simple cry, which goes straight to the heart: "Remember my bonds."

He wished their remembrance because he needed their sympathy. Like the old rags put round the ropes by which the prophet was hauled out of his dungeon, the poorest bit of sympathy twisted round a fetter makes it chafe less. The petition helps us to conceive how heavy a trial Paul felt his imprisonment, to be little as he said about it, and bravely as he bore it. He wished their remembrance too, because his bonds added weight to his words. His sufferings gave him a right to speak. In times of persecution confessors are the highest teachers, and the marks of the Lord Jesus borne in a man's body give more authority than diplomas and learning. He wished their remembrance because his bonds might encourage them to steadfast endurance if need for it should arise. He points to his own sufferings, and would have them take heart to bear their lighter crosses and to fight their easier battle.

One cannot but recall the words of Paul's Master, so like these in sound, so unlike them in deepest meaning. Can there be a greater contrast than between "Remember my bonds," the plaintive appeal of a weak man seeking sympathy, coming as an appendix, quite apart from the subject of the letter, and "Do this in remembrance of Me," the royal words of the Master? Why is the memory of Christ's death so unlike the memory of Paul's chains? Why is the one merely for the play of sympathy, and the enforcement of his teaching, and the other the very centre of our religion? For one reason alone. Because Christ's death is the life of the world, and Paul's sufferings, whatever their worth, had nothing in them that bore, except indirectly, on man's redemption. "Was Paul crucified for you?" We remember his chains, and they give him sacredness in our eyes. But we remember the broken body and shed blood of our Lord, and cleave to it in faith as the one sacrifice for the world's sin.

And then comes the last word: "Grace be with you." The apostolic benediction, with which he closes all his letters, occurs in many different stages of expression. Here it is pared down to the very quick. No shorter form is possible—and yet even in this condition of extreme compression, all good is in it.

All possible blessing is wrapped up in that one word, Grace. Like the sunshine, it carries life and fruitfulness in itself. If the favour and kindness of God, flowing out to men so far beneath Him, who deserve such different treatment, be ours, then in our hearts will be rest and a great peacefulness, whatever may be about us, and in our characters will be all beauties and capacities, in the measure of our possession of that grace.

That all-productive germ of joy and excellence is here parted among the whole body of Colossian Christians. The dew of this benediction falls upon them all—the teachers of error if they still held by Christ, the Judaisers, the slothful Archippus, even as the grace which it invokes will pour itself into imperfect natures and adorn very sinful characters, if beneath the imperfection and the evil there be the true affiance of the soul on Christ.

That communication of grace to a sinful world is the end of all God's deeds, as it is the end of this letter. That great revelation which began when man began, which has spoken its complete message in the Son, the heir of all things, as this Epistle tells us, has this for the purpose of all its words— whether they are terrible or gentle, deep or simple—that God's grace may dwell among men. The mystery of Christ's being, the agony of Christ's cross, the hidden glories of Christ's dominion are all for this end, that of His fulness we may all receive, and grace for grace. The Old Testament, true to its genius, ends with stern onward-looking words which point to a future coming of the Lord and to the possible terrible aspect of that coming—"Lest I come and smite the earth with a curse." It is the last echo of the long drawn blast of the trumpets of Sinai. The New Testament ends, as our Epistle ends, and as we believe the weary history of the world will end, with the benediction: "The grace of our Lord Jesus Christ be with you all."

That grace, the love which pardons and quickens and makes good and fair and wise and strong, is offered to all in Christ. Unless we have accepted it, God's revelation and Christ's work have failed as far as we are concerned. "We therefore, as fellow-workers with Him, beseech you that ye receive not the grace of God in vain."

THE EPISTLE TO PHILEMON

I

"Paul, a prisoner of Christ Jesus, and Timothy our brother, to Philemon our beloved and fellow-worker, and to Apphia our sister, and to Archippus our fellow-soldier, and to the Church in thy house: Grace to you and peace from God our Father and the Lord Jesus Christ."—Philem. 1–3 (Rev. Ver.).

This Epistle stands alone among Paul's letters in being addressed to a private Christian, and in being entirely occupied with a small though very singular private matter; its aim being merely to bespeak a kindly welcome for a runaway slave who had been induced to perform the unheard-of act of voluntarily returning to servitude. If the New Testament were simply a book of doctrinal teaching, this Epistle would certainly be out of place in it; and if the great purpose of revelation were to supply material for creeds, it would be hard to see what value could be attached to a simple, short letter, from which no contribution to theological doctrine or ecclesiastical order can be extracted. But if we do not turn to it for discoveries of truth, we can find in it very beautiful illustrations of Christianity at work. It shows us the operation of the new forces which Christ has lodged in humanity—and that on two planes of action. It exhibits a perfect model of Christian friendship, refined and ennobled by a half-conscious reflection of the love which has called us "no longer slaves but friends," and adorned by delicate courtesies and quick consideration, which divines with subtlest instinct what it will be sweetest to the friend to hear, while it never approaches by a hair-breadth to flattery, nor forgets to counsel high duties. But still more important is the light which the letter casts on the relation of Christianity to slavery, which may be taken as a specimen of its relation to social and political evils generally, and yields fruitful results for the guidance of all who would deal with such.

It may be observed, too, that most of the considerations which Paul urges on Philemon as reasons for his kindly reception of Onesimus do not even need the alteration of a word, but simply a change in their application, to become worthy statements of the highest Christian truths. As Luther puts it, "We are all God's Onesimuses"; and the welcome which Paul seeks to secure for the returning fugitive, as well as the motives to which he appeals in order to secure it, do shadow forth in no uncertain outline our welcome from God, and the treasures of His heart towards us, because they are at bottom the same. The Epistle then is valuable, as showing in a concrete instance how the Christian life, in its attitude to others, and especially to those who have injured us, is all modelled upon God's forgiving love to us. Our Lord's parable of the forgiven servant who took his brother by the throat finds here a commentary, and the Apostle's own precept, "Be imitators of God, and walk in love," a practical exemplification.

Nor is the light which the letter throws on the character of the Apostle to be regarded as unimportant. The warmth, the delicacy, and what, if it were not so spontaneous, we might call tact, the graceful ingenuity with which he pleads for the fugitive, the perfect courtesy of every word, the gleam of playfulness—all fused together and harmonized to one end, and that in so brief a compass and with such unstudied ease and complete self-oblivion, make this Epistle a pure gem. Without thought of effect, and with complete unconsciousness, this man beats all the famous letter-writers on their own ground. That must have been a great intellect, and closely conversant with the Fountain of all light and beauty, which could shape the profound and far-reaching teachings of the Epistle to the Colossians, and pass from them to the graceful simplicity and sweet kindliness of this exquisite letter; as if Michael Angelo had gone straight from smiting his magnificent Moses from the marble mass to incise some delicate and tiny figure of Love or Friendship on a cameo.

The structure of the letter is of the utmost simplicity. It is not so much a structure as a flow. There is the usual superscription and salutation, followed, according to Paul's custom, by the expression of his thankful recognition of the love and faith of Philemon and his prayer for the perfecting of these. Then he goes straight to the business in hand, and with incomparable persuasiveness pleads for a welcome to Onesimus, bringing all possible reasons to converge on that one request, with an ingenious eloquence born of earnestness. Having poured out his heart in this pleasure adds no more but affectionate greetings from his companions and himself.

In the present section we shall confine our attention to the superscription and opening salutation.

I. We may observe the Apostle's designation of himself, as marked by consummate and instinctive appreciation of the claims of friendship, and of his own position in this letter as a suppliant. He does not come to his friend clothed with apostolic authority. In his letters to the Churches he always puts that in the forefront, and when he expected to be met by opponents, as in Galatia, there is a certain ring of defiance in his claim to receive his commission through no human intervention, but straight from heaven. Sometimes, as in the Epistle to the Colossians, he unites another strangely contrasted title, and calls himself also "the slave" of Christ; the one name asserting authority, the other bowing in humility before his Owner and Master. But here he is writing as a friend to a friend, and his object is to win his friend to a piece of Christian conduct which may be somewhat against the grain. Apostolic authority will not go half so far as personal influence in this case. So he drops all reference to it, and, instead, lets Philemon hear the fetters jangling on his limbs—a more powerful plea. "Paul, a prisoner," surely that would go straight to Philemon's heart, and give all but irresistible force to the request which follows. Surely if he could do anything to show his love and gratify even momentarily his friend in prison, he would not refuse it. If this designation had been calculated to produce effect, it would have lost all its grace; but no one with any ear for the accents of inartificial spontaneousness, can fail to hear them in the unconscious pathos of these opening words, which say the right thing, all unaware of how right it is.

There is great dignity also, as well as profound faith, in the next words, in which the Apostle calls himself a prisoner "of Christ Jesus." With what calm ignoring of all subordinate agencies he looks to the true author of his captivity! Neither Jewish hatred nor Roman policy had shut him up in Rome. Christ Himself had riveted his manacles on his wrists, therefore he bore them as lightly and proudly as a bride might wear the bracelet that her husband had clasped on her arm. The expression reveals both the author of and the reason for his imprisonment, and discloses the conviction which held him up in it. He thinks of his Lord as the Lord of providence, whose hand moves the pieces on the board—Pharisees, and Roman governors, and guards, and Cæsar; and he knows that he is an ambassador in bonds, for no crime, but for the testimony of Jesus. We need only notice that his younger companion Timothy is associated with the Apostle in the superscription, but disappears at once. The reason for the introduction of his name may either have been the slight additional weight thereby given to the request of the letter, or more probably, the additional authority thereby given to the junior, who would, in all likelihood, have much of Paul's work devolved on him when Paul was gone.

The names of the receivers of the letter bring before us a picture seen, as by one glimmering light across the centuries, of a Christian household in that Phrygian valley. The head of it, Philemon, appears to have been a native of, or at all events a resident in, Colossæ; for Onesimus, his slave, is spoken of in the Epistle to the Church there as "one of *you*." He was a person of some standing and wealth, for he had a house large enough to admit of a "Church" assembling in it, and to accommodate the Apostle and his travelling companions if he should visit Colossæ. He had apparently the means for large pecuniary help to poor brethren, and willingness to use them, for we read of the refreshment which his kindly deeds had imparted. He had been one of Paul's converts, and owed his own self to him; so that he must have met the Apostle,—who had probably not been in Colossæ,—on some of his journeys, perhaps during his three years' residence in Ephesus. He was of mature years, if, as is probable, Archippus, who was old enough to have service to do in the Church (Col. iv. 17), was his son.

He is called "our fellow-labourer." The designation may imply some actual co-operation at a former time. But more probably, the phrase, like the similar one in the next verse, "our fellow-soldier," is but Paul's gracefully affectionate way of lifting these good people's humbler work out of its narrowness, by associating it with his own. They in their little sphere, and he in his wider, were workers at the same task. All who toil for furtherance of Christ's kingdom, however widely they may be parted by time or distance, are fellow-workers. Division of labour does not impair unity of service. The field is wide, and the months between seedtime and harvest are long; but all the husbandmen have been engaged in the same great work, and though they have toiled alone shall "rejoice together." The first man who dug a shovelful of earth for the foundations of Cologne Cathedral, and he who fixed the last stone on the topmost spire a thousand years after, are fellow-workers. So Paul and Philemon, though their tasks were widely different in kind, in range, and in importance, and were carried on apart and independent of each other, were fellow-workers. The one lived a Christian life and helped some humble saints in an insignificant, remote corner; the other flamed through the whole then civilized western world, and sheds light to-day: but the obscure, twinkling taper and the blazing torch were kindled at the same source, shone with the same light, and were parts of one great whole. Our narrowness is rebuked, our despondency cheered, our vulgar tendency to think little of modest, obscure service rendered by commonplace people, and to exaggerate the worth of the more conspicuous, is corrected by such a thought. However small may be our capacity or sphere, and however solitary we may feel, we may summon up before the eyes of our faith a mighty multitude of apostles, martyrs, toilers in every land and age as *our*—even our—work-fellows. The field stretches far beyond our vision, and many are toiling in it for Him, whose work never comes near ours. There are differences of service, but the same Lord, and all who have the same master are companions in labour. Therefore Paul, the greatest of the servants of Christ, reaches down his hand to the obscure Philemon, and says, "He works the work of the Lord, as I also do."

In the house at Colossæ there was a Christian wife by the side of a Christian husband; at least, the mention of Apphia here in so prominent a position is most naturally accounted for by supposing her to be the wife of Philemon. Her friendly reception of the runaway would be quite as important as his, and it is therefore most natural that the letter bespeaking it should be addressed to both. The probable reading "our sister" (R.V.), instead of "our beloved" (A.V.), gives the distinct assurance that she too was a Christian, and like-minded with her husband.

The prominent mention of this Phrygian matron is an illustration of the way in which Christianity, without meddling with social usages, introduced a new tone of feeling about the position of woman, which gradually changed the face of the world, is still working, and has further revolutions to affect. The degraded classes of the Greek world were slaves and women. This Epistle touches both, and shows us Christianity in the very act of elevating both. The same process strikes the fetters from the slave and sets the wife by the side of thc husband, "yoked in all exercise of noble end,"—namely, the proclamation of Christ as the Saviour of all mankind, and of all human creatures as equally capable of receiving an equal salvation. That annihilates all distinctions. The old world was parted by deep gulfs. There were three of special depth and width, across which it was hard for sympathy to fly. These were the distinctions of race, sex, and condition. But the good news that Christ has died for all men, and is ready to live in all men, has thrown a bridge across, or rather has filled up, the ravine; so the Apostle bursts into his triumphant proclamation, "There is neither Jew nor Greek, there is neither bond nor free, there is neither male nor female; for ye are all one in Christ Jesus."

A third name is united with those of husband and wife, that of Archippus. The close relation in which the names stand, and the purely domestic character of the letter, make it probable that he was a son of the wedded pair. At all events, he was in some way part of their household, possibly some kind of teacher and guide. We meet his name also in the Epistle to the Colossians, and, from the nature of the reference to him there, we draw the inference that he filled some "ministry" in the Church of Laodicea. The nearness of the two cities made it quite possible that he should live in Philemon's house in Colossæ and yet go over to Laodicea for his work.

The Apostle calls him "his fellow-soldier," a phrase which is best explained in the same fashion as is the previous "fellow-worker," namely, that by it Paul graciously associates Archippus with himself, different as their tasks were. The variation of *soldier* for *worker* probably is due to the fact of Archippus' being the bishop of the Laodicean Church. In any case, it is very beautiful that the grizzled veteran officer should thus, as it were, clasp the hand of this young recruit, and call him his comrade. How it would go to the heart of Archippus!

A somewhat stern message is sent to Archippus in the Colossian letter. Why did not Paul send it quietly in this Epistle instead of letting a whole Church know of it? It seems at first sight as if he had chosen the harshest way; but perhaps further consideration may suggest that the reason was an instinctive unwillingness to introduce a jarring note into the joyous friendship and confidence which sounds through this Epistle, and to bring public matters into this private communication. The warning would come with more effect from the Church, and this cordial message of goodwill and confidence would prepare Archippus to receive the other, as rain showers make the ground soft for the good seed. The private affection would mitigate the public exhortation with whatever rebuke may have been in it.

A greeting is sent, too, to "the Church in thy house." As in the case of the similar community in the house of Nymphas (Col. iv. 15), we cannot decide whether by this expression is meant simply a Christian family, or some little company of believers who were wont to meet beneath Philemon's roof for Christian converse and worship. The latter seems the more probable supposition. It is natural that they should be addressed; for Onesimus, if received by Philemon, would naturally become a member of the group, and therefore it was important to secure their good will.

So we have here shown to us, by one stray beam of twinkling light, for a moment, a very sweet picture of the domestic life of that Christian household in their remote valley. It shines still to us across the centuries, which have swallowed up so much that seemed more permanent, and silenced so much that made far more noise in its day. The picture may well set us asking ourselves the question whether we, with all our boasted advancement, have been able to realize the true ideal of Christian family life as these three did. The husband and wife dwelling as heirs together of the grace of life, their child beside them sharing their faith and service, their household ordered in the ways of the Lord, their friends Christ's friends, and their social joys hallowed and serene—what nobler form of family life can be conceived than that? What a rebuke to, and satire on, many a so-called Christian household!

II. We may deal briefly with the apostolic salutation, "Grace to you and peace from God our Father and the Lord Jesus Christ," as we have already had to speak of it in considering the greeting to the Colossians. The two main points to be observed in these words are the comprehensiveness of the Apostle's loving wish, and the source to which he looks for its fulfilment. Just as the regal title of the King, whose Throne was the Cross, was written in the languages of culture, of law, and of religion, as an unconscious prophecy of His universal reign; so, with like unintentional felicity, we have blended here the ideals of good which the East and the West have framed for those to whom they wish good, in token that Christ is able to slake all the thirsts of the soul, and that whatsoever things any races of men have dreamed as the chiefest blessings, these are all to be reached through Him and Him only.

But the deeper lesson here is to be found by observing that "grace" refers to the action of the Divine heart, and "peace" to the result thereof in man's experience. As we have noted in commenting on Col. i. 2, "grace" is free, undeserved, unmotived, self-springing love. Hence it comes to mean, not only the deep fountain in the Divine nature, that His love, which, like some strong spring, leaps up and gushes forth by an inward impulse, in neglect of all motives drawn from the lovableness of its objects, such as determine our poor human loves, but also the results of that bestowing love in men's characters, or, as we say, the "graces" of the Christian soul. They are "grace," not only because in the æsthetic sense of the word they are beautiful, but because, in the theological meaning of it, they are the products of the giving love and power of God. "Whatsoever things are lovely and of good report," all nobilities, tendernesses, exquisite beauties, and steadfast strengths of mind and heart, of will and disposition—all are the gifts of God's undeserved and open-handed love.

The fruit of such grace received is peace. In other places the Apostle twice gives a fuller form of this salutation, inserting "mercy" between the two here named; as also does St. John in his second Epistle. That fuller form gives us the source in the Divine heart, the manifestation of grace in the Divine act, and the outcome in human experience; or as we may say, carrying on the metaphor, the broad, calm lake which the grace, flowing to us in the stream of mercy, makes, when it opens out in our hearts. Here, however, we have but the ultimate source, and the effect in us.

All the discords of our nature and circumstances can be harmonized by that grace which is ready to flow into our hearts. Peace with God, with ourselves, with our fellows, repose in the midst of change, calm in conflict, may be ours. All these various applications of the one idea should be included in our interpretation, for they are all included in fact in the peace which God's grace brings where it lights. The first and deepest need of the soul is conscious amity and harmony with God, and nothing but the consciousness of His love as forgiving and healing brings that. We are torn asunder by conflicting passions, and our hearts are the battleground for conscience and inclination, sin and goodness, hopes and fears, and a hundred other contending emotions. Nothing but a heavenly power can make the lion within lie down with the lamb. Our natures are "like the troubled sea, which cannot rest," whose churning waters cast up the foul things that lie in their slimy beds; but where God's grace comes, a great calm hushes the tempests, "and birds of peace sit brooding on the charmed wave."

We are compassed about by foes with whom we have to wage undying warfare, and by hostile circumstances and difficult tasks which need continual conflict; but a man with God's grace in his heart may have the rest of submission, the repose of trust, the tranquillity of him who "has ceased from his own works": and so, while the daily struggle goes on and the battle rages round, there may be quiet, deep and sacred, in his heart.

The life of nature, which is a selfish life, flings us into unfriendly rivalries with others, and sets us battling for our own hands, and it is hard to pass out of ourselves sufficiently to live peaceably with all men. But the grace of God in our hearts drives out self, and changes the man who truly has it into its own likeness. He who knows that he owes everything to a Divine love which stooped to his lowliness, and pardoned his sins, and enriched him with all which he has that is worthy and noble, cannot but move among men, doing with them, in his poor fashion, what God has done with him.

Thus, in all the manifold forms in which restless hearts need peace, the grace of God brings it to them. The great river of mercy which has its source deep in the heart of God, and in His free, undeserved love, pours into poor, unquiet spirits, and there spreads itself into a placid lake, on whose still surface all heaven is mirrored.

The elliptical form of this salutation leaves it doubtful whether we are to see in it a prayer or a prophecy, a wish or an assurance. According to the probable reading of the parallel greeting in the second Epistle of John, the latter would be the construction; but probably it is best to combine both ideas, and to see here, as Bengel does in the passage referred to in John's Epistle, "votum cum affirmatione" — a desire which is so certain of its own fulfilment, that it is a prophecy, just because it is a prayer.

The ground of the certainty lies in the source from which the grace and peace come. They flow "from God the Father and the Lord Jesus Christ." The placing of both names under the government of one preposition implies the mysterious unity of the Father with the Son; while conversely St. John, in the parallel passage just mentioned, by employing two prepositions, brings out the distinction between the Father, who is the fontal source, and the Son, who is the flowing stream. But both forms of the expression demand for their honest explanation the recognition of the divinity of Jesus Christ. How dare a man, who thought of Him as other than Divine, put His name thus by the side of God's, as associated with the Father in the bestowal of grace? Surely such words, spoken without any thought of a doctrine of the Trinity, and which are the spontaneous utterance of Christian devotion, are demonstration, not to be gainsaid, that to Paul, at all events, Jesus Christ was, in the fullest sense, Divine. The double source is one source, for in the Son is the whole fulness of the Godhead; and the grace of God, bringing with it the peace of God, is poured into that spirit which bows humbly before Jesus Christ, and trusts Him when He says, with love in His eyes and comfort in His tones, "My grace is sufficient for thee"; "My peace give I unto you."

II

"I thank my God always, making mention of thee in my prayers, hearing of thy love, and of the faith which thou hast toward the Lord Jesus, and toward all the saints; that the fellowship of thy faith may become effectual, in the knowledge of every good thing which is in you, unto Christ. For I had much joy and comfort in thy love, because the hearts of the saints have been refreshed through thee, brother." —Philem. 4–7 (Rev. Ver.).

Paul's was one of those regal natures to which things are possible that other men dare not do. No suspicion of weakness attaches to him when he pours out his heart in love, nor any of insincerity when he speaks of his continual prayers for his friends, or when he runs over in praise of his converts. Few men have been able to talk so much of their love without betraying its shallowness and self-consciousness, or of their prayers without exciting a doubt of their manly sincerity. But the Apostle could venture to do these things without being thought either feeble or false, and could unveil his deepest affections and his most secret devotions without provoking either a smile or a shrug.

He has the habit of beginning all his letters with thankful commendations and assurances of a place in his prayers. The exceptions are 2 Corinthians, where he writes under strong and painful emotion, and Galatians, where a vehement accusation of fickleness takes the place of the usual greeting. But these exceptions make the habit more conspicuous. Though this is a habit, it is not a form, but the perfectly simple and natural expression of the moment's feelings. He begins his letters so, not in order to please and to say smooth things, but because he feels lovingly, and his heart fills with a pure joy which speaks most fitly in prayer. To recognise good is the way to make good better. Teachers must love if their teaching is to help. The best way to secure the doing of any signal act of Christian generosity, such as Paul wished of Philemon, is to show absolute confidence that it will be done, because it is in accordance with what we know of the doer's character. "It's a shame to tell Arnold a lie: he always trusts us," the Rugby boys used to say. Nothing could so powerfully have swayed Philemon to grant Paul's request, as Paul's graceful mention of his beneficence, which mention is yet by no means conscious diplomacy, but instinctive kindliness.

The words of this section are simple enough, but their order is not altogether clear. They are a good example of the hurry and rush of the Apostle's style, arising from his impetuosity of nature. His thoughts and feelings come knocking at "the door of his lips" in a crowd, and do not always make their way out in logical order. For instance, he begins here with thankfulness, and that suggests the mention of his prayers, *v.* 4. Then he gives the occasion of his thankfulness in *v.* 5, "Hearing of thy love and of the faith which thou hast," etc. He next tells Philemon the subject matter of his prayers in *v.* 6, "That the fellowship of thy faith may become effectual," etc. These two verses thus correspond to the two clauses of *v.* 4, and finally in *v.* 7 he harks back once more to his reasons for thankfulness in Philemon's love and faith, adding, in a very lovely and pathetic way, that the good deeds done in far off Colossæ had wafted a refreshing air to the Roman prison house, and, little as the doer knew it, had been a joy and comfort to the solitary prisoner there.

I. We have,—then, here the character of Philemon, which made Paul glad and thankful. The order of the language is noteworthy. Love is put before faith. The significance of this sequence comes out by contrast with similar expressions in Ephesians i. 15: "Your faith in the Lord Jesus, and love unto all the saints" (A.V.) and Colossians i. 4: "Your faith in Christ Jesus, and the love which ye have toward all the saints," where the same elements are arranged in the more natural order, corresponding to their logical relation; viz., faith first, and love as its consequence. The reason for the change here is probably that Onesimus and Epaphras, from whom Paul would be likely to hear of Philemon, would enlarge upon his practical benevolence, and would naturally say less about the root than about the sweet and visible fruit. The arrangement then is an echo of the talks which had gladdened the Apostle. Possibly, too, love is put first, because the object of the whole letter is to secure its exercise towards the fugitive slave; and seeing that the Apostle would listen with that purpose in view, each story which was told of Philemon's kindness to others made the deeper impression on Paul. The order here is the order of analysis, digging down from manifestation to cause: the order in the parallel passages quoted is the order of production ascending from root to flower.

Another peculiarity in the arrangement of the words is that the objects of love and faith are named in the reverse order to that in which these graces are mentioned, "the Lord Jesus" being first, and "all the saints" last. Thus we have, as it were, "faith towards the Lord Jesus" imbedded in the centre of the verse, while "thy love ... toward all the saints," which flows from it, wraps it round. The arrangement is like some forms of Hebrew poetical parallelism, in which the first and fourth members correspond, and the second and third, or like the pathetic measure of *In Memoriam*, and has the same sweet lingering cadence; while it also implies important truths as to the central place in regard to the virtues which knit hearts in soft bonds of love and help, of the faith which finds its sole object in Jesus Christ.

The source and foundation of goodness and nobility of character is faith in Jesus the Lord. That must be buried deep in the soul if tender love toward men is to flow from it. It is "the very pulse of the machine." All the pearls of goodness are held in solution in faith. Or, to speak more accurately, faith in Christ gives possession of His life and Spirit, from which all good is unfolded; and it further sets in action strong motives by which to lead to every form of purity and beauty of soul; and, still further, it brings the heart into glad contact with a Divine love which forgives its Onesimuses, and so it cannot but touch the heart into some glad imitation of that love which is its own dearest treasure. So that, for all these and many more reasons, love to men is the truest visible expression, as it is the direct and necessary result, of faith in Christ. What is exhaled from the heart and drawn upwards by the fervours of Christ's self-sacrificing love is faith; when it falls on earth again, as a sweet rain of pity and tenderness, it is love.

Further, the true object of faith and one phase of its attitude towards that object are brought out in this central clause. We have the two names which express, the one the divinity, the other the humanity of Christ. So the proper object of faith is the whole Christ, in both His natures, the Divine-human Saviour. Christian faith sees the divinity in the humanity, and the humanity around the divinity. A faith which grasps only the manhood is maimed, and indeed has no right to the name. Humanity is not a fit object of trust. It may change; it has limits; it must die. "Cursed be the man that maketh flesh his arm," is as true about faith in a merely human Christ as about faith in any other man. There may be reverence, there may be in some sense love, obedience, imitation; but there should not be, and I see not how there can be, the absolute reliance, the utter dependence, the unconditional submission, which are of the very essence of faith, in the emotions which men cherish towards a human Christ. The Lord Jesus only can evoke these. On the other hand, the far off splendour and stupendous glory of the Divine nature becomes the object of untrembling trust, and draws near enough to be known and loved, when we have it mellowed to our weak eyes by shining through the tempering medium of His humanity.

The preposition here used to define the relation of faith to its object is noteworthy. Faith is "toward" Him. The idea is that of a movement of yearning after an unattained good. And that is one part of the true office of faith. There is in it an element of aspiration, as of the soaring eagle to the sun, or the climbing tendrils to the summit of the supporting stem. In Christ there is always something beyond, which discloses itself the more clearly, the fuller is our present possession of Him. Faith builds upon and rests in the Christ possessed and experienced, and just therefore will it, if it be true, yearn towards the Christ unpossessed. A great reach of flashing glory beyond opens on us, as we round each new headland in that unending voyage. Our faith should and will be an ever-increasing fruition of Christ, accompanied with increasing perception of unreached depths in Him, and increasing longing after enlarged possession of His infinite fulness.

Where the centre is such a faith, its circumference and outward expression will be a widely diffused love. That deep and most private emotion of the soul, which is the flight of the lonely spirit to the single Christ, as if these two were alone in the world, does not bar a man off from his kind, but effloresces into the largest and most practical love. When one point of the compasses is struck deeply and firmly into that centre of all things, the other can steadily sweep a wide circle. The widest is not here drawn, but a somewhat narrower, concentric one. The love is "toward all saints." Clearly their relation to Jesus Christ puts all Christians into relation with one another. That was an astounding thought in Philemon's days, when such high walls separated race from race, the slave from the free, woman from man; but the new faith leaped all barriers, and put a sense of brotherhood into every heart that learned God's fatherhood in Jesus. The nave of the wheel holds all the spokes in place. The sun makes the system called by its name a unity, though some planets be of giant bulk and swing through a mighty orbit, waited on by obedient satellites, and some be but specks and move through a narrow circle, and some have scarce been seen by human eye. All are one, because all revolve round one sun, though solemn abysses part them, and though no message has ever crossed the gulfs from one to another.

The recognition of the common relation which all who bear the same relation to Christ bear to one another has more formidable difficulties to encounter to-day than it had in these times when the Church had no stereotyped creeds and no stiffened organizations, and when to the flexibility of its youth were added the warmth of new conviction and the joy of a new field for expanding emotions of brotherly kindness. But nothing can absolve from the duty. Creeds separate, Christ unites. The road to "the reunion of Christendom" is through closer union to Jesus Christ. When that is secured, barriers which now keep brethren apart will be leaped, or pulled down, or got rid of somehow. It is of no use to say, "Go to, let us love one another."

That will be unreal, mawkish, histrionic. "The faith which thou hast toward the Lord Jesus" will be the productive cause, as it is the measure, of "thy love toward all the saints."

But the love which is here commended is not a mere feeling, nor does it go off in gushes, however fervid, of eloquent emotion. Clearly Philemon was a benefactor of the brotherhood, and his love did not spend only the paper money of words and promises to pay, but the solid coin of kindly deeds. Practical charity is plainly included in that love of which it had cheered Paul in his imprisonment to hear. Its mention, then, is one step nearer to the object of the letter. Paul conducts his siege of Philemon's heart skilfully, and opens here a fresh parallel, and creeps a yard or two closer up. "Surely you are not going to shut out one of your own household from that wide-reaching kindness." So much is most delicately hinted, or rather, left to Philemon to infer, by the recognition of his brotherly love. A hint lies in it that there may be a danger of cherishing a cheap and easy charity that reverses the law of gravity, and *in*creases as the square of the distance, having tenderness and smiles for people and Churches which are well out of our road, and frowns for some nearer home. "He that loveth not his brother whom he hath seen, how shall he love" his brother "whom he hath not seen?"

II. In *v.* 6 we have the apostolic prayer for Philemon, grounded on the tidings of his love and faith. It is immediately connected with "the prayers" of *v.* 4 by the introductory "that," which is best understood as introducing the subject matter of the prayer. Whatever then may be the meaning of this supplication, it is a prayer for Philemon, and not for others. That remark disposes of the explanations which widen its scope, contrary, as it seems to me, to the natural understanding of the context.

"The fellowship of thy faith" is capable of more than one meaning. The signification of the principal word and the relation expressed by the preposition may be variously determined. "Fellowship" is more than once used in the sense of sharing material wealth with Christ's poor, or more harshly and plainly, charitable contribution. So we find it in Romans xv. 26 and 2 Corinthians ix. 13. Adopting that meaning here, the "of" must express, as it often does, the origin of Philemon's kindly gifts, namely, his faith; and the whole phrase accords with the preceding verse in its view of the genesis of beneficence to the brethren as the result of faith in the Lord.

The Apostle prays that this faith-begotten practical liberality may become efficacious, or may acquire still more power; *i.e.* may increase in activity, and so may lead to "the knowledge of every good thing that is in us." The interpretation has found extensive support, which takes this as equivalent to a desire that Philemon's good deeds might lead others, whether enemies or friends, to recognise the beauties of sympathetic goodness in the true Christian character. Such an explanation hopelessly confuses the whole, and does violence to the plain requirements of the context, which limit the prayer to Philemon. It is *his* "knowledge" of which Paul is thinking. The same profound and pregnant word is used here which occurs so frequently in the other epistles of the captivity, and which always means that deep and vital knowledge which knows because it possesses. Usually its object is God as revealed in the great work and person of Christ. Here its object is the sum total of spiritual blessings, the whole fulness of the gifts given us by, and, at bottom, consisting of, that same Christ dwelling in the heart, who is revealer, because He is communicator, of God. The full, deep knowledge of this manifold and yet one good is no mere theoretical work of the understanding, but is an experience which is only possible to him who enjoys it.

The meaning of the whole prayer, then, put into feebler and more modern dress is simply that Philemon's liberality and Christian love may grow more and more, and may help him to a fuller appropriation and experience of the large treasures "which are in us," though in germ and potentiality only, until brought into consciousness by our own Christian growth. The various readings "in us," or "in you" only widen the circle of possessors of these gifts to the whole Church, or narrow it to the believers of Colossæ.

There still remain for consideration the last words of the clause, "unto Christ" They must be referred back to the main subject of the sentence, "may become effectual." They seem to express the condition on which Christian "fellowship," like all Christian acts, can be quickened with energy, and tend to spiritual progress; namely, that it shall be done as to the Lord. There is perhaps in this appended clause a kind of lingering echo of our Lord's own words, in which He accepts as done unto Him the kindly deeds done to the least of His brethren.

So then this great prayer brings out very strongly the goal to which the highest perfection of Christian character has still to aspire. Philemon was no weakling or laggard in the Christian conflict and race. His attainments sent a thrill of thankfulness through the Apostle's spirit. But there remained "very much land to be possessed"; and precisely because he had climbed so far, does his friend pray that he may mount still higher, where the sweep of view is wider, and the air clearer still. It is an endless task to bring into conscious possession and exercise all the fulness with which Christ endows His feeblest servant. Not till all that God can give, or rather has given, has been incorporated in the nature and wrought out in the life, is the term reached. This is the true sublime of the Christian life, that it begins with the reception of a strictly infinite gift, and demands immortality as the field for unfolding its worth. Continual progress in all that ennobles the nature, satisfies the heart, and floods the mind with light is the destiny of the Christian soul, and of it alone. Therefore unwearied effort, buoyancy, and hope which no dark memories can dash nor any fears darken should mark *their* temper, to whom the future offers an absolutely endless and limitless increase in the possession of the infinite God.

There is also brought out in this prayer the value of Christian beneficence as a means of spiritual growth. Philemon's "communication of faith" will help him to the knowledge of the fulness of Christ. The reaction of conduct on character and growth in godliness is a familiar idea with Paul, especially in the prison epistles. Thus we read in his prayer for the Colossians, "fruitful in every good work, and increasing in the knowledge of God." The faithful carrying out in life of what we already know is not the least important condition of increasing knowledge. If a man does not live up to his religion, his religion shrinks to the level of his life. Unoccupied territory lapses. We hold our spiritual gifts on the terms of using them. The practice of convictions deepens convictions; not that the exercise of Christian graces will make theologians, but it will give larger possession of the knowledge which is life.

While this general principle is abundantly enforced in Scripture and confirmed by experience, the specific form of it here is that the right administration of wealth is a direct means of increasing a Christian's possession of the large store treasured in Christ. Every loving thought towards the sorrowful and the needy, every touch of sympathy yielded to, and every kindly, Christlike deed flowing from these, thins away some film of the barriers between the believing soul and a full possession of God, and thus makes it more capable of beholding Him and of rising to communion with Him. The possibilities of wealth lie, not only in the direction of earthly advantages, but in the fact that men may so use it as to secure their being "received into everlasting habitations." Modern evangelical teachers have been afraid to say what Paul ventured to say on this matter, for fear of obscuring the truth which Paul gave his life to preach. Surely they need not be more jealous for the doctrine of "justification by faith" than he was; and if he had no scruples in telling rich men to "lay up in store for themselves a good foundation for the time to come," by being "ready to communicate," they may safely follow. There is probably no more powerful cause of the comparative feebleness of average English Christianity than the selfish use of money, and no surer means of securing a great increase in the depth and richness of the individual Christian life than the fuller application of Christian principle, that is, of the law of sacrifice, to the administration of property.

The final clause of the verse seems to state the condition on which Philemon's good deeds will avail for his own growth in grace, and implies that in him that condition is fulfilled. If a man does deeds of kindness and help to one of these little ones, as "unto Christ," then his beneficence will come back in spiritual blessing on his own head. If they are the result of simple natural compassion, beautiful as it is, they will reinforce *it*, but have no tendency to strengthen that from which they do *not* flow. If they are tainted by any self-regard, then they are not charitable deeds at all. What is done for Christ will bring to the doer more of Christ as its consequence and reward. All life, with all its varied forms of endurance and service, comes under this same law, and tends to make more assured and more blessed and more profound the knowledge and grasp of the fulness of Christ, in the measure in which it is directed to Him, and done or suffered for His sake.

III. The present section closes with a very sweet and pathetic representation of the Apostle's joy in the character of his friend.

The "for" of *v.* 7 connects not with the words of petition immediately before, but with "I thank my God" (*v.* 4), and gives a graceful turn—graceful only because so unforced and true—to the sentence. "My thanks are due to you for your kindness to others, for, though you did not think of it, you have done me as much good as you did them." The "love" which gives Paul such "great joy and consolation" is not love directed to himself, but to others; and the reason why it gladdened the Apostle was because it had "refreshed the hearts" of sorrowful and needy saints in Colossæ. This tender expression of affectionate joy in Philemon's good deeds is made wonderfully emotional by that emphatic "brother" which ends the verse, and by its unusual position in the sentence assumes the character of a sudden, irrepressible shoot of love from Paul's heart towards Philemon, like the quick impulse with which a mother will catch up her child, and cover it with caresses. Paul was never ashamed of showing his tenderness, and it never repels us.

These final words suggest the unexpected good which good deeds may do. No man can ever tell how far the blessing of his trivial acts of kindness, or other pieces of Christian conduct, may travel. They may benefit one in material fashion, but the fragrance may reach many others. Philemon little dreamed that his small charity to some suffering brother in Colossæ would find its way across the sea, and bring a waft of coolness and refreshing into the hot prison house. Neither Paul nor Philemon dreamed that, made immortal by the word of the former, the same transient act would find its way across the centuries, and would "smell sweet and blossom in the dust" to-day. Men know not who are their audiences, or who may be spectators of their works; for they are all bound so mystically and closely together, that none can tell how far the vibrations which he sets in motion will thrill.

This is true about all deeds, good and bad, and invests them all with solemn importance. The arrow shot travels beyond the archer's eye, and may wound where he knows not. The only thing certain about the deed once done is, that its irrevocable consequences will reach much farther than the doer dreamed, and that no limits can be set to the subtle influence which, for blessing or harm, it exerts.

Since the diameter of the circle which our acts may fill is unknown and unknowable, the doer who stands at the centre is all the more solemnly bound to make sure of the only thing of which he can make sure, the quality of the influence sent forth; and since his deed may blight or bless so widely, to clarify his motives and guard his doings, that they may bring only good wherever they light.

May we not venture to see shining through the Apostle's words the Master's face? "Even as Christ did for us with God the Father," says Luther, "thus also doth St. Paul for Onesimus with Philemon"; and that thought may permissibly be applied to many parts of this letter, to which it gives much beauty. It may not be all fanciful to say that, as Paul's heart was gladdened when he heard of the good deeds done in far-off Colossæ by a man who "owed to him his own self" so we may believe that Christ is glad and has "great joy in our love" to His servants and in our kindliness, when He beholds the poor work done by the humblest for His sake. He sees and rejoices, and approves when there are none but Himself to know or praise; and at last many, who did lowly service to His friends, will be surprised to hear from His lips the acknowledgment that it was Himself whom they had visited and succoured, and that they had been ministering to the Master's joy when they had only known themselves to be succouring His servants' need.

III

"Wherefore, though I have all boldness in Christ to enjoin thee that which is befitting, yet for love's sake I rather beseech, being such a one as Paul the aged, and now a prisoner also of Jesus Christ; I beseech thee for my child, whom I have begotten in my bonds, Onesimus; who was aforetime unprofitable to thee, but now is profitable to thee, and to me." —Philem. 8–11 (Rev. Ver.).

After honest and affectionate praise of Philemon, the Apostle now approaches the main purpose of his letter. But even now he does not blurt it out at once. He probably anticipated that his friend was justly angry with his runaway slave, and therefore, in these verses, he touches a kind of prelude to his request with what we should call the finest tact, if it were not so manifestly the unconscious product of simple good feeling. Even by the end of them he has not ventured to say what he wishes done, though he has ventured to introduce the obnoxious name. So much persuading and sanctified ingenuity does it sometimes take to induce good men to do plain duties which may be unwelcome.

These verses not only present a model for efforts to lead men in right paths, but they unveil the very spirit of Christianity in their pleadings. Paul's persuasives to Philemon are echoes of Christ's persuasives to Paul. He had learned his method from his Master, and had himself experienced that gentle love was more than commandments. Therefore he softens his voice to speak to Philemon, as Christ had softened His to speak to Paul. We do not arbitrarily "spiritualize" the words, but simply recognise that the Apostle moulded his conduct after Christ's pattern, when we see here a mirror reflecting some of the highest truths of Christian ethics.

I. Here is seen love which beseeches where it might command. The first word, "wherefore," leads back to the preceding sentence, and makes Philemon's past kindness to the saints the reason for his being asked to be kind now. The Apostle's confidence in his friend's character, and in his being amenable to the appeal of love, made Paul waive his apostolic authority, and sue instead of commanding. There are people, like the horse and the mule, who understand only rough imperatives, backed by force; but they are fewer than we are apt to think, and perhaps gentleness is never wholly thrown away. No doubt, there must be adaptation of method to different characters, but we should try gentleness before we make up our minds that to try it is to throw pearls before swine.

The careful limits put to apostolic authority here deserve notice. "I might be much bold in Christ to command." He has no authority in himself, but he has "in Christ." His own personality gives him none, but his relation to his Master does. It is a distinct assertion of right to command, and an equally distinct repudiation of any such right, except as derived from his union with Jesus.

He still further limits his authority by that noteworthy clause, "that which is befitting." His authority does not stretch so far as to create new obligations, or to repeal plain laws of duty. There was a standard by which his commands were to be tried. He appeals to Philemon's own sense of moral fitness, to his natural conscience, enlightened by communion with Christ.

Then comes the great motive which he will urge, "for love's sake," —not merely his to Philemon, nor Philemon's to him, but the bond which unites all Christian souls together, and binds them all to Christ. "That grand, sacred principle," says Paul, "bids me put away authority, and speak in entreaty." Love naturally beseeches, and does not order. The harsh voice of command is simply the imposition of another's will, and it belongs to relationships in which the heart has no share. But wherever love is the bond, grace is poured into the lips, and "I enjoin" becomes "I pray." So that even where the outward form of authority is still kept, as in a parent to young children, there will ever be some endearing word to swathe the harsh imperative in tenderness, like a sword blade wrapped about with wool, lest it should wound. Love tends to obliterate the hard distinction of superior and inferior, which finds its expression in laconic imperatives and silent obedience. It seeks not for mere compliance with commands, but for oneness of will. The lightest wish breathed by loved lips is stronger than all stern injunctions, often, alas! than all laws of duty. The heart is so tuned as only to vibrate to that one tone. The rocking stones, which all the storms of winter may howl round and not move, can be set swinging by a light touch. Una leads the lion in a silken leash. Love controls the wildest nature. The demoniac, whom no chains can bind, is found sitting at the feet of incarnate gentleness. So the wish of love is all-powerful with loving hearts, and its faintest whisper louder and more constraining than all the trumpets of Sinai.

There is a large lesson here for all human relationships. Fathers and mothers, husbands and wives, friends and companions, teachers and guides of all sorts, should set their conduct by this pattern, and let the law of love sit ever upon their lips. Authority is the weapon of a weak man, who is doubtful of his own power to get himself obeyed, or of a selfish one, who seeks for mechanical submission rather than for the fealty of willing hearts. Love is the weapon of a strong man who can cast aside the trappings of superiority, and is never loftier than when he descends, nor more absolute than when he abjures authority, and appeals with love to love. Men are not to be dragooned into goodness. If mere outward acts are sought, it may be enough to impose another's will in orders as curt as a soldier's word of command; but if the joyful inclination of the heart to the good deed is to be secured, that can only be done when law melts into love, and is thereby transformed to a more imperative obligation, written not on tables of stone, but on fleshy tables of the heart.

There is a glimpse here into the very heart of Christ's rule over men. He too does not merely impose commands, but stoops to entreat, where He indeed might command. "Henceforth I call you not servants, but friends"; and though He does go on to say, "Ye are My friends, if ye do whatsoever I command you," yet His commandment has in it so much tenderness, condescension, and pleading love, that it sounds far liker beseeching than enjoining. His yoke is easy, for this among other reasons, that it is, if one may so say, padded with love. His burden is light, because it is laid on His servant's shoulders by a loving hand; and so, as St. Bernard says, it is *onus quod portantem portat*, a burden which carries him who carries it.

II. There is in these verses the appeal which gives weight to the entreaties of love. The Apostle brings personal considerations to bear on the enforcement of impersonal duty, and therein follows the example of his Lord. He presents his own circumstances as adding power to his request, and as it were puts himself into the scale. He touches with singular pathos on two things which should sway his friend. "Such a one as Paul the aged." The alternative rendering "ambassador," while quite possible, has not congruity in its favour, and would be a recurrence to that very motive of official authority which he has just disclaimed. The other rendering is every way preferable. How old was he? Probably somewhere about sixty—not a very great age, but life was somewhat shorter then than now, and Paul was, no doubt, aged by work, by worry, and by the unresting spirit that "o'er-informed his tenement of clay." Such temperaments as his soon grow old. Perhaps Philemon was not much younger; but the prosperous Colossian gentleman had had a smoother life, and, no doubt, carried his years more lightly.

The requests of old age should have weight. In our days, what with the improvements in education, and the general loosening of the bonds of reverence, the old maxim that "the utmost respect is due to children," receives a strange interpretation, and in many a household the Divine order is turned upside down, and the juniors regulate all things. Other still more sacred things will be likely to lose their due reverence when silver hairs no longer receive theirs.

But usually the aged who are "such" aged "as Paul" was, will not fail of obtaining honour and deference. No more beautiful picture of the bright energy and freshness still possible to the old was ever painted than may be gathered from the Apostle's unconscious sketch of himself. He delighted in having young life about him — Timothy, Titus, Mark, and others, boys in comparison with himself, whom yet he admitted to close intimacy as some old general might the youths of his staff, warming his age at the genial flame of their growing energies and unworn hopes. His was a joyful old age too, notwithstanding many burdens of anxiety and sorrow. We hear the clear song of his gladness ringing through the epistle of joy, that to the Philippians, which, like this, dates from his Roman captivity. A Christian old age should be joyful, and only it will be; for the joys of the natural life burn low, when the fuel that fed them is nearly exhausted, and withered hands are held in vain over the dying embers. But Christ's joy "remains," and a Christian old age may be like the polar midsummer days, when the sun shines till midnight, and dips but for an imperceptible interval ere it rises for the unending day of heaven.

Paul the aged was full of interest in the things of the day; no mere "praiser of time gone by," but a strenuous worker, cherishing a quick sympathy and an eager interest which kept him young to the end. Witness that last chapter of the second Epistle to Timothy, where he is seen, in the immediate expectation of death, entering heartily into passing trifles, and thinking it worth while to give little pieces of information about the movements of his friends, and wishful to get his books and parchments, that he might do some more work while waiting for the headsman's sword. And over his cheery, sympathetic, busy old age there is thrown the light of a great hope, which kindles desire and onward looks in his dim eyes, and parts "such a one as Paul the aged" by a whole universe from the old whose future is dark and their past dreary, whose hope is a phantom and their memory a pang.

The Apostle adds yet another personal characteristic as a motive with Philemon to grant his request: "Now a prisoner also of Christ Jesus." He has already spoken of himself in these terms in *v.* 1. His sufferings were imposed by and endured for Christ. He holds up his fettered wrist, and in effect says, "Surely you will not refuse anything that you can do to wrap a silken softness round the cold, hard iron, especially when you remember for

Whose sake and by Whose will I am bound with this chain." He thus brings personal motives to reinforce duty which is binding from other and higher considerations. He does not merely tell Philemon that he ought to take back Onesimus as a piece of self-sacrificing Christian duty. He does imply that highest motive throughout his pleadings, and urges that such action is "fitting" or in consonance with the position and obligations of a Christian man. But he backs up this highest reason with these others: "If you hesitate to take him back because you ought, will you do it because I ask you? and, before you answer that question, will you remember my age, and what I am bearing for the Master?" If he can get his friend to do the right thing by the help of these subsidiary motives, still, it is the right thing; and the appeal to these motives will do Philemon no harm, and, if successful, will do both him and Onesimus a great deal of good.

Does not this action of Paul remind us of the highest example of a similar use of motives of personal attachment as aids to duty? Christ does thus with His servants. He does not simply hold up before us a cold law of duty, but warms it by introducing our personal relation to Him as the main motive for keeping it. Apart from Him, Morality can only point to the tables of stone and say: "There! that is what you ought to do. Do it, or face the consequences." But Christ says: "I have given Myself for you. My will is your law. Will you do it for My sake?" Instead of the chilling, statuesque ideal, as pure as marble and as cold, a Brother stands before us with a heart that beats, a smile on His face, a hand outstretched to help; and His word is, "If ye love Me, keep My commandments." The specific difference of Christian morality lies not in its precepts, but in its motive, and in its gift of power to obey. Paul could only urge regard to him as a subsidiary inducement. Christ puts it as the chief, nay, as the sole motive for obedience.

III. The last point suggested by these verses is the gradual opening up of the main subject matter of the Apostle's request. Very noteworthy is the tenderness of the description of the fugitive as "my child, whom I have begotten in my bonds." Paul does not venture to name him at once, but prepares the way by the warmth of this affectionate reference. The position of the name in the sentence is most unusual, and suggests a kind of hesitation to take the plunge, while the hurried passing on to meet the objection which he knew would spring immediately to Philemon's mind is almost as if Paul laid his hand on his friend's lips to stop his words,—"Onesimus then is it? that good-for-nothing!" Paul admits the indictment, will say no word to mitigate the condemnation due to his past worthlessness, but, with a playful allusion to the slave's name, which conceals his deep earnestness, assures Philemon that he will find the formerly inappropriate name, Onesimus—i.e. profitable—true yet, for all that is past. He is sure of this, because he, Paul, has proved his value. Surely never were the natural feelings of indignation and suspicion more skilfully soothed, and never did repentant good-for-nothing get sent back to regain the confidence which he had forfeited, with such a certificate of character in his hand!

But there is something of more importance than Paul's inborn delicacy and tact to notice here. Onesimus had been a bad specimen of a bad class. Slavery must needs corrupt both the owner and the chattel; and, as a matter of fact, we have classical allusions enough to show that the slaves of Paul's period were deeply tainted with the characteristic vices of their condition. Liars, thieves, idle, treacherous, nourishing a hatred of their masters all the more deadly that it was smothered, but ready to flame out, if opportunity served, in blood-curdling cruelties—they constituted an ever-present danger, and needed an ever-wakeful watchfulness. Onesimus had been known to Philemon only as one of the idlers who were more of a nuisance than a benefit, and cost more than they earned; and he apparently ended his career by theft. And this degraded creature, with scars on his soul deeper and worse than the marks of fetters on his limbs, had somehow found his way to the great jungle of a city, where all foul vermin could crawl and hiss and sting with comparative safety. There he had somehow come across the Apostle, and had received into his heart, filled with ugly desires and lusts, the message of Christ's love, which had swept it clean, and made him over again. The Apostle has had but short experience of his convert, but he is quite sure that he is a Christian; and, that being the case, he is as sure that all the bad black past is buried, and that the new leaf now turned over will be covered with fair writing, not in the least like the blots that were on the former page, and have now been dissolved from off it, by the touch of Christ's blood.

It is a typical instance of the miracles which the gospel wrought as every-day events in its transforming career. Christianity knows nothing of hopeless cases. It professes its ability to take the most crooked stick and bring it straight, to flash a new power into the blackest carbon, which will turn it into a diamond. Every duty will be done better by a man if he have the love and grace of Jesus Christ in his heart. New motives are brought into play, new powers are given, new standards of duty are set up. The small tasks become great, and the unwelcome sweet, and the difficult easy, when done for and through Christ. Old vices are crushed in their deepest source; old habits driven out by the force of a new affection, as the young leaf-buds push the withered foliage from the tree. Christ can make any man over again, and does so re-create every heart that trusts to him. Such miracles of transformation are wrought to-day as truly as of old. Many professing Christians experience little of that quickening and revolutionising energy;

many observers see little of it, and some begin to croak, as if the old power had ebbed away. But wherever men give the gospel fair play in their lives, and open their spirits, in truth and not merely in profession, to its influence, it vindicates its undiminished possession of all its former energy; and if ever it seems to fail, it is not that the medicine is ineffectual, but that the sick man has not really taken it. The low tone of much modern Christianity and its dim exhibition of the transforming power of the gospel is easily and sadly accounted for without charging decrepitude on that which was once so mighty, by the patent fact that much modern Christianity is little better than lip acknowledgment, and that much more of it is wofully unfamiliar with the truth which it in some fashion believes, and is sinfully negligent of the spiritual gifts which it professes to treasure. If a Christian man does not show that his religion is changing him into the fair likeness of his Master, and fitting him for all relations of life, the reason is simply that he has so little of it, and that little so mechanical and tepid.

Paul pleads with Philemon to take back his worthless servant, and assures him that he will find Onesimus helpful now. Christ does not need to be besought to welcome His runaway good-for-nothings, however unprofitable they have been. That Divine charity of His forgives all things, and "hopes all things" of the worst, and can fulfil its own hope in the most degraded. With bright, unfaltering confidence in His own power He fronts the most evil, sure that He can cleanse; and that, no matter what the past has been, His power can overcome all defects of character, education, or surroundings, can set free from all moral disadvantages adhering to men's station, class, or calling, can break the entail of sin. The worst needs no intercessor to sway that tender heart of our great Master whom we may dimly see shadowed in the very name of "Philemon," which means one who is loving or kindly. Whoever confesses to him that he has "been an unprofitable servant," will be welcomed to His heart, made pure and good by the Divine Spirit breathing new life into him, will be trained by Christ for all joyful toil as His slave, and yet His freedman and friend; and at last each once fugitive and unprofitable Onesimus will hear the "Well done, good and faithful servant!"

IV

"Whom I have sent back to thee in his own person, that is, my very heart: whom I would fain have kept with me, that in my behalf he might minister unto me in the bonds of the gospel: but without thy mind I would do nothing; that thy goodness should not be as of necessity, but of free will." — Philem. 12–14 (Rev. Ver.).

The characteristic features of the Epistle are all embodied in these verses. They set forth, in the most striking manner, the relation of Christianity to slavery and to other social evils. They afford an exquisite example of the courteous delicacy and tact of the Apostle's intervention on behalf of Onesimus; and there shine through them, as through a semi-transparent medium, adumbrations and shimmering hints of the greatest truths of Christianity.

I. The first point to notice is that decisive step of sending back the fugitive slave. Not many years ago the conscience of England was stirred because the Government of the day sent out a circular instructing captains of men-of-war, on the decks of which fugitive slaves sought asylum, to restore them to their "owners." Here an Apostle does the same thing—seems to side with the oppressor, and to drive the oppressed from the sole refuge left him, the horns of the very altar. More extraordinary still, here is the fugitive voluntarily going back, travelling all the weary way from Rome to Colossæ in order to put his neck once more beneath the yoke. Both men were acting from Christian motives, and thought that they were doing a piece of plain Christian duty. Then does Christianity sanction slavery? Certainly not; its principles cut it up by the roots. A gospel, of which the starting-point is that all men stand on the same level, as loved by the one Lord, and redeemed by the one cross, can have no place for such an institution. A religion which attaches the highest importance to man's awful prerogative of freedom, because it insists on every man's individual responsibility to God, can keep no terms with a system which turns men into chattels. Therefore Christianity cannot but regard slavery as sin against God, and as treason towards man. The principles of the gospel worked into the conscience of a nation destroy slavery. Historically it is true that as Christianity has grown slavery has withered. But the New Testament never directly condemns it, and by regulating the conduct of Christian masters, and recognising the obligations of Christian slaves, seems to contemplate its continuance, and to be deaf to the sighing of the captives.

This attitude was probably not a piece of policy or a matter of calculated wisdom on the part of the Apostle. He no doubt saw that the Gospel brought a great unity in which all distinctions were merged, and rejoiced in thinking that "in Christ Jesus there is neither bond or free"; but whether he expected the distinction ever to disappear from actual life is less certain. He may have thought of slavery as he did of sex, that the fact would remain, while yet "we are all one in Christ Jesus." It is by no means necessary to suppose that the Apostles saw the full bearing of the truths they had to preach, in their relation to social conditions. They were inspired to give the Church the principles. It remained for future ages, under Divine guidance, to apprehend the destructive and formative range of these principles.

However this may be, the attitude of the New Testament to slavery is the same as to other unchristian institutions. It brings the leaven, and lets it work. That attitude is determined by three great principles. First, the message of Christianity is primarily to individuals, and only secondarily to society. It leaves the units whom it has influenced to influence the mass. Second, it acts on spiritual and moral sentiment, and only afterwards and consequently on deeds or institutions. Third, it hates violence, and trusts wholly to enlightened conscience. So it meddles directly with no political or social arrangements, but lays down principles which will profoundly affect these, and leaves them to soak into the general mind. If an evil needs force for its removal, it is not ready for removal. If it has to be pulled up by violence, a bit of the root will certainly be left and will grow again. When a dandelion head is ripe, a child's breath can detach the winged seeds; but until it is, no tempest can move them. The method of violence is noisy and wasteful, like the winter torrents that cover acres of good ground with mud and rocks, and are past in a day. The only true way is, by slow degrees to create a state of feeling which shall instinctively abhor and cast off the evil. Then there will be no hubbub and no waste, and the thing once done will be done for ever.

So has it been with slavery; so will it be with war, and intemperance, and impurity, and the miserable anomalies of our present civilization. It has taken eighteen hundred years for the whole Church to learn the inconsistency of Christianity with slavery. We are no quicker learners than the past generations were. God is patient, and does not seek to hurry the march of His purposes. We have to be imitators of God, and shun the "raw haste" which is "half-sister to delay."

But patience is not passivity. It is a Christian's duty to "hasten the day of the Lord," and to take part in the educational process which Christ is carrying on through the ages, by submitting himself to it in the first place, and then by endeavouring to bring others under its influence. His place should be in the van of all social progress. It does not become Christ's servants to be content with the attainments of any past or present, in the matter of the organization of society on Christian principles. "God has more light to break forth from His word." Coming centuries will look back on the obtuseness of the moral perceptions of nineteenth century Christians in regard to matters of Christian duty which, hidden from us, are sun-clear to them, with the same half-amused, half-tragic wonder with which we look back to Jamaica planters or South Carolina rice growers, who defended slavery as a missionary institution, and saw no contradiction between their religion and their practice. We have to stretch our charity to believe in these men's sincere religion. Succeeding ages will have to make the same allowance for us, and will need it for themselves from their successors. The main thing is, for us to try to keep our spirits open to all the incidence of the gospel on social and civic life, and to see that we are on the right side, and trying to help on the approach of that kingdom which does "not cry, nor lift up, nor cause its voice to be heard in the streets," but has its coming "prepared as the morning," that swims up, silent and slow, and flushes the heaven with an unsetting light.

II. The next point in these verses is Paul's loving identification of himself with Onesimus.

The A.V. here follows another reading from the R.V.; the former has "thou therefore receive him, that is, mine own bowels." The additional words are unquestionably inserted without authority in order to patch a broken construction. The R.V. cuts the knot in a different fashion by putting the abrupt words, "himself that is, my very own heart," under the government of the preceding verb. But it seems more probable that the Apostle began a new sentence with them, which he meant to have finished as the A.V. does for him, but which, in fact, got hopelessly upset in the swift rush of his thoughts, and does not right itself grammatically till the "receive him" of *v.* 17.

In any case the main thing to observe is the affectionate plea which he puts in for the cordial reception of Onesimus. Of course "mine own bowels" is simply the Hebrew way of saying "mine own heart." We think the one phrase graceful and sentimental, and the other coarse. A Jew did not think so, and it might be difficult to say why he should. It is a mere question of difference in localizing certain emotions. Onesimus was a piece of Paul's very heart, part of himself; the unprofitable slave had wound himself round his affections, and become so dear that to part with him was like cutting his heart out of his bosom. Perhaps some of the virtues, which the servile condition helps to develop in undue proportion, such as docility, lightheartedness, serviceableness, had made him a soothing and helpful companion. What a plea that would be with one who loved Paul as well as Philemon did! He could not receive harshly one whom the Apostle had so honoured with his love. "Take care of him, be kind to him as if it were to me."

Such language from an Apostle about a slave would do more to destroy slavery than any violence would do. Love leaps the barrier, and it ceases to separate. So these simple, heart-felt words are an instance of one method by which Christianity wars against all social wrongs, by casting its caressing arm around the outcast, and showing that the abject and oppressed are objects of its special love.

They teach too how interceding love makes its object part of its very self; the same thought recurs still more distinctly in *v.* 17, "Receive him as myself." It is the natural language of love; some of the deepest and most blessed Christian truths are but the carrying out of that identification to its fullest extent. We are all Christ's Onesimuses, and He, out of His pure love, makes Himself one with us, and us one with Him. The union of Christ with all who trust in Him, no doubt, presupposes His Divine nature, but still there is a human side to it, and it is the result of His perfect love. All love delights to fuse itself with its object, and as far as may be to abolish the distinction of "I" and "thou." But human love can travel but a little way on that road; Christ's goes much farther. He that pleads for some poor creature feels that the kindness is done to himself when the former is helped or pardoned. Imperfectly but really these words shadow forth the great fact of Christ's intercession for us sinners, and our acceptance in Him. We need no better symbol of the stooping love of Christ, Who identifies Himself with His brethren, and of our wondrous identification with Him, our High Priest and Intercessor, than this picture of the Apostle pleading for the runaway and bespeaking a welcome for him as part of himself. When Paul says, "Receive him, that is, my very heart," his words remind us of the yet more blessed ones, which reveal a deeper love and more marvellous condescension, "He that receiveth you receiveth Me," and may reverently be taken as a faint shadow of that prevailing intercession, through which he that is joined to the Lord and is one spirit with Him, is received of God as part of Christ's mystical body, bone of His bone, and flesh of His flesh.

III. Next comes the expression of a half-formed purpose which was put aside for a reason to be immediately stated. "Whom I would fain have kept with me"; the tense of the verb indicating the incompleteness of the desire. The very statement of it is turned into a graceful expression of Paul's confidence in Philemon's goodwill to him, by the addition of that "on thy behalf." He is sure that, if his friend had been beside him, he would have been glad to lend him his servant, and so he would have liked to have had Onesimus as a kind of representative of the service which he knows would have been so willingly rendered. The purpose for which he would have liked to keep him is defined as being, "that he might minister to me in the bonds of the Gospel." If the last words be connected with "me," they suggest a tender reason why Paul should be ministered to, as suffering for Christ, their common Master, and for the truth, their common possession. If, as is perhaps less probable, they be connected with "minister," they describe the sphere in which the service is to be rendered. Either the master or the slave would be bound by the obligations which the Gospel laid on them to serve Paul. Both were his converts, and therefore knit to him by a welcome chain, which made service a delight.

There is no need to enlarge on the winning courtesy of these words, so full of happy confidence in the friend's disposition, that they could not but evoke the love to which they trusted so completely. Nor need I do more than point their force for the purpose of the whole letter, the procuring a cordial reception for the returning fugitive. So dear had he become, that Paul would like to have kept him. He goes back with a kind of halo round him, now that he is not only a good-for-nothing runaway, but Paul's friend, and so much prized by him. It would be impossible to do anything but welcome him, bringing such credentials; and yet all this is done with scarcely a word of direct praise, which might have provoked contradiction. One does not know whether the confidence in Onesimus or in Philemon is the dominant note in the harmony. In the preceding clause, he was spoken of as, in some sense, part of the Apostle's very self. In this, he is regarded as, in some sense, part of Philemon. So he is a link between them. Paul would have taken his service as if it had been his master's. Can the master fail to take him as if he were Paul?

IV. The last topic in these verses is the decision which arrested the half-formed wish. "I was *wishing* indeed, but I *willed* otherwise." The language is exact. There is a universe between "I wished" and "I willed." Many a good wish remains fruitless, because it never passes into the stage of firm resolve. Many who wish to be better will to be bad. One strong "I will" can paralyse a million wishes.

The Apostle's final determination was, to do nothing without Philemon's cognisance and consent. The reason for the decision is at once a very triumph of persuasiveness, which would be ingenious if it were not so spontaneous, and an adumbration of the very spirit of Christ's appeal for service to us. "That thy benefit" — the good done to me by him, which would in my eyes be done by you — "should not be as of necessity, but willingly." That "as" is a delicate addition. He will not think that the benefit would really have been by constraint, but it might have looked as if it were.

Do not these words go much deeper than this small matter? And did not Paul learn the spirit that suggested them from his own experience of how Christ treated him? The principle underlying them is, that where the bond is love, compulsion takes the sweetness and goodness out of even sweet and good things. Freedom is essential to virtue. If a man "could not help it" there is neither praise nor blame due. That freedom Christianity honours and respects. So in reference to the offer of the gospel blessings, men are not forced to accept them but appealed to, and can turn deaf ears to the pleading voice, "Why will ye die?" Sorrows and sins and miseries without end continue, and the gospel is rejected, and lives of wretched godlessness are lived, and a dark future pulled down on the rejecters' heads — and all because God knows that these things are better than that men should be forced into goodness, which indeed would cease to be goodness if they were. For nothing is good but the free turning of the will to goodness, and nothing bad but its aversion therefrom.

The same solemn regard for the freedom of the individual and low estimate of the worth of constrained service influence the whole aspect of Christian ethics. Christ wants no pressed men in His army. The victorious host of priestly warriors, which the Psalmist saw following the priest-king in the day of his power, numerous as the dewdrops, and radiant with reflected beauty as these, were all "willing" — volunteers. There are no conscripts in the ranks. These words might be said to be graven over the gates of the kingdom of heaven, "Not as of necessity, but willingly." In Christian morals, law becomes love, and love, law. "Must" is not in the Christian vocabulary, except as expressing the sweet constraint which bows the will of him who loves to harmony, which is joy, with the will of Him who is loved. Christ takes no offerings which the giver is not glad to render. Money, influence, service, which are not offered by a will moved by love, which love, in its turn, is set in motion by the recognition of the infinite love of Christ in His sacrifice, are, in His eyes, nought. An earthenware cup with a drop of cold water in it, freely given out of a glad heart, is richer and more precious in His sight than golden chalices swimming with wine and melted pearls, which are laid by constraint on His table. "I delight to do Thy will" is the foundation of all Christian obedience; and the servant had caught the very tone of the Lord's voice when he said, "Without thy mind I will do nothing, that thy benefit should not be, as it were, of necessity, but willingly."

V

"For perhaps he was therefore parted from thee for a season, that thou shouldest have him for ever; no longer as a servant, but more than a servant, a brother beloved, specially to me, but how much rather to thee, both in the flesh and in the Lord. If then thou countest me a partner, receive him as myself. But if he hath wronged thee at all, or oweth thee aught, put that to mine account; I Paul write it with mine own hand, I will repay it: that I say not unto thee how that thou owest to me even thine own self besides." —Philem. 15–19 (Rev. Ver.).

The first words of these verses are connected with the preceding by the "for" at the beginning; that is to say, the thought that possibly the Divine purpose in permitting the flight of Onesimus was his restoration, in eternal and holy relationship, to Philemon, was Paul's reason for not carrying out his wish to keep Onesimus as his own attendant and helper. "I did not decide, though I very much wished, to retain him without your consent, because it is possible that he was allowed to flee from you, though his flight was his own blamable act, in order that he might be given back to you, a richer possession, a brother instead of a slave."

I. There is here a Divine purpose discerned as shining through a questionable human act.

The first point to note is, with what charitable delicacy of feeling the Apostle uses a mild word to express the fugitive's flight. He will not employ the harsh naked word "ran away." It might irritate Philemon. Besides, Onesimus has repented of his faults, as is plain from the fact of his voluntary return, and therefore there is no need for dwelling on them. The harshest, sharpest words are best when callous consciences are to be made to wince; but words that are balm and healing are to be used when men are heartily ashamed of their sins. So the deed for which Philemon's forgiveness is asked is half veiled in the phrase "he was parted."

Not only so, but the word suggests that behind the slave's mutiny and flight there was another Will working, of which, in some sense, Onesimus was but the instrument. He "*was* parted" —not that he was not responsible for his flight, but that, through his act, which in the eyes of all concerned was wrong, Paul discerns as dimly visible a great Divine purpose.

But he puts that as only a possibility: "*Perhaps* he departed from thee."——He will not be too sure of what God means by such and such a thing, as some of us are wont to be, as if we had been sworn of God's privy council. "Perhaps" is one of the hardest words for minds of a certain class to say; but in regard to all such subjects, and to many more, it is the motto of the wise man, and the shibboleth which sifts out the patient, modest lovers of truth from rash theorists and precipitate dogmatisers. Impatience of uncertainty is a moral fault which mars many an intellectual process; and its evil effects are nowhere mote visible than in the field of theology. A humble "perhaps" often grows into a "verily, verily"—and a hasty, over-confident "verily, verily," often dwindles to a hesitating "perhaps." Let us not be in too great a hurry to make sure that we have the key of the cabinet where God keeps His purposes, but content ourselves with "perhaps" when we are interpreting the often questionable ways of His providences, each of which has many meanings and many ends.

But however modestly he may hesitate as to the application of the principle, Paul has no doubt as to the principle itself: namely, that God, in the sweep of His wise providence, utilizes even men's evil, and works it in, to the accomplishment of great purposes far beyond their ken, as nature, in her patient chemistry, takes the rubbish and filth of the dunghill and turns them into beauty and food. Onesimus had no high motives in his flight; he had run away under discreditable circumstances, and perhaps to escape deserved punishment. Laziness and theft had been the hopeful companions of his flight, which, so far as he was concerned, had been the outcome of low and probably criminal impulses; and yet God had known how to use it so as to lead to his becoming a Christian. "With the wrath of man Thou girdest Thyself," twisting and bending it so as to be flexible in Thy hands, and "the remainder Thou dost restrain," How unlike were the seed and the fruit—the flight of a good-for-nothing thief and the return of a Christian brother! He meant it not so; but in running away from his master, he was running straight into the arms of his Saviour. How little Onesimus knew what was to be the end of that day's work, when he slunk out of Philemon's house with his stolen booty hid away in his bosom! And how little any of us know where we are going, and what strange results may evolve themselves from our actions! Blessed they who can rest in the confidence that, however modest we should be in our interpretation of the events of our own or of other men's lives, the infinitely complex web of circumstance is woven by a loving, wise Hand, and takes shape, with all its interlacing threads, according to a pattern in His hand, which will vindicate itself when it is finished!

The contrast is emphatic between the short absence and the eternity of the new relationship: "for a season"—literally an hour—and "for ever." There is but one point of view which gives importance to this material world, with all its fleeting joys and fallacious possessions. Life is not worth living, unless it be the vestibule to a life beyond. Why all its discipline, whether of sorrow or joy, unless there be another, ampler life, where we can use to nobler ends the powers acquired and greatened by use here? What an inconsequent piece of work is man, if the few years of earth are his all! Surely, if nothing is to come of all this life here, men are made in vain, and had better not have been at all. Here is a narrow sound, with a mere ribbon of sea in it, shut in between grim, echoing rocks. How small and meaningless it looks as long as the fog hides the great ocean beyond! But when the mist lifts, and we see that the narrow strait leads out into a boundless sea that lies flashing in the sunshine to the horizon, then we find out the worth of that little driblet of water at our feet. It connects with the open sea, and that swathes the world. So is it with "the hour" of life; it opens out and debouches into the "for ever," and therefore it is great and solemn. This moment is one of the moments of that hour. We are the sport of our own generalisations, and ready to admit all these fine and solemn things about life, but we are less willing to apply them to the single moments as they fly. We should not rest content with recognising the general truth, but ever make conscious effort to feel that *this* passing instant has something to do with our eternal character and with our eternal destiny.

That is an exquisitely beautiful and tender thought which the Apostle puts here, and one which is susceptible of many applications. The temporary loss may be eternal gain. The dropping away of the earthly form of a relationship may, in God's great mercy, be a step towards its renewal in higher fashion and for evermore. All our blessings need to be past before reflection can be brought to bear upon them, to make us conscious how blessed we were. The blossoms have to perish before the rich perfume, which can be kept in undiminished fragrance for years, can be distilled from them. When death takes away dear ones, we first learn that we were entertaining angels unawares; and as they float away from us into the light, they look back with faces already beginning to brighten into the likeness of Christ, and take leave of us with His valediction, "It is expedient for you that I go away." Memory teaches us the true character of life. We can best estimate the height of the mountain peaks when we have left them behind. The softening and hallowing influence of death reveals the nobleness and sweetness of those who are gone. Fair country never looks so fair as when it has a curving river for a foreground; and fair lives look fairer than before, when seen across the Jordan of death.

To us who believe that life and love are not killed by death, the end of their earthly form is but the beginning of a higher heavenly. Love which is "in Christ" is eternal. Because Philemon and Onesimus were two Christians, therefore their relationship was eternal. Is it not yet more true, if that were possible, that the sweet bonds which unite Christian souls here on earth are in their essence indestructible, and are affected by death only as the body is? Sown in weakness, will they not be raised in power? Nothing of them shall die but the encompassing death. Their mortal part shall put on immortality. As the farmer gathers the green flax with its blue bells blooming on it, and throws it into a tank to rot, in order to get firm fibre which cannot rot, and spin it into a strong cable, so God does with our earthly loves. He causes all about them that is perishable to perish, that the central fibre, which is eternal, may stand clear and disengaged from all that was less Divine than itself. Wherefore mourning hearts may stay themselves on this assurance, that they will never lose the dear ones whom they have loved in Christ, and that death itself but changes the manner of the communion, and refines the tie. They were as for a moment dead, but they are alive again. To our bewildered sight they departed and were lost for a season, but they are found, and we can fold them in our heart of hearts for ever.

But there is also set forth here a change, not only in the duration but in the quality of the relation between the Christian master and his former slave, who continues a slave indeed, but is also a brother. "No longer as a servant, but more than a servant, a brother beloved, specially to me, but how much rather to thee, both in the flesh and in the Lord." It is clear from these words that Paul did not anticipate the manumission of Onesimus. What he asks is, that he should not be received *as* a slave. Evidently then he is to be still a slave in so far as the outward fact goes—but a new spirit is to be breathed into the relationship. "Specially to me"; he is more than a slave to me. I have not looked on him as such, but have taken him to my heart as a brother, as a son indeed, for he is especially dear to me as my convert. But however dear he is to me, he should be more so to thee, to whom his relation is permanent, while to me it is temporary. And this Brotherhood of the slave is to be felt and made visible "both in the flesh"—that is, in the earthly and personal relations of common life, "and in the Lord"—that is, in the spiritual and religious relationships of worship and the Church.

As has been well said, "In the flesh, Philemon has the brother for his slave; in the Lord, Philemon has the slave for his brother." He is to treat him as his brother therefore both in the common relationships of every-day life and in the acts of religious worship.

That is a pregnant word. True, there is no gulf between Christian people now-a-days like that which in the old times parted owner and slave; but, as society becomes more and more differentiated, as the diversities of wealth become more extreme in our commercial communities, as education comes to make the educated man's whole way of looking at life differ more and more from that of the less cultured classes, the injunction implied in our text encounters enemies quite as formidable as slavery ever was. The highly educated man is apt to be very oblivious of the brotherhood of the ignorant Christian, and he, on his part, finds the recognition just as hard. The rich mill-owner has not much sympathy with the poor brother who works at his spinning-jennies. It is often difficult for the Christian mistress to remember that her cook is her sister in Christ. There is quite as much sin against fraternity on the side of the poor Christians who are servants and illiterate, as on the side of the rich who are masters or cultured. But the principle that Christian brotherhood is to reach across the wall of class distinctions is as binding to-day as it was on these two good people, Philemon the master and Onesimus the slave.

That brotherhood is not to be confined to acts and times of Christian communion, but is to be shown and to shape conduct in common life. "Both in the flesh and in the Lord" may be put into plain English thus: A rich man and a poor one belong to the same church; they unite in the same worship, they are "partakers of the one bread," and therefore, Paul thinks, "are one bread." They go outside the church door. Do they ever dream of speaking to one another outside? "A brother beloved in the Lord"—on Sundays, and during worship and in Church matters—is often a stranger "in the flesh" on Mondays, in the street and in common life. Some good people seem to keep their brotherly love in the same wardrobe with their Sunday clothes. Philemon was bid, and all are bid, to wear it all the week, at market as well as church.

II. In the next verse, the essential purpose for which the whole letter was written is put at last in an articulate request, based upon a very tender motive. "If then thou countest me as a partner, receive him as myself," Paul now at last completes the sentence which he began in *v.* 12, and from which he was hurried away by the other thoughts that came crowding in upon him. This plea for the kindly welcome to be accorded to Onesimus has been knocking at the door of his lips for utterance from the beginning of the letter; but only now, so near the end, after so much conciliation, he ventures to put it into plain words; and even now he does not dwell on it, but goes quickly on to another point. He puts his requests on a modest and yet a strong ground, appealing to Philemon's sense of comradeship—"if thou countest me a partner"—a comrade or a sharer in Christian blessings. He sinks all reference to apostolic authority, and only points to their common possession of faith, hope, and joy in Christ. "Receive him as myself." That request was sufficiently illustrated in the preceding chapter, so that I need only refer to what was then said on this instance of interceding love identifying itself with its object, and on the enunciation in it of great Christian truth.

III. The course of thought next shows—Love taking the slave's debts on itself.

"If he hath wronged thee, or oweth thee aught." Paul makes an "if" of what he knew well enough to be the fact; for no doubt Onesimus had told him all his faults, and the whole context shows that there was no uncertainty in Paul's mind, but that he puts the wrong hypothetically for the same reason for which he chooses to say, "was parted" instead of "ran away," namely, to keep some thin veil over the crimes of a penitent, and not to rasp him with rough words. For the same reason, too, he falls back upon the gentler expressions, "wronged" and "oweth," instead of blurting out the ugly word "stolen." And then, with a half-playful assumption of lawyer-like phraseology, he bids Philemon put that to his account. Here is my autograph—"I Paul write it with mine own hand"—I make this letter into a bond. Witness my hand; "I will repay it." The formal tone of the promise, rendered more formal by the insertion of the name—and perhaps by that sentence only being in his own handwriting—seems to warrant the explanation that it is half playful; for he could never have supposed that Philemon would exact the fulfilment of the bond, and we have no reason to suppose that, if he had, Paul could really have paid the amount. But beneath the playfulness there lies the implied exhortation to forgive the money wrong as well as the others which Onesimus had done him.

The verb used here for *put to the account of* is, according to the commentators, a very rare word; and perhaps the singular phrase may be chosen to let another great Christian truth shine through. Was Paul's love the only one that we know of which took the slave's debts on itself? Did anybody else ever say, "Put that on mine account"? We have been taught to ask for the forgiveness of our sins as "debts," and we have been taught that there is One on whom God has made to meet the iniquities of us all. Christ takes on Himself all Paul's debt, all Philemon's, all ours. He has paid the ransom for all, and He so identifies Himself with men that He takes all their sins upon Him, and so identifies men with Himself that they are "received as Himself." It is His great example that Paul is trying to copy here. Forgiven all that great debt, he dare not rise from his knees to take his brother by the throat, but goes forth to show to his fellow the mercy which he has found, and to model his life after the pattern of that miracle of love in which is his trust. It is Christ's own voice which echoes in "put that on mine account."

IV. Finally, these verses pass to a gentle reminder of a greater debt: "That I say not unto thee how that thou owest to me even thine own self besides."

As his child in the Gospel, Philemon owed to Paul much more than the trifle of money of which Onesimus had robbed him; namely his spiritual life, which he had received through the Apostle's ministry. But he will not insist on that. True love never presses its claims, nor recounts its services. Claims which need to be urged are not worth urging. A true, generous heart will never say, "You ought to do so much for me, because I have done so much for you." To come down to that low level of chaffering and barter is a dreadful descent from the heights where the love which delights in giving should ever dwell.

Does not Christ speak to us in the same language? We owe ourselves to Him, as Lazarus did, for He raises us from the death of sin to a share in His own new, undying life. As a sick man owes his life to the doctor who has cured him, as a drowning man owes his to his rescuer, who dragged him from the water and breathed into his lungs till they began to work of themselves, as a child owes its life to its parent—so we owe ourselves to Christ. But He does not insist upon the debt; He gently reminds us of it, as making His commandment sweeter and easier to obey. Every heart that is really touched with gratitude will feel, that the less the giver insists upon his gifts, the more do they impel to affectionate service. To be perpetually reminded of them weakens their force as motives to obedience, for it then appears as if they had not been gifts of love at all, but bribes given by self-interest; and the frequent reference to them sounds like complaint. But Christ does not insist on His claims, and therefore the remembrance of them ought to underlie all our lives and to lead to constant glad devotion.

One more thought may be drawn from the words. The great debt which can never be discharged does not prevent the debtor from receiving reward for the obedience of love. "I will repay it," even though thou owest me thyself. Christ has bought us for His servants by giving Himself and ourselves to us. No work, no devotion, no love can ever repay our debt to Him. From His love alone comes the desire to serve Him; from His grace comes the power. The best works are stained and incomplete, and could only be acceptable to a Love that was glad to welcome even unworthy offerings, and to forgive their imperfections. Nevertheless He treats them as worthy of reward, and crowns His own grace in men with an exuberance of recompense far beyond their deserts. He will suffer no man to work for Him for nothing; but to each He gives even here great reward *in* keeping His commandments, and hereafter "an exceeding great reward," of which the inward joys and outward blessings that now flow from obedience are but the earnest His merciful allowance of imperfections treats even our poor deeds as rewardable; and though eternal life must ever be the *gift* of God, and no claim of merit can be sustained before His judgment seat, yet the measure of that life which is possessed here or hereafter is accurately proportioned to and is, in a very real sense, the consequence of obedience and service, "If any man's work abide, he shall receive a reward," and Christ's own tender voice speaks the promise, "I will repay, albeit I say not unto thee how thou owest to Me even thine own self besides." Men do not really possess themselves unless they yield themselves to Jesus Christ. He that loveth his life shall lose it, and he that loseth himself, in glad surrender of himself to his Saviour, he and only he is truly lord and owner of his own soul. And to such an one shall be given rewards beyond hope and beyond measure—and, as the crown of all, the blessed possession of Christ, and in it the full, true, eternal possession of himself, glorified and changed into the image of the Lord who loved him and gave Himself for him.

VI

"Yea, brother, let me have joy of thee in the Lord refresh my heart in Christ. Having confidence in thine obedience I write unto thee, knowing that thou wilt do even beyond what I say. But withal prepare me a lodging: for I hope that through your prayers I shall be granted unto you.

"Epaphras, my fellow prisoner in Christ Jesus, saluteth thee; and so do Mark, Aristarchus, Demas, Luke, my fellow workers.

"The grace of our Lord Jesus Christ be with your spirit. Amen."—Philem. 20–25 (Rev. Ver.).

We have already had occasion to point out that Paul's pleading with Philemon, and the motives which he adduces, are expressions, on a lower level, of the greatest principles of Christian ethics. If the closing salutations be left out of sight for the moment, there are here three verses, each containing a thought which needs only to be cast into its most general form to show itself as a large Christian truth.

I. Verse 20 gives the final moving form of the Apostle's request. Onesimus disappears, and the final plea is based altogether on the fact that compliance will pleasure and help Paul. There is but the faintest gleam of a possible allusion to the former in the use of the verb from which the name Onesimus is derived—"Let me have *help* of thee"; as if he had said, "Be you an Onesimus, a helpful one to me, as I trust he is going to be to you." "Refresh my heart" points back to *v.* 7, "The hearts of the saints have been refreshed by thee," and lightly suggests that Philemon should do for Paul what he had done for many others. But the Apostle does not merely ask help and refreshing; he desires that they should be of a right Christian sort. "In Christ" is very significant. If Philemon receives his slave for Christ's sake and in the strength of that communion with Christ which fits for all virtue, and so for this good deed—a deed which is of too high and rare a strain of goodness for his unaided nature,—then "in Christ" he will be helpful to the Apostle. In that case the phrase expresses the element or sphere in which the act is done. But it may apply rather, or even also, to Paul, and then it expresses the element or sphere in which he is helped and refreshed. In communion with

Jesus, taught and inspired by Him, the Apostle is brought to such true and tender sympathy with the runaway that his heart is refreshed, as by a cup of cold water, by kindness shown to him. Such keen sympathy is as much beyond the reach of nature as Philemon's kindness would be. Both are "in Christ." Union with Him refines selfishness, and makes men quick to feel another's sorrows and joys as theirs, after the pattern of Him who makes the case of God's fugitives His own. It makes them easy to be entreated and ready to forgive. So to be in Him is to be sympathetic like Paul, and placable as He would have Onesimus. "In Christ" carries in it the secret of all sweet humanities and beneficence, is the spell which calls out fairest charity, and is the only victorious antagonist of harshness and selfishness.

The request for the sake of which the whole letter is written is here put as a kindness to Paul himself, and thus an entirely different motive is appealed to. "Surely you would be glad to give me pleasure. Then do this thing which I ask you." It is permissible to seek to draw to virtuous acts by such a motive, and to reinforce higher reasons by the desire to please dear ones, or to win the approbation of the wise and good. It must be rigidly kept as a subsidiary motive, and distinguished from the mere love of applause. Most men have some one whose opinion of their acts is a kind of embodied conscience, and whose satisfaction is reward. But pleasing the dearest and purest among men can never be more than at most a crutch to help lameness or a spur to stimulate.

If however this motive be lifted to the higher level, and these words thought of as Paul's echo of Christ's appeal to those who love Him, they beautifully express the peculiar blessedness of Christian ethics. The strongest motive, the very mainspring and pulsing heart of Christian duty, is to please Christ. His language to His followers is not, "Do this because it is right," but, "Do this because it pleaseth Me." They have a living Person to gratify, not a mere law of duty to obey. The help which is given to weakness by the hope of winning golden opinions from, or giving pleasure to, those whom men love is transferred in the Christian relation to Jesus. So the cold thought of duty is warmed, and the weight of obedience to a stony, impersonal law is lightened, and a new power is enlisted on the side of goodness, which sways more mightily than all the abstractions of duty. The Christ Himself makes His appeal to men in the same tender fashion as Paul to Philemon. He will move to holy obedience by the thought—wonderful as it is—that it gladdens Him. Many a weak heart has been braced and made capable of heroisms of endurance and effort, and of angel deeds of mercy, all beyond its own strength, by that great thought, "We labour that, whether present or absent, we may be well-pleasing to Him."

II. Verse 21 exhibits love commanding, in the confidence of love obeying. "Having confidence in thine obedience I write unto thee, knowing that thou wilt do even beyond what I say." In *v.* 8 the Apostle had waived his right to enjoin, because he had rather speak the speech of love, and request. But here, with the slightest possible touch, he just lets the note of authority sound for a single moment, and then passes into the old music of affection and trust. He but names the word "obedience," and that in such a way as to present it as the child of love, and the privilege of his friend. He trusts Philemon's obedience, because he knows his love, and is sure that it is love of such a sort as will not stand on the exact measure, but will delight in giving it "pressed down and running over."

What could he mean by "do more than I say"? Was he hinting at emancipation, which he would rather have to come from Philemon's own sense of what was due to the slave who was now a brother, than be granted, perhaps hesitatingly, in deference to his request? Possibly, but more probably he had no definite thing in his mind, but only desired to express his loving confidence in his friend's willingness to please him. Commands given in such a tone, where authority audibly trusts the subordinate, are far more likely to be obeyed than if they were shouted with the hoarse voice of a drill-sergeant. Men will do much to fulfil generous expectations. Even debased natures will respond to such appeal; and if they see that good is expected from them, that will go far to evoke it. Some masters have always good servants, and part of the secret is that they trust them to obey. "England expects" fulfilled itself. When love enjoins there should be trust in its tones. It will act like a magnet to draw reluctant feet into the path of duty. A will which mere authority could not bend, like iron when cold, may be made flexible when warmed by this gentle heat. If parents oftener let their children feel that they had confidence in their obedience, they would seldomer have to complain of their disobedience.

Christ's commands follow, or rather set, this pattern. He trusts His servants, and speaks to them in a voice softened and confiding. He tells them His wish, and commits Himself and His cause to His disciples' love.

Obedience beyond the strict limits of command will always be given by love. It is a poor, grudging service which weighs obedience as a chemist does some precious medicine, and is careful that not the hundredth part of a grain more than the prescribed amount shall be doled out. A hired workman will fling down his lifted trowel full of mortar at the first stroke of the clock, though it would be easier to lay it on the bricks; but where affection moves the hand, it is delight to add something over and above to bare duty. The artist who loves his work will put many a touch on it beyond the minimum which will fulfil his contract. Those who adequately feel the power of Christian motives will not be anxious to find the least that they durst, but the most that they can do. If obvious duty requires them to go a mile, they will rather go two, than be scrupulous to stop as soon as they see the milestone. A child who is always trying to find out how little would satisfy his father cannot have much love. Obedience to Christ is joy, peace, love. The grudging servants are limiting their possession of these, by limiting their active surrender of themselves. They seem to be afraid of having too much of these blessings. A heart truly touched by the love of Jesus Christ will not seek to know the lowest limit of duty, but the highest possibility of service.

> "Give all thou canst; high heaven rejects the lore
> Of nicely calculated less or more."

III. Verse 22 may be summed up as the language of love, hoping for reunion. "Withal prepare me a lodging: for I hope that through your prayers I shall be granted unto you." We do not know whether the Apostle's expectation was fulfilled. Believing that he was set free from his first imprisonment, and that his second was separated from it by a considerable interval, during which he visited Macedonia and Asia Minor, we have yet nothing to show whether or not he reached Colossæ; but whether fulfilled or not, the expectation of meeting would tend to secure compliance with his request, and would be all the more likely to do so, for the very delicacy with which it is stated, so as not to seem to be mentioned for the sake of adding force to his intercession.

The limits of Paul's expectation as to the power of his brethren's prayers for temporal blessings are worth noting. He does believe that these good people in Colossæ could help him by prayer for his liberation, but he does not believe that their prayer will certainly be heard. In some circles much is said now about "the prayer of faith"—a phrase which, singularly enough, is in such cases almost confined to prayers for external blessings,—and about its power to bring money for work which the person praying believes to be desirable, or to send away diseases. But surely there can be no "faith" without a definite Divine *word* to lay hold of. Faith and God's promise are correlative; and unless a man has God's plain promise that A. B. will be cured by his prayer, the belief that he will is not faith, but something deserving a much less noble name. The prayer of faith is not forcing our wills on God, but bending our wills to God's. The prayer which Christ has taught in regard to all outward things is, "Not my will but Thine be done," and, "May Thy will become mine." That is the prayer of faith, which is always answered. The Church prayed for Peter, and he was delivered; the Church, no doubt, prayed for Stephen, and he was stoned. Was then the prayer for him refused? Not so, but if it were prayer at all, the inmost meaning of it was "be it as Thou wilt"; and that was accepted and answered. Petitions for outward blessings, whether for the petitioner or for others, are to be presented with submission; and the highest confidence which can be entertained concerning them is that which Paul here expresses: "I *hope* that through your prayers I shall be set free."

The prospect of meeting enhances the force of the Apostle's wish; nor are Christians without an analogous motive to give weight to their obligations to their Lord. Just as Paul quickened Philemon's loving wish to serve him by the thought that he might have the gladness of seeing him before long, so Christ quickens His servant's diligence by the thought that before very many days He will come, or they will go—at any rate, they will be with Him,—and He will see what they have been doing in His absence. Such a prospect should increase diligence, and should not inspire terror. It is a mark of true Christians that they "love His appearing." Their hearts should glow at the hope of meeting. That hope should make work happier and lighter. When a husband has been away at sea, the prospect of his return makes the wife sing at her work, and take more pains or rather pleasure with it, because his eye is to see it. So should it be with the bride in the prospect of her bridegroom's return. The Church should not be driven to unwelcome duties by the fear of a strict judgment, but drawn to large, cheerful service, by the hope of spreading her work before her returning Lord.

Thus, on the whole, in this letter, the central springs of Christian service are touched, and the motives used to sway Philemon are the echo of the motives which Christ uses to sway men. The keynote of all is love. Love beseeches when it might command. To love we owe our own selves beside. Love will do nothing without the glad consent of him to whom it speaks, and cares for no service which is of necessity. Its finest wine is not made from juice which is pressed out of the grapes, but from that which flows from them for very ripeness. Love identifies itself with those who need its help, and treats kindnesses to them as done to itself. Love finds joy and heart solace in willing, though it be imperfect, service. Love expects more than it asks. Love hopes for reunion, and by the hope makes its wish more weighty. These are the points of Paul's pleading with Philemon. Are they not the elements of Christ's pleading with His friends?

He too prefers the tone of friendship to that of authority. To Him His servants owe themselves, and remain for ever in His debt, after all payment of reverence and thankful self-surrender. He does not count constrained service as service at all, and has only volunteers in His army. He makes Himself one with the needy, and counts kindness to the least as done to Him. He binds Himself to repay and overpay all sacrifice in His service. He finds delight in His people's work. He asks them to prepare an abode for Him in their own hearts, and in souls opened by their agency for His entrance. He has gone to prepare a mansion for them, and He comes to receive account of their obedience and to crown their poor deeds. It is impossible to suppose that Paul's pleading for Philemon failed. How much less powerful is Christ's, even with those who love Him best?

IV. The parting greetings may be very briefly considered, for much that would have naturally been said about them has already presented itself in dealing with the similar salutations in the epistle to Colossæ. The same people send messages here as there; only Jesus called Justus being omitted, probably for no other reason than because he was not at hand at the moment. Epaphras is naturally mentioned singly, as being a Colossian, and therefore more closely connected with Philemon than were the others. After him come the two Jews and the two Gentiles, as in Colossians.

The parting benediction ends the letter. At the beginning of the epistle Paul invoked grace upon the household "from God our Father and the Lord Jesus Christ." Now he conceives of it as Christ's gift. In him all the stooping, bestowing love of God is gathered, that from Him it may be poured on the world. That grace is not diffused like stellar light, through some nebulous heaven, but concentrated in the Sun of Righteousness, who is the light of men. That fire is piled on a hearth that, from it, warmth may ray out to all that are in the house.

That grace has man's spirit for the field of its highest operation. Thither it can enter, and there it can abide, in union more close and communion more real and blessed than aught else can attain. The spirit which has the grace of Christ with it can never be utterly solitary or desolate.

The grace of Christ is the best bond of family life. Here it is prayed for on behalf of all the group, the husband, wife, child, and the friends in their home Church. Like grains of sweet incense cast on an altar flame, and making fragrant what was already holy, that grace sprinkled on the household fire will give it an odour of a sweet smell, grateful to men and acceptable to God.

That wish is the purest expression of Christian friendship, of which the whole letter is so exquisite an example. Written as it is about a common, every-day matter, which could have been settled without a single religious reference, it is saturated with Christian thought and feeling. So it becomes an example of how to blend Christian sentiment with ordinary affairs, and to carry a Christian atmosphere everywhere. Friendship and social intercourse will be all the nobler and happier, if pervaded by such a tone. Such words as these closing ones would be a sad contrast to much of the intercourse of professedly Christian men. But every Christian ought by his life to be, as it were, floating the grace of God to others sinking for want of it to lay hold of, and all his speech should be of a piece with this benediction.

A Christian's life should be "an epistle of Christ" written with His own hand, wherein dim eyes might read the transcript of His own gracious love, and through all his words and deeds should shine the image of his Master, even as it does through the delicate tendernesses and gracious pleadings of this pure pearl of a letter, which the slave, become a brother, bore to the responsive hearts in quiet Colossæ.